BANKERS AND CATTLEMEN

BANKERS
AND
CATTLEMEN

GENE M. GRESSLEY

UNIVERSITY OF NEBRASKA PRESS · LINCOLN

First Bison Book printing: March 1971

Bison Book edition reproduced from the first (1966) edition by
arrangement with Alfred A. Knopf, Inc.

FOR

M.M.G., L.M.G.

AND

J.B.G., D.E.G. AND *D.R.G.*

TWO GENERATIONS—

ONE EAST, ONE WEST

PREFACE

It is a prosaic observation that the cattle industry has captured its share of the printed word in the literature of the West. Much of this verbiage has been devoted to an emotional rendering of the folk-saga theme of what must be conceded was a very dramatic period in American history. The scene is predictable—the lone cowboy, sitting astride a magnificent horse on a high bluff, silhouetted against the twilight sky, with the muted bawling of milling cattle heard in the distance. All this is calculated to bring tears to the eyes of the most hardened cowhand or television viewer. This is the West that was, they say; this is the West that is gone.

The earthier and harder side of life on the range—the long drives when more dust was swallowed than water; the stench of the bunkhouse; the grease-filled plates; the broken leg, with a doctor fifty miles distant; the constant tug of war with the local or Eastern banker—all are forgotten, buried in the mush of sentimentality.

That fiction and fable have survived rather than fact and history is perhaps inevitable, since so many of the firsthand "I remember when" accounts are the products of senility. Being too old to ride, a few energetic cowboys turned to writing, or at least to hiring their Boswells from the East. In the latter case, when he (or she) turned out to be "some young fool journalist," the cowhand delightedly let his imagination roam. As one old-time ranch manager said to the writer, "The ones that knew and made the history, didn't tell it."

Another cause of the emotionalism that affects so much of the literature is the scenic side of the West. The West is indeed a place of immense beauty, grandeur, and silence. It would take a calloused soul not to be awestruck at sight of the Grand Tetons, the vast haunted desert of the Navajos, and the enormity of desolate space in eastern Montana and the Dakotas, filled only by the "big sky" and the flat, broad prairie. The solitude, the loneliness, and the emptiness have been themes developed by a small handful of literati: Willa Cather, Eugene Manlove Rhodes, Mary Austin, Ole Rölvaag, Mari Sandoz, Mildred Walker, and Jack Schaefer. The scenario writer or scriptwriter, denied the talent of a Rhodes or a Cather, too commonly produces only the froth.

More significant for the economic historians of the cattle industry than the literary effusion of the range epic has been the total absence of any memoir, maudlin or not, from the managerial and financial side of the industry. Entrepreneurs, Eastern or Western, have not been prolific autobiographers, but in the cattle industry this vacuum is especially striking. Only one financial figure, John Clay, left a narrative that is both detailed enough and significantly interpretive to be of broad value. Historians can only lament the fact that men such as Lyman Gage and Geoffrey Snydacker, who, as officers of the First National Bank of Chicago, played such an active role in cattle financing, did not write their reminiscences. Unfortunately, not even their personal papers on this aspect of their careers have survived.

The purpose of this study has been to trace the main configurations of Eastern investment in the cattle industry. Several topics are probed in detail: the motivations behind investment; the

Western attorney's role in channeling investment for his Eastern client; the industry's heavy reliance on Eastern financing; the inherent complexities in communication between the investor and the manager on the range; the commission firm; and the decline of the industry, to which the companies responded with panic and panaceas.

Obviously the writer does not believe that economic history should be the sole preoccupation of the historian of the American West. He would suggest that the economic phase of Western history is but one of the many historical blanks that could be filled in. In a very frequently quoted article written over a decade ago, Earl Pomeroy noted that a "reorientation" was long overdue for the history of the American West. It still is. All too often today the "classic" work on an area of the West such as mining, the fur trade, or the cattle industry was the standard tome twenty years ago.

Any scholar in search of a topic is quickly confronted with a myriad of possibilities. The whole transfer of capital from East to West is only partially comprehended. Irrigation and reclamation have scarcely received treatment, and then only sketchily. Western urbanization is at once a field so broad and so neglected that it frightens all but the most persevering. More territorial studies of the nature of those of Earl Pomeroy and Howard Lamar are desperately needed. We know astonishingly little about Western political evolution, let alone its ramifications with the Eastern political scene. Industrialization has been studiously ignored. There are scarcely a dozen sound corporate histories; those that do exist, such as Gerald White's history of Standard Oil of California, demonstrate the huge potential of research on business history in the West. The federal-state relationships, let alone the federal largesse which has been lavished on the West, remain a subject of intense dispute but little enlightenment. The fertile field of state administrative policy, the value of which has recently been demonstrated by Gerald Nash's study of California, is an empty one. The histories of Western education, in spite of such histrionic titles as "Beacon of Mountain and Plain," are not beacons nor even flashlights. Land policy, exceedingly complex, has received some of the best scholarly effort from Professors Allan Bogue, Paul W. Gates, and Leslie Decker; however, an immense part of the domain has yet to receive even a scowl from weary historians. Indeed, the field of land tenure is as broad as the patience of the researcher. The topical list could be extended; it is limited only by one's imagination.

Historians with a regional orientation must first of all be historians with a national frame of reference; they must escape the curse of historical myopia. They must switch from squinting at their feet to gazing across the landscape. At this point in time, it is hardly exciting to note that Western institutions have been strongly influenced by Eastern precedents. Yet historians of the West for years have blithely been treating their topics in geographic as well as intellectual isolation. Certainly monographic studies are imperative, if we are to construct the broader theses which will stand the test of historical scrutiny a generation from now. Nevertheless, monographic history must avoid the narrow confines of provincialism; too many Western historians have surrounded themselves with a barbed-wire curtain. In search of the specific, they need to be acutely aware of the relation of their topics to the broader scene. A study of railroad development in North Dakota may be both valuable and interesting, but if it excludes the interaction with national railroad operation for the same period, it becomes history in a test tube.

This, then, is a study of Eastern capital in the frontier economy, with specific attention to the range cattle industry. The writer hopes that some of the methodological techniques and conclusions will have relevance for historians investigating other economic sectors of the American West. Though there were some problems unique for the investor in the cattle industry, the pattern of Eastern investment, whether it was in the Black Jack Mining Company, the Cactus Creek Oil Company, or the Suffolk Cattle Company, was remarkably the same.

In the absence of published sources, the writer has depended to a great extent on manuscript collections. As for the geographical connotations of "East" and "West," the popular hundredth meridian will serve as well as any other delineation. For this study, the economic implication of these geographic terms is more important, for East is considered a sophisticated, mature economic system, and West an underdeveloped region requiring inputs of capital for its economic growth. Obviously there were wide gradations of economic development in both regions.

That historical research in the twentieth century is a cooperative enterprise is evident to anyone engaging in such research. Gone is the age of the Brahmin scholar, sitting in splendid isolation in a dimly lit study, composing a multi-volume epic on some grand theme for which the world is his historical stage. In over seven years of research, my obligations have become many, my debts unrepayable. First, my deep gratitude is to Professor Earl Pomeroy of the University of Oregon for his suggestive comments, criticism, and assistance. His insights provided the stimulus for an intensive re-examination of many a dogmatic assumption.

Dr. James Ranz, former director of libraries and now dean of academic affairs of the University of Wyoming, not only gave encouragement but also made available the necessary time to undertake this work. Dr. John T. Fey, president of the University of Wyoming created the academic climate and freedom which made completion of this study possible. Dr. George Duke Humphrey, president emeritus of the University of Wyoming, provided the initial impetus, when there were "a thousand other tasks" to be done. Dr. Ray W. Frantz, Jr., director of libraries, University of Wyoming, will discover numerous of his stylistic suggestions popping up in the narrative.

To Professors Ralph Hidy and Arthur Johnson of the Harvard School of Business Administration, who through a business history fellowship enabled me to spend a summer of uninterrupted research at Cambridge, my sincerest thanks. They also suggested fertile lines of study about the interaction of East and West at the weekly luncheon sessions at Kresge Hall. To Professor Wallace Farnham of the University of Wyoming, who punctured with considerable adroitness several fond theories, my belated thanks. Professors Wendell H. Stephenson, Kenneth W. Porter, and James Tattersall, all of the University of Oregon, took time from their busy schedules to read the entire manuscript and make helpful criticisms. Dr. John Schlebecker, Smithsonian Institution, contributed several excellent queries.

Mrs. Agnes Wright Spring, former state historian of Colorado and Wyoming, has come up time and time again with that bit of elusive information from a seemingly inexhaustible fount of knowledge. Though she didn't know it at the time, she first suggested the topic more than a decade ago in one of those volatile luncheon sessions among the staff of the Colorado State Historical Society. Mr. Lamar Moore of Winslow, Arizona, whose detailed knowledge of the cattle industry is unexcelled, opened his library and gave freely of his time and knowledge. Mrs. Elsa Spear Byron of one of the pioneer families in Wyoming experienced the cyclical fortunes of the cattle industry; her insights into the psychology of cattlemen were more helpful than she realized.

Mr. Joe Watt, president of the Wyoming Stock Growers Association and trustee of the University of Wyoming, foresaw years ago the necessity of preserving the history of the cattle industry in the West. His contributions are apparent in the records of the American National Cattlemen's Association at the University of Wyoming and the rare books in the Wyoming Stock Growers Collection in the University's library. Robert Hanesworth, past secretary, and Dean Prosser, present secretary of the Wyoming Stock Growers Association, have been unfailingly helpful. Without the dutiful attentions of Miss Alice Smith and Mr. Russell Thorp, former secretaries of the Stock Growers, this organization's invaluable historical records would have ended up with so much other history—on the dump. Donald R. Ornduff, editor of the *American Hereford Journal*, took considerable interest and offered assistance in the project from its initiation.

Dr. William Fitzhugh, Jr., of Monterey, California, and Ernest C. Miller of Warren, Pennsylvania, both donated rare Western Americana to the Western History Research Center. Without their timely assistance, the research for this volume would have been immeasurably more difficult.

This study would have been shallow or perhaps nonexistent without the willingness of descendents of personages prominent

in the cattle industry to release their family archives. Carlile
Bolton-Smith of Washington, D.C., not only answered a plethora
of questions regarding his grandfather, but also opened his personal file of material on Francis Smith and Company. Hiram Dow
of Roswell, New Mexico, spent two days digging out material
and regaling the writer with his remarkable knowledge of the
history of New Mexico. Mrs. Jean Craig Evans of Belle Fourche,
South Dakota, provided manuscript material and recollections of
the activities of her father, James T. Craig. Mrs. William Coffee,
at the last moment, uncovered a valuable ledger of the Lakota
Cattle Company, which furnished the documentary substantiation
required on the fascinating operation of Clarence King in the
West.

Colonel James T. Padgitt of San Antonio served as a gracious
host over a weekend, and shared his own unpublished manuscripts,
as well as the papers of his grandmother, Mrs. Mabel Day Lea,
whose fight to save her estate is one of the most astounding tales
in cattle history. Also, by giving me access to the H. K. Thurber
papers, Colonel Padgitt made a major contribution to this work.
The Hughes brothers, William, Charles, and Lafayette, and Mr.
T. C. Trudgin of Denver opened up William Hughes's papers for
my examination. Over a period of several years, Mr. Arthur
Lafrentz of New York City related the experiences of his father,
Mr. F. W. Lafrentz, as secretary of the Swan Land and Cattle
Company. Mrs. Jack Nason of Spearfish, South Dakota, devoted
an entire Sunday morning to her reminiscences of the Weare and
Clay operations in South Dakota. Mr. T. B. Hord of Alliance,
Nebraska, donated both his time and his grandfather's immensely
valuable letterbooks. Miss Emily Painter of Greeley, Colorado,
related by the hour recollections of her father, John Painter, and
his early activities in the cattle industry. Mrs. Margaret Trimble
Pease of New York City presented the Western History Research
Center with a delightful and enlightening group of letters by her
father, Richard Trimble, written home during his days in Wyoming in the early 1880's. Congressman William Henry Harrison
of Wyoming gave permission to utilize the papers of his father,
Russell B. Harrison, heretofore closed.

Archivists and librarians over the country were consistently generous in their response to persistent inquiries and were courteous hosts upon visitations. I am especially indebted to Mr. Robert Lovett, curator of manuscripts, Baker Library, Harvard University; Mr. Charles Shelter, curator, West Virginia Collection, West Virginia University Library, Morgantown; Mr. Michael Kennedy, director, Mrs. Vivian Paladin, associate editor, and Miss Mary Dempsey, librarian, of the Montana State Historical Society, Helena; Dr. Alexander Moffitt, librarian, and Miss Llerena Friend, director, of the Eugene C. Barker Texas History Center, University of Texas Library, Austin; Dr. Lucille Kane, curator of manuscripts, Minnesota Historical Society, St. Paul; Miss Josephine L. Harper, manuscripts section head, State Historical Society of Wisconsin, Madison; Miss Elfrieda Lang, assistant curator of manuscripts, Eli Lilly Library, Indiana University, Bloomington; Dr. David Otis Kelley, librarian, University of New Mexico Library, Albuquerque; Mr. Martin Schmitt, curator, Oregon Collection, University of Oregon, Eugene; Mr. C. Boone McClure, museum director, Panhandle Plains Historical Museum, Canyon; Dr. Seymour V. Connor, director, Mr. Sylvan Dunn, archivist, Southwest Collection, Texas Technological College, Lubbock; Mrs. Alys Freeze, head, Western History Department, Denver Public Library, Denver; and Mrs. Enid Thompson, librarian, and Mrs. Laura Eckstrom, assistant librarian, State Historical Society of Colorado, Denver.

It has been my good fortune to have a number of secretaries and assistants who have contributed to the mechanics of this study. Mrs. Esther Kelley, administrative secretary of the University of Wyoming Library, read not one but four versions of the manuscript. Without her eagle awareness, many a slip would have gone by. Mrs. Claire Doll, Mrs. Joyce L. Dion, and Mrs. Sonia Thorn all typed various drafts; Mrs. Mary Lee Neithold, Mrs. Susan Quinlivan, Mrs. Bonnie Pendleton, Mrs. Ruth Ann Haug, Mrs. Kaye Miller, Mrs. Joy Toomey, Mrs. Karen Parker, and Mrs. Linda Erickson, all contributed research assistance and all have my appreciation for their help.

One does not have to be kin to Thomas Wolfe to realize that

beside every author stands a good editor. Angus Cameron of Knopf was unfailingly patient, generous, and helpful in answering queries and offering advice. Though sorely tried, he never lost his perspective.

A look at the prefaces of historical tomes makes it obvious that there would be little historical writing without the assistance of the historian's wife; the present writer is no exception. As critic, proofreader, and murderer of her husband's stylistic "little darlings," as Quiller-Couch so aptly puts it, Joyce performed brilliantly. To Deborah Ellyn and David Randolph, who patiently put up with their father's neglect and vacant stares, while he was daydreaming in another century, my thanks for being indulgent.

GENE M. GRESSLEY

Laramie, Wyoming
December 1, 1965

CONTENTS

I

WALL STREET
page 3

II

CAREY AVENUE
page 39

III

"You couldn't keep me out"
THE EASTERN INVESTOR
page 62

IV

"We, the undersigned . . ."
ORGANIZATION AND CAPITALIZATION
page 89

X
BALANCE SHEET
page 273

BIBLIOGRAPHY
page 299

INDEX
follows page 320

ILLUSTRATIONS

Unless otherwise indicated, all illustrations are courtesy of the Western History Research Center, University of Wyoming.

BANKERS AND CATTLEMEN

I

WALL STREET

On a cold, bone-chilling December evening in 1880 in Franklin, Pennsylvania, the gaslights were ablaze in the Exchange Hotel. The western Pennsylvania community was holding a farewell reception for one of its "most distinguished and illustrious citizens," in the words of one of the main orators. After enduring speeches by the mayor, the president of the local bar, and the representative to the state legislature, the audience sat until nearly midnight before the guest of honor rose to respond.

Samuel C. T. Dodd presented a ponderous appearance. Short, rotund, double-chinned, with a trim walrus mustache—to which would be added a thick set of side-whiskers in later years—Dodd reminded one New York journalist of Grover Cleveland.[1] He was affable, philosophical, erudite, and witty. A rather "Scattergood Baines" type of lawyer, with gravy on his ascot, he suggested to some an "old time, sound, shrewd, kindly country lawyer."[2]

While he would retain the posture of a small-town Midwestern lawyer all his life, he stood before his friends this evening to explain his changing his abode from Franklin to New York City. The task was doubly difficult, for he was leaving to join what many in the audience regarded as "the enemy"—the Standard Oil Company. Typically, he took refuge in humor: "Why, then, do I go away? Well, as the ministers say when they get a call to a higher salary, it seems to be the Lord's will." Then there was a missionary motive: "I expect New York has need of me—but I expect New York will be a long time finding it out. Boss Tweed is dead; John Kelly has fallen; Jay Gould seems to be busy with his stock affairs; and Beecher lives in Brooklyn. It seems there ought to be somebody living in New York."[3]

In reality, Dodd had little reason to apologize to his friends. No official had ever joined Standard with less of an opportunity for accumulating a fortune. Dodd refused to draw a salary in excess of $25,000 and all Rockefeller's offers of stock options were consistently spurned. He thereby forfeited the assurance of becoming a multi-millionaire. Soon after his arrival at 26 Broadway, the Standard Oil International office, Dodd was asked to devise a legal structure wherein all the Standard operations could be carried out under one corporate entity.[4] After considering and discarding several forms, Dodd outlined the advantages of a "trust" operation. He recommended to the Standard officials that they create a corporation in each state in which Standard had a heavy investment. Superimposed on these state corporations

[1] New York *Daily Graphic*, April 3, 1889.
[2] New York *Evening Post*, January 19, 1905.
[3] Franklin *Spectator*, undated clipping. Dodd Scrapbook, Dodd Collection, Petroleum History and Research Center, University of Wyoming.
[4] Enlightening discussions of the evolution of the Standard Oil Trust are in Ralph and Muriel Hidy: *Pioneering in Big Business* (New York: Harper; 1955), 40–9; Allan Nevins: *Study in Power*, 2 vols. (New York: Scribner; 1953), I, 382–402.

would be a "corporation of corporations," or a trust, which would hold the voting stock of forty companies. Trust certificates would be issued to the companies on a percentage basis, according to the amount of stock contributed, and the management of the entire organization would reside in the trustees. The dividends would be declared to the individual companies by the trustees in proportion to the number of certificates they held.

The Standard Oil trust agreement, signed on January 2, 1882, inaugurated a new era of industrial combination. Samuel C. T. Dodd had, more than any other individual, made feasible the gigantic industrial corporation which became synonymous with American economic life for the next thirty years. Dodd cringed at being labeled "the father of trusts," but if he was not the father, he was the closest relative. Though, as chief counsel, Dodd gave complete loyalty to the Standard Oil Company, he did not necessarily condone all the imaginative uses of the trust device.

In speech after speech and pamphlet after pamphlet, Dodd meticulously defined his view of "monopoly versus combination."[5] In an essay issued shortly after the Standard Oil trust became publicly known, Dodd maintained: "A mistake is made when we unite the terms 'Combination and Monopoly.' There is, in fact, no necessary relation between them." Furthermore, he argued, "without combinations, without partnerships, without joint stock associations, without corporations, the business of the world would stagnate." They are "as indispensable to the manufactures and commerce of this nineteenth century as air is to our existence."[6] Dodd described the many blessings that flowed from combination: "lower prices, cheaper transportation, lower manufacturing costs, and 'greater productivity' of wealth." If combination degenerated into monopoly, it was the fault of our laws, not the system itself. "In other words, the evil is not in combination but

[5] The most helpful pamphlets and articles in extracting Dodd's position on monopoly are his *Combinations: Their Uses and Abuses, with a History of the Standard Oil Trust* (New York: 1888); *Trusts* (Boston: 1889); "The Present Legal Status of Trusts," *Harvard Law Review*, VII (November 1893), 157–69; *Aggregated Capital* (New York: 1893); *A Statement of Pending Legislation and Its Consequences* (New York: n.d.); *Memories of S. C. T. Dodd, Written for His Children and Friends* (New York: 1907).

[6] Dodd: *Combinations: Their Uses and Abuses.*

in its purpose and result."[7] Addressing himself to the attacks on combination, Dodd maintained that the villains were socialists, the corporations' own inadequate public relations, and especially the newspapers, whose only motive was to get a story. All these reasons would be readily appreciated by the business community of several generations later.

Though Dodd was in and of his age, he escaped the invective widely and indiscriminately flung at the "robber barons." Sitting on the porch of his home in Twilight Park, in the heart of the Catskills, as a New York newspaperman found him in 1905, Dodd was the picture of contentment.[8] He had fostered a revolution in economic association, yet he never reaped the great financial rewards enjoyed by his compatriots, Rockefeller, Rogers, Flagler, or Pratt. Looking across the Catskills from his porch, Sam Dodd was the selfsame shrewd, able, dedicated lawyer with a high sense of integrity who had said good-bye to his friends in Franklin, Pennsylvania, a quarter of a century before.

Eighteen hundred miles to the west of Franklin, and two years previous to Mr. Dodd's departure, a young man who had just alighted from an eastbound Union Pacific train strode quickly up to the desk of the Inter-Ocean Hotel. Cheyenne, as an entrepôt of the West, was accustomed to oddities in dress and manner. But the guest registering at the Inter-Ocean on the afternoon of April 28, 1879, startled even the jaded sensibilities of the natives. There he stood, for the wonderment of all, resplendent in silk stockings, linen shirt, green wrinkled velveteen breeches and jacket, and low-cut shoes. He carefully inscribed "Clarence King" on the register.[9]

The desk clerk may or may not have recognized the name. If he did not, the chances are that he was illiterate, for his new guest's

[7] Ibid.

[8] New York *Evening Post*, January 19, 1905.

[9] The most comprehensive biography of Clarence King is Thurman Wilkins's *Clarence King* (New York: Macmillan; 1958). Additional biographical material on King is available in William R. Thayer: *The Life and Letters of John Hay*, 2 vols. (Boston: Houghton Mifflin & Co.; 1915); Century Association: *Clarence King Memoirs* (New York: G. P. Putnam's Sons; 1904); and Tyler Dennett: *Life and Letters of John Hay* (New York: Dodd, Mead & Co.; 1933).

mountaineering feats had been splashed across the pages of the national newspapers for a decade. Clarence King first came West in 1863, to make a geologic appraisal of the Comstock Lode in Nevada; then he joined the California Geological Survey. By 1866, a magnificent scientific scheme had taken shape in his febrile imagination: why not undertake a survey along the fortieth parallel from eastern Colorado to the California border? Such an expedition would include not only the geology of the region but also information on natural history and a survey of the mining industry. When King presented his systematic plan to Congress, he was amazed at the favorable reception. He discovered that his cause had not been hindered by his naming a peak for Senator Conness, a potent member of the committee. As King later admitted, this was a stroke of political genius.

During the next ten years, King crossed and recrossed the vast region along the fortieth parallel. So successful was his work, his publicity, and his political adeptness that in 1878 he was appointed the first director of the United States Geological Survey. He welcomed the opportunity of spending more time in the capital city, for he was a member of that close and brilliant entourage of intellectuals who congregated at the Lafayette Square home of Henry Adams.[1]

The Adams salon of 1607 H Street was a highly exclusive and intimate group. Here John Hay and his wife, Henry and Mrs. Adams, and Clarence King founded the minuscule "Five of Hearts Club." In the sanctuary of the Adams home, they harpooned society, lampooned political corruption, and listened with high merriment to Clarence King's tales of the West, or to John Hay's satirical comments on some inept senator. King excelled as a wit and a raconteur. In the Adams parlor he was the center of the stage, with his flashing blue eyes, Vandyke beard, and white linen shirts. In one celebrated exchange, Adams referred to the "polar" condition of Boston society, to which King glacially re-

[1] One of the best insights into the intellectual "emotionality" of Lafayette Square is to be found in Ernest Samuels: *Henry Adams, The Middle Years* (Cambridge: Harvard University Press; 1958), 143–80.

torted: "Boston was 1,387,453 years under the ice, and then the Adamses came."[2]

As an investor in the West, King gambled with the fervor of a Gould or a Converse. As he lay dying, his body burning up with tuberculosis in the hot southwestern sun, he lamented to John Hay: "I fear that I stayed too long in pure science and got a bent for the philosophical and ideal side of life too strong for any adaptation to commercial affairs."[3] For King, investment was a matter of economic survival; a financial chess game in stock on the exchange held little attraction. Capitalizing on his scientific acumen, he had done "tolerably well" after leaving the survey in 1881. Most of his attention was given to mining ventures, although he did reap amazing dividends from several cattle companies in Wyoming and Nebraska. The depression of 1893 devastated his financial and emotional reserve, so much so that he escaped into insanity. King had already authored his own epitaph —"more scientist" than entrepreneur.

While Clarence King was slipping on the glacial slopes of the Sierra Nevadas, a grand opening was taking place near the tip of Manhattan. Thousands of visitors streamed into 120 Broadway in May 1870. According to newspaper accounts, one of the architectural wonders of New York had just been completed: a seven-story office building, the center of which was a forty-by-one-hundred-foot "atrium" surrounded by marble Corinthian columns.[4] The most discussed and abused feature was its two steam-powered elevators: everyone in Manhattan wanted to ride those elevators!

The building and the company housed therein were the creation of one man—Henry Baldwin Hyde. As founder of the Equitable Life Assurance Company, Hyde was happiest when he was constructing, whether it was his Jekyll Island, Georgia, retreat, or devising a new policy to proselytize "assurants" from New York Life or Mutual Life, two of his most active competitors. Hyde would remind anyone that this fitted in with the Equitable cor-

[2] Ibid., 172.
[3] Dennett: *John Hay*, 161.
[4] R. Carlyle Buley: *The Equitable Life Assurance Society of the United States* (New York: Appleton-Century-Crofts; 1959), 29–31.

porate goal—growth. Much to the disgust of some of his stock-holders, the president of Equitable always insisted that dividends came after "growth."

Hyde was an imposing figure—almost six feet tall, lithe, slightly stooped-shouldered, with an aquiline nose, bushy eye-brows over sunken eyes, and a cleft in his chin, especially notice-able in his youth. His personality was as dynamic as his physical appearance. One historian noted that when he talked about his favorite subject, insurance, "there was a certain peculiar pose, a sway of the body, a sort of bird-like cocking of the head; the hand flashed to keep pace with the mind. . . . People spoke of the hypnotic quality of his eyes."[5] Close associates were aware of another quality, his incisive intellect, which made him an entre-preneurial genius in the insurance field. Hyde never squandered his hours. There were numerous stories of his fanatical devotion to conserving time. In his youth, he possessed a seemingly inex-haustible energy, coupled with a zealous attention to detail, quali-ties that were reflected in the startling rise of the Equitable Life Assurance Company to its position as "the strongest in the world." Equitable maintained this enviable leadership until shortly after Hyde's death.[6]

In 1895, he issued a directive to the employees in the home of-fice: "Mr. Hyde has been considerably annoyed by persons wish-ing to see him for business purposes following him to his house uptown. When Mr. Hyde remains away from his office, he does so for the very purpose of being private."[7] This outburst may have been symptomatic of Hyde's increasing weariness. Two years later he confessed to his vice-president, James W. Alexander: "Mr. McCall and Mr. Perkins[8] are able men and comparatively young men and it is hard for me having so many outside things to do after all the work I have done and at the age I have attained to

---

[5] Ibid., 14–15.
[6] Far and away the best analysis of the life insurance business in the nine-teenth century is Morton Keller's *Life Insurance Enterprise, 1885–1910* (Cambridge: Harvard University Press; 1963).
[7] "Memorandum," March 26, 1895. Hyde Collection, Baker Library, Har-vard University.
[8] Two officials of the New York Life Insurance Company.

match them."[9] Hyde realized that he had exhausted his physical energy, and by 1899 he was dead.

As an innovator in the field of life insurance, Hyde was the entrepreneurial equal of a Morgan or a Harriman. The tontine policy he ingeniously devised one day in 1865 was a brilliant stroke of salesmanship. Under this policy, the insured who were willing to gamble on longevity could pass up immediate dividends for a paid-up policy in a comparatively short time. For example, one might take out a life insurance policy at the age of thirty-five and be paid up approximately at the age of fifty. The extra dividends accruing to the policy would be utilized to reduce future premiums and purchase an annuity.[1] An Equitable salesman had a phenomenal psychological advantage when discussing a policy with a potential customer: he could talk in terms of life rather than death. Hyde was, in effect, offering his "assurants" a chance to gamble, not on the hereafter, but on life.

It was only a relatively few blocks from 120 Broadway to 210 Madison Avenue, but it might well have been another country, another time. J. Pierpont Morgan would have approved of the medieval splendor of Hyde's surroundings, but in personality the two men were opposites. Flamboyant Hyde loved publicity and was burning up with nervous energy; Morgan was taciturn, stolid, and domineering.

A visitor ushered into the library of the Morgan residence saw first the great man's bulbous and inflamed red nose. Then, as the fascination diminished, he might glance at the hazel eyes, so penetrating and intense that he was immediately uncomfortable.[2] Edward Steichen, the famous photographer, recalled that meeting this gaze was like meeting the headlights of an oncoming train. As the first awkward moments passed, the visitor might focus on the whole man: his huge head, prominent features, flourishing

[9] Henry B. Hyde to James Alexander, March 27, 1895. Hyde Collection, Baker Library, Harvard University.

[1] Buley: *The Equitable Life Assurance Society*, 29–31.

[2] A remarkable biography is Frederick Lewis Allen's *The Great Pierpont Morgan* (New York: Harper; 1949). All other biographies are pale beside Allen's; nevertheless, these are useful—Herbert L. Satterlee: *J. Pierpont Morgan* (New York: Macmillan; 1939); John K. Winkler: *Morgan the Magnificent* (New York: Vanguard Press; 1930).

walrus mustache, and broad shoulders. It took Morgan's business associates months, and sometimes years, to feel at ease in his presence.

J. Pierpont Morgan was not easily forgotten, either by his visitors or by his era. When your eye finally shifted from the man to his surroundings, you were quickly aware of opulence—not ostentatious display, but, as one biographer has noted, "solid comfort." There were the massive ornate desk in the library, with two lamps, several chairs bordered with heavy fringe, long bejeweled lights hanging down from a high ceiling. Morgan was proud of these lights; like many of his possessions, these electric lights were the first in a New York residence.[3] The floors were covered with a flowered carpet, the walls were hung with paintings, and bric-a-brac was everywhere. J. Pierpont Morgan was a collector—of people, yachts, art, corporations, and money (not necessarily in that order).

The Gilded Age could well have been christened the Age of Morgan. But this honorific title never achieved popularity because it was also the Age of Harriman, Gould, Rockefeller, and Rogers. Any Wall Street broker would have admitted that Morgan possessed unusual, if not unique, talents, which were readily apparent in the "Morgan method" of corporate organization. His accomplishments as a fiscal reorganizer and a consolidator of business enterprise were legendary.

A year before his death, he was summoned to Washington, D.C., to appear before the Pujo Committee, which was investigating the "money trust" in the United States. To an incredulous inquisitor, Samuel Untermyer, Morgan insisted that the primary prerequisite for success in Wall Street was not money but character. Regardless of the way in which Untermyer put his questions, Morgan's answers were always the same. The dialogue between the investigator and the witness ended with:

UNTERMYER: For instance, if he has got Government bonds, or railroad bonds, and goes in to get credit, he gets it, and on the security of those bonds, does he

[3] The tribulations of "electrifying" the Morgan manor are in Matthew Josephson: *Edison* (New York: McGraw-Hill; 1959), 291–3.

not? He does not get it on his face or his character, does he?

MORGAN: Yes, he gets it on his character.

UNTERMYER: I see; then he might as well take the bonds home,
had he not?

MORGAN: Because a man I do not trust could not get money
from me on all the bonds in Christendom.

UNTERMYER: That is the rule all over the world?

MORGAN: I think that is the fundamental basis of business.[4]

If Untermyer had been privy to Morgan's private exchange
with Isaac Ellwood, barbed-wire entrepreneur of De Kalb, Illinois,
during the consolidation of the Federal Steel Corporation, he
might have been less skeptical of Morgan's sincerity. Uneasy
about the progress of the negotiations, Ellwood had requested
more "of your private opinion" from Morgan. Morgan assured
Ellwood that the negotiations were proceeding satisfactorily, for,
as "you and I know, we are dealing with men of character."[5]
Whether or not Ellwood was mollified by Morgan's answer, he
did not have the temerity to question it.

That Untermyer and Morgan failed to understand each other
was not surprising. Untermyer heralded the Progressive era, while
Morgan symbolized all that the Progressive believer distrusted—
monopoly, economic inequality, and above all, corruption, a sin
which the Progressive damned with fervor in oratory and in
print.

Never before in American finance had so much capital been
so mobile or so many investors willing to take such high risks.
If it was whispered that a new "trust" had the support of a
Morgan, Harriman, or Forbes, nervous brokers were soon signal-
ing orders from the floor of the stock exchange. The speculative
craze was part and parcel of the confused financial atmosphere
infecting the 1880's and 1890's.[6] Industrial fragmentation and

[4] New York *Times,* December 20, 1912.

[5] J. Pierpont Morgan to Isaac Ellwood, August 8, 1898. Ellwood Collection,
Western History Research Center, University of Wyoming.

[6] A recent, able economic history of this period is Ray Ginger's *Age of
Excess* (New York: Macmillan; 1965). Other views of this era are offered in
Edward C. Kirkland: *Industry Comes of Age* (New York: Holt, Rinehart

disorder were the rule, not the exception. Henry L. Higginson, Boston broker, lamented to his friend Thomas Sturgis: "Someone may be understanding the market fluctuations, I would feel a lot easier, if I did."[7] Obviously it had been an exasperating day for Higginson, for he did not often indulge in confessions of this nature.

Into this unregulated atmosphere stepped the investment banker. It was men with a touch of the Morgan genius who, when confronted with disorganization and financial confusion, inspired confidence, enforced regulation, and sought order. A bankrupt corporation with some tangible but entangled assets was a challenge to the Morgans, Kuhns, Belmonts, and Schiffs. A galaxy of corporations—the Northern Pacific, the New York Central, United States Steel, Edison Electric Light, and International Harvester—owed their brilliance to Morgan's talent. By the time Czolgosz nervously aimed a pistol at William McKinley, the corporate builder was yielding to the corporate organizer, the investment house.

Morgan as financier, Hyde as entrepreneur, Dodd as corporate lawyer, and King as literary scientist were representative of the magnificence of the age. If it was an age of excess, it was also an age of talents. Undeniably it was an age of unrest, as the audiences crowding into the small-town railroad stations to hear the socialist and populist oratory of Eugene V. Debs, Ignatius Donnelly, or "Pitchfork" Ben Tillman would have been the first to tell you. Yet if there was a style that characterized the Gilded Age, it was set by burgeoning industrial wealth and technological development, which were managed by a corrupt corporate officialdom. Few would have denied that the vortex of this financial activity swirled around the tip of Manhattan—Wall Street.

One Pepys of Wall Street, James Medbery, saw "the glory of Wall Street . . . in its magnificent opportunities for satisfying in a few months the demands of civilization. It is the greatest

and Winston; 1961); H. Wayne Morgan (ed.): *The Gilded Age: A Reappraisal* (Syracuse: Syracuse University Press; 1963); and Thomas C. Cochran: *Railroad Leaders* (Cambridge: Harvard University Press; 1953).

[7] Henry L. Higginson to Thomas Sturgis, October 24, 1891. Higginson Collection, Baker Library, Harvard University.

money-making and money-losing spot on the globe."[8] Since Medbery was an "insider," his statement sounded authoritative, even though he was inclined to be carried away by the "romance" of the clatter and babbling of the stock exchange.

If really pressed, Medbery might have conceded that some of the glory of Wall Street was tarnished by the antics of speculators along the Street. Medbery was careful to define class strata. First, there were the outsiders, whom he defined as "not merely the promiscuous and intermittent body of individuals with small purses and large desires, but also merchants, manufacturing capitalists, bank officers, and citizens who have relied upon their fortunes."[9] Then came the "operators," "men who move noiselessly, spread their nets, gather in a great harvest, retire, reappear, but love not the glory of notoriety nor the *eclat* of a large clientele."[1] The latter were the great deceivers, for manipulation was their art and craft. As Medbery perceived, "the master-spirit which has controlled the destiny of the market is content to leave the world to its surmises."[2]

Despite Medbery's description of voodoo-like manipulation on Wall Street, there was much acute discernment in his analysis. Operators did move with quiet precision, though not as unfailingly as Medbery in *Men and Mysteries of Wall Street* would have one believe. The flamboyance of the Jerome brothers,[3] while it made excellent advertising copy, was definitely atypical of the prototype of a successful financier. The Harrimans, Converses, and Morgans played a close-to-the-chest game in Wall Street. The pawns created the noise; the kings were silent.

To move with dispatch, knowledge, and profit in and out of the financial byways of the stock market required an attentiveness and a diligence that taxed the most sophisticated financier. There has seldom been a time in the history of Wall Street when more fluctuation occurred than during the last quarter of the nineteenth

[8] James K. Medbery: *Men and Mysteries of Wall Street* (Boston: Fields, Osgood and Co.; 1870).

[9] Ibid., 194.

[1] Ibid., 154.

[2] Ibid.

[3] A delightful biography of Leonard Jerome is Anita Leslie's *The Remarkable Mr. Jerome* (New York: Holt; 1954).

century. Rapacious manipulators were only a minor part of the financial syndrome. The burgeoning industrial growth, fed by a booming population both native and immigrant, the exploitation of natural resources at a rapacious rate, a rapidly expanding transporation system—all contributed to the dynamism of the economy. The opening up of huge bonanza farming lands produced a cornucopia of agricultural products for both export and home consumption. A favorable political climate—and though it was not as balmy as many have assumed, politician and industrialist were able to walk arm in arm—pervaded the age. As a natural consequence of these forces in the economy, there were cyclonic periods of boom and depression, with a majority of the capitalists tacking first one way and then another to ride out recurring financial storms.[4]

The oracle of the New York financial district, the *Commercial and Financial Chronicle*, did its best to be either optimistic or pessimistic, as the mood of the day demanded. In the *Chronicle*'s annual "Retrospects" of the preceding year's economic developments, the editors were unfazed by contradicting a previous judgment. In general, though, it was good business to be optimistic, and frequently the staid columns glowed with bright auguries. Whether in a time of prosperity or depression, the editorials of the *Chronicle* provided an excellent index to businesscycle palpitations in the nineteenth century. The editor's diagnosis of an upswing in business in 1882-3 was clearly accurate: railroad construction had leaped from 2,665 miles in 1878 to 11,569 in 1882.[5] Though 1883 was a year of contraction, manufacturing and outside bank clearings indicate that in some ways it showed more business activity than did 1882. In 1884 there was a slide in the economy, a situation the *Chronicle* editor attributed to political upheavals. Yet it was the decline in railroad construction, rather than oratory, that froze the economy. Employment figures broke with the fall in railroad construction; unemployment in turn precipitated a depression throughout the nation; a bank panic

---

[4] The cyclic nature of the Victorian era and earlier is contained in Rendigs Fels: *American Business Cycles, 1865-1897* (Chapel Hill: University of North Carolina Press; 1959).

[5] *Historical Statistics of the United States* (Washington, 1960), 427.

then triggered a stock market crash. On May 8 the brokerage firm of Grant and Ward failed, bringing down with it the Marine National Bank, which had indiscreetly overcertified a $750,000 Grant and Ward check.[6] In rapid succession, two other events occurred which seemed to signify impending disaster for the whole Street. The president of the Second National Bank embezzled three million dollars, and the discovery of the theft promptly closed the bank's doors. Rumors that the Metropolitan Bank was also unsound then precipitated a run on it the day after the collapse of the Second National, and the Metropolitan had no alternative except to cease business. For all these fast-shutter sequences of ill fortune, there was a decided upturn in the economy in September 1884.

Though the recovery was not as fast as the editor would have had his readers believe. Crops in late 1884 reached near-bumper proportions, but were not enough to influence either railroad profits or exports. Indeed, it was not until the latter half of 1886 that railroad construction and agricultural exports picked up enough to rouse the slumbering economy. The intensity of the contraction of 1887–8 went virtually unrecognized by the financial community, and the *Chronicle* in 1889 only gave a hint that 1888 had been a year of unsettled conditions. But if Wall Street had fully appreciated the decline in railroad construction in the second half of 1887 and in 1888, coupled with the accompanying drop in real estate values and building, there would have been a wave of apprehension. That the financial community failed to recognize the setback can be attributed to the decided upswing of 1888 through 1892. Specifically, the cycle began in April 1888 and lasted through May 1891.[7] Although railroad construction fell, rail freight rose, building construction increased markedly, and credit eased, thereby creating a favorable trade balance. Although the *Chronicle*'s editor did identify some of these signs, by 1890 he became too preoccupied with the silver problem and the tariff to give much attention to business recovery.

[6] Fels: *American Business Cycles*, 128–35.
[7] Ibid., 164.

The 1893 downswing was marked by the spectacular failure of the Philadelphia and Reading, along with a shaky stock situation in steel, banks, and railroads. In assessing the causes of this depression, the *Chronicle* blamed two evils: the silver question and the inadequate banking system. The newspaper was partially accurate on both counts. The usual seasonal increase in money supply did not materialize, and the silver agitation precipitated a contraction four months earlier than it probably would have occurred otherwise. The period 1893–5, in sum, was one of transition. The *Chronicle* missed the disquieting indications which corporations nationwide were watching. The Venezuela uproar, the silver issue, and low investment opportunities held recovery back in 1895–6. However, in 1897 there was an overall upswing, the result of a surge in grain exports and the renewed willingness of financiers to search out investment possibilities.

The *Chronicle*'s editor, while untutored in the language of the Schumpeterian business cycle, had little difficulty in diagnosing the hills and valleys in his economic environment, though he did attribute them to the wrong factors from time to time. Some economic historians have referred to the 1883–97 period as "the years of the long depression"; yet such a phrase overemphasizes the dismalness of this era. Without doubt, the monetary situation was a powerful and unsettling factor in the situation, but it was hardly the scapegoat that the *Chronicle* made it. Obviously, no one sector of the economy can be singled out as totally responsible for the fluctuation, but from the evidence available, crops and railroad construction were prime ingredients in the cyclic economic health of these two decades.

This, in skeletal outline, is the milieu in which the Eastern financier operated during the Gilded Age. The image of the Wall Street broker has been nursed into a flourishing mythology by "inside" writers such as James Medbery: Jim Fisk, clutching his breast as he tumbles down the stairs, murdered over an amorous affair;[8] Jay Gould, squeezing all the assets out of the Kansas

8 W. A. Swanberg: *Jim Fisk: The Career of an Improbable Rascal* (New York: Scribner; 1959).

Pacific Railroad;[9] little prune-faced Daniel Drew, with a wicked scowl, terrorizing the Erie Railroad; dashing Leonard Jerome, riding around upper Manhattan in his tallyho by night and making dramatic coups by day.[1] As with most mythology, a pupa of substance is surrounded by a cocoon of fiction. The religious and parsimonious William E. Dodge,[2] sad-faced John D. Rockefeller (sans his public relations man, Ivy Lee), and the diligent Charlemagne Tower[3] do not provide the same gaudy copy.

Historians and public alike have alternated between casting the nineteenth-century entrepreneur as a robber baron with bulging pockets, and portraying him as a benevolent figure with a luxuriant white beard, passing out philanthropic gifts to create a literate America.[4] The capitalist's actual role in the nineteenth century probably lies somewhere in the no-man's-land between these trenches.

In an era dominated by the rise of corporate behemoths, the entrepreneur, with the mist of laissez faire in his eyes, saw in the

[9] A well-researched, sympathetic, and imaginative biography is Julius Grodinsky's *Jay Gould, His Business Career, 1887–1896* (Philadelphia: University of Pennsylvania Press; 1957).

[1] Leslie: *The Remarkable Mr. Jerome.*

[2] A calm, almost dispassionate account of William E. Dodge's career is in Richard Lowitt: *A Merchant Prince of the Nineteenth Century* (New York: Columbia University Press; 1954).

[3] A good biography of Charlemagne Tower (almost better than the subject merits) is Hal Bridges: *Iron Millionaire* (Philadelphia: University of Pennsylvania Press; 1952).

[4] The literature on the "robber barons" thesis of nineteenth-century capitalism is massive, diffuse, and not infrequently more emotional than enlightening. The following are a selection of the most incisive opera: Edward C. Kirkland: *Business in the Gilded Age: The Conservatives' Balance Sheet* (Madison: University of Wisconsin Press; 1952); Allan Nevins and Matthew Josephson: "Should American History Be Rewritten?" *Saturday Review of Literature,* XXXVII (February 6, 1954), 9–10; Charles A. Barker: *Henry George* (New York: Oxford University Press; 1955); Thomas C. Cochran: *Railroad Leaders, 1845–1890: The Business Mind in Action* (Cambridge: Harvard University Press; 1953); Ralph W. Hidy and Muriel E. Hidy: *Pioneering in Big Business, 1882–1911* (New York: Harper and Brothers; 1955); Edward C. Kirkland: *Men, Cities and Transportation: A Study in New England History, 1820–1910,* 2 vols. (Cambridge: Harvard University Press; 1948); Francis W. Gregory and Irene D. Neu: "The American Industrial Elite in the 1870's: Their Social Origins," in W. Miller (ed.): *Men in Business: Essays in the History of Entrepreneurship* (Cambridge: Harvard University Press; 1952); Thomas C. Cochran: "The Legend of the Robber Barons," *Pennsylvania Magazine of History and Biography,* LXXIV (July

West a region ripe for exploitation. The Eastern financier saw opportunity beckoning on every hand. The essence of American business philosophy in the nineteenth century is found in contemporary expressions regarding competition. Whether the entrepreneur ever pored over the tomes of Darwin and Spencer or listened to the platform eloquence of John Fiske is a moot question; what is sure, however, is that the "survival of the fittest" and the rest of the perfumed potpourri of Social Darwinist dogma was in the businessman's ether.[5]

S. C. T. Dodd blandly remarked in his autobiography that he had known of no instances in which the Standard Oil Trust had curried legislative favor.[6] What is even more remarkable is that, from a personal standpoint, the ethereal Mr. Dodd was probably being truthful. When urged by Rockefeller to take stock in Standard Oil, Dodd refused: "I considered myself similar to a judge, and desired to keep myself perfectly free from bias on any questions that I had to pass on." However, Dodd showed a slight twinge of regret as he remarked: "On account of this conscientious scruple, I narrowly escaped growing rich like the rest."[7]

1950), 307–21; Irwin G. Wyllie: *The Self-Made Man in America: The Myth of Rags to Riches* (New Brunswick: Rutgers University Press; 1954); John Tipple: "The Anatomy of Prejudice," *Business History Review*, XXXIII (Winter 1959), 510–23; John Tipple: "The Robber Baron in the Gilded Age: Entrepreneur or Iconoclast?" in Morgan (ed.): *The Gilded Age;* Chester McArthur Destler: "The Opposition of American Business Men to Social Control During the 'Gilded Age,'" *Mississippi Valley Historical Review*, XXXIX (March 1953), 641–72; Chester McArthur Destler: "Entrepreneurial Leadership among the 'Robber Barons': A Trial Balance," *Journal of Economic History, Supplement*, VI (1946), 28–49; Chester McArthur Destler: "Wealth Against Commonwealth, 1894–1944," *American Historical Review*, L (October 1944), 49–69; Vernon Louis Parrington: *Main Currents in American Thought* (New York: Harcourt, Brace & Co.; 1930), III, 405–21; Chester McArthur Destler: *Henry Demarest Lloyd and the Empire of Reform* (Philadelphia: University of Pennsylvania Press; 1963); Matthew Josephson: *The Robber Barons: The Great American Capitalist, 1861–1901* (New York: Harcourt, Brace & Co.; 1934).

5 Two works which inevitably appear in footnotes to discussions of Social Darwinism, a tribute to both their erudition and their "quotablity," are Richard Hofstadter: *Social Darwinism in American Thought* (Boston: Beacon Press; 1955), and Henry S. Commager: *The American Mind* (New Haven: Yale University Press; 1950).

6 Dodd: *Memories of S. C. T. Dodd* (New York: 1907).

7 Ibid., 35.

Like the Dodds, the Jubilee Jim Fisks are also atypical of nineteenth-century entrepreneurs. Coming much closer to the mean were men like the ironmonger Charlemagne Tower, or the lumberman Henry Sage.[8] Tight-fisted Henry Sage's single criterion of a successful administrator was the "test of profit." One of Sage's maxims was: "Hire men *low* and pay them from the store." If he ever considered that this was labor exploitation, he quickly banished such insidious thoughts from his head.

Sage would have applauded the sentiment of Charles E. Perkins, president of the Chicago, Burlington, and Quincy Railroad, who knowingly commented to his Chicago merchant, Levi Leiter: "Practically all of our business is competitive and if a service is not sold today because the price is unsatisfactory, that which might have been sold today is never sold." Later on, Perkins expressed his theory of competition in a statement that William Graham Sumner would have been proud to claim: "To deny the Railroads the natural right to combine is an interference with the natural laws of competition which is certain to work injury to the whole people."[9]

The petroleum magnate of West Virginia, John J. Carter, supported Perkins's viewpoint when he jotted in his notebook: "Either the economy will have to find its natural way, or we will not be able to survive. . . . Competition is not ruined by combination, but only by unwise combination."[1] Isaac Ellwood, the barbed-wire king of De Kalb, Illinois, unfamiliar with and unconcerned with economic theory, heartily concurred with his friend and business associate John W. Gates: "I agree with you, either we go along with combination [later the American Steel and Wire Company] or we lose our advantage of competition."[2] That Ellwood in effect had produced a *non sequitur* was of little moment.

[8] A useful biography of Sage is Anita Shafer Goodstein: *Henry W. Sage, 1814–1897: Biography of a Businessman* (Ithaca: Cornell University Press; 1962).

[9] Thomas C. Cochran: *Railroad Leaders, 1845–1890: the Business Mind in Action* (Cambridge: Harvard University Press; 1953), 448.

[1] John J. Carter Diary, July 11, 1892. Carter Collection, Humble Oil Corporation, Tulsa, Oklahoma.

[2] Isaac Ellwood to John W. Gates, February 17, 1899. Ellwood Collection, Western History Research Center, University of Wyoming.

For several years before this statement to Gates, the barbed-wire industry had maintained a trade association or "pool" which monopolized the productive capacity of the industry.[3]

The views of the industrialists of the nineteenth century regarding competition were often contradictory at best. These capitalists would mouth platitudinous phrases on the marvels of free enterprise, while signing a monopolization agreement aimed at the negation of these very ideas. With his emphasis on profit, that shrewd financier from upper New York State, Henry Sage, sliced through the labyrinth of honorifics pertaining to the control of production.[4] Sage argued that any philosophical debate on free enterprise versus a closed market was mere exercise unless it dealt with the basic issue of which system would yield the most profit.

Along with the idea of profit came a strong conviction based on the Social Darwinist–Horatio Alger premise that success was an individualistic accomplishment,[5] independent of environment. In rural America, all farm boys had the same chance on the golden stairs to success. The tone of this creed was caught by the St. Louis brewer August Busch in a magnificent bombast to his old, good, and true friend Richard Kerens. In one of those maudlin old-grad reminiscences, Busch recalled the good old days that never were.

> I enjoyed your kind letter of the 31st ultimate very much, reminding me of the happy days of '73 and '74 when we were both young and full of courage and dash. Even at that time they prophesied that we two would make a career and we did and I think deserved what we did accomplish. We were successful because we had the perseverance and energy and because we were determined to get there. We were on hand day and night in all sorts of weather afraid of nothing. The boys of today seem

[3] Earl Hayter: "An Iowa Farmer's Protective Association," *The Iowa Journal of History* (June 1934), 331–62.

[4] Goodstein: *Henry W. Sage, 1814–1897.*

[5] An incisive dissection of the success cult is in Irvin G. Wyllie's *The Self-Made Man in America; The Myth of Rags to Riches* (New Brunswick, N.J.: Rutgers University Press; 1954). A light biography which purports to reveal the Alger myth is John Tebbel: *From Rags to Riches* (New York: Macmillan; 1963).

weaker, they do not seem to display the spirit and I think this is the reason there is so much distress.[6]

With a potential market full of lush sentimentality such as this, it is easy to see why the Beadle dime novel was a sensation. What is more, these captains of industry reiterated the "grand and glorious" so often that they began to believe it. Why not? When dusk came, one could ride one's hansom home to a Victorian brownstone mansion sitting amid the green lawns of a hundred-acre estate—badges of material success which one had earned in one's lifetime. And this was all the more impressive when one could recall less comfortable surroundings of one's youth in an unpainted farmhouse[7] (although the circumstances were not as dire as one related to one's grandchildren). These idyllic images corresponded to reality for only a few thousand millionaires in the late nineteenth century; yet it is this elite who have given us our picture of the Gilded Age.

There was more than a little superficiality to these Horatio Alger-like recollections, yet there was also a degree of truth which even Henry Lloyd would have had to concede. The ambitious Henry Baldwin Hyde, in a letter to his son, recalled the vicissitudes of rising in the business world. His son had recently suffered a minor reverse, and the letter was calculated to uplift his spirits.

A number of years ago I organized a company called the Equitable Trust of Connecticut, raised all the capital stock myself, got my friends into it, etc. I put a man in as President who had been begging me for a position for about twenty years by the name of Jonathan Edwards. He made up his mind he was losing his dignity by such a close connection with the Equitable. . . . Soon after the company was organized . . . to lend money in the West, its directors were exceedingly gilt-edged men, all very rich, they lent their money very unwisely taking poor security. I protested from week to week, but with no other result than to make myself unpopular. I resigned and told them that the company was going to destruction as fast as it possibly could and that they would soon be on the rocks. The company

[6] Adolphus Busch to Richard Kerens, February 2, 1899. Elkins Collection, University of West Virginia Library.
[7] Wyllie: *The Self-Made Man in America*, 72–109.

afterwards failed. . . . Temporary defeat is sometimes more valuable than victory. It puts a keener edge on the sword and a finer point on the nerves. . . . Hold your wind, bide your time, act wisely no matter if the other fellow is ahead for the moment. You will lay him out cold in the end. "All things come to him who waits" even getting even with one's enemies. One of the most fearful things you will have to learn is how few men are in the world that are honorable and can be relied upon. The longer you live the more you will find out what miserable stuff the average human nature is made of. Men who remain true under fire are exceedingly rare.[8]

In offering this "Lord Chesterfield" advice, Hyde was in substance espousing a philosophy developed over a lifetime. For the Hydes of the nineteenth-century world success was a matter of time and application. The Puritan ethic was only slowly yielding to the grinding of institutions like the Equitable Life Assurance Company.[9]

The quotable Andrew Carnegie, whose beliefs seem so absurdly crass to twentieth-century America, gave no quarter to the inequities of environment. "We accept and welcome, therefore, as conditions to which we must accommodate ourselves, great inequality of environment; the concentration of business, industrial and commercial, in the hands of the few and the law of competition."[1] As a concordance to this philosophy, Carnegie noted that the "rich man's boy" was to be pitied, for it was from the poor classes that "so many strong, eminent, self-reliant men have always sprung and always must spring."[2] These sentiments fell on receptive ears. The majority of Americans enjoyed hearing a mixture of "motherhood" and Social Darwinism in Fourth of July orations.

Indeed, these patriotic sentiments might be the only uplifting

[8] Henry Hyde to James Hyde, April 29, 1897. Hyde Collection, Baker Library, Harvard University.

[9] A shrewdly conceived essay on the Puritan ethic and the age of success is Louis Wright's "Franklin's Legacy to the Gilded Age," *Virginia Quarterly Review*, XXII (Spring 1946), 268–79.

[1] Andrew Carnegie: *The Gospel of Wealth and Other Timely Essays* (New York: Century Company; 1900), 4.

[2] Ibid., xii.

aspect of being crowded in front of a hexagonal bandstand set judiciously in "the square" with the Civil War cannon nearby. Many a farmer remembered, with discomfort, the hot, humid afternoons when sweat poured down his face and through his shirt.

In a business-dominated era, Americans were firmly committed to the ideals of the business community; laissez faire and free competition were perfectly palatable principles to the majority of the electorate. This is not to dismiss flippantly the strong protest movements in the "mauve decade," but, with few exceptions, they failed to win the hearts or the pocketbooks of the mass of the American public.

While Carnegie blatantly trumpeted his "religious fervor" for the creed of Social Darwinism, some businessmen felt that it was the better part of valor and wisdom to point out the positive side of the philosophy they were defending. T. Jefferson Coolidge, the Boston entrepreneur whose investments spread from shoe factories to railroads, wrote Henry Cabot Lodge in support of the wool tariff: "Verily the gods make mad and whom do they wish to destroy? The country should be told it can not be prosperous if the industries of the country are ruined and then end in the workingmen being idle and in want."[3]

A common defense of the entrepreneur's rapacity was that, even if the costs were high, the end justified the means. The Bostonian leader of the Chicago, Burlington, and Quincy clique, John Murray Forbes, defended Oakes Ames to a colleague:

> It was a hard job Oakes Ames had to do in those times and I did not hanker after joining him in the undertaking when he would have given me as good terms as he did his Congressional partners. The Road was much better built—quicker and its work better than such a plan promised or would have been accomplished under any but so strong and energetic a head as Ames. I have always tried to avert blame from him for the mistakes he made.
>
> Were he back here as just the head of this enterprise Gould

[3] T. Jefferson Coolidge to Henry Cabot Lodge, April 1, 1887. Coolidge Collection, Baker Library, Harvard University.

could never attempt the barefaced monopoly that he is now aiming at.[4]

The biographer of Jay Gould, in summing up his career, saw justification for Gould's life in public benefit.[5] Americans had gained from the new roads, smashed traffic pools, and lowered rate structures.

A close business associate of Forbes, Charles E. Perkins, president of the Burlington, became thoroughly disgusted with the Iowa legislative attacks on his railroad and vigorously defended the Eastern capitalist: "People can make money on farms and other industries than ours . . . and it is only the Eastern capitalist who cannot use his money to advantage at home who is willing to risk it in Western railroads."[6] Perkins was in effect saying that we should protect the flow of Eastern capital if for no other reason than to support the principle of entrepreneurial risk taking.

Henry Sage thought the *raison d'être* for the businessman was self-evident. In forceful language, he emphasized the increasingly high standard of living enjoyed by the populace. Where else in the world was life so good for so many? In addition, private industrial fortunes had endowed American public life with tremendous cultural advantages—and all this in a Christian atmosphere![7]

The New York broker Jacob Schiff shared in Sage's religiosity, but went even further in doing battle for the business community. As an occupant of Wall Street for almost half a century, Schiff had observed the rise and fall of numerous brokerage firms, and thought he knew why the names of some concerns had become household words, while others had long since been obliterated. "The reason is to be sought in the fact that they have been more honest."[8] As far as Schiff could perceive, the morality of

[4] Cochran: *Railroad Leaders, 1845–1890*, 336.
[5] Julius Grodinsky: *Jay Gould* (Philadelphia: University of Pennsylvania Press; 1957), 610–11.
[6] Cochran: *Railroad Leaders, 1845–1890*, 98.
[7] Goodstein: *Henry W. Sage, 1814–1897*, 46.
[8] Cyrus Alder: *Jacob Henry Schiff: His Life and Letters* (Garden City: Doubleday, Doran and Co.; 1929), I, 23.

Wall Street had been steadily improving since he first walked the four blocks years before.

If needed, further justification for great wealth could be found in the idea of stewardship. In his lordly manner, Carnegie summed up this philosophy: "The fundamental idea of the gospel of wealth is that surplus wealth should be considered as a sacred trust to be administered by those into whose hand it falls, during their lives, for the good of the community."[9] Jacob Schiff's wide philanthropic interest exemplifies Carnegie's ideal. Schiff's fortune not only endowed the chair for German culture at Cornell, a Judaic library in the Library of Congress, and the American School of Oriental Research in Jerusalem; it supported victims of the Galveston flood as well.[1] T. Jefferson Coolidge, of Boston, believed: "It is our duty to give of our wealth to causes *worthy* of our support."[2] Specifically, he made the comment to badger a wayward Harvard alumnus to contribute; but, in general, the phrase "worthy of our support" furnished a loophole large enough to please even the most discriminating philanthropist. Coolidge faced a peculiar problem in answering the requests that came in his mail. With the given name of Jefferson, he was fair game to all fund raisers for any Jefferson association. In response to a plea from Jefferson Medical College, he unhesitatingly wrote: "As to my equipping a chemical laboratory . . . I have no doubt of the excellence of the institution . . . but I cannot afford to give to every college with the name of Jefferson."[3]

Henry Hyde, who was never accused of excessive generosity, told his business associate James Alexander: "The giving you have done for your parish church will give you pleasure long after memories of your business success are gone. We should all enjoy our money this way."[4] This was good advice, which Hyde man-

[9] Carnegie: *The Gospel of Wealth,* 54.

[1] Alder: *Jacob Henry Schiff: His Life and Letters,* II, 18, 35, 37, 111.

[2] T. Jefferson Coolidge to Edward Briddle, March 26, 1899. Coolidge Collection, Baker Library, Harvard University.

[3] T. Jefferson Coolidge to William M. Farr, January 2, 1899. Ibid.

[4] Henry Hyde to James Alexander, September 8, 1897. Hyde Collection, Baker Library, Harvard University.

aged successfully to ignore. As far as he was concerned, it was little disgrace to die enshrouded in one's millions.

Some millionaires were more enthusiastic disciples of Carnegie's philanthropic stewardship than Hyde. In a crude attempt to divine a pattern in the bequests of America's four thousand, the *Review of Reviews* in 1893 conducted a survey of the fruits of philanthropy in America's cities.[5] The *Review*, reflecting the influence of W. T. Stead and Henry D. Lloyd, insisted that the great American fortunes were the product of "social opportunities rather than mere creative power of their holders."[6] Therefore, the public should benefit from the "golden sheaves," especially all manner of public institutions. The *Review* then took its readers on a city-by-city tour, spotlighting in each the millionaires and their benefactions.

The favorite philanthropy in Cleveland was educational institutions; in Cincinnati, culture, especially music; in Detroit, hospitals; in San Francisco, institutions of higher learning; in Philadelphia, a bohemian mixture of science, arctic expeditions, and the "ennoblement" of the American Indian. The *Review* had no bashfulness when it came to lampooning the public spirit of millionaires. Boston, which had the second largest number of great fortunes, was castigated: "It is to be regretted that they cannot give a better account of themselves."[7] In contrast, the millionaires of another coastal city, Baltimore, were lauded for "their timely and purposeful gifts."[8]

It is doubtful that America's millionaires were entranced by the *Review of Reviews* argument for the social use of their wealth, but as the nineteenth century passed, they were beginning to consider the ways and means of philanthropic giving. Typically, they approached the problem in the same fashion as they had attacked that of business organization. If trusts were good business devices, then they were a good philanthropic stratagem. The first

5 Albert Shaw: "America's Millionaires and Their Public Gifts," *Review of Reviews*, VII (February 1893), 48–60.
6 Ibid., 49.
7 Ibid., 59.
8 Ibid., 58.

decade in the twentieth century was as much the era of foundation "trusts" as it was of corporate trusts: the Rockefeller Institute for Medical Research, 1901; the General Education Board,
1902; the Carnegie Foundation for the Advancement of Teaching,
1905; the Russell Sage Foundation, 1907; the Carnegie Corporation of New York, 1911.

Whether the financier of Wall Street in New York or Federal
Square in Boston merited Carl Schurz's epithet "robber barons"
remains a rhetorical question. A few facts are self-evident: (1)
unparalleled industrial growth occurred in the last three decades
of the nineteenth century; (2) the opening of the West offered
a unique field for economic development; (3) immense fortunes
were amassed on an unprecedented scale; (4) from these fortunes
mushroomed foundations, which were of undeniable public benefit. In sum, the ultimate public gains and losses from this massive
accumulation of wealth are not easily calculable.

Whatever social "calculus" is used, it is clear that labor suffered in the Gilded Age. Without question, some nineteenth-
century capitalists were shrewd, ruthless speculators. There were
a few stocks on Wall Street which might have been purchased
on "growth potential" and which by some freak chance escaped
manipulation. However, in the main the stock market in the last
quarter of the nineteenth century was a gambling affair, as much so
as the faro tables in the "last-chance" saloons in the storied West.

Undoubtedly much of the smog surrounding the image of the
"robber baron" is owing to the vehemence of the attack on this
image and the stubbornness of the defense. Whether you view
the captains of industry as creative entrepreneurs or malevolent
exploiters, part of the industrial growth of the nineteenth century
was incontestably their creation. Whether the cost to society
exceeded the benefits will remain in dispute. Although the muck-
rakers strafed the robber barons for amassing their millions, they
disregarded the capitalists' philanthropic creations until after 1910,[9]

[9] The studies on American philanthropy, with a few minor exceptions,
are distinguished neither by quantity nor by quality. Some of the more useful
are F. Emerson Andrews: *Philanthropic Giving* (New York: Russell Sage

undoubtedly on the biblical injunction that it is more blessed to
give than to receive.

This, then, was the capitalistic environment from which the
Eastern investor cast his attention toward the enormous resources
of the American West. If ever a region deserved to be called "underdeveloped," it was the land of plain and mountain beyond the
hundredth meridian from the bony rib of the Cascades to the
Sierra Nevadas. In 1880, the total population of the Mountain
West (which included Arizona, Colorado, Idaho, Montana, Nevada, New Mexico, Utah, and Wyoming, according to the Census
Bureau) numbered 653,119.[1] The most populous of these states
was Colorado, with 194,320; the least populous was Nevada, with
20,789. In comparison, Maine, with an area of 33,215 square miles,
as against these eight states' 863,888, had a population of 648,936.
The total population for the United States was 50,189,209. In the
next decennial census, these eight states doubled in population,
reaching 1,213,935. Colorado was still ahead, with 413,249—approximately one third of the total. Wyoming supplanted Nevada
as the least populous, with 62,555. The Mountain West could
congratulate itself, as Maine's population had increased by only
20,000; now the total of the eight states approximated the population of Mississippi or California. At the century mark, the
Mountain States had a population of 1,674,657; Colorado continued its lead, with 539,700, and Nevada again took last place
with 42,335. Mississippi and California kept pace, with their population increasing at a rate matching that of the Mountain States.[2]

These were the souls, but what were people doing in the West
in 1880? Roughly 20 per cent were on farms or ranches; another

---

Foundation; 1950); Merle Curti: "The History of American Philanthropy
as a Field of Research," *American Historical Review*, LXII (January 1957),
352–63; Amos G. Warner: *American Charities* (New York: Crowell; 1894);
Raymond G. Fosdick: *The Story of the Rockefeller Foundation* (New
York: Harper & Row; 1952); Irvin G. Wyllie: "The Reputation of the
American Philanthopists," *Social Service Review*, XXXII (September 1958),
215–22; Allan Nevins: *Study in Power;* Dwight MacDonald: *The Ford
Foundation* (New York: Reynal; 1956).

[1] *Historical Statistics of the United States,* 12.
[2] Ibid.

20 per cent worked in mines; 10 per cent were employed in factories; and 7 per cent had jobs in the transportation industries. The
rest fell into miscellaneous occupations such as domestic service,
government and military duty, and unskilled labor.[3] In 1900 the
percentages were roughly the same. Agriculture increased to 28
per cent, mineral extraction to 12 per cent, manufacturing to 11
per cent, and transportation to 9 per cent.[4] The significance of
these figures is highlighted when compared with those of the
United States as a whole. In 1900 the labor force was split, 35 per
cent going to agriculture, 10 to 18 per cent to manufacturing, 10
per cent to mining, and 5 per cent to transportation.[5]

The Westerner was most likely to be a miner, stock raiser, or
railroader in 1880. His son in 1900 was likely to follow in his
father's footsteps. A majority of the states were dependent to a
crippling extent on a single economic base: Wyoming on the
range cattle industry, Arizona and, to a lesser extent, Nevada on
mining. These export industries (whose products were marketed
outside the region) were essential not only for economic growth
but for survival. An area can by stringent means build a self-
sufficient economy, as Utah has graphically demonstrated.[6] But
Utah's theocratic-economic oligarchy was obviously a unique
system of government in West or East. Utah also had the dynamic
momentum provided by strong tide of immigration.

The advent of the railroad opened up the Eastern market dra-
matically and quickly changed the pastoral village base which
had been the caste mark of the Mountain West.[7] With the

[3] Leonard Arrington: *The Changing Economic Structure of the Mountain West, 1850–1950* (Logan: Utah State University Press; 1963), 42–3.
[4] Ibid., 44–5.
[5] Ibid.
[6] Leonard Arrington: *Great Basin Kingdom: An Economic History of
the Latterday Saints, 1830–1890* (Cambridge: Harvard University Press;
1958).
[7] For treatment of the merchant-capitalists, the following are pertinent:
J. Evetts Haley: *Charles Shreiner* (Austin: Texas State Historical Assoc.;
1944); William Parish: *The Charles Ifeld Company* (Cambridge: Harvard
University Press; 1961); Floyd S. Fireman: "The Spiegelbergs of New
Mexico: Merchants and Bankers, 1844–1893," *Southwestern Studies*, I
(Winter 1964), 1–48.

metamorphosis from village economies into cities serving as distribution points, there grew up in the West a local hierarchy of entrepreneurial leadership. In the pre-railroad, merchant-capitalist era, the local businessman depended almost exclusively on the credit of, or outright financing from, an Eastern wholesaler. The Western banker was at a decided disadvantage in competing for business; unable to offer such attractive credit or interest rates, he was one of the weakest links in the economic chain. He would have to be intolerably obtuse not to realize that there was often little reason for his existence.

The influx of immigration with the railroad altered but did not overturn the merchant-capitalist power, in part for the obvious reason that much of the West remained a hinterland cut off from the radial influence of the railroad. Also, even after the maturing economy would have justified a stronger place for the banking institution, the merchant-capitalist proved formidable competition for the town banker. P. A. Gushurst, a storekeeper of Lead, South Dakota, retained not only his economic dominance but his local political power as well, long after Lead had been transformed from an isolated village economy into a distributing point for the surrounding region.[8] But in larger metropolises, with heavy inputs of capital and a booming population, the merchant-capitalist's strategic status was quickly and thoroughly undermined.

Eastern investors and corporations commonly employed a local attorney or banker as their Western spokesman and adviser. There remains a need in Western history for a discerning study of the influence of legal institutions in Western development. One hypothesis, based on fragmentary evidence, has led this writer to propose that legal advisers were to Eastern investors of 1880–1900 what the merchant-capitalists were in 1850–80. As Western manager of large inputs of Eastern capital, the Western lawyer was in a unique position to abet or discourage various sectors in his local economy. The career of the famous Wolcott brothers

[8] Rodman W. Paul: *Mining Frontiers of the Far West, 1848–1880* (New York: Holt, Rinehart and Winston; 1963), 190–1. Also, Gushurst Collection, Western History Research Center, University of Wyoming.

of Colorado offers an illustration. Edward Oliver Wolcott was born in Massachusetts in 1848, served in the Civil War, graduated from Yale in 1866, and received his law degree from Harvard in 1871.[9] Then, after spending the summer in New England, he moved to Georgetown, Colorado. Here he joined his brother, Henry R. Wolcott, who had arrived in the Centennial State two years before. Edward Wolcott quickly gained a reputation as the attorney to retain if one was enmeshed in the intricacies of mining law. In 1889, and again in 1895, he was elected to the United States Senate. Henry Wolcott's success in business paralleled his brother's rise in the bar. In quick succession, he became treasurer of the Colorado Smelting and Mining Company, vice-president of the Colorado Fuel and Iron Company, and president of the Colorado Telephone Company.

In the early 1890's both Henry and Edward Wolcott became the "confidants" of Henry Hyde, president of the Equitable Life Assurance Company. The Hyde-Wolcott alliance was a mutually advantageous one; Hyde persistently asked the Wolcotts for their opinion on lucrative investment opportunities and on "general conditions out there." This favorite phrase of Hyde's could be translated into "Tell me the political and business gossip." In the late spring of 1895, Henry Wolcott offered Hyde a résumé of the signs and portents of the economic climate in the Rockies, concluding: "I have greater faith than ever in this city. . . . The right kind of people have come to make Denver a home and we have no rival for several hundred miles in either direction."[1] Wolcott's opinion of the future of Denver must have sounded convincing to Hyde, for he soon financed the construction of two "downtown" office buildings, the Boston and Equitable "skyscrapers."

In July of the same year, Hyde toyed with the idea of buying into the First National Bank of Denver. He asked the Wolcotts to "search, search every nook and cranny of their operations—

[9] Biographical sketches of Edward Oliver Wolcott and Henry R. Wolcott are in Wilbur F. Stone: *History of Colorado*, (Chicago: J. J. Clarke; 1918), II, 9–10, 12–13.

[1] Henry Wolcott to Henry Hyde, April 6, 1895. Hyde Collection, Baker Library, Harvard University.

then tell me what you believe."[2] With the influential connections that the Wolcotts possessed among Denver's "four hundred," this was a relatively easy assignment. Edward Wolcott responded: "I fear in some matters they have been placing too much confidence in the statements made to them by their customers."[3] The Wolcotts cast no aspersions on David Moffat, principal stockholder in the Denver and Rio Grande Western, but they considered briefly the unattractive possibility of approaching him to ask for a personal guarantee of loss against suspicious accounts. Hyde dismissed this possibility with the curt statement: "We would not wish to cast stones, where we only have doubt, no matter how strong."[4] Hyde sensibly assumed that once Moffat's transactions were questioned, further negotiation would be impossible. Hyde kept relentless pressure on the Wolcotts to uncover "as deep as you can without throwing up the whole game."[5] Henry Wolcott, in an attempt to satiate Hyde's curiosity once and for all, advised "against you purchasing stock. . . . Moffat's a rich man, but he is not always as conservative as he should be. All this is very confidential."[6] Hyde yielded to Wolcott's judgment, for this was the last time he questioned the brothers on the First National Bank's affairs. The Wolcotts' uneasiness was justified when the Moffat financial empire collapsed in 1911.

Another fruitful and long-term relationship involved J. C. Young, a Cedar Rapids, Iowa, attorney, and J. Horace Harding, son-in-law of Jay Cooke's son-in-law, Charles D. Barney, and trustee for the Jay Cooke estate in bankruptcy. In the days of his dreams of empire, Jay Cooke acquired heavy landholdings in the upper Midwest.[7] As a land broker and legal adviser, Cooke came in contact with J. C. Young, who had been speculating for some years in the "land of ten thousand lakes." Young managed rentals,

[2] Henry Hyde to Edward O. Wolcott, July 17, 1895. Ibid.

[3] Edward O. Wolcott to Henry Hyde, August 3, 1895. Ibid.

[4] Henry Hyde to Henry Wolcott, August 10, 1895. Ibid.

[5] Ibid., September 5, 1895.

[6] Henry Wolcott to Henry Hyde, September 21, 1895. Ibid.

[7] The most helpful biography of Jay Cooke, especially from an entrepreneurial standpoint, is Henrietta Larson: *Jay Cooke* (Cambridge: Harvard University Press; 1936).

sold and exchanged parcels of real estate, and kept Cooke—and later Harding—up to date on the political crosscurrents of the upper Mississippi region.

Young had an unsophisticated policy of speculation: "The situation is just this, when one does not need money and has faith and assurance and is willing to take chances of long time land, it will pay, but if he does not want to be bothered with care and details of long winded investments he should sell."[8] As for himself, he was buying, "for I believe in this country, I may want to run for the Senate someday, you know, and I want to have plenty of possessions and be identified with the farmers."[9] The Young-Harding-Cooke relationship lasted for over fifteen years, until most of the Cooke estate was liquidated. As Harding admitted in an aside in a letter to Jay Cooke at his summer retreat on Gibraltar Island in Lake Erie, Young's managerial and legal initiative "has saved us time and money, but I wish that he would cut short his letters."[1] Harding's irritation came from a letter he had just received from Young: "My dear friend, I am sort of a sensitive plant ready to sacrifice everything for my friends and I feel hurt if they do not understand me." Young's wilted spirits and "gloomy depths" did not last long, for he was soon describing the "new mortgage sale, which if we manage right will make fortunes for all of us."[2]

For all the minor vexations, Young's shrewd management enabled Cooke's estate to reap a good long-term profit. After a two-year probation period, Harding left the decisions in the West largely up to Young. The clearance of titles, mortgage sales, collection of rents, boundary disputes, railroad lobbying, and legal housekeeping all were handled with considerable deftness by the Cedar Rapids attorney. Harding offered advice and supplied capital, but Young handled the daily details and suggested the next business policy. Locked in this partnership, both parties were

[8] J. C. Young to J. Horace Harding, November 29, 1892. Cooke Collection, Baker Library, Harvard University.
[9] Ibid.
[1] J. Horace Harding to Jay Cooke, March 9, 1891. Ibid.
[2] J. C. Young to J. Horace Harding, November 30, 1891. Ibid.

basically satisfied, for Young and Harding realized that their individual success had come from mutual cooperation.

The Wolcott-Hyde, Young-Harding relationships represent the type of East-West association which was both common and profitable in the nineteenth and early twentieth centuries. Railroads retained "local counselors" along the entire length of their rights-of-way. Carl Pforzheimer of New York, the first broker to trade petroleum stocks of companies based in the Rockies, had legal advisers in Denver and Cheyenne to keep him informed. The Curtis family of Jamestown, New York, when they became entranced over the possibilities of Wyoming oil, hired the Denver attorney Warwick Downing, one of the ablest in the petroleum industry.[3] The Livermore family of Boston depended on their local attorney in Telluride, Colorado,[4] to guide their property transactions in Colorado mining. Marshall Field and Levi Leiter had "counsel and advice" from lawyers near their widely scattered Western properties.

Cases of Eastern investor–Western attorney alliances could be indefinitely multiplied. The attorney in the West occupied a pivotal place in the capital flow between East and West, although the full nature of this influence needs further investigation. As political and economic adviser, knowledgeable as to Western conditions and shrewdly cognizant of his Eastern client's *modus operandi*, the Western attorney had influence restricted only by his ineptness. Obviously, if he betrayed a client's trust or misrepresented a business proposition, his career would be short and unhappy. Young dismissed one assistant with the sarcastic note: "Should we have foolishly followed your advice, we would all be in jail, where you should be."[5] If, on the other hand, he served his Eastern client adeptly, his power was incalculable. One grate-

[3] Downing Collection, Petroleum History and Research Center, University of Wyoming.

[4] Livermore Collection, Western History Research Center, University of Wyoming; E. B. Adams: *My Association with a Glamorous Man . . . Bulkeley Wells* (Grand Junction, Colorado: 1961).

[5] J. C. Young to Andrew Gilbreth, June 10, 1892. Cooke Collection, Baker Library, Harvard University.

ful Duluth investor wrote his Idaho Springs, Colorado, attorney: "You will now know how fully indebted we feel to you. Our family has been the brunt of unethical actions out there time and again, but in the four years, you have never caused us a day of regret."[6] Accompanying the letter was pecuniary proof of their regard.

From the early 1870's Dun and Bradstreet, as the financial intelligence for Eastern investors, hired squads of young lawyers to make "confidential" investigations of Western businesses. In communities of fifteen hundred or less, one can imagine how discreet these inquiries were. The field reports, in sharp, cryptic, and sometimes brutal phrases, related age, occupation, acquaintances, credit standing, mobility, and character. Fluidity was the most conspicuous characteristic of Western society as shown in the Dun and Bradstreet reports. Western institutions were in flux; mobility, geographical and occupational, was commonplace.

Isaac Blake, trying his best to establish the Continental Oil Company in Cheyenne, received the Dun and Bradstreet man's tentative approval in November 1874: "Good char[acter] & hon[est], can't say as to capacity hasn't be[e]n tried yet."[7] September 11 found the Continental Oil Company expanding and "considered a sound institution though yet a new concern." July 15, 1876, "still in bus[iness] expanding to new towns ap[p]ears to be making money."[8] The young legal sleuths employed by Dun and Bradstreet could be withering in their "confidences," however. One young lawyer-businessman was described as "age 32, a pretty fair lawyer but bears a bad repu[tation] at one time threatened with a criminal prosecution in debt now."[9] Somehow this man must have been able to redeem himself, for he later became a senator and one of the most prominent financial figures in the Centennial State. Another businessman was curtly dismissed with the phrase: "Fair hab[its] tho' he lives up to his in-

---

[6] W. Ray Russell to E. L. Regennitter, October 23, 1895. Regennitter Collection, Western History Research Center, University of Wyoming.
[7] "The West," vol. 3, Dun and Bradstreet Collection, Baker Library, Harvard University.
[8] Ibid.
[9] Ibid., vol. 1, 13.

come & is not believed to have much respons[ibility] of his own."[1] Again, this young man presumably saw the light of salvation, as he was one of the organizers and later chief executive of the Colorado Fuel and Iron Corporation.

An intriguing facet of the Dun and Bradstreet inquiries was the emphasis on small Western communities and even smaller "main street" businesses. The stores along the boardwalks of South Pass City's A Avenue received as critical a credit inspection as the largest emporium in Denver. Also, from year to year Dun and Bradstreet would select a geographical area for intense credit analysis: in 1870, it was northern Wyoming and southern Montana; in 1872, Indian territory which later became Oklahoma; in 1873, southern and central California.

It is evident that Dun and Bradstreet were responding to the demands of their clients. When the proprietor of the Miner's Delight bar of South Pass City wrote to a wholesaler for goods in Chicago or Omaha, the merchants obviously wanted to know something of the credit standing of this frontier merchant-capitalist. Above all, the Dun and Bradstreet records reveal the tight mercantile connections between East and West. The supplier in Omaha and Chicago might have considerably more business from stores in small Midwest communities with the names of Polo, Illinois, or Kentland, Indiana, which could easily be checked on; but an order from a store in North Park, Colorado, presented a credit-rating challenge to be met by Dun and Bradstreet.

That the American economy underwent a cataclysmic upheaval in the last three decades of the nineteenth century is indisputable. That tremendous economic growth accompanied this period of turmoil is also clear. Gross national product leaped from $9 billion in 1870 to $46 billion at the turn of the century.[2] The value of mineral products rose from $301 million in 1880 to $914 million two decades later.[3] Capital investment in major manufacturing went from more than $2 billion in 1879 to more than $11 billion

[1] Ibid., 16.
[2] *Historical Statistics of the United States*, 139. These estimates are in 1929 dollar values.
[3] Ibid., 350.

twenty-five years later.[4] The operating railroad mileage increased from 60,000 in 1870 to 258,000 in 1900.[5]

The nation had never experienced such a radical change in it economy. New access to immense national resources gave enough capital to the financial community (led by entrepreneur, or robber baron, as you will) to satisfy their most imperial dreams. Assisted by a classical laissez-faire policy and a Social Darwinist economic philosophy, by a friendly political atmosphere and a series of imaginative legal devices, the capitalist of the nineteenth century was sanctified with the climate of opinion and the practical opportunity necessary to give free rein to his entrepreneurial whims.

The United States of 1900 was a drastically different country from that of 1870, just as the American West of 1900 bore little resemblance to the West of 1870. Not that Eastern capital and immigration had eliminated all the traces of an underdeveloped region; many indications of the immature economy of the West still remained in the mid-twentieth century. Nevertheless, there had been a remarkable transformation. Instead of one transcontinental railroad, there were now five; a fivefold increase in population had taken place; urbanization had started; and for the first time the resources of the West were being developed on a wide and systematic basis. Owen Wister had sensed this transformation as early as 1885 when he jotted in his Western journal on the evening of July 16:

> The details of the Life here are interesting. Wish I could find out all about it—and master it—theoretically. It's a life as strange as any country has seen, and it will slowly make room for Cheyennes, Chicagos, and ultimately inland New Yorks—everything reduced to the same prairie-like level or utilitarian civilization. Branans and Beeches [families of Wyoming] will give way to Tweeds and Jay Goulds—and the ticker will replace the rifle.[6]

[4] Ibid., 411.
[5] Ibid., 427-9.
[6] "Wister Journal," July 16, 1885. Wister Collection, Western History Research Center, University of Wyoming.

II

CAREY AVENUE

ᴧ B CY ᴼ ND ⊥ ೭
◇ ʌ ㅂ ϒ ☜
エ ō ℞
Ϙ

As Nathan Addison Baker, sometime schoolteacher, law student, and "artistic" printer, walked down Ferguson (later Carey) Avenue in Cheyenne on a May morning in 1868, he reflected on the future of Cheyenne and the West. Striding past the flapping entrances of the tents in which Cheyenne's population lived, Baker began to formulate an editorial that would appear the following morning in his paper, the Cheyenne *Leader*, under the masthead "Future of the Plains." The editor of the *Leader* left little room for debate about what that future would be.

That a future of the greatest importance is in store for the western plains, no one who has traveled over and lived upon them for any considerable length of time can doubt . . . this country will make stock raising a specialty, since it is one of the most profitable branches of industry which it is possible for civilized man to engage in.[1]

While Baker was not unique among frontier editors in forecasting a magnificent destiny for the West, he was one of the first to devote himself to publicizing the cattle industry. In the next two years, the *Leader* carried sixty-three articles proclaiming the "wondrous" development of the cattle industry. The message, though chronicled in variant styles, was remarkably consistent—Wyoming was the cattleman's paradise.

The reasons, Baker claimed, were obvious. Nature had lavished her bounty on Wyoming. The grasses of the plains and mountain valleys were "exceedingly" nutritious. Good water was "everywhere" abundant. The mild winters—flannel-shirt weather—reduced the necessity for winter feeding. In fact, so his argument went, it was cheaper to count on a small 2 or 3 per cent loss during the winter than to feed. Sheltered valleys protected the cattle during the infrequent winter storms. In addition, this flourishing range had the advantage that it was free government domain. Baker undoubtedly had on the same spectacles as the rainmaker Melbourne of two decades later.[2] Only a small labor force was required, because herds did not need close supervision in such a temperate climate. The Union Pacific Railroad provided "cheap" (many cattlemen would have vigorously dissented) and rapid transportation to market. Because of these railroad facilities, he envisioned Cheyenne becoming the "Greatest Cattle Market" in the country.[3] Buyers were already coming from Chicago; it was only necessary to construct extensive stockyards, and the Magic City of the Plains would rival Chicago as a market.[4]

Given all these factors conducive to cattle raising, how could

[1] Cheyenne *Leader*, May 8, 1868.
[2] Clark C. Spence: "Melbourne, the Australian Rain Wizard," *Annals of Wyoming*, XXXIII (April, 1961), 5–18.
[3] Cheyenne *Leader*, September 9, 1870.
[4] Cheyenne *Leader*, September 20, 1875; February 7, 1871; February 23, 1875.

one escape making a fortune? The lesson was clear: Only the most improvident and careless businessman would have difficulty in reaping a handsome profit for a small expenditure of labor and capital.[5]

While few other journalists may have reached such heights of enthusiasm, many were developing the same theme. A Laramie, Wyoming, newspaperman became so fervent over the prospects of the cattle industry that he was aroused to write:

> The East—and by that we mean everything east of the Missouri River—is getting discouraged in competing with the great stock growing plains of this country . . . and is going out of business, leaving the trans-Missouri country to supply the beef of the world.[6]

The *Colorado Chieftain* declared that the "sleek fat" cattle coming down from the lush winter range would dispel the myth of the Great American Desert.[7] The Denver *Tribune* regretted that the furor over mining and railroad speculation had resulted in the neglect of the cattle industry.[8] Any business, the *Tribune* contended, which would pay a 15 or 20 per cent dividend deserved the serious attention of an investor. (Written at the height of the cattle boom, this statement was, to say the least, remarkable. The Denver editor had evidently just glanced East to the plains and discovered the cattle industry.) The Las Vegas *Optic* predicted the day when all northern New Mexico would be "dotted with cattle as thick as the prairies of Illinois."[9]

Newspaper editors, *sui generis*, are not reputed for their reserve when speaking about the economic opportunities of their home localities. Although the fact has been slighted in studies of this era, enthusiasm was already widespread a decade before the cattle boom began. By 1875, spirited publicity had developed which was aimed at drawing Eastern capital to the West. The

[5] Laramie *Sentinel*, May 1, 1876; October 21, 1874; September 16, 1882; July 14, 1883.
[6] Laramie *Sentinel*, August 6, 1881.
[7] *Colorado Chieftain*, June 10, 1869.
[8] Denver *Tribune*, August 12, 1882.
[9] Las Vegas *Daily Optic*, May 10, 1881.

bulk of it was erratically fashioned, exaggerated, and ineffective, but there was a cumulative force which acted perhaps as much on the West as on the East, for Western editors and readers began to be mesmerized by their own pronouncements. Merris C. Barrow, editor of the Douglas *Budget* and locally known as the "Sage Brush Philosopher," wrote a Wisconsin relative: "Agricultural possibilities, primarily cattle raising, are unlimited."[1]

If frontier newspapers waxed eloquent over the golden prospects of the West, their rhetoric paled beside the ballyhoo of promoter-publicists. Promoters themselves frequently verged on eccentricity. Of four whose writings successively captured the imaginations of wide audiences, one was a physician, one a journalist, one a general, and one a German baron. Only the baron was not associated with a railroad.

Dr. Hiram Latham, former surgeon of the Union Pacific Railroad, as he titled himself, was the earliest railroad press agent for the cattle country of the northern plains. His *Trans-Missouri Stock Raising*,[2] which was published in 1871, set the tone and molded the pattern to be followed by future prophets. Latham had served as a surgeon in the Union Army before coming West. He was recalled much later by a Laramie, Wyoming, resident as a "most interesting character. A tall erect person . . . full of anecdotes and a charming talker, a man of culture and education."[3]

As most of the publicists did to some degree, Latham adopted his own advice. The year his book appeared, he was one of the organizers of the Wyoming Stock Graziers Association, predecessor of the Wyoming Stock Growers Association.[4] He and a partner had already established a ranch on the Laramie plains, and the Laramie *Sentinel* noted that Dr. Latham owned the

---

[1] M. C. Barrow to Nellis Galbreath, April 8, 1893, Combs Collection, Western History Research Center, University of Wyoming.

[2] Hiram Latham: *Trans-Missouri Stock Raising; The Pasture Lands of North America: Winter Grazing* . . . (Denver: Old West Publ. Co.; 1962).

[3] Nancy Fillmore Brown: "Girlhood Recollections of Laramie in 1870 and 1871," *Wyoming Historical Society Quarterly Bulletin*, I (January 15, 1924), 12.

[4] Laramie *Sentinel*, April 14, 1871.

finest cattle in the immediate region.[5] A visionary Latham most certainly was, but his aspirations as a cattleman were also undeniable.

Latham traveled widely to spread his message that the trans-Missouri country was the "future dependence of the East for wool, mutton and horses." In the columns of the Laramie *Sentinel* habitual references are made to Dr. Latham's interludes in the East. The Denver *Rocky Mountain Daily News*, reporting an address before the Colorado Stock Growers in 1873, quoted Latham as urging his audience: "Never cease your efforts till every acre of grass in Colorado is eaten annually; till your beef is consumed in every market."[6] A few weeks after this speech, Latham was in Cheyenne raising three hundred dollars from affluent citizenry to advertise the city as a cattle market. "There is no time to lose," Latham advised, "if we expect to reap any benefit from the cattle trade this coming season. We can just as well have a hundred thousand cattle brought to this market every year as not, if we only take hold and push things."[7]

For Latham, public relations and business evidently did not mix, for in December 1873 his cattle ranch was declared bankrupt.[8] Next the itinerant Dr. Latham turned up in Japan as superintendent of a railway system and an official in the Imperial College. In the late 1880's he was huckstering real estate in northern California. The death of this facsimile of George Francis Train occurred in 1902 in Alameda, California.[9]

Latham's *Trans-Missouri Stock Raising*, which first appeared as a series of articles in the Omaha *Herald*, was an effusive testimonial to the wonders of the West as grazing country. Each chapter discussed a specific geographic area along the Union Pacific, its agricultural potential and market (present or anticipated), and the profits to be realized immediately. It is not sur-

[5] Laramie *Sentinel*, February 8, 1871.

[6] *Rocky Mountain Daily News*, February 2, 1873.

[7] Cheyenne *Leader*, February 24, 1873.

[8] Laramie *Sentinel*, December 22, 1873.

[9] A biographical sketch of Hiram Latham is in Robert H. Burns, Andrew S. Gillespie, and Willing G. Richardson: *Wyoming's Pioneer Ranches* (Laramie: Top-of-the-World Press; 1955), 57–60.

prising that, with the exception of Texas, Dr. Latham found the best grazing land in the country along the Union Pacific Railroad. His debt to the Union Pacific is clear from the copious references to his sponsor which adorn the narrative.

As for the book's style, Latham employed the technique of incorporating testimonial letters from prominent personages in the West. Whenever he desired to buttress his argument, he presented letters from Army officers, bankers, and politicians giving laudatory opinions on subjects ranging from winter grazing to the milk production of a dairy herd.[1] He also offered figures on the cost of raising livestock on the plains, but he did not use a device popular in later books—reaching for a mythical investment figure and then, with abacus-like agility, calculating the amount of profit which would accrue to the investor after a three-year interval. As the doctor demonstrated little restraint in his other sales tactics, undoubtedly this one never occurred to him.

After Latham left to superintend a narrow-gauge railway in Japan, the Union Pacific sponsored another author, one who eclipsed the doctor in both loquacity and power of imagination. The title of Robert Strahorn's first book, *The Hand-Book of Wyoming and Guide to the Black Hills and Big Horn Regions for Citizen, Emigrant and Tourist*,[2] showed that he intended his work for a select clientele—every prospective traveler on the Union Pacific.

Strahorn first saw Denver on an August day in 1870.[3] A one-time journalist from Sedalia, Missouri, he was looking for a job on a newspaper in the eleven-year-old, mile-high community. Soon he did obtain a position, not as a reporter, but as a printer's devil, and not on the *Rocky Mountain Daily News*, Denver's leading eight-page clarion, but on the Black Hawk *Journal*, in a

[1] Latham: *Trans-Missouri Stock Raising*, 13–22, 50–2, 76–86.

[2] Robert E. Strahorn: *The Hand-Book of Wyoming and Guide to the Black Hills and Big Horn Regions for Citizen, Emigrant and Tourist* (Cheyenne [Chicago: Knight and Leonard]; 1877).

[3] The biographical sketch is derived from Robert E. Strahorn's autobiography, "Ninety Years of Boyhood" (manuscript, College of Idaho, Caldwell; 1942). Strahorn crammed his reminiscences with irrelevant minutiae.

mining town thirty-five miles west of Denver. However, his residence in the center of the "richest square mile on earth" was of short duration. In a few months, Strahorn was back in Denver, reporting for several newspapers (including the *Rocky Mountain Daily News*) and supervising the circulation department of the Denver *Tribune*. As an avocation, he published the *Colorado Agricultural and Stock Journal*, confessing that the only reason for "choosing that field was that all others were done to death, with only one other agricultural and stock journal within a thousand miles."[4]

Strahorn's career in Colorado abruptly ended when he enlisted as a war correspondent with General Crook, who was engaged in the Rosebud campaign of 1876.[5] He began to dispatch stories to the Chicago *Tribune*, the *Rocky Mountain Daily News*, the Omaha *Republican*, and, sporadically, to the New York *Times*. In a lull in the campaigning during the winter of 1876, Strahorn wrote his *Hand-Book*, a task which he accomplished with alacrity, concluding it in ninety days.

On a trip from Cheyenne to Illinois in September 1877, Strahorn stopped off at Omaha to see Thomas Kimball, general passenger agent for the Union Pacific. Kimball was just leaving for Wisconsin on a fishing trip with Jay Gould, president of the Union Pacific, but he managed to spend a few minutes with the young author, and he stuffed a copy of the *Hand-Book* in his valise before he escaped to the Wisconsin woods.

Years later Strahorn reminisced: "My prosy literary production served its purpose. . . . It settled my coveted entrance into the great railroad game, for, upon Kimball's return to Headquarters, he got in touch with me and the arrangement was hastily consummated."[6] Strahorn's first assignment was to write a book "of several hundred pages which would describe the resources and the attractions of *all* the country west of the Missouri." This was to be followed by a flood of leaflets, maps, and brochures, some

[4] Ibid., 72.
[5] For Crook's career, see Martin F. Schmitt (ed.): *General George Crook, His Autobiography* (Norman: University of Oklahoma Press; 1946).
[6] Strahorn: "Ninety Years of Boyhood," 243.

of which would be translated into foreign languages. In doing the research for his new book, the author was to travel four thousand miles in Union Pacific land.

Before leaving Omaha, Strahorn asked his new employer for advice. "Well, Robert," Kimball cautioned, "bear in mind that everything you write will be discounted at least fifty per cent. At the same time don't forget that everything like this first book to be circulated by the Union Pacific must bear your name as author."[7] Anonymous and "original"—these were the criteria the Union Pacific dictated to Strahorn for his *To the Rockies and Beyond*.[8]

Thirty days after taking on his assignment, Strahorn, travel-weary from jostling in the Union Pacific palace cars, dropped five hundred pages of manuscript on Kimball's desk with the explanation: "The book moved quickly." Kimball had only one change to propose: a credit line to the *Rocky Mountain Daily News* should be deleted from a statistical table. "Why?" queried the author, puzzled. Because it impaired "originality," was the answer. Evidently plagiarism was not considered a deterrent to uniqueness.[9]

Both the publicity department and Strahorn prospered under the Gould regime, even if the Union Pacific stock did not. Jay Gould operated on the theory that if a book which cost a dollar to print would sell a hundred-dollar ticket (the fare from Omaha to the Pacific Coast), then print more books. Though this seemed indisputable logic to the publicity-minded Gould, the austere Charles Francis Adams replaced Gould as president, and Strahorn felt "cold shivers" run down his spine during their first meeting. Adams quickly cut off the publicity department's funds, and Strahorn resigned.

His departure from the Union Pacific by no means signaled

[7] Ibid., 244.
[8] Robert E. Strahorn: *To the Rockies and Beyond, or a Summer on the Union Pacific Railroad and Branches. Saunterings in the Popular Health, Pleasure, and Hunting Resorts of Nebraska, Dakota, Wyoming, Colorado, New Mexico, Utah, Montana, and Idaho.* (Omaha: Omaha Republican Print; 1878).
[9] Strahorn: "Ninety Years of Boyhood," 246–50.

an end to his railroad activities, however. He assisted the financing
of the Fairhaven Northern and Southern railroads in Puget Sound.
Then from 1890 to 1898 he was a broker in Boston, specializing
in municipal and state bonds. Ironically, Strahorn returned to the
Union Pacific under the Harriman aegis, to advise on the development of the Pacific Northwest roads in the Harriman empire.

During his tenure with the Union Pacific, Strahorn had written
five books[1] and innumerable pamphlets. As publicity for the cattle industry, *The Hand-Book of Wyoming* was favored by newspaper editors, who filled long columns in their sheets with
Strahorn's pronouncements. The *Hand-Book* followed the format of other promotional literature. An eleven-page introduction,
offering a brief history of Wyoming from the period of the
Spanish exploitations, opened mellifluously: "Since the time when
Isabella pawned her jewels to procure an outfit for Columbus,
the desire to discover the golden sands of the West has not
lessened."[2] Strahorn did not stay long with the Spanish, however;
in eight paragraphs he was already tramping over the Big Horns
with the Connor expedition of 1865. Following this introduction,
his account of Wyoming covered subjects ranging from the
"bountiful" forests to woman suffrage. The last six chapters dealt
with the Big Horn and Black Hills regions (one was flippantly
headed "The Recent Jaunt of Generals Sheridan and Crook").

Nowhere was Strahorn's inspirational prose more apparent than
in the *Hand-Book* section on stock raising, which featured a
financial statement of a "reliable" Cheyenne stock dealer. Four
pages were devoted to statistical tables illustrating one fact—
the immense profits to be realized from raising cattle.[3] The first
table consisted of a ledger sheet for an investment made in July
1874 of 750 Texas steers, which were promptly turned loose to

---

[1] There were, in addition to *Hand-Book of Wyoming* and *To the Rockies
and Beyond, Montana and Yellowstone National Park* (Kansas City: 1881),
The Resources and Attractions of Idaho Territory (Boise: 1881), and *The
Resources of Montana Territory and Attractions of Yellowstone National
Park* (Helena: 1879).
[2] Strahorn: *Hand-Book of Wyoming*, 2.
[3] Ibid., 28–30.

roam the range. After the cattle were fattened for three years on "succulent" grasses, and after an additional 3,200 head were purchased, the fortunate owner had netted a profit of $36,200 on an original investment of $10,400. In the second table, the author projected the earnings from breeding cattle, with the assurance: "The estimates are made from actual experience, and the profits are as free from exaggeration as in the previous showing."[4] This table demonstrated that on the basis of 1,000 Texas cows and 40 bulls, representing a total expenditure of $15,000, a profit of $68,915 accumulated in five years' time.

Expenses were omitted and losses conveniently minimized in Strahorn's predictions, though later he acknowledged that his estimate of a 2 per cent loss was on the low side. As to profits, Strahorn suggested:

> . . . to the wonderful and often exaggerated results placed upon paper in relation to this industry, a few words may not be amiss. A steady profit of twenty-five per cent per annum is really a common result. Forty and fifty per cent have been realized, but the writer who lays down such figures as an average is very liable to get his reputation involved.[5]

After writing with such conservatism on the cattle industry, Strahorn concluded, appropriately enough, with a rhapsodic passage on the wonders of the transcontinental railroad: "In a little over three years this mighty Western continent was spanned, the foundation for half a dozen grand states laid, and a region believed to be irredeemable turned into one vast mine of production."[6] Perhaps it was only a quirk of fate that this tall, lean, frock-coated missionary ended up in a pulpit on wheels, instead of in a nave.

A decade following the appearance of *Trans-Missouri Stock Raising* and four years after the publication of *The Hand-Book of Wyoming*, General James S. Brisbin brought out *The Beef Bonanza; or, How to Get Rich on the Plains.*[7] The title was in-

[4] Ibid., 29.
[5] Ibid., 35.
[6] Ibid., 248.
[7] James S. Brisbin: *The Beef Bonzana; or, How to Get Rich on the Plains* (Philadelphia: J. B. Lippincott; 1881).

dicative that what followed would not be a pessimistic economic treatise. Indeed, the General saw more gold in the grass than either Strahorn or Latham, or, for that matter, most gold seekers. Where Strahorn had allotted four pages to statistical "proof" of huge profits, Brisbin used fifty-one, most of them devoted to a listing of cattle kings and their reputed returns.

Why was a general in the frontier army so enraptured by the cattle industry? Promotion was the answer: after twelve years' service in a succession of army posts, Brisbin discovered a way to augment his income. If he were to write a promotional book that the Union Pacific distributed, his reputation would enable him to act as broker between Western cattlemen and Eastern investors.

Born in 1837 in Boalsborg, Pennsylvania, the author of *Beef Bonanza* was both a lawyer and editor of the *Centre Democrat* in that community when the Civil War began.[8] He enlisted in the Union Army as a private, quickly advanced to second lieutenant, and was wounded in the first battle of Bull Run. Brisbin went on to distinguish himself, rapidly moving up in rank until 1865, when he became a brigadier general in the volunteers. Deciding he liked shiny epaulets and the metallic clank of the saber, he joined the Sixth Cavalry in 1866. After two years he was commissioned a major in the Second Cavalry, and he spent the remaining twenty-three years of his life on Western army posts. He died in 1892 in Philadelphia, where he had gone because of ill health. The obituary in the New York *Times* said: "Gen. Brisbin was among the first to promote cattle grazing in the West and the transcontinental railways."

The most pervasive characteristic of *Beef Bonanza* was its complete lack of restraint in describing the fortunes to be made in the cattle industry. Indeed, it seemed as though one had only to place a few steers on the open range, then in a short time the owner would magically become a millionaire. Appearing at the

[8] The biographical data is based on Brisbin's obituary in the New York *Times,* January 15, 1892, and on Gilbert C. Fite's foreword to the University of Oklahoma reprint of James S. Brisbin's *Beef Bonanza; or, How to Get Rich on the Plains* (Norman: University of Oklahoma Press; 1959).

height of the expansionist mood in the cattle industry, Brisbin's book appealed to both Eastern investors and Western cattlemen. Chapter headings such as "Great Lands and Great Owners," "Estimated Fortunes," "Money to be Made," "Millions in Beef," "Great Lands in the Southwest," and "Great Opportunities" set the tone.

Although Strahorn had suggested that prudent management was advisable, and Latham had conceded that not everyone made a fortune, the General denied that there was any risk at all. His preface, blending Horace Greeley's inspirational style with biblical rhetoric, stated:

> It does not matter where the emigrant settles in the West, so [long] he comes, and he will almost anywhere soon find himself better off than if he had remained in the East . . . to the discouraged let me say, be of good heart and come West, for what has been occurring in the East during the last two hundred years is now occurring in the West, only with ten fold more rapidity.[9]

In addition to its financial tables and exuberant prophecy, *Beef Bonanza* carried the usual testimonial letters and quotations from the West's leading citizens, some of whom had endorsed Dr. Latham's book years before. Nor were the testimonial letters the General's only debt to Dr. Latham; a number of sentences and statistics had more than a family resemblance to those in *Trans-Missouri Stock Raising*.[1] The fact that the Union Pacific Railroad was a major subscriber to both books may have freed Brisbin's conscience. Brisbin regarded Latham's writing as company property, to be used and reused by company publicists. The General was not unique in the matter of borrowing from promotional literature, however. Material written by Latham, Strahorn, and Brisbin himself cropped up with amazing frequency in cattle-company prospectuses and newspaper and periodical articles. Apparently, repetition did not dull the magnetism of their appeal, or the gloss of their honesty.

[9] Ibid., 14–15.
[1] For the "borrowing" from Latham see Jeff C. Dyke's introduction to the Old West Publishing Company reprint of Hiram Latham's *Trans-Missouri Stock Raising* (Denver: 1962).

In the spring of 1883, a year after *Beef Bonanza* appeared, Brisbin wrote to John B. Thomas of Cheyenne, offering to act as agent in the West or abroad to obtain capital so that "you may increase your lands and profits." His services were courteously and firmly declined.[2] Evidently this discouragement did not dampen Brisbin's brokerage ambitions; two years later, Samuel T. Hauser, mining magnate of Helena, Montana, and a partner in the Pioneer Cattle Company, responded favorably to his overture. By some historians Hauser would be referred to as a "minor" robber baron; he was "minor" only in the sense that he was outwitted by the "majors." Hauser proposed that if the General negotiated the sale of 24,500 head of cattle of the Pioneer Cattle Company in England or elsewhere, "I will personally guarantee your expenses of $3,500.00, and if you sell the cattle, will present you with a $25,000 investment—at least."[3] However, whether Brisbin turned down Hauser's conditions, or the Army denied his requested leave, the contract was never consummated.

In many ways, the most eccentric and histrionic of the promoters was Baron Walter von Richthofen, whose volume *Cattle-Raising on the Plains*[4] was unfortunately issued in 1885, the year before the cattle market collapsed. A Junker, Richthofen arrived in Denver in 1877,[5] and, casting himself as an entrepreneur, immediately plunged into Denver's economic and social life. In an amazingly short time he was involved in suburban Denver real estate, the San Souci Beer Gardens, the Corkscrew Club for foreign gentlemen marooned in Denver, an interurban railroad, and, for good measure, a zoo complete with a bear pit.[6] In the year in which his opus appeared, Richthofen also organized the Western Land Company, which established the town of Montclair in

2 James S. Brisbin to John B. Thomas, April 18, 1883. Dunder Collection, Western History Research Center, University of Wyoming.

3 Samuel Hauser to James S. Brisbin, January 22, 1885. Letterbook, 1883–1885, Hauser Collection, Historical Society of Montana.

4 Baron Walter von Richthofen: *Cattle-Raising on the Plains of North America* (New York: Appleton; 1885).

5 I am indebted to Mrs. Agnes Wright Spring, state historian emerita, State Historical Society of Colorado, for sharing her personal biographical file on Baron von Richthofen, which includes a valuable questionnaire completed by the Baron's daughter.

6 Denver *Times*, May 9, 1898.

east Denver. Tallyhos carried prospective real estate buyers from downtown Denver. For excursionists from Nebraska, however, Richthofen set up a tent city—which the local commentators soon christened "the Baron's circus."[7]

A divorce, the building of a quarter-million-dollar "castle," and the panic of 1893—in that order—dissipated the Baron's fortunes. Forsaking Colorado, Richthofen next turned up in London, where he attempted to entice wealthy Englishmen to join him in a mining syndicate to speculate in Cripple Creek stock. When this venture failed, he returned to Denver, and there he died in the spring of 1898 following an appendectomy.

Cattle-Raising on the Plains, which lacked none of the hyperbole of the previous promotional literature, celebrated the glories of ranch life and of the abundant grass in the "former" Great American Desert. In one chapter, "Cattle Raising, a Legitimate and Safe Business," the author, with mining stock lotteries in mind, assured his readers: "There are no risks beyond losses arising from natural causes, which can be calculated down to a percentage per annum and none arising from speculation. . . . There is not the slightest element of uncertainty in cattle raising."[8] Three chapters were devoted to an assessment of a hypothetical ranch and the magnificent economic rewards for the owner. Compared with the work of the earlier publicists, Richthofen's discussion was more sophisticated and his financial tables were more complicated; but the prophecy at the conclusion was just as outlandish—156 per cent profit in six years on an investment of approximately half a million dollars.

The fleeting fame of a prophet was denied Richthofen when the cattle market collapsed in 1886. The Georgetown, Colorado, *Courier*, referring to a visit of the Baron in 1887, snidely remarked that he "had written a book on cattle, which was once well received."[9]

Concurrently with the promotional books, prospectuses and immigration booklets were being published by Western cattle-

[7] Louisa W. Arps: *Denver in Slices* (Denver: Sage Books; 1959), 155–63.
[8] Richthofen: *Cattle-Raising on the Plains*, 54.
[9] Georgetown *Courier*, June 12, 1887.

men in the search for Eastern gold. For example, A. T. Babbitt, manager of the successful Standard Cattle Company, printed on company stationery a ten-page "inquiry" into the cattle market, past, present, and future. In this piece, titled "The Grazing Interest and the Beef Supply," Colonel Babbitt could not repress the observation:

> The statement has been repeatedly made, and to my knowledge never questioned, that the history of this business records *no case of failure* where reasonable care has been bestowed, together with the employment of capital adequately proportioned to the volume of business carried on.[1]

Though Babbitt's pamphlet was originally intended for distribution among his friends in the Cheyenne Club and their relatives in the East, it also reached financial houses in New York and Chicago. Thomas Sturgis, secretary of the Wyoming Stock Growers Association and Babbitt's intimate friend, dispatched 500 copies each to John Clay and Company in Chicago and to Clark, Dodge and Company in New York, with a note asking them: "Please give these to your clients."[2]

While few prospectuses were as firmly utopian as Babbitt's, all were full of optimism. The Ames Cattle Company, located in Beaverhead County, Montana, urged Eastern investors: "Send your subscription with all due speed, before our capitalization is fulfilled."[3] The Capitol Freehold Land and Investment Company, owners of the enormous XIT Ranch, were not above claiming: "Of all property in the United States, land in New States, and cattle, have hitherto yielded the steadiest profit, even in the fact of great commercial depression."[4] One investor recalled this sentence in 1893 and gleefully taunted the manager with it.

Some company prospectuses parodied promoters and journalists

---

[1] A. T. Babbitt: "The Grazing Interest and the Beef Supply" (Cheyenne: March 10, 1884), 4.
[2] Thomas Sturgis to John Clay; Thomas Sturgis to Clark, Dodge and Company, April 18, 1885. Wyoming Stock Growers Association Collection, Western History Research Center, University of Wyoming.
[3] Ames Cattle Company: *Prospectus* (Boston: 1884), 2.
[4] Capitol Freehold Land and Investment Company: *Prospectus* (Chicago: 1886), 1.

in their prognostication of profits. The prospectus of the Western Philanthropic Society of New York, which had holdings in New Mexico, forecast: "Over a five year period annual profits of forty-six per cent are typical."[5] And according to the Albany Land and Cattle Company of Wyoming: "The profits of the business are large, which accounts for the eagerness with which investments are made. . . . Careful estimates made by leading dealers place the profits of the average herd at thirty-five to forty per cent over and above the losses and expenses."[6]

One of the most elaborate prospectuses was that of the Yellowstone Cattle Company of Montana, which not only included the ubiquitous table of earnings, but also quoted at length from a contemporary article in *Scientific American*, "Why Beef Is Dear." The cattle market, according to this article, was bound to increase, because the exportation of beef together with home consumption had far exceeded home supply.[7]

Many of the prospectuses salted a few prominent names of Eastern families on the title page: the Oelrichs, Thurber, Gage, Gould, and Harrison were favorites. These lists from the "four hundred" were not entirely pseudo, as many members of wealthy Eastern families did have stock in cattle companies. In fact, in spite of all the prospectuses, promoters' volumes, immigration pamphlets, and newspaper articles, the Eastern investor more often than not gravitated to the cattle industry through family connections. Western cattlemen were always looking for new investors, and in many instances, with the aid of commission companies and publicity, they succeeded. But frequently when loans were needed, close associates, relatives, and family friends were the best source.

In addition to company prospectuses, a plethora of pamphlets was published by the state and territorial immigration bureaus, crammed with embellished prose on the "resources" of their regions. It is impossible to assess the impact, in numbers or in spirit,

[5] Western Philanthropic Society of New York: *Prospectus* (New York: 1879), 1.
[6] Albany Land and Cattle Company: *Prospectus* (Cheyenne: 1884).
[7] Yellowstone Cattle Company: *Prospectus* (Helena: 1883).

which these booklets had on the Wall Street or Federal Square investor. Cattlemen, recognizing another avenue of publicity, in some cases actually composed the sections of those brochures dealing with livestock. In 1883, Russell Harrison, son of Benjamin Harrison and secretary of the Montana Stock Growers Association, wrote the secretary of the Wyoming Stock Growers Association, Thomas Sturgis, that he was in "the throes of finishing a piece for a new immigration pamphlet."[8]

Besides helping to fabricate some of these promotion pieces, cattlemen occasionally underwrote the cost. Charles B. Eddy, recently a New York financier and now a New Mexico cattleman, in a letter to his partner, Captain Joseph Lea, founder of the New Mexico city of Roswell, suggested that they pay for a territorial publication, as "no one else is inclined to do so."[9] Charles O'Donel, manager of the Red River Valley Company (owner of the huge Bell Ranch in New Mexico), wrote his largest stockholder, Louis G. Stoddard, in New Haven, Connecticut, for permission to subscribe to a joint effort among cattle growers for a territorial publication. O'Donel and his associate had only a nominal interest in colonization schemes for their ranch; their real motivation was capital, not people.[1] John L. Routt, Colorado cattleman and later governor of Colorado, in a letter to William Paxton, an influential cattleman and stockyard owner in Nebraska, requested "all available" information concerning the activities of Nebraska cattlemen in promoting the state.[2]

These sporadic efforts by cattlemen to influence territorial publications can hardly be called successful. Aimed at all classes and economic interests of Easterners, the territoral brochures sometimes ignored the cattle industry altogether. For example, one

[8] Russell B. Harrison to Thomas Sturgis, December 9, 1883. Wyoming Stock Growers Association Collection, Western History Research Center, University of Wyoming.

[9] Charles B. Eddy to Joseph C. Lea, July 18, 1889. Dow Collection, Roswell, New Mexico.

[1] Charles O'Donel to Louis Stoddard, August 22, 1902. Bell Ranch Collection, University of New Mexico Library.

[2] John L. Routt to William Paxton, August 8, 1884. Western Range Cattle Industry Collection, State Historical Society of Colorado.

of them said: "Wyoming possesses resources that offer extraordinary inducements to the capitalist, the miner, the farmer and
all persons seeking homes in the West."[3] The common pattern
allotted only two or three pages to stock raising—even, strangely
enough, in territories and states dominated by livestock interests.

The commissioners of immigration evolved a standard format
for their publicity "news-sheets."[4] A history of the territory
and an account of its geographic wonders would be followed by
descriptions of the soil, climate, wild game, and agricultural and
industrial potentialities. County profiles listing these "bountiful"
assets for each section dominated the rest of the narrative. Occasionally, after a discursive treatise on one county, an author
would state forthrightly: "What is said of one county will generally apply to all." At least one could admire a forthright as well
as realistic admission. A concluding passage provided a synopsis
of the Homestead Law and other land legislation.

The style of the "resource" pamphlet often had a saccharine
quality: The valleys were "gardens of Eden," the mountains
"majestic and heavily timbered," the rivers "sparkling," the water
"delicious," the atmosphere "clear and bracing." Occasionally
in the perfumed prose came a real prevarication, as when James
Foster, in his Outlines of History of the Territory of Dakota,
insisted: "The dread of deep snow, and cold winters in so high a
northern latitude is altogether imaginary."[5] Cattlemen, especially
during the winter of 1886–7 hardly considered their losses a mirage.

The impact, either favorable or adverse, that the "resource"
booklets had on the Eastern investor is problematical. Though the
Western cattleman regarded the territorial and state pamphlets

[3] Board of Immigration: The Territory of Wyoming, Its History, Soil,
Climate, Resources, Etc. (Laramie City: Daily Sentinel Print; 1874), 3.
[4] The examples of immigration and publicity booklets are numerous.
Department of Immigration and Statistics: Resources of Dakota (Sioux
Falls, Dakota: Argus-Leader Co.; 1887); Granville Stuart: Montana and The
Northwest Territory . . . (Chicago: 1879); Texas As It is: or, the Main
Facts in a Nut-Shell (Weatherford, Texas: 1876) are but a few of the
multitude.
[5] James Foster: Outlines of History of the Territory of Dakota and Emi-
grant's Guide to the Free Lands of the Northwest (Yankton, Dakota
Territory: M'Intyre & Foster Printers; 1870).

as another medium in his propaganda barrage, official territorial efforts did not greatly interest him.

The catastrophic slump of the cattle market in 1886 and 1887 muffled promotion. Yet as the flight of Eastern capital from the West after the winter of 1886–7 has been exaggerated, so has the cessation of promotional literature. While the flamboyant promoter-publicists fled the cattle industry for more lucrative fields, the railroads and the state immigration bureaus issued booklets in a never ending cascade. Unquestionably the emphasis of this publicity shifted to the homesteader, but the cattleman was not neglected.

And even yet, an occasional publicist would suddenly appear. William M. Thayer in his garrulous volume *The Marvels of the New West*, published in 1889, discounted the decline in the Western cattle industry.[6] "The profits of stock raising are marvellous," insisted Thayer. "For this reason, men endure hardships and brave dangers, dwelling apart from friends and civilized society. The prospect of speedy fortunes reconciles them to privations for the time being."[7] Thayer saw nothing incongrous in reaching back a decade for his prophecy. Without irony, he quoted one of the tables of profits forecast by A. A. Hayes in *Harper's Monthly* of 1879.

Thayer finished his book on a Social Darwinist note, with fundamentalist overtones. "These facts indicate that the New West will decide the destiny of our land. . . . Perils beset this portion of our country, it is true . . . but this is God's battle, in which 'one will chase a thousand, and two put ten thousand to flight.' "[8] What tremendous perils awaited the birth of this "New Western Man"? Thayer explained:

> Mammonism, Mormonism, Socialism, Skepticism, and Theism are mighty obstacles to the rise and progress of our western domain; but the holy trinity of Liberty, Education, and Christianity, which the Anglo-Saxon race believe, will prove more

6 William M. Thayer: *The Marvels of the New West* (Norwich, Conn.: Henry Bill Pub.; 1889).
7 Ibid., 547.
8 Ibid., 713.

than a match for them. . . . This race has laid the foundation of our Western empire, and started it off in a career of unexampled prosperity.[9]

On the warm, humid afternoon of June 30, 1885, a young and handsome member of Philadelphia's Main Line society boarded the Pennsylvania Limited "all eager" for the "grand adventure" —a journey to the American West. This scion of one of the City of Brotherly Love's famous families would do more to create the myth of the West than all the Lathams, Strahorns, and Thayers combined. For from his pen would come a tale which would captivate the imagination of the country.

The Virginian, Wister's chivalric cowboy, was a veritable knight in buckskin, who rode out of the West into the parlors of the East. Never again for many Americans would the image of the West be anything but the West of Owen Wister, although for the immigrants who creaked West in wagons, followed plowshares, or stiffened their backs hunting for gold, the West of Bret Harte, Willa Cather, or Ole Rölvaag held more reality. Not that *The Virginian* was totally Wister's imagination; far from it, for Wister saw many of the scenes which he described so vividly. After him, however, came hordes of manufacturers of blood and thunder who picked up the Wister "formula," but seldom strayed from the Genesee Valley of New York or the coast of Maine.

Few Americans went West with a more perceptive or appreciative eye than Owen Wister. As the Union Pacific rolled through Nebraska in July 1885, Wister the "tourist" was "agog":

One must come to the West to realize what one may have most probably believed all one's life long—that it is a very much bigger place than the East—and future America is just bubbling and seething in bare legs and pinafores here. I don't wonder a man never comes back after he has once been here for a few years.[1]

The expanse of the country was overpowering: "It reminds me of the northern part of Spain. The same vast stretches of

[9] Ibid., 714.
[1] Wister Journal, July 2, 1885. Wister Collection, Western History Research Center, University of Wyoming.

barren green back to the sky line or to rising ground." But he also relished the landscape's detail: "Just now we stopped at a station where a black pig was drinking the drops that fell from the locomotive tank, and a pile of whitened cattle bones lay nearby." His exurberance increased with the miles; he gushed: "It looks really like what it scientifically is—space—a few prairie dogs. The air is delicious. As if it had never been in any one's lungs before. I like this continual passing of green void."[2]

Wister had been on the Wolcott ranch near Douglas, Wyoming, only a month before he wrote his first notes on the cowboy. Though fascinated by their character, he retained more perspective than many a later Eastern Brahmin. In his journal Wister reported one conversation with the foreman of the Wolcott "spread":

Tom King, the foreman, says he likes this life and will never go East again. On Miss Irwin's inquiry whether he will not get tired of it when he grows old—he replied that cowboys never live long enough to get old. They don't I believe. They're a queer episode in the history of this country. Purely nomadic and leaving no race or posterity, for they don't marry. I am told they're without any moral sense whatever. Perhaps they are—but I wonder how much less they have than the poor classes in New York?[3]

Early in his stay on the Wolcott ranch, Wister decided that the "New Western Man" would overpower the nation. "I feel more certainly than ever, that no matter how completely the East may be the headwaters from which the West has flown . . . it won't be a century before the West is simply the true America with thought, type and life of its own kind." Why? "We Atlantic Coast people, all varnished with Europe, and some of us having a good lot of Europe in our marrow besides, will vanish from the face of the earth. We're no type—no race—we're transient." Then, in a Rip Van Winkle aside, he wished he "could come back in two hundred years and see a townful of real Americans—not a collection of revolutionary scions of English families and emigrants

2 Ibid., July 3, 1885.
3 Ibid., August 6, 1885.

arrived yesterday from Cork and Bremen for that is what our Eastern cities are today."[4]

However, a fortnight had not passed before Wister became more pessimistic about the coming fate of the Westerner. Much to his chagrin, he discovered that this new man did not necessarily want to be unique. "The one idea of Western city people is to have a town as good as New York—in New York the English importations at present antagonize." Regardless of the contemporary attitude of New Yorkers toward the British, Wister could take little solace in this fact, for he wondered if the immigrant in a few years would not be totally adopted. If so, "good day to my theory of an American civilization here—it will slowly New Yorkify, and rot. We'll have horses better bred than the women who ride them, and dogs with pedigrees longer than their master's."[5]

Until the West should change, however, Wister felt that it was a land far greater than the motley cities of the East, and he portrayed its promise in *The Virginian*. The constant repetition of the myth of the West, whether by America's imaginative writers or by the publicity mills of the West's Carey Avenues, had some part in encouraging the flow of capital from the East to West.

Although the most potent influence on the Eastern investor was the advice of friends, relatives, and investment associations, young Richard Trimble was not the only investor to come West and then to send home Strahorn and Latham's books. The records of the Wyoming Stock Growers Association contain a myriad of queries from Easterners regarding opportunities for investment. Should the investor take only a moderate initial stock subscription, the stealthy rumors of enormous profits filtering back East would lure him to want a bigger stake in the cattle company. As a pump primer, the Western promotion had a prominent role.

The fact has been little credited that the banker and cattleman on Carey Avenue propagated the image of a favorable economic milieu in the West a full ten years before the heaviest investment in the cattle industry occurred. It was not just a chauvinistic

[4] Ibid., July 10, 1885.
[5] Ibid., July 21, 1885.

campaign on the part of the Westerners: capital was extremely tight in the West. When a 24 per cent yearly interest was not uncommon, the scarcity of money was obviously uppermost in Western consciousness.

The Carey Avenue merchant, aside from capital necessity, was convinced of the West's economic destiny. As he sat in his Morris rocker in the evening reading the Cheyenne *Leader*, he could be in complete agreement with the editorial "Future of the Plains." He willingly succumbed to the opiate of his own propaganda, so much so that the collapse of 1886–7 left him bewildered. His newspapers, whether in Miles City, Cheyenne, Pueblo, or Santa Fe, reflected a startled disillusionment.

The railroads, promoters, and newspapers had been amazingly successful in advertising the Western country. In retrospect, what seems most incredible about this accomplishment was the poor quality of the publicity exhortations. "Thirty-Day" books from title page to finis could not be accused of being cleverly contrived, let alone well written. Ungrammatical, full of grandiose phrases and inane hyperbole, the literature reeked a synthetic odor. Yet well-constructed sentences are superfluous if the reader is convinced that he is soon to be a millionaire. Further, perspective is distorted when one is behind a mahogany desk in a financial house 2,000 miles from one's investment.

III

"You couldn't keep me out"

THE EASTERN INVESTOR

⅄ᗷ CY ⊘ ND ⊥ ⅄
◇ ⅄ ⊕ ⅄ ◔
⊥ ⊖ ℞
Ⅎ

One year out of Harvard, Hubert E. Teschemacher, class of 1878, joined his fellow classmate Frederic deBillier in forming a cattle company with headquarters forty miles north of Cheyenne. In quest of capital Teschemacher journeyed East in the winter of 1881–2. His visit, as he described it to his associate in the West, was a "curious mixture of reverie and business, both immensely exhausting."[1]

Whether success was due to his recreational pursuits in his club

[1] H. E. Teschemacher to Fred deBillier, December 9, 1881. Dunder Collection, Western History Research Center, University of Wyoming.

or to his knocking on office doors in Boston's Federal Square, by the spring of 1882 Teschemacher had assurances of the $250,000 requisite for the incorporation of the Teschemacher and deBillier Cattle Company.[2] Teschemacher evidently was as magnetic a salesman as James Brisbin or Hiram Latham, for after his return West, Joseph Ames, a friend and Boston banker, wrote him that he would subscribe $10,000 worth of stock and that his father, Joseph Ames, Sr., also wanted to put up $10,000. When Ames had the temerity to remind his father of other heavy financial commitments, the senior Ames declared: "You couldn't keep me out."[3]

What is remarkable is that other financiers in the East during the late 1870's and early 1880's were just as enthusiastically investing in cattle companies. Why did the Eastern investor want to send his gold West? Obviously he expected profits, but there were hundreds of schemes promising rich rewards. True, the Brisbins, Lathams, and Strahorns had softened the hard shell of Eastern investment reserve. But it took more than promotional literature to keep capital flowing from Eastern financial centers to the Western range.

More often than not, the Eastern financier's interest was aroused by a friend or relative who had already succumbed to having his name embossed on a stock certificate. Any recital of the boards of directors of cattle companies discloses the fact that Eastern businessmen loved company when investing. John and Charles Arbuckle, New York coffee manufacturers, joined their friend Horace K. Thurber, wholesale grocer and shipping magnate, in purchasing stock in the PO Ranch near Cheyenne, Wyoming, and in the Lea Cattle Company of Roswell, New Mexico. The eminent geologist Clarence King interested Abraham S. Hewitt, ironmonger and son-in-law of Peter Cooper, and the New York publisher James Gordon Bennett in placing their

[2] For the rise and fall of this concern see Gene M. Gressley: "Teschemacher and deBillier Cattle Company," *Business History Review*, XXXIII (Summer 1959), 121–37.

[3] Joseph Ames, Jr., to H. E. Teschemacher, April 11, 1882. Dunder Collection, Western History Research Center, University of Wyoming.

capital in ranches in Nebraska and Wyoming.[4] Levi Leiter, Chicago real estate magnate, induced Marshall Field and his mercantile partner, R. M. Fair, to become directors in the Pratt-Ferris Cattle Company—an enormous enterprise which eventually had holdings in Nebraska, Wyoming, and South Dakota.

Philetus Sawyer, the Wisconsin lumberman, on a visit to the Lone Star State in 1871, became so enamored of the prospects of Texas ranching that he went back to Wisconsin and incorporated the Sawyer Cattle Company. Eventually, Sawyer became the proud possessor of 269 sections of land in west Texas.[5] His infectious enthusiasm spread to E. C. Kellogg, an Oshkosh lumberman, who loaned substantial amounts to Texas cattlemen. Quincy Shaw, the developer of the Calumet and Hecla mines, and Alexander Agassiz, the son of the renowned geologist Louis Agassiz, provided a fellow Bostonian, N. R. Davis, with capital to start the N. R. Davis Cattle Company in Wyoming and Nebraska. They also lent Thomas Sturgis, secretary of the Wyoming Stock Growers Association and president of the Union Cattle Company of Cheyenne, a substantial sum for expansion. Davis complained that Shaw was not the most congenial backer, for Shaw habitually reminded him, when the annual reports of the N. R. Davis Company appeared, that "the profits you expected and I anticipated have never been seen."[6]

Group investment, of course, was not restricted to the cattle industry. The Leiters and Fields had real estate holdings scattered over the Midwest; the Sawyers and the Kelloggs possessed a sizable timber tract in Wisconsin and adjoining states; the Thurbers and Arbuckles invested in South America, a land of promise, especially in coffee plantations. The investment clique, whether in cattle or coffee, was the pattern in nineteenth-century financial

[4] Scattered references to Hewitt's activities in the cattle industry are in Allan Nevins: *Abram S. Hewitt* (New York: Harper; 1935), 450–9, 544.

[5] An abbreviated account of the Sawyers in Texas is in Grace M. Connelly: "The Bar-S Ranch," *West Texas Historical Association Yearbook*, XXXIII (October 1957), 94–104. Sawyer's career and remarks on his cattle interests are in Richard N. Current: *Pine Logs and Politics* (Madison: State Historical Society of Wisconsin; 1950).

[6] Quincy Shaw to N. R. Davis, August 10, 1880. Thorp Collection, Western History Research Center, University of Wyoming.

circles. Of course there were also many lone operators, but they did not predominate in the cattle corporations of the 1880's.

Another motivation, besides investor fellowships, was the tendency of Eastern financiers to invest in cattle companies after they had acquired other economic interests in the West. Railroad executives capitalized on their distinct advantage and captured huge slices of the Western domain. Sidney Dillon,[7] Thomas C. Durant, and Oliver Ames located a ranch near North Platte, Nebraska. General Jack Casement, a construction contractor for the Union Pacific, bought up land in Kansas, Nebraska, and Colorado and soon had herds on his acreage. John B. Alley, Union Pacific director, usurped the presidency of the Palo Blanco Ranch Company in New Mexico after Stephen Dorsey became tainted in the Star Route fraud. Shortly after the New York Central built extensive cattle yards in Kansas City, William K. Vanderbilt organized a livestock company in Colorado.[8]

Joseph Glidden, Isaac Ellwood, and Henry Sanborn, entrepreneurs in the De Kalb, Illinois, barbed-wire industry, followed their product to west Texas. Sanborn founded Amarillo, and Ellwood surrounded Lubbock with his ranches. C. M. Tilford and H. J. Tilford, distillers, because of their backing of W. V. Johnson's tannery in Louisville, sought an economical source of hides and established the Kentucky Cattle Raising Company in Texas.[9]

Mining speculation frequently led the investor to explore other financial opportunities. It was after "Uncle" Rufus Hatch, New York stockbroker, began visiting Colorado yearly to inspect his mines that he considered investing in Colorado and Nebraska

[7] The Kansas City *Livestock Indicator*, on October 16, 1884, asserted: "Sidney Dillon, noted ex-potentate of the Union Pacific is one of the heaviest cattle owners in the West. The firm of which he is principal is known as Dillon & Co. Isaac Dillon is in the company and as a manager of the business, lives on a ranch near North Platte. The cattle are numbered by the thousands on a thousand hills. Some in the Platte Valley, others on Snake River country. The headquarters known as Stone Ranch, is in the valley near O'Fallon station and surrounded by a splendid range."

[8] Denver *Daily Tribune*, April 20, 1879.

[9] Nellie W. Spikes and Temple A. Ellis: *Through the Years; A History of Crosby County, Texas* (San Antonio: Naylor Co.; 1952), 97–114.

ranching properties.[1] Trenor W. Park had floated the nefarious
Emma Silver Mining Company in Utah six years before his association with Charles Greene in New Mexico and Arizona.
Fifteen years before the enormous XIT Ranch was founded in
Texas, John V. Farwell placed a fortune in the Snowy Range
near Encampment, Wyoming, in fruitless search of a "paying
proposition."[2]

Many a banker and commission man became entangled—often
reluctantly—in a Western cattle scheme in order to protect his
investment. To Godfrey Snydacker of the First National Bank
of Chicago fell the task of untangling the books of the insolvent
Swan Land and Cattle Company.[3] He quickly passed this chore on
to John Clay, a prominent Chicago broker and commission man.
Other commission men, such as Joseph Rosenbaum, whose office
was near Clay's in the Rookery Building in Chicago, controlled
several corporations in Montana. R. G. Hunter and A. D. Evans,
members of a Kansas City commission firm, manipulated cattle
companies in Texas, Kansas, Nebraska, and Colorado.

Nelson Morris, Chicago packer, accumulated ranches in Texas,
Wyoming, and Montana over a fifteen-year period. One Texas
newspaper complained that Morris had never even seen his 250,-
000-acre ranch in that beloved state.[4] While Morris may never
have surveyed his Texas landscape, he certainly wanted it understood that he was a cattleman to the core. In a letter to Thomas
Sturgis, secretary of the Wyoming Stock Growers Association,
he protested emphatically against an association ruling on the
assessment of cattle, and said: "You know I am one of you, thoroughly familiar with your problems and I might add my sympathy has been worth a great deal to you on occasion."[5] This

[1] Denver *Republican,* June 21, 1881.
[2] Ample proof of unrewarding mining claims is in the Farwell ledger,
now in Cheyenne, Wyoming, in the possession of Mrs. Edgar Boice, the
daughter of Robert MacIntosh, Farwell's manager.
[3] A clear and concise tale of the Swan empire is related by John Clay in
My Life on the Range (Chicago: 1924), 200–29.
[4] San Antonio *Daily Express,* quoted in Kansas City *Livestock Indicator,*
March 19, 1884.
[5] Nelson Morris to Thomas Sturgis, February 21, 1881. Wyoming Stock
Growers Association Collection, Western History Research Center, University of Wyoming.

declaration of brotherhood may have been skeptically regarded by many Western cattlemen, especially at fall shipping time, but it revealed an additional rationale for Morris's ranch ownership.

Whether an investor's attraction to mining, banking, tanneries, or railroads preceded his casting capital into the cattle business, or vice versa, is not of momentous consequence. Patently clear is that investment in one sector of the West's economy repeatedly brought entrepreneurial curiosity and capital to other sectors as well. Once the financier discerned a horizon of unlimited potential for profit in the West, he usually increased and diversified his investments. The fluctuating popularity of mining, railroad, and cattle stocks resulted in a cyclical dearth of capital in a number of years, but seldom a wholesale divorcement at any one time.

The urge to invest, however, was not confined to the industrial and business elite. Scrambling around in their outdoor laboratories, scientists who had come to the West succumbed as quickly as Wall Street financiers to the stock certificates emblazoned with the head of a steer. Clarence King, on his way to the Pacific Coast, stopped off at the Cheyenne Club, the lavish home away from home for the Eastern financier, and when he departed he was a partner not only in N. R. Davis and Company but also in several other cattle schemes.[6] George Bird Grinnell, whose tomes on the American Indian brought him fame as an anthropologist and ethnologist, pre-empted a ranch near Lander, Wyoming,[7] while Alexander Agassiz joined his brother-in-law, Boston copper magnate Quincy Shaw, in buying a ranch near North Platte, Nebraska.[8]

The scientist refused to react to his investments as an experiment in quest of scientific formula. Clarence King alternated between praising his partner and bombarding him with demands for information about their company's finances.[9] In reality, King

---

[6] Thurman Wilkins in his biography *Clarence King* (New York: Macmillan; 1958), sketched the N. R. Davis and Dakota Cattle Company operation; see pp. 217–29.

[7] Laramie *Daily Boomerang*, October 15, 1886.

[8] Cheyenne *Leader*, February 15, 1879.

[9] Clarence King to N. R. Davis, September 8, 1879. King Collection, Princeton University Library.

had little basis for complaint, as N. R. Davis shrewdly disposed of most of the cattle before the market collapsed. Alexander Agassiz, on the other hand, had serious cause for dissatisfaction with his company. After undergoing vicissitudes which would test the stamina of the strongest stockholders, he lost a substantial sum.

At the other end of society's spectrum were the wayward Eastern scions whose families, seeking relief from their sons' embarrassing philandering, banished them to the West with high hopes of redemption, or at least of retribution. The English re-mittance man—the third or fourth son of a wealthy family in *Burke's Peerage*—was shuttled to the American West for the same reason. Dissipation on a ranch appeared more difficult to come by than in London or New York, and after a year in the high altitude, perhaps the black sheep might even be fit to re-enter polite society.[1]

The young Easterner first glimpsing his exile from the window of a grimy red-plush Pullman car, indubitably considered his rela-tives sadists. Even the charitable John Clay's description of the Magic City of the Plains was hardly inviting: "Cheyenne was then as now an enigma. It stands out on the prairie, desolate, wind swept, but lying on a gentle incline southwards."[2] What a rude awakening it must have been for more than one Eastern "cousin" who, visiting the Cheyenne Club, saw imported wine flowing freely and entertainment furnished by the graceful Lily Langtry.[3] One Eastern guest was astounded to see a member con-

[1] One Irish rancher-to-be, William French, revealed his emotions when he contemplated leaving Ireland: "On November 4, 1883, I left Ireland, having taken passage on the Royal Mail Steamship *Arizona* at that time con-sidered to be one of the greyhounds of the North Atlantic Fleet. I had no definite plans, only the desire to better my fortune . . . so far my life had been that of a younger son. I was devoted to sport and had some slight military experience and a smattering of law." *Some Recollections of a West-ern Ranchman* (New York: Frederick A. Stokes; 1928), 1.
[2] Clay: *My Life on the Range*, 3.
[3] The Friday edition, June 27, 1884, of the St. Louis *Globe-Democrat* gossiped: " 'There goes Lily's cowboy adorer,' said an idler at the Baldwin Bar. . . . His name is H. Oelrichs and his native land England. He is brother of the big steamship man of that name, and doubtless made the acquaintance of Lily on the other side of that Atlantic. He is rich in land and cattle on the plains and hills of Wyoming Territory. . . ."

currently playing tennis, carrying on a chess game at the side of the court, and quenching his thirst with hasty gulps of bourbon! The astonished Owen Wister would note in his diary: "No wonder they like the club at Cheyenne. Went there with Dick Trimble and had a drink. It's the pearl of the prairies."[4]

The number of sons sent West defies computation, but the fact that errant offsprings figured in the establishment of a number of ranches in the West is evident from only a cursory inspection of the records of incorporation.

At any rate, by accident or premeditation, Eastern investors were coming into the cattle industry in large numbers by the late 1870's. What manner of men were most of them? An analysis was made of 93 such investors on the basis of age, background, investments, occupations, residence, marital status, and religion.[5] The average ascertainable age of 71 of the men at the time they first subscribed to stock in a cattle company was forty-two. The oldest, James Converse, Boston dry-goods merchant, was seventy-six when he first backed Hubert E. Teschemacher in the Tesche-

---

[4] Wister Journal, July 3, 1885. Wister Collection, Western History Research Center, University of Wyoming.

[5] The 93 investors were selected chiefly on the basis of the availability of sources, representativeness as to occupation and investment pattern, and to a lesser extent on the significance of their investment. Marshall Field's records are far scarcer than Russell B. Harrison's, whose investment was only a tenth that of Fields. If their capital investment was less than $10,000 they were automatically excluded. Care was taken that the investors selected did not fall at one end of the "rainbow" of speculator versus conservative in their investment approach. However, as indicated later, this polarization of conservative against speculator often fades out on intensive examination. A strong argument can be made that any investment in the nineteenth-century West was speculative!

The Eastern investors surveyed were Alexander Agassiz, John B. Alley, Azel Ames, Joseph Ames, S. Reed Anthony, Charles Arbuckle, John Arbuckle, Robert Bacon, J. H. Barron, James G. Bennett, John Bigelow, Henry Blair, George R. Blanchard, August Busch, Jerome Increase Case, Jack Stephen Casement, John V. Clark, William A. Clark, John Clay, Edmund Converse, James Converse, Edward Creighton, B. W. Crowinshield, Frederick Ogden deBillier, George P. Denny, Sidney Dillon, Stephen B. Elkins, I. L. Ellwood, R. D. Evans, R. M. Fair, N. K. Fairbanks, John V. Farwell, Marshall Field, John H. Flagler, "Jack" Forrest, D. B. Gardner, Joseph Glidden, David M. Goodrich, William C. Greene, Augustus Gurnee, Jacob B. Haish, Russell B. Harrison, Rufus Hatch, Abram S. Hewitt, R. G. Hunter, Robert Ingersoll, W. V. Johnson, C. E. Judson, E. C. Kellogg, George Kellogg, Clarence King, Augustus

macher and deBillier Cattle Company. The youngest, John V. Clark of Chicago, had barely reached nineteen when he assumed a dominant role in the Porter Land and Livestock Company of Colorado.

The West may have been a young man's land, but the Eastern financier who purchased a stake in the cattle industry was mature, both in age and in financial judgment. Inasmuch as the life expectancy of the American male was forty-eight years, the investor had passed the prime of life. More than one financier recognized this fact and lamented that his money was being handled by young and inexperienced managers. Isaac Ellwood told his son: "The major success of a ranch, my friends in Texas tell me, is due to choosing a good manager."[6]

The Eastern businessman who sent his capital to the Western range was not a flighty youth prone to gambling in the stock market, but rather a mature financier, who, by the time his name appeared on the incorporation papers of a cattle company, had fifteen to twenty years of financial experience. Men of this caliber and background hardly plead ignorance of the financial risks which they were taking; and yet some did bemoan their tragic fate as if they were neophytes. Portus B. Weare, for example, complained to his nephew:

> You have no idea or at least you seem to have no realization of what I have been through for you. Many a young man would have jumped at the opportunity to succeed at the proposition I made you. I do not mean to be overly hard on you as I am frank to admit if I had known more of the chances I would

Kountze, Levi Leiter, E. M. McGillin, J. W. Macrum, John A. McShane, Benjamin B. Mitchell, James Moore, Nelson Morris, Joy Morton, Charles May Oelrichs, Harry Oelrichs, Herman Oelrichs, Trenor W. Park, Duncan C. Plumb, J. W. Powper, Henry A. Rice, William Rockefeller, Theodore Roosevelt, Joseph Rosenbaum, Henry B. Sanborn, Philetus Sawyer, Isaac Newton Seligman, Jesse Seligman, Joseph Seligman, Edmund Seymour, Quincy Adams Shaw, D. W. Smith, Chester Allyn Snider, Geoffrey Snydacker, E. G. Stoddard, H. E. Teschemacher, Horace K. Thurber, C. M. Tilford, H. J. Tilford, Charlemagne Tower, Richard Trimble, William Vanderbilt, Julius Wadsworth, Portus B. Weare, Ellerton P. Whitney, William C. Whitney, and Eugene Williams.

[6] Isaac Ellwood to William Ellwood, November 26, 1890. Ellwood Collection, Western History Research Center, University of Wyoming.

have been more reluctant to send you West with my money.[7]

Where did these seasoned entrepreneurs live? Not surprisingly, over half the investors in the sample which was studied had their offices in either New York or Boston. Chicago ranked third with 15 financiers, and the same were scattered across America's heartland: 4 in St. Louis, 4 in Louisville, 3 in Omaha, and 4 in De Kalb. The remainder were spread over a diffuse area from Poughkeepsie to Charleston, West Virginia, to Oshkosh, Wisconsin.[8] Only 4 financiers could be considered Southerners, if one includes Louisville in this regional classification. With little distortion, it could be said that the membership of the Union League Club of Chicago, the Union League Club of New York, and the Harvard Club of Boston controlled the major portion of Eastern capital in the range cattle industry.

Geography plagued many an Eastern investor. Communication

[7] Portus Weare to Henry Weare, July 7, 1885. Weare Letterbook, 1885-7, Nason Collection, Spearfish, South Dakota.

[8] The residences divided as follows: *Boston*—Alexander Agassiz, John B. Alley, Joseph Ames, Azel Ames, S. Reed Anthony, George Blanchard, Edmund Converse, James Converse, B. W. Crowinshield, George Denny, R. D. Evans, John H. Flagler, Augustus Gurnee, C. E. Judson, J. P. Powper, Henry A. Rice, Quincy A. Shaw, H. E. Teschemacher, Ellerton P. Whitney; *New York*—Charles Arbuckle, John Arbuckle, Robert Bacon, James G. Bennett, Jr., John Bigelow, Frederick O. deBillier, William Clark, Sidney Dillon, William C. Greene, Rufus Hatch, Abram S. Hewitt, Augustus Kountze, Charles Oelrichs, Herman Oelrichs, Harry Oelrichs, Trenor W. Park, William Rockefeller, Theodore Roosevelt, Jesse Seligman, Joseph Seligman, Edmund Seymour, Horace K. Thurber, Richard Trimble, William Vanderbilt, Julius Wadsworth, William C. Whitney; *Chicago*—Henry Blair, John V. Clark, John Clay, R. M. Fair, N. K. Fairbanks, John V. Farwell, Marshall Field, William Forrest, Levi Leiter, Nelson Morris, Joy Morton, Duncan C. Plumb, Joseph Rosenbaum, Godfrey Snydacker, Portus B. Weare; *Concord, New Hampshire*—J. H. Barron; *Philadelphia*—Isaac Seligman; *St. Louis*—August Busch, Eugene Williams, R. G. Hunter, C. A. Snider; *New Haven*—E. G. Stoddard; *Racine, Wisconsin*—Jerome I. Case; *Painesville, Ohio*—Jack S. Casement; *Omaha*—Edward Creighton, John A. McShane, J. W. Macrum; *De Kalb, Illinois*—Isaac Ellwood, Joseph Glidden, Jacob Haish, Henry Sanborn; *Akron, Ohio*—David M. Goodrich; *Indianapolis*—Russell B. Harrison; *Buffalo, Illinois*—John B. Hunter; *Peoria, Illinois*—Robert Ingersoll; *Louisville, Kentucky*—C. M. Tilford, H. J. Tilford, W. V. Johnson, James Moore; *Oshkosh, Wisconsin*—George Kellogg, Philetus Sawyer, E. C. Kellogg; *Washington, D.C.*—Clarence King; *Cleveland*—E. M. McGillin; *Troy, New York*—Benjamin B. Mitchell, Charlemagne Tower; *Charleston, West Virginia*—Stephen B. Elkins, D. W. Smith.

over a 2,000-mile expanse persistently led to confusion and even distrust. Quincy Shaw, the Boston entrepreneur, complained to N. R. Davis:

> You should return to Boston more often so your stockholders could discuss our common affairs with you. There is some belief here that your prolonged absence is due to unfortunate news you should relate. Please write—soon![9]

Some of the Eastern financiers expected, even demanded, detailed reports from their managers; but, while they might wish to be well informed, they had little inclination to reside at their ranches for extended periods of time. A month's visit was delightful; a longer one led to boredom. In a letter to his son William, Isaac Ellwood wrote:

> I am glad you like ranch life. I have never found it occupied me after two weeks. It is good you are making the rounds with Arnett [the ranch manager]. He can tell you much about the business. This shouldn't take you long to learn. Have you thought about more education, since we talked in May? I wish you would think seriously about the future.[1]

Like many of the financiers in the sample, Ellwood was eager for his son to go to college; and also like many of them, he had not had much education himself. Ellwood's abbreviated tenure in the classroom was hardly unique. Of the 93 investors analyzed, only 25 attended college, and 19 of these graduated.[2] Sketchy

[9] Quincy Shaw to N. R. Davis, March 26, 1885. Dunder Collection, Western History Research Center, University of Wyoming.

[1] Isaac Ellwood to William Ellwood, September 17, 1889. Ellwood Collection, Western History Research Center, University of Wyoming.

[2] Those matriculating at a college were: John Arbuckle, Washington and Jefferson College; Robert Bacon, Harvard University; Henry Blair, University of Chicago–Williston Seminary; John V. Clark, St. Ignatius College; John Clay, University of Edinburg; Frederick deBillier, Harvard University; Stephen B. Elkins, University of Missouri; John V. Farwell, Mt. Morris Seminary; David M. Goodrich, Harvard University; Russell B. Harrison, Lafayette College; Abram S. Hewitt, Columbia University; Clarence King, Yale University; Benjamin B. Mitchell, Louisburg University; Harry Oelrichs, Columbia University; Theodore Roosevelt, Harvard University; E. G. Stoddard, Yale Unversity; Richard Trimble, Harvard University; Julius Wadsworth, Yale University; William C. Whitney, Yale University; Charlemagne Tower, Lafayette College. Occasionally one investor had matriculated at two Ivy League schools. William C. Whitney and Frederick deBillier attended both Yale and Harvard.

biographical material indicates that only 37 went beyond the sixth grade. The memoirs of investors are full of words such as "meager," "rudimentary," and "limited" when delineating their education.

This was the age of the self-made man, a time when education might be desirable but was far from an essential ingredient of success. The 25 in the study who had enrolled in colleges came mostly from wealthy, well-established families, and they mostly selected Ivy League schools for their "hallowed" academic careers. In all, 7 were alumni of Harvard, 3 of Columbia, and 4 of Yale, and the rest represented colleges from Washington and Jefferson to the University of Missouri. Only 3—Theodore Roosevelt, William C. Whitney, and Charlemagne Tower—achieved sufficient academic excellence to merit election to Phi Beta Kappa, and only 3 earned a degree beyond the bachelor's. William C. Whitney, New York lawyer and financier, attended Yale and graduated from Harvard Law School. Stephen B. Elkins, senator from West Virginia and owner of the major coal reserves in that state, graduated from the University of Missouri in 1860 and returned there after the Civil War to earn a master of arts degree in 1863. Russell B. Harrison, secretary of the Montana Stock Growers Association and son of President Benjamin Harrison, received the degree of master of engineering from Lafayette College.

Whether or not the Eastern financiers benefited from a broad education, there is no testimony to suggest that they scorned education, or were even blasé in their attitude toward education. Their philanthropic activities alone are an index of their concern. Abram Hewitt gave liberally to Cooper Union, founded by his father-in-law. Edward Creighton, whose biographer described his schooling as "very rudimentary," donated a major portion of his estate to the establishment of Creighton University. Isaac Ellwood presented Northern Illinois State College with handsome gifts, and through his political influence did much to assure adequate legislative appropriations. Marshall Field and Henry Blair contributed generously to the University of Chicago; Stephen B. Elkins to Davis-Elkins College; and William C. Whitney to his alma mater, Yale.

Admittedly, few Eastern entrepreneurs were imbued with sufficient missionary zeal to donate to struggling Western educational institutions. An exception was Horace K. Thurber, who replied, when his manager, Joseph Lea, wrote him regarding the establishment of a college at Roswell:

> I do not think you should name the college after me. It is much better to appeal to local interest. Thurber College, as much as I enjoy the sound of the name, will not be as popular locally as Roswell University. I agree we should do all we can to foster the college. Give them as many choice lots as you deem necessary and *all* the political support in the territory that you can bring to bear.[3]

Lea followed Thurber's dictum. The new school, founded in 1891, was called Goss Military Institute for the first superintendent, and was later renamed New Mexico Military Institute.[4]

That the educated and polished Eastern financiers nourished educational institutions is hardly astonishing; that the Western ranchmen gave substantial funds to education is more worthy of note. The John W. Iliff fortune, the estate of the largest cattle raiser on the plains, went to establish the Iliff School of Theology in Denver. Though some inspiration for this gift came from Bishop Warren of the Methodist Episcopal Church (who later married Mrs. Iliff), the deeply religious John Iliff, who would allow neither smoking nor drinking among his cowboys, would have applauded. John and Dudley Snyder, brothers who were extensive stock growers all the way up the 100th meridian from Texas, assumed the management and part ownership of the Iliff herds. The Snyders created Georgetown College in their home community in Texas and their benefactions sustained the college over the years.

[3] H. K. Thurber to Joseph C. Lea, October 4, 1889. Padgitt Collection, San Antonio, Texas. Thurber reiterated this sentiment five weeks later in another letter to Lea, November 13, 1889.
[4] The beginnings of the New Mexico Military Institute appear in James T. Padgitt: "Early History of the New Mexico Military Institute," *West Texas Historical Association Yearbook*, XXXIV (October 1958), 67–81. See also, J. R. Kelly: *History of the New Mexico Military Institute* (Roswell, New Mexico: 1953), 1–22.

Inside the Sturgis-Goodell Ranch.

*An interior view of the other side
of the cattle business, Senator John B. Kendrick's home.*

A. J. Seligman. A member of a famous international family banking firm, who discovered that the game of finance in frontier Montana could be every bit as rough and exciting as Wall Street.

Hubert Teschemacher. As a young Harvard graduate and friend of Theodore Roosevelt, he sought his fortune on the Laramie River in territorial Wyoming.

Thomas Sturgis. Secretary of the Wyoming Stock Growers Association, official of several national cattlemen's associations, he was one of the most respected cattlemen west of the 98th meridian. When a piece of legislation needed passage or a federal appointment demanded attention, "See Tom Sturgis" became a byword.

Isaac Ellwood. Barbed-wire king, a founder of the American Steel and Wire Company. More than any single man he transformed the range into a ranch economy.

Range and "city" architecture; ABOVE: *a Bandlands ranch house (Sylvane M. Ferris in rig);* BELOW: *16th Street, Cheyenne, 1868.*

Roundup and chuckwagon scenes; ABOVE: *the way the cow-boy really looked; the photographer interrupts chow;* BELOW: *cow outfit cook making pies;* ABOVE RIGHT: *grub in the shade, "deluxe" style;* CENTER: *coffee break at the chuck-wagon;* BELOW RIGHT: *Dakota Territory cowboys pause while branding to have their picture "took."*

Cow country domestic scenes; ABOVE: *return to the home place from Miles City, 1884, with kitchen, grub house, and bunkhouse in background;* CENTER: *bunkhouse interior with cowboy impedimenta;* BELOW: *bunkhouse on the OW Ranch; cowhands entertaining themselves with fiddle, banjo, and a boxing match.*

M. E. Post, *miner, stockman, banker. Going deeply in debt after the failure of his Cheyenne, Deadwood, Miles City banking firm, Post lived to recoup a fortune in California real estate, paying off all his indebtedness dollar for dollar.*

Owen Wister, ABOVE RIGHT. *"From his pen the cowboy myth soared into the imagination of the country"—Frances Kemble Wister Stokes.*

Asa Mercer, BELOW LEFT. *Staunch friend, then violent enemy of the cattleman, Asa Mercer's career was an enigmatic one.*

George Searight, BELOW RIGHT. *President of the Dolores Land and Cattle Company in Texas, the failure of which in 1886 was an ominous signal for the range depression that followed.*

TOP: *a certificate for seven shares of Wyoming Land and Cattle Company stock;* BELOW LEFT: *Burton C. Mossman, manager of the Aztec Land and Cattle Company, Limited, in his office at the Hashknife Ranch in Holbrook, Arizona, 1900;* BELOW RIGHT: *poster of a cattle forwarding agent for the Union Pacific Railroad. The fine print reads: "Persons driving Cattle from Montana and Idaho, and passing by Soda Springs and the Bear Lake Settlements, will cross over from Bear River to the head of Little Muddy and follow down that stream, over a good road, to within a mile and a half of the junction of the Little with the Big Muddy, where they will cross a bridge and find a rich pasture, extending many miles; good water & perfect security for their stock, within convenient distance of the stockyards."*

CATTLE MEN READ THIS!

Great Inducements to those who wish to

Ship Cattle on the U. P. Railroad !!

Having entered into special arrangements with the U. P. R. R. Company, by which I can ship Cattle East at greatly reduced rates, and having selected a point between Carter and Church Buttes Stations some ten miles East of the former place, near the junction of the Big and Little Muddies, and having Constructed Commodious Lots and Extensive Enclosures, and the Company having put in a Switch capable of holding 40 Cars, I will be Prepared to Commence Shipping on or before the 15th of the Present Month, and will be able to promptly ship any Number of cattle that may be Offered.

The cattle yards are in an enclosure of some 400 acres, and stock scales and all conveniences for shipping will be furnished. If parties do not wish to ship themselves, I will purchase at good prices all shipping cattle that may be offered. As cattle are now bearing excellent prices East, it would be well for persons to bring their Cattle forward as soon as possible.

For further particulars, address

W. A. CARTER,
Fort Bridger, Wyo. Ter.

Fort Bridger, July 2, 1877.

Charles Goodnight, the onetime partner of John Adair of the famous JA Ranch, founded Goodnight College in the Texas town named for him. The school was under Baptist supervision for a few years but closed for want of students and funds. Its demise led the cowman to note drolly: "My school house business has been real expensive—paying for the other fellows."[5] Judge Carey, cattleman and sometime governor of Wyoming, had a custom of traveling from Cheyenne to Laramie every spring to present funds for anonymous scholarships to the president of the University of Wyoming.

Investors in the cattle industry, according to the sample studied, were mainly merchants, bankers, financiers, and industrialists, although there was also a small group of professional men.[6]

Of the 93 in the sample, 12 listed their occupation as mercantilist; 7 of these owned dry-goods emporiums. The founder of a Cleve-

[5] Quoted in J. Evetts Haley: *Charles Goodnight* (Boston: Houghton Mifflin; 1936), 452.

[6] Their occupational classification broke down into: *Mercantilists*— Charles Arbuckle (wholesale grocer), John Arbuckle (wholesale grocer), John H. Barron (dry goods), Edmund Converse (dry goods), R. M. Fair (dry goods), James Converse (dry goods), B. W. Crowinshield (dry goods), John V. Farwell (dry goods), Marshall Field (dry goods), E. M. McGillin (dry goods), Benjamin B. Mitchell (wholesale druggist), Horace K. Thurber (wholesale grocer), J. W. Powper (dry goods); *Bankers*—Joseph Ames, S. Reed Anthony, Robert Bacon, Henry Blair, John V. Clark, C. E. Judson, Augustus Gurnee, Augustus Kountze, D. C. Plumb, Isaac Seligman, Jesse Seligman, Joseph Seligman, Quincy Shaw, Godfrey Snydacker, E. G. Stoddard, Richard Trimble, Eugene Williams; *Financiers*—Alexander Agassiz (broker), Azel Ames (broker), George R. Blanchard (commission), William A. Clark (broker), John Clay (commission), Frederick deBillier (broker), George P. Denny (commission), N. K. Fairbanks (real estate), William Forrest (commission), Rufus Hatch (broker), R. G. Hunter (commission), J. W. Macrum (commission), Levi Leiter (real estate), Charles Oelrichs (broker), Harry Oelrichs (broker), Henry A. Rice (broker), Joseph Rosenbaum (commission), Edmund Seymour (broker), D. W. Smith (commission), Chester Snider (commission), H. E. Teschemacher (broker), Julius Wadsworth (real estate), Portus B. Weare (commission), Ellerton P. Whitney (broker), William C. Whitney (broker); *Industrialists*—John B. Alley (railroads), August Busch (distiller), J. I. Case (farm implements), Jack S. Casement (railroads), Edward Creighton (telegraph), Sidney Dillon (railroads), Isaac Ellwood (wire), R. D. Evans (rubber), John H. Flagler (steel), Joseph Glidden (wire), David M. Goodrich (rubber), William C. Greene (copper), Jacob Haish (wire), Abram S. Hewitt (steel), W. V. Johnson (distiller), George Kellogg (lumber), E. C. Kellogg (lumber), John A. McShane (stockyards), James Moore (distiller), Nelson Morris (packer), Joy Morton (salt), Herman Oelrichs

land, Ohio, department store, E. M. McGillin,[7] lost his estate in
the cattle industry. Except that he was of Irish birth, little is
known about McGillin before he appeared in Cleveland in 1876
as president of "E. M. McGillin Co., Importers and Retailers of
Dry Goods." The concern obviously prospered, for by 1882
McGillin owned ranches scattered from Texas to Montana. After
the market crash of 1886–7, he conceived the idea of organizing
the cattle raisers in the West and the cattle feeders in the East in
a gigantic trust to control the market. One journalist stated that
McGillin's goal was the transference of merchandising techniques
to the cattle industry.[8] The scheme failed, however, owing to several factors—the individualistic temperament of the cattlemen,
a sluggish market, inadequate capital, and the unyielding opposition of the packers. If this was McGillin's dream, it was an abortive one.

Another prominent mercantilist, Marshall Field of Chicago,
through his stock in the Pratt-Ferris Cattle Company, the Weare
Land and Livestock Company, and a number of other firms, participated in ranching enterprises in Montana, South Dakota,
Nebraska, and Wyoming. In contrast to many Easterners in the
cattle industry, Field retained his stock long after the cattle boom.
He did not withdraw from Pratt-Ferris until the early 1900's.
That he did so indicated either a remarkable endurance or a
resignation to futility. George Weare gossiped to another officer
of the Weare Land and Cattle Company, C. M. Favonite:

> The truth is the Field interests have not seemed well satisfied
> with their investment for several years, while the Weare inter-
> ests have worked hard and cheap and honestly to make the Co.
> a success. Perhaps the Fields have been plundered so much by

---

(shipping), Trenor W. Park (shipping), William Rockefeller (oil), Henry
Sanborn (wire), Philetus Sawyer (lumber), C. M. Tilford (distiller), H. J.
Tilford (distiller), Charlemagne Tower (iron), William H. Vanderbilt
(railroads); *Professional Men*—James G. Bennett (publisher), John Bigelow
(author), Stephen B. Elkins (lawyer, politician), Russell B. Harrison
(lawyer), Robert Ingersoll (lawyer), Clarence King (geologist), Theodore
Roosevelt (lawyer, politician).

[7] Los Angeles *Times*, November 3, 1919; Cleveland *Plain Dealer*, August
29, 1899, November 4, 1920.

[8] Denver *Republican*, February 10, 1887.

those associated with them in similar deals, that a fair deal makes them lonesome.[9]

The miseries of the cattle situation afflicted all segments of the Eastern business community, but none endured more or complained more loudly than the bankers, who slightly outnumbered the mercantilists. By reputation conservatives, the bankers were no more successful than others in avoiding the pitfalls of a poor risk. Augustus Kountze and his brothers, Herman, Luther, and Charles B., had immense holdings not only in cattle but also in real estate, lumber, and railroads. The banking firm of Kountze Brothers included banks in Denver, Indianapolis, Omaha, and New York. The Kountze brothers' greatest entanglement in the cattle industry came from their association with Shanghai Pierce, the boisterous and flamboyant cattleman of the gulf coast of Texas. In 1885, Pierce concluded an agreement with the Kountzes to select 200,000 acres and purchase 12,000 yearlings.[1] The Kountzes supplied the capital; for his services Pierce received one sixth of the profits from the cattle. Despite a rather tempestuous relationship, both parties benefited from the agreement.

The Kountzes' excursion into the cattle industry was a triumph compared with that of many bankers. S. Reed Anthony, the Boston banker, was embroiled with the M. E. Post Company Bank in Cheyenne and the Santa Fe National Bank which brought him a series of emotionally wracking experiences. In spite of Anthony's admonitions, Post extended loans on inadequate security to a number of cattlemen during the expansion of the early 1880's. By 1887, much of this paper was worthless because of nonpayment of loans. The Cheyenne *Leader* on January 14, 1887, proclaimed that the Magic City was "startled by the failure of the private banking house of M. E. Post to open." Anthony pleaded with another Cheyenne friend, Hubert E. Teschemacher, to come to Post's aid: "I feel," wrote Anthony, "that some of his friends must assist

[9] George Weare to C. M. Favonite, February 26, 1897. Weare Letterbook 2, Nason Collection, Spearfish, South Dakota.

[1] Details of the Pierce-Kountze partnership are in Chris Emmett: *Shanghai Pierce* (Norman: University of Oklahoma Press; 1953), 69, 75–104, 154–5, 174–96.

or we will all suffer irreparable damage."[2] Providentially Anthony's dire predictions did not come to pass; Post paid off most of his creditors in full and left Wyoming for California, where he soon enjoyed more prosperity than he had known in Cheyenne.

Another sizable occupational grouping of Eastern investors consisted of manufacturers or industrialists, among whom Isaac Ellwood of De Kalb, Illinois, through his production and sale of barbed wire, became one of the most strongly attracted by the West. As a hardware merchant, Ellwood in 1874 grasped the potential of the simplified barbed wire invented by his neighbor Joseph Glidden, and the Ellwood concern became the largest producer of barbed wire in the United States. By the middle 1880's, the De Kalb merchant had put "venture" capital into railroads, mines, farm mortgages, and three Texas ranches totaling 246,347 acres. The ranches cost over $2,000,000 in cattle, land, and improvements,[3] and by 1889 they represented over 25 per cent of Ellwood's total invested capital.

Ellwood was captivated by his Texas interests. From May until December 1889, a flurry of letters passed between Ellwood and his manager, W. T. Carpenter. The De Kalb financier was giving advice on every subject from the best time to ship calves, to the number of windmills to be erected on twenty sections of land. Ellwood lavished attention on every detail of the ranch's development. He personally selected the pedigreed bulls to be sent to the ranch and the machinery to be used, and he hired some of the employees in his Chicago office. This minute supervision, so uncharacteristic of many Eastern investors, strained relations with his managers. On July 3, 1890, Ellwood wrote to Carpenter:

I can realize you are having trouble straightening Ellwood out as to what is going on. But send me more letters explaining

[2] S. Reed Anthony to H. E. Teschemacher, January 6, 1887. Teschemacher and deBillier Collection, Western History Research Center, University of Wyoming. A biographical sketch of M. E. Post, as well as a number of fascinating personal letters, are in Philip W. Whitely: "A Pioneer Story in Western Cover," *Brand Book of the Denver Westerners* (Denver: 1952), 298–324.

[3] Ledger, 1889–91. Ellwood Collection, Western History Research Center, University of Wyoming.

your problems so I can understand what you are doing. I can not go to Texas on every problem you face—nor do I imagine you would want me to do so.[4]

This placating letter alleviated the tension for a short period, but until the 1890's when Ellwood's son William assumed the managerial duties from De Kalb, the managers devoted much time to "straightening Ellwood out."

Ellwood differed from most entrepreneurs in his attitude toward improvements on his ranches. His correspondence was laced with phrases such as: "I want the finest equipped ranch in Texas," and "be sure you use good material in the building."[5] William Ellwood fervently maintained that it was his father's improvements which enabled the ranch to show a profit in the early 1900's.

Ample resources permitted Ellwood to indulge in his "show place" philosophy. Among the groups of investors studied, the financiers (exclusive of bankers) were inclined to the opposite approach, tending to be chary of what they termed "prodigal use of capital." Stockbrokers and commission men, all too often trapped into rescuing a company on the brink of financial collapse, consistently exhorted their managers to guard the company's exchequers. Among these conservatives was John Clay, a Scot who devoted a lifetime to protecting British investments in the West. So successfully did he resuscitate defunct firms that he became an ex officio adviser to dozens of Western cattlemen. Another financier, Francis Smith of San Antonio, Memphis, and Indianapolis, who was commission agent for numerous British investment companies and American insurance companies investing in real estate and cattle, admonished borrowers to survey their financial requirements in view of their assets. A characteristic letter from Smith to a debtor read:

I am informed that during my absence you attempted to extend your loan. In fairness you should agree that we have been more than a little generous in our treatment of your past extensions. I can not in good conscience allow you more than 60

[4] Isaac Ellwood to W. T. Carpenter, July 3, 1890. Ibid.
[5] Isaac Ellwood to W. T. Carpenter, April 22, 1890. Ibid.

days to complete payment of your loan. I hope you will be able to comply with this request.[6]

Among the other financiers, Portus B. Weare, a Chicago broker and commission agent, would have applauded Smith's sentiments. Blunt and caustic, Weare kept up a barrage of communications to his nephew, Henry Weare, manager of the Weare Land and Livestock Company in South Dakota, Montana, and Wyoming.[7] Whenever his nephew, tiring of his uncle's missives, sought solace from his father, George Weare, he usually received a reply that went: "Uncle Portus's business ability should not be questioned."[8]

Whether or not Portus Weare's business acuman was infallible, he had certainly had a varied and prosperous career. Born on New Year's Day, 1842, he was the son of a country banker in Iowa. At the age of twenty he launched the commission firm of P. B. Weare and Company in Chicago, and within five years he had a "comfortable fortune," made by exporting prairie chickens from the American West to the British Isles and the European continent. Later he sent buffalo robes overseas until the extermination of the buffalo herds finished this lucrative trade. Weare then went into the grain-brokerage business, erecting sixty-five elevators in Illinois, Nebraska, and Iowa. In 1877 he organized the Weare Land and Livestock Company, which four years later had 50,000 head of cattle grazing on the public domain in Montana, Wyoming, and South Dakota. Another of his enterprises, founded in 1891, was the North America Trading and Transport Company, which had great success as a supplier to the miners in the Yukon and the rest of western Canada.[9] George Weare's laconic comment that "Uncle

[6] Francis Smith to W. A. Cross, October 19, 1899. Letterbook 3, Smith Collection, H. P. Drought and Company, San Antonio, Texas.

[7] John Clay found Weare of a "breezy nature—an optimist of the most outspoken kind, rich in repartee coated with humorous varnish which made him popular wherever he went." *My Life on the Range* (Chicago: 1924), 111. If Clay could have read the Weare business correspondence, he might have altered this opinion. Portus B. Weare possessed high integrity, a shrewd business sense, and plain speech. There was little in his correspondence which would show him as loquacious or "breezy."

[8] George Weare to Henry Weare, November 12, 1887. Weare Letterbook 2, Nason Collection, Spearfish, South Dakota.

[9] *National Cyclopedia of American Biography*, X (New York: J. T. White; 1909), 475.

Portus's business ability should not be questioned" was not said facetiously!

After the disastrous market collapse of 1887, Portus Weare advised his nephew:

> As to my own feeling in the matter of liquidation, I would call the Directors together and lay the true condition of affairs before them and ask them to take action and relieve the management of the charge that surely will be laid at your door of concealing the fact of our losses. You know as well as I do that these lossess will appear in a few months. You therefore should not be defenseless when called to account about them as you most certainly will be if you don't forestall the charges.[1]

The Weare Land and Livestock Company not only weathered the financial crisis and adjusted to a radically reduced range; it also managed to make a substantial profit before its liquidation in 1908.

The remaining investors in the sample studied were professional men, some of whom were in politics. For these highly individual men—personages such as Clarence King, the erudite geologist; John Bigelow, editor, diplomat, and author; and Stephen B. Elkins, lawyer, industrialist, and politician—flout a common denominator. Of this group, Elkins had the longest association with the West and the most influential role in its development. Born in Perry County, Ohio, in 1841, he moved West to Missouri during his adolescence and later graduated from the University of Missouri. After serving in the Civil War, he formed a law partnership in Santa Fe with Thomas B. Catron, a man who brilliantly manipulated New Mexico politics for fifty years. Catron had full empathy for his partner's political ambitions. The decade following Elkins's arrival in Santa Fe, he practiced law, negotiated the sale of the Maxwell Land Grant, and became the territorial delegate to the U.S. House of Representatives.[2]

The neophyte delegate entered the Washington political and

---

[1] Portus Weare to Henry Weare, November 12, 1887. Weare Letterbook 2, Nason Collection, Spearfish, South Dakota.

[2] A highly favorable, uncritical, impressionistic, and disappointing biography is Oscar D. Lambert: *Stephen Benton Elkins* (Pittsburgh: University of Pittsburgh; 1955).

social scene a wealthy man, for the Santa Fe National Bank, which he had helped to organize, thrived beyond all expectations. Land speculation, a passion of his life, also cushioned his bank balance. In later life Elkins wrote: "All the time I was in New Mexico I kept putting my money in land whenever I saw the opportunity of buying a good deal of land at ten cents an acre and from that upward."[3] At the time he made this averment, he controlled 100,000 acres of coal and timber land in West Virginia, 80,000 acres in Maryland, and uncounted acres in New Mexico. Elkins was not quite the classic Horatio Alger hero, however; his Eastern holdings were assembled under the aegis of his father-in-law, Senator H. G. Davis, the largest landholder in West Virginia.

After leaving Congress in 1875, Elkins decided that his future was in the East, not the West. He opened law offices in Washington and later in New York. The same year that he joined the Washington legal circles, he was appointed to the Republican National Committee, a post he jealously refused to relinquish for over a decade. Elkins's exchange of New Mexico for West Virginia residency did not signal an abandonment of his Western investments; on the contrary, his avaricious appetite for real estate never abated, in spite of the immense holdings he already had. Elkins's drive to own more and more land was not completely headlong, however; he tempered his acquisitive instincts in more than one instance when a deal seemed hazardous. In the summer of 1886, Samuel T. Hauser, A. V. Davis, and Granville Stuart were trying to sell him the Pioneer Cattle Company of Montana. Wiser after their ill-fated experience with General Brisbin, this time the Montanans chose as broker Russell B. Harrison, son of Senator (later President) Benjamin Harrison, and himself secretary of the Montana Stock Growers Association. The selection was not by chance. The Harrison and Elkins families were intimate both politically and socially. When Benjamin Harrison left the presidency, Elkins selected a site for the president's retirement residence,[4] but Harrison spurned the offer and returned to his Indiana home.

[3] Ibid., 50.
[4] Ibid., 154.

Harrison found the negotiations hard going, however. On August 5, 1886, Hauser received a dispirited letter from him:

I enclose a clipping from the New York Tribune of today containing the notice of the death on Tuesday of John T. Elkins, a brother of S. B. Elkins. It is a very sad and sudden death. His death for the present will interfere seriously with the sale of the pioneer herd, as he was working with me to close up the remainder of the money. . . . While I was engaged in this work and at a time when I thought I was about successful, came the very discouraging news about the drought and the death of cattle in the West and Southwest. They were not willing to go forward with the negotiations. For that reason I have abandoned all hope until fall.[5]

But even in October, Harrison wrote Hauser: "We might as well forget the whole project."[6] Five months' work had led only to frustration.

Because of Elkins's long and close friendship with Thomas Catron, New Mexico land and banking remained favorite investments of his. The ponderous correspondence between the two men discloses that Elkins lobbied in Washington for Catron's projects in return for Catron's advice on New Mexico investments. Many a dream became a political reality when Tom Catron wrote: "Dear Steve . . . "

The collaboration between Elkins and Catron in the reorganization of the American Valley Company is a case in point. Originally a cattle concern guided by the Texas cattleman W. S. Slaughter,[7] the company floundered in 1893 owing to drought, severe winters, and poor administration. The 4,000 cattle surviving from a herd

5 Russell B. Harrison to Samuel Hauser, August 5, 1886. Hauser Collection, Historical Society of Montana, Helena.

6 Russell B. Harrison to Samuel Hauser, October 29, 1886. Ibid.

7 Slaughter conducted the affairs of the American Valley Company on an expensive scale for a short time. The San Marcial *Reporter* noted on November 10, 1888: "W. B. Slaughter, gen. manager of American Valley Co. . . . spends much of his time in Los Angeles where his company has its own slaughter pens and retail markets, shipping their beef direct from the New Mexico range." On March 16, 1889, the same newspaper commented: "The American Valley Cattle Co. will clear its range of all surplus stock this spring and remove them north and to the Ind. Terr. The company expects to be able to gather fully 15,000 head for removal."

of 20,000 were sold and an $11-per-share dividend was bestowed on the stockholders. The 12,000-acre range remained intact, however.[8] Seeing and seizing an opportunity, Catron quietly began communicating with dissident stockholders, and within only four months he had secured 3,000 shares and the controlling stock of the company. The rumors of Catron's activities mystified the Santa Fe business community,[9] but there was little to be puzzled about. In several notes Catron sent Elkins he revealed his motive:

> The ranch interests as they now stand comprise about 12,000 acres of patented land; and after acquiring a few more properties for which I am negotiating we will have the range controlled over a wide area.[1]

Elkins agreed to be a director of the company and to purchase $25,000 worth of stock. Further, he lobbied unceasingly with the Interior and Justice departments to clear the muddled patents on the land. Catron acknowledged this strategic assistance with the comment: "You have always been a loyal friend when I need help the most."[2]

For all Elkins's gratuities the American Valley Company turned out to be one of the few unprofitable Elkins-Catron schemes— owing, Catron claimed, to poor management by Charles Elmendorf, who was vice-president and manager of the company. Certainly Elkins and Catron had followed what was usually a successful working pattern for them. Whether they were floating a mining company, organizing a bank, or speculating in real estate, Catron initiated the promotion, provided part of the capital, and supervised the organization, while Elkins assumed a large share of the financing and created the essential favorable political atmosphere in Washington.

The Eastern investors were unified in their antagonism to celibacy. There were only 2 bachelors among the sample of 93:

[8] Charles Elmendorf to William Watson, April 14, 1900. Catron Collection, University of New Mexico Library.
[9] Charles A. Spiess to Miguel Otero, July 25, 1899. Otero Collection, University of New Mexico Library.
[1] Thomas Catron to Stephen B. Elkins, October 20, 1899. Catron Collection, University of New Mexico Library.
[2] Thomas Catron to Stephen B. Elkins, December 4, 1900. Ibid.

Charles Arbuckle of the Arbuckle Coffee family and the New York stockbroker, Harry Oelrichs. In fact, 14 married twice, and the Boston ironmonger John Haldane Flagler married thrice. When Horace K. Thurber learned of the marriage of his New Mexico partner and manager, Joseph C. Lea, he immediately sent felicitations: "The news of your marriage has just come. I am delighted as I know a good wife if treated right, can be a wonderful helpmate. Please give my best to Mrs. Lea."[3] From all indications, few of the Eastern financiers dissented from Thurber's marital philosophy. Of the 91, 74 were fathers, and one, August Busch, sired fourteen children. The progeny averaged a little more than three per family (for the country as a whole, the 1900 census listed 4.7 per family).

As to their investment habits, the Eastern financiers, for all their emotional reaction, were opposed to "sitting on one stock," as the XIT investor Abner Taylor put it. There were a few exceptions, such as Edward McGillin, Cleveland dry-goods merchant, and Horace K. Thurber, New York wholesaler, who both invested their major capital in cattle companies. But much more typical was John Haldane Flagler, the Boston entrepreneur, whose widespread dabbling in oil, railroads, steel, real estate, and cattle drove his broker to distraction. When one of his managers, John B. Thomas of the Suffolk Cattle Company, implored Flagler to agree to increased capitalization, he found the Easterner adamant. After Thomas's second urgent letter, Flagler replied:

I have never agreed with the philosophy that one should sacrifice all assets to take advantage of a momentary "golden opportunity." I believe I have prevented more than one disappointment by successfully ignoring temporary enthusiasm.[4]

Undoubtedly Flagler basked in the wisdom of his self-restraint when, two years later, the company with the "golden opportunity" was tarnished with bankruptcy.

While Eastern entrepreneurs were loath to oversubscribe in one

3 H. K. Thurber to Joseph C. Lea, May 28, 1889. Padgitt Collection, San Antonio, Texas.
4 John H. Flagler to John B. Thomas, April 29, 1884. Dunder Collection, Western History Research Center, University of Wyoming.

stock, they did have their *enfant gates*. Mining promotion aroused their greatest enthusiasm. Of the 71 investors on which there was enough data to perceive their investment structure, 23 speculated in mining stock. Trenor Park, N. K. Fairbanks, Levi Leiter, and Marshall Field were especially susceptible to mining ventures. Likewise, Isaac Ellwood had an investment in the Delores Mining Company of Mexico and Colorado which "stabilized" at over three million dollars; but beyond this point he developed sales resistance. When Ellwood arrived at his Texas ranch in November 1894, he found a letter from John B. Farish, a mining engineer of Denver and a close adviser, who outlined his latest claim, emphasizing that Ellwood would ignore this offer at his own peril.

> Mr. Richards [Farish's partner] thinks we are making a mistake in offering to part with any portion of the property . . . without doing anything more on the property, we could dispose of our option for a good profit to ourselves. I, therefore, feel that the proposition to you is very fair, and even a liberal one.[5]

But Ellwood was not in an expansive mood:

> You will have to look elsewhere for your capital. I am just tied up with other obligations. If the mine is as promising as you indicate, you will have no trouble interesting other men. In the meantime, should my dividends from the Delores increase sufficiently to warrant further investment, I may consider your proposition.[6]

Aside from the Eastern investors' attraction to the glitter of gold-mining opportunities, their timidity about committing more funds to the cattle industry (which became more pronounced in the late 1880's) is understandable. The absence of dividends—in some cases, since the corporation's inception—hardly instilled confidence or encouraged the advancing of more capital.

But the investor's seesaw reaction of entrancement and then disenchantment with the cattle industry exasperated more than one

[5] John B. Farish to Isaac Ellwood, November 12, 1894. Ellwood Collection, Western History Research Center, University of Wyoming.
[6] Isaac Ellwood to John B. Farish, November 17, 1894. Ibid.

manager. J. H. Wilson of Marion, Ohio, a major stockholder in
the Dilworth Cattle Company of Montana, complained to his
manager. J. N. Tolman, that expenses were too high and dividends
too low, and he refused to invest more until this situation was
rectified. Making little attempt to disguise his disgust, Tolman
replied:

> I was surprised to receive your latest. . . . As near as I can
> make out, I am charged with making too much expense and
> improvements on the ranch. . . . I have tried to run the ranch
> as cheaply as possible consistent with good business principles.
> If the company does not want any more work on the land and
> pay for this improvement at a fair price then the company be
> hanged! You can not expect a company to pay dividends if you
> do not continue to support it.[7]

Disagreements between managers and investors were numerous on
many counts, yet more disputes hinged on Eastern reluctance to
continue supplying funds than on any other subject.

In cataloging the religious affiliations of the Eastern investors,
one receives the impression that these men were not overly concerned with the world of the spirit. The one exception, John V.
Farwell, the XIT stockholder, was deeply religious. On the other
hand, the son of a Congregational minister, Robert G. Ingersoll,
who was a lawyer and partner in the Dorsey ranch in New
Mexico, took delight in shocking nineteenth-century America
with his atheistic doctrines.

Between the pious Farwell and the antichrist Ingersoll, most
investors fell in their adherence to grace. Only 31 mentioned a
religious affiliation. Their affirmation followed a predictable
denominational pattern: 4 Roman Catholics, 4 Jews, and 23
Protestants. Of the Protestants, there were 12 Episcopalians, 5
Congregationalists, 3 Presbyterians, 1 Baptist, 1 Dutch Reformed,
and 1 Unitarian. Considering the New England origins of the
financiers, the dominance of the Protestant sects, particularly
Episcopalians and Congregationalists, is not surprising. However,

---

[7] J. N. Tolman to J. H. Wilson, March 23, 1893. Tolman Collection,
Clark, Wyoming.

the proportionate number of Jewish and Roman Catholic faiths provides little consolation to those proponents of an adaptation of the Weber-Tawney thesis in American society. The vacuum in biographical accounts relating to the religious affiliations of these men suggests that the Eastern investor may have purchased his pew in Christ's Church, but he seldom occupied it.

In sum, to define a "typical" Eastern investor is hazardous, but retouching and reducing the composite etching to a portrait may bring a sharper image. In most instances, he had been born in the late 1830's or the early 1840's, and lived in New York or Boston. His education seldom went beyond elementary school, but whether it did or not, he was a generous supporter of education. If he had the good fortune to matriculate at college, he usually chose one of the Ivy League schools.

He chose his vocation in a predictable pattern. The most frequent occupational choices were, first, industrialist (distiller, railroad builder, or steel official were favored categories); second, financier, specifically a broker or a commission agent; third, banker; and fourth, merchant (particularly a dry-goods merchant or wholesale grocer).

The Eastern investor's original curiosity about the cattle industry sometimes arose because he had other investments in the West, usually in mining, railroads, or real estate. When he actually came to investment in cattle, he commonly followed the "associative spirit." He liked company, particularly friends or relatives.

Finally, the Eastern investor enthusiastically shunned bachelorhood. He was definitely a family man, in accord with the social mores of the time.

In economic philosophy, investment temperament, and individual personality, the Eastern investor in the cattle industry blended into the financial behaviorism about him. His Western investment, because of frequency of failures, conceivably gave him a higher proportion of traumatic shocks than his neighboring Wall Street financier, but he was much more a part of, rather than separated from, the business milieu of his age.

IV

"We, the undersigned..."

ORGANIZATION & CAPITALIZATION

ᴧ B CY ᴕ ND ⊥ ⅏
ᴼ A ⇙ ᴑ
ᴵ ᴓ ᴙ
ᴓ

Edward Page of Boston, in a fit of nervous frustration, dashed off a note to his partner-manager in Cheyenne: "For God's sake use any form of partnership suitable to the laws of Wyoming, but do something in the way of an agreement before you proceed to buy cattle."[1]

Until Eastern and foreign capital poured into the West, the partnership, or what was loosely termed "association," was the most popular type of organization. Limited in scope, uncomplicated in specifics, the partnership agreement fulfilled the legal

[1] Edward Page to John B. Thomas, April 9, 1878. Dunder Collection, Western History Research Center, University of Wyoming.

requirements of the day. However, its very simplicity provided the seedbed for future altercations between partners.

In typical legal style, the first words of the partnership contract invariably were: "We the Undersigned . . ." After the names and addresses of the partners, it gave the amount of capital, the length of corporate existence, the *raison d'être* of the partnership (which might encompass everything from opening a mine to establishing a town), the basis for division of profits, the stipulations for withdrawal from partnership, and the disposal of assets in the event of death or disability of either or both partners.

In the beginning, the partners quickly agreed upon most of these provisions, the amount of capitalization having previously been discussed. It was the organizational details—the hiring of a manager and the securing of land and cattle—which brought to the fore any latent friction. Many of these disputes were caused by the Eastern investor's failure to comprehend the financial responsibilities which he had as a cattle king. The Western partner, who might also be manager, was amazingly inarticulate in explaining financial requirements, and his silence served to delay but not to avert his partner's inevitable wrath.

A common agreement was that the Western partner-manager would take his profits from the annual cattle sales at a specified percentage or amount. The Eastern investor understandably became irritated when the annual profits were absorbed by the Western partner, leaving him little, if any, return for the use of his capital. In view of the wide and free public domain, the low cost of Texas cattle, and the cheap cowhand labor, the Easterner often panicked at the diminished state of the company finances after a year's operation. James T. Gardner of Albany, New York, complained vigorously to his partner, George McClellan: "When we agreed to associate, you said we could establish a company with $40,000. You now have expended almost $48,000 and still you have the bravery to tell me that the end is not in sight."[2] Gardner's letter, which ran for twelve pages, appeared

[2] James T. Gardner to George B. McClellan, December 22, 1881. McClellan Collection, Western History Research Center, University of Wyoming.

calculated to intimidate McClellan. In a petulantly systematic fashion, Gardner proceeded to disagree with everything McClellan had undertaken—his land purchases, the cattle he had bought, his hiring of "inebriated" cowboys, and his rumored absence from the ranch. The Albany capitalist could not fathom why the purchase of so much land was essential "if no one besides ourselves is there to occupy it." As to cattle: "I hear Oregon cattle are better and in the long run cheaper than those Texas ones." On the employees: "Be sure to hire sober men: I shudder at the thought of our cattle running around on the plains cared for by some fuzzy minded cowboy."

While most other investors managed to exercise more self-control than Gardner, their criticisms of policy just as often left both them and their partners exhausted. Daniel C. Bacon, a Boston stockbroker, questioned his partner, John Painter of Roggen, Colorado, as to how much capital must be "sunk in land." Informed that $15,000 would cover it, Bacon assented. Five months later, when this sum had evaporated and their range was still not secure, he asked to be released from the partnership. Painter agreed, requesting only "a modest sum" for his time and effort.[3]

A recurring clash of temperaments broke up more than one promising partnership. Silas Guthrie, who went West from Marion, Ohio, in the early 1880's founded a ranch near Newcastle, Wyoming, and formed a partnership with Charles J. Webb and Company of Philadelphia. Although this association managed to hold together for over a decade, disagreement marred it from the beginning. At one point John Willidin, treasurer of the company, wrote: "It has long since been evident to me, as it probably has been to you, that our partnership was a mistake."[4] One can almost hear the sigh of relief as Guthrie replied: "Your discontent has bothered me for some time. I am willing to sever our partnership, if some mutually acceptable agreement can be worked out."[5] The last phrase is the key to the continuation of the partnership;

[3] Daniel C. Bacon to John E. Painter, February 14, 1891. Painter Collection, Greeley, Colorado.

[4] John Willidin to Silas Guthrie, April 23, 1882. Guthrie Collection, Western History Research Center, University of Wyoming.

[5] Silas Guthrie to John Willidin, May 16, 1882. Ibid.

stymied on the division of assets, the members stayed together for another twelve years.

Guthrie and Willidin's tenuous acceptance of an uneasy business marriage rather than an unsatisfactory divorce was the alternative many partners reisgned themselves to, even though it often took years of bickering. Most partners' altercations, not surprisingly, erupted over the splitting of profits, or rather the fact that there were no earnings to divide. Occasionally each partner contributed an equal amount of capital to the company treasury and then acquiesced in the misleading euphony of share and share alike. Thus Clarence King and N. R. Davis's agreement was dignified with the accustomed flourish:

> In the event the business continues three years from July first that at the expiration of that time N. R. Davis and Clarence King to (have) equal shares in all property real and personal either purchased with the original capital or accrued in the course of business—all profits from the business to be shared equally from the start.[6]

More commonly, however, the Eastern backer contributed the larger share of capital and the Western partner offered the main asset—described as "managerial talents"—plus a small amount of money.

The heavy initial outlay and slow return brought wails from the Eastern investors before they had really suffered financial loss. Richard Lake, Chicago financier, wrote his partner Henry Blair that "my money would be much better placed in Chicago real estate than in Western cattle, which tend to disappear more than they multiply."[7] Blair, who was also from Chicago and who held as much stock as Lake did, retorted: "You are at least receiving a return on your share without the managerial obligations."[8] Blair had cause for anger, as his recompense for managerial problems came to a miserly one sixth more of the stock than Lake's.

While not always satisfactory, the Blair-Lake pattern in which

[6] Clarence King–N. R. Davis Partnership Agreement, August 22, 1871. Princeton University Library.

[7] Richard Lake to Henry Blair, August 3, 1884. Henry Blair Collection, Western History Research Center, University of Wyoming.

[8] Henry Blair to Richard Lake, September 8, 1884. Ibid.

the investor-manager partner was reimbursed through an alloca-
tion of additional stock became the accepted form. Less frequently, the managing partner received a salary. John Thomas
and Henry Rogers's partnership agreement specified that Thomas
would receive $1,200 a year for assuming managerial responsi-
bilities. However, since the salary was contingent on Rogers's
shares first accruing a 6 per cent dividend, Thomas was rarely paid,
a fact which led him to remark laconically: "I wish I had more
shares, then I would receive less than nothing."[9]

If partnerships were uneasy alliances, a partner's demise seldom
brought a financial rebirth. When the Irishman John Adair died,
his partner Charles Goodnight was left with the vexation of dealing with a vacillating widow and an alleged illegitimate son who
was imbued with avaricious desires. Goodnight finally settled for
the leaner end of the bargain, just to shed the unpleasant arrangement and salvage something.[1]

The Boston manufacturer James Converse discovered that when
he dissolved his partnerships, he found himself committed to paying the "managerial expense," amounting to a tidy sum. After
several such disconcerting experiences, it took all of velvet-tongued
Hubert Teschemacher's powers of persuasion to induce Converse
even to contemplate being a stockholder in the Teschemacher and
deBillier Cattle Company. In response to Teschemacher's eloquently worded letter describing the delights in store for a
Western cattle investor, Converse commented: "Once a fool,
twice the wiser the next time. I know your integrity and enthusiasm, but the fact is you cannot guarantee the return I can get in
the East."[2] Nevertheless, Teschemacher's persistence triumphed,
and Converse subscribed to $10,000 in Teschemacher and deBillier.

Of course, not all partnerships were fraught with dissension and
distrust; some had a remarkable degree of serenity. More often

[9] John B. Thomas to Henry Rogers, January 6, 1881. Dunder Collection,
Western History Research Center, University of Wyoming.
[1] J. Evetts Haley: *Charles Goodnight* (Boston: Houghton Mifflin; 1936),
326–33.
[2] E. C. Converse to H. E. Teschemacher, January 18, 1882. Teschemacher
and deBillier Collection, Western History Research Center, University of
Wyoming.

than not, however, these were family partnerships rather than a combination of Eastern investor and Western manager-investor. One family enterprise was operated by two brothers from Dayton, Ohio, Valentine and William Dickey, who had a meteoric career on the plains. Before they reached the age of thirty, their brand appeared on cattle from the Indian territory to Dakota.[3] But when William died in 1886, his brother proved incapable of mastering the tangled business affairs. With great difficulty, Valentine Dickey repaid their debts to Thomas Nelson,[4] the British publisher, and to the First National Bank of Chicago. Then he liquidated their holdings at less than twenty-five cents on the dollar and, discouraged in spirit and ill in health, died four years after his brother.[5]

The Snyder brothers, Dudley, John, and Tom, of Georgetown, Texas, also achieved eminence that their competitors could well envy. As with so many cattlemen, the Snyders established their business by trailing cattle north from Texas, first to Abilene and then later to Cheyenne. In 1877 they contracted with John Iliff to deliver 17,500 cattle during the next year, and they completed the deal in July 1878, six months after Iliff's death.[6] The Snyders then purchased a major interest in the Iliff herds and assumed their management. Before the market collapsed in 1886–7, the overextended Snyders sensed their vulnerable financial position and attempted to curtail their operations. John lamented to his brother Dudley in February 1885: "I have been to the banks here [Cheyenne] and in Denver, but no encouragement. I wish I could sell anything we have."[7] By January 1886, John was completely disconsolate. "I think by shaping up the horse shoe business so as to not have to drive any of them up here we can probably shape our business here so as to get out. . . . I do not want to spend an-

[3] Kansas City *Livestock Indicator*, April 10, 1890; July 22, 1886; October 7, 1887. *Northwestern Livestock Journal*, December 3, 1886.
[4] John Clay: *My Life on the Range* (Chicago: 1924), 92–4.
[5] Kansas City *Livestock Indicator*, April 10, 1890.
[6] Agnes Wright Spring: "A Genius for Handling, John W. Iliff," *When Grass Was King* (Boulder: University of Colorado Press; 1956), 414.
[7] J. W. Snyder to D. H. Snyder, February 2, 1885. Snyder Collection, University of Texas.

other winter here for I have certainly done all I agreed to do in the very best way I could do."[8]

John Snyder had his wish; he never spent another winter on the Northern plains. Returning to Texas, the Snyder brothers recouped their losses and enjoyed prosperity for a few years, but by 1899 their luck turned bad again. Relating details of an exhausting mine operation in Mexico, Dudley assured his friend Isaac Ellwood: "Don't think I'm crazy or visionary or like a drowning man grabbing at a straw when I tell you I am still down in Sinaloa, Mexico, dickering with mines."[9] Totally discouraged a year later, Dudley asked Ellwood for a job: "Please don't think for a moment I would feel humiliated in managing your business after having owned the greater part of it."[1] The Snyders had come the full circle.

A partnership much more successful, though not as long-lived, as that of the Snyders developed in Omaha in the burgeoning post-Civil War era. The Creighton brothers, builders of the Pacific Telegraph, and the Kountze brothers, financiers and bankers, who controlled financial institutions scattered from New York to the West, possessed the ingredients essential for a flourishing enterprise. The Creighton-Kountze alliance was blessed from the beginning with assets that many cattle companies never achieved: shrewd business judgment, sufficient capital, a compatability forged in former associations. In addition, their confidence was buoyed up by immense profits pouring in from Colorado mines.

Charles Brown, Creighton's secretary, first got the idea which grew into another successful partnership. In the days of the construction of the Pacific Telegraph, Brown had astutely observed that the Laramie plains in Southern Wyoming appeared to be excellent cattle country.[2] Brown depicted to Creighton, in vivid terms, the region's winter protection, luxuriant grass, and abundant water—all adding up to a cattleman's Eden. Swayed by

[8] J. W. Snyder to D. H. Snyder, January 11, 1886. Ibid.
[9] D. H. Snyder to Isaac Ellwood, July 27, 1899. Ellwood Collection, Western History Research Center, University of Wyoming.
[1] D. H. Snyder to Isaac Ellwood, December 17, 1900. Ibid.
[2] Barbara Sorensen: "A King and a Prince among Pioneers; John and Edward Creighton" (M. A. Thesis, Creighton University, 1962).

his secretary's opinions as well as his own observations, Creighton, with the assistance of the Kountze brothers and the First National Bank of Omaha, financed Thomas Alsop and Charles Hutton in a ranch on the Laramie plains in 1868. The Creighton-Alsop-Hutton partnership achieved an enviable record, not only in inaugurating a thriving cattle firm, but also in conducting a brokerage business, by purchasing Colorado cattle and then trailing them to and selling them at a railroad point on the North Platte. The Creighton-Alsop-Hutton firm had all the components for success: Eastern backers who were conversant with the land of the prairies, understood the risks involved, and were willing to gamble sufficient capital, plus two experienced cattlemen who devoted their time to minute supervision of the ranch rather than to social life in Cheyenne. Adequate capital, shrewd management, and persistent attention virtually assured the prosperity of any cattle company.

Three partnerships—the Dickey brothers, the Snyder brothers, and the Creighton-Alsop-Hutton combination—reflected the blemishes as well as the advantages inherent in partnerships of the cattle industry. In theory, the partnership offered a vehicle for additional capital supply to the West and at the same time enabled the neophyte Eastern investor, theoretically, an opportunity to secure responsible advice and management in an underdeveloped area. Yet a striking commentary on these early agreements is the high percentage of partnerships between Western cattlemen and an Eastern financial figure. In the shadowy background sat the silent participant—a bank, commission firm, or Eastern investor. This refusal of the financial backer to become more implicated, both financially and managerially, often spelled disaster for the partnership. The rationale for his reticence may have been furnished by Charles G. Francklyn, American advisor to the British Cunards, who wrote to an associate: "Most of my friends are hesitant to place more of their money into the cattle business, which they can not control though some of them have regretted this of late."[3] Many financiers would not have argued for total

[3] Charles G. Francklyn to Andrew Dunham, March 9, 1885. Western Range Cattle Industry Collection, State Historical Society of Colorado, Denver.

power over corporate affairs, but they desired more influence than they usually had. Thus as early as 1879, not every investor was being influenced by the boom psychology. Another very evident problem for the investor was his entanglement in other investments: railroads, mining, and iron often offered quicker and larger returns.

For all the hazards and dissensions embodied in "agreements between parties," the partnership as a legal entity offered a simplified mode of business operation with the limited financial resources of early cattle companies. The intense demand for cattle, reflected in the prices on the Chicago market and the subsequent high consumer prices, made modestly successful partnerships take on the warm glow of phenomenal prosperity.

Several factors combined toward the end of the 1870's to stain the attractiveness of the partnership. The restriction of the range against the encroachment of small cattlemen and farmers forced large cattle companies to consider the purchase of public domain, or at least the sections controlling the water rights. This factor, combined with the easier access to markets through intensive railroad construction and the increasing tendency to discern fortunes on every range, made an increase in capital not only highly desirable, but essential. The logical solution, which many partners perceived concurrently, was incorporation. Besides increasing the number of stockholders and thereby the financial resources, incorporation offered "limited liability," which held great charm for many financiers. In fact, the absence of this provision in partnership agreements created tremendous introspection between partners. Any hint of falling fortunes in his firm sent the neurotic Eastern partner into depressive moods. Western cattlemen were as susceptible to the jitters as Easterners. Living in Boston for the winter, John Thomas one chilly morning received a particularly discouraging letter from his partner, Henry Hay, in Cheyenne. After spending several days in brooding contemplation of his partner's letter, scrutinizing every phrase, Thomas painfully composed a reply:

> Your letter with the horrible news that our cattle and sheep sales will no more than pay our expense and interest arrived here

last week. What went wrong? How could this happen? I just can't understand what happened. Send me *immediately* a copy of our journal, be sure you outline the expenses in detail. There must be a leak somewhere.[4]

In his next letter, Hay did his best to calm his partner's nerves by telling him that the outlook was not so bleak as originally forecast. Yet he could not conceal his irritation at Thomas's aspersions on his management. He concluded with the comment: "I doubt whether you could or anybody could have done any better this winter. We are no worse or better than the Durbins, Careys or others."[5]

Incorporation of joint-stock firms did not banish fear or suspicion from investor-manager relationships, but it did seem to allay some of the attacks of panic. While contemporary evidence is slight, one suspects that Eastern investor and Western cattlemen alike understood more about the inherent dangers of the cattle business than they ever committed to paper. There is a synthetic tone to the anguished wrangling at cattle conventions and the injured private comments in letters. It was easy to submerge these fears in the boom years, when rumors of promised rewards filtered through the smoky haze of most gentlemen's clubs.

Though the joint-stock company swiftly became the accepted mode in the cattle country, the partnership was not completely submerged. Family partnerships, especially, survived through the heyday of incorporation. Indeed, family concerns which later incorporated became the dominant financial arrangement.

The legal artistry of the incorporation agreement followed a standard and unimaginative pattern. After giving the state law to which the company owed its legal life, article one followed with "The name of this corporation and by which it shall be known in law is. . . ." Article two detailed the purposes of the corporation: "owning, raising, buying, selling and dealing in meat, cattle, horses, sheep and land." Perpetually reluctant to miss any good opportunity, the incorporators often included town lots,

---

[4] John B. Thomas to Henry Hay, November 18, 1877. Dunder Collection, Western History Research Center, University of Wyoming.
[5] Henry Hay to John B. Thomas, December 21, 1877. Ibid.

mining, and even street railways in the objects of the corporation. Article three stated: "The corporation is capitalized in the sum of one hundred thousand and the number af shares thereof is four thousand." In rare instances this sentence was amended by a subsequent clause: "The amount of said stock actually paid in at the date hereof is. . . ." In common practice this phrase was shunned by directors for the reason that the majority of corporation's stock was not subscribed until long after the incorporation papers were filed in the dank territorial or state capital basement. The regrets were many and the self-recriminations sincere when the directors were called upon to explain the ghost of watered stock which revisited the company in later existence. Article four gave the corporate bases of operation—for example: "The operations of this corporation shall be carried on in Weld County, in the State of Colorado and the office for the transaction of business with the State of Illinois shall be kept at Cook County, Illinois." The final article listed the existence of the corporation. Then above the affixed gold seal, with two scraps of red ribbon, were inscribed the names of the incorporators.

The filing of incorporation papers may have signified that the company was about to come into existence, or it may have indicated only a dream on the part of a couple of promoters, or it may have meant a truce in the altercations of the incorporators. The hammering out of corporate agreements exposed the raw nerves of numerous incorporators. Corporations frequently rose out of the ashes of a decreased partnership, a fact which alone assured disagreement. One trustee described the manner of incorporation thus: "The owner having a herd of cattle valued at $150,000 would take out a charter for a corporation with the capital of $300,000, sell his cattle to the corporation for 51 per cent of the stock and sell to those desiring to engage in this profitable enterprise the remaining stock for cash."[6] In such a manner fortunes were made.

The crux of numerous disputes lay in how much the assets of the

[6] Mrs. J. Lee Jones and Rupert N. Richardson: "Colorado City, the Cattlemen's Capital," *West Texas Historical Association Yearbook*, XIX (October 1943), 40.

deceased partnership should be valued at when put into the joint-stock company. Especially bothersome to many trustees was the appraisal, which seemed designed to deceive: "And the corporation assumes the good will of said partnership." How could anyone divine a partnership's good will? In reality, good will meant the bonus the partners would receive for consenting to sell. Alexander Agassiz and Quincy Shaw, in a joint letter to N. R. Davis, complained about the good-will clause in their contract, and about a mysterious $12,378.80 which suddenly appeared in the first annual statement as a liability. Where did this sum originate? queried Shaw and Agassiz.[7] In answer Davis said that the amount was a holdover from the former partnership. The very thought appalled them; they insisted that if this were the case the sum should be immediately stricken from the company's books. "It appears to us that the books concerning the contract business should be started from this point distinct from any former accounts."[8]

As a case study in incorporation frustration, few negotiations excelled those of John Thomas. His attempt to create the Suffolk Cattle Company brought him to the edge of a nervous breakdown. From the spring of 1883 to the spring of 1884, Thomas journeyed from Cheyenne to Boston on three separate occasions in an effort to entice his partner, Edward Page, to place the assets of Thomas and Page in the proposed Suffolk Cattle Company. From the first, Page remained obdurate, insisting that he would have no part of any scheme that did not give him a "major voice in the company." As far as Page was concerned, a "major voice" translated into complete control. Thomas argued that the assets of the Thomas and Page partnership alone were more than enough to give them the decisive say. Page refused to be mollified and with a compulsion which seemed to Thomas a mania, held out for 51 per cent of the stock.

As a last resort, Thomas acquiesced the only course that lay open, namely, to negotiate with the other stockholders. Finally

[7] Quincy Shaw and Alexander Agassiz to N. R. Davis, December 30, 1879. Russell Thorp Collection, Western History Research Center, University of Wyoming.
[8] Ibid.

after weeks of personal conferences and haranguing in Boston, he managed to persuade all but two stockholders to give Page the control he demanded. One stockholder wrote him: "I will never agree to this foolhardy arrangement if I were not convinced of your honesty."[9] At that point Page, worn down by Thomas's cajoling, yielded to a compromise settlement: while he would not be allotted 51 per cent of the stock, he would be given a veto power on all expenditures of the company over $1,000, a power which in theory should enable him to safeguard his investment. This amazing solution, born of frustration, was doomed to failure.

Thomas left Boston in late March, exhausted but exhilarated over the outcome of his bargaining. He had been in Cheyenne only two weeks when he received a letter from Page reneging on his promise: "I feel there are too many dangers in the company you propose"—and as a final insult: "Why do you not put your money with me in real estate here?"[1] Thomas was in despair; after three days of agonizing he sent a letter to his friend and fellow stockholder, Joseph Ames, in Boston. "I got everything in shape as I told you when Page and son kicked over the traces and refused to come into the company altho' I had their assent that they would. They now want me to take their stocks at par and let them out in that way at about 93,000. This I will not consent to do. . . . I am thoroughly disgusted."[2]

By the middle of May, Thomas had regained his composure, although he was far from happy. He wrote Ames: "I finally got them [Pages] to come to $75,000, still much higher than their interest is worth." On the more pleasant subject of the future of the Suffolk Cattle Company, Thomas was more eloquent. "Now as regards to the outlook, I can only say that both the herd (Thomas and Page) and the range proved to exceed my fondest anticipation."[3]

After another year, Thomas remained convinced of the wonder-

[9] T. W. Iselin to John B. Thomas, November 22, 1883. Dunder Collection, Western History Research Center, University of Wyoming.

[1] Edward Page to John B. Thomas, April 3, 1884. Ibid.

[2] John Thomas to Joseph Ames, April 22, 1884. Ibid.

[3] John Thomas to Joseph Ames, May 17, 1884. Ibid.

ful prospects in store for the Suffolk Cattle Company. He wrote to his Bostonian friend Henry Rogers: "Everything pertaining to the Suffolk Cattle Company is in good shape. . . . you need not fear my doing my best for my own sake and yours. My interest in this outcome is far larger than anyone else's."[4] Within a year the Suffolk Cattle Company was fighting for its financial survival. Resignedly, Thomas decided that the fates were inevitably against him and the cattle industry was for others. Even though his exhilarating hopes of becoming a cattle king had faded, Thomas stayed on in Cheyenne until the autumn of 1910, when he finally returned to Boston.

Fortunately, not all incorporators had to suffer the way Thomas did. At the same time as the Suffolk Cattle Company bargaining, John V. Farwell was negotiating relatively easily with the English on a loan for the XIT Ranch. Refused capital in theUnited States, Farwell departed for Europe in 1885 to borrow money abroad. Initially the English businessmen were reluctant to finance Farwell unless an English company was formed. Farwell wrote his partner, Abner Taylor, for advice. Taylor promptly responded that he and his associate would consent to three "modes of organizing a company":

> 1st—the land to be put in the Company at $10,000,000 and the stock for that amount issued and delivered as we give title. $5,000,000 5 per cent debentures to be issued. $2,000,000 to be sold and the money invested in cattle and improvements on the land. $3,000,000 to be sold and the money paid to the owners of the land, at the rate of $1.00 per acre as they deliver title. The promoters to furnish a market for the $5,000,000 debentures at par for which they are to receive $2,500,000 of stock.

> 2nd—The company to issue $12,000,000 of stock. $2,000,000 at par to be taken to be invested in cattle and improvements on the land. $3,000,000 of 5 per cent debentures to be issued and sold at par and the money paid to the owners of the land at the rate of $1.00 per acre as they deliver title. $3,000,000 of the capital stock to be delivered to the promoters to pay them for finding a market for the $2,000,000 of stock and the $2,000,000

4 John Thomas to Henry Rogers, June 6, 1885. Ibid.

of debentures. $10,000,000 of stock to be delivered pro-rata to the owners as they deliver title.

3rd—$1,000,000 of stock preferred for a 20 per cent dividend for 5 years then to be taken up with a 5 per cent debenture. This money to be invested in cattle and improvements on the land. Also $1,000,000 of 5 per cent debentures to be sold at par and the money invested in the same way. $2,000,000 of 5 per cent debentures to be delivered to the owners of the land at the rate of $1.00 per acre as they deliver title. The promoters to find a market for these debentures at par. $9,000,000 of the common stock to be issued and delivered to the owners of the land as they deliver title.[5]

The English financiers, recognizing the shrewdness of these terms, balked at Taylor's proposition and insisted that if any financing was to be had it would be on their own stipulations. Farwell acquiesced to the English ultimatum, and the Capitol Company, as the American owners were known, conveyed the land to the new English organization, the Capitol Freehold Land and Investment Company. From its headquarters in England, the new company then sold debentures bearing interest of not more than 7 per cent. The debentures matured at specific periods of five, seven, and ten years, but could be called in by the company on an official notice of six months.[6] The XIT, on the basis of this loan and the glamour and magnitude of the Capitol Company's operation, was often assumed to be an English company. In reality, the Farwells and the Taylors kept tight control of it. John Farwell returned to the States to be elected managing director of the company. When the last bonds were redeemed in 1909, the foreign company ceased to exist.

Once a corporate structure had achieved a semblance of reality, and the stockholders had compromised on their conflicting ambitions, the primary chore remained—selling the stock. Usually the incorporators or directors of the new company already had subscribed the greater part of the capitalization. Once the corpora-

[5] A. Taylor to John V. Farwell, February 17, 1885. XIT Letterbook, 1883-5, XIT Collection, Panhandle Plains Museum, Canyon, Texas.
[6] J. Evetts Haley: *The XIT Ranch of Texas, and the Early Days of the Llano Estacado* (Norman: University of Oklahoma Press; 1953), 72.

tion was launched, however, the subscribers all too frequently had second thoughts about their pledges. Colonel Jay L. Torrey, who achieved national reputation and acclaim for leading a group of cowboy roughriders in the Spanish-American War (though his regiment never saw Cuba, bogging down instead in a Florida swamp), reminded a director of his Embar Cattle Company that his subscription was due. He received a short reply:

> My dear Colonel, I have come to the conclusion that I must have been drunk on the day I agreed to take your stock. I feel in five years (maybe less) that it will be worthless. I hope you will not be offended when I reduce my stock undertaking to $3,000 [instead of the $7,500 he had originally agreed on]. A cheque is enclosed[7]

Torrey haughtily replied that a director with such a lack of confidence did not deserve to be included on the Embar Cattle Company's board. He returned the check.[8]

If all the incorporators purchased their shares, additional stock was then issued to give the superficial impression of legitimacy to the announced capitalization. The sale of this stock beyond the original subscription became, to put it mildly, a difficult task. The most effective, but by no means sure, method was for the directors to peddle the stock among their relatives and business acquaintances. Understandably, new or prospective shareholders were reluctant to take an interest in a cattle corporation when they had not participated in its organization and would have no voice in its future policies. By the same token, the original stockholders were reluctant to give up any measure of control to people who were contributing less to the company than they were themselves. One dissatisfied stockholder expressed this feeling in a letter to Ora Haley of Colorado and Wyoming: "You can not expect confidence in your management when you show no confidence in your stockholders."[9] Haley solved the problem with alacrity by purchasing the stock of this disgruntled investor

[7] G. W. E. Griffeth to Jay L. Torrey, January 9, 1887. Torrey Collection, Western History Research Center, University of Wyoming.

[8] Jay L. Torrey to G. W. E. Griffeth, February 11, 1887. Ibid.

[9] Clifford Danks to Ora Haley, September 17, 1879. Western Range Cattle Industry Collection, State Historical Society of Colorado, Denver.

in addition to the majority of outstanding shares in his company.

There was, then, in reality, a vast chasm between actual capital subscribed and the imaginative figure boldly printed on the incorporation papers. The total amount of incorporation capital for Montana, Wyoming, Colorado, and New Mexico is available for the years 1880 to 1900; yet to recite these figures without adopting extreme caution is to engage in Alice in Wonderland economics. If allowances are made for the exaggerated capital figures and the bogus incorporations, the incorporations can be a mercurial indicator of the relative amounts of investment among these states. On a yearly basis the figures also assume some significance as a charting of the pinnacles and craters in the flow of capital East to West.

For the last two decades of the nineteenth century, the total number of incorporated cattle companies in Montana reached 181; in Wyoming, 188; in Colorado, 324; and in New Mexico, 186. The aggregate capitalization for these respective states came to $27,141,800 for Montana, $94,095,800 for Wyoming, $102,015,000 for Colorado, and $61,340,500 for New Mexico.[1]

The problems in interpreting these figures are immediately apparent. Colorado, with 324 companies, had a total of only $102,015,000 in capitalization. Were the legal provisions for incorporation in the Centennial State especially lenient? The answer is no: statutory requirements for incorporation in the four states show no meaningful differences. The large number of corporations and small aggregate capitalization in Colorado is explained rather by the nature of the agricultural economy. The early development of irrigation together with a mild climate and a rich soil combined to encourage a more intensive farming as opposed to a ranching economy. The reduced acreage essential for a productive farming and stock raising concern mitigated the necessity for huge amounts of capital.[2] An interesting corollary was that it also lessened the speculative craze so conspicuous in other states. Colorado certainly had its quota of gamblers, but

[1] Incorporation records. Ibid.
[2] A. T. Steinel: *History of Agriculture in Colorado* (Ft. Collins: State Agricultural College; 1926).

they gravitated to the mining industry, not the cattle industry. No one in the cattle industry of the Centennial State came close to the financial gyrations of Wilson Waddingham[3] in New Mexico or James Reavis[4] in Arizona, Montana, and Wyoming.

Montana's low capitalization figure on an aggregate and per company basis presents another problem in interpretation. That Montana's agricultural foundation of the 1880's radically differed from Colorado's is evident: there were pockets of intensive agriculture, yet a casual glance at a map of Montana's agricultural regions for the period before 1900 shows the enormous extent of rangeland versus fertile loam. The mining industry, though, was economically comparable to that of Colorado. In spite of the booming capital demands of Montana and Colorado's mining industry, there is no testimony that investors starved other sectors of these states' economy. Nor were there substantial variations in entrepreneurial leadership. The speculative psyches of F. Augustus Heinze[5] and H. A. W. Tabor[6] possessed more similarities than differences. What, then, does account for the almost five to one discrepancy in investment? Part of the solution is that numer-

[3] The press of the 1889's reveled in chronicling the exploits of Wilson Waddingham. The Cimarron *News Press* concerned itself more than most newspapers. On March 18, 1882, a headline appeared stating that "Wilson Waddingham has organized a big stock company and will stock the Pablo Montoya Grant in the eastern part of S. M. County. The Grant contains 653,469 acres." On April 8, 1882: "W. Waddingham who made a cool million and a half out of the Robinson Mine in Colorado has purchased 6,400 head of cattle for his ranch, and will reach there in July." Waddingham's affairs eventually reached such a confused state that a year after his death, Charles Elmendorf wrote a friend: "Truly the affairs of the Waddingham estate are in a strange condition, and it seems to me that the estate is to be completely swamped unless there is some change brought soon." Charles Elmendorf to E. P. Baker, May 21, 1900. Catron Collection, University of New Mexico.

[4] One way to describe James Reavis would be as a combination of John Law, P. T. Barnum, and Baron Munchausen. His remarkable career is sketched in Donald M. Powell's *The Peralta Grant* (Norman: University of Oklahoma Press; 1960).

[5] A sketch of the career of F. Augustus Heinze and his impact on Montana is in Joseph K. Howard's interpretive *Montana; High, Wide and Handsome* (New Haven: Yale University Press; 1943), 68–84.

[6] The tale of the rise and fall of the house of Tabor runs in the vein of melodramatic Victorian opera. Of the numerous volumes about the Tabors, Lewis C. Gandy's *The Tabors* (New York: Press of the Pioneers; 1934) is the least distressing.

ous cattle companies with sizable operations in Montana were incorporated in another state, frequently Texas. Enormous corporations such as the XIT, Berry and Boice, the Matador, and the Continental Land and Cattle Company[7] all had their northern range in Montana. The cattle census for 1884, as a case in point, listed Montana with 770,940 head of cattle at an assessed appraisal of $22,988,280. The fact that the valuation of Montana's herds for *one* year came within four million dollars of the total capitalization of all companies incorporated in the state for *twenty* years is illustrative of the number of "imported" cattle, especially considering that the $27,141,800 represented an inflated amount.[8] Furthermore, in none of the other three states are the figures at all comparable.

Other factors which in some degree influenced the slower growth of Montana's cattle industry were the retarded railroad development, the smaller population, and the slower development of the economy as a whole. By the 1880's railroads interlaced Colorado, but in Montana the Northern Pacific awaited completion and the Great Northern was only an idea in the fertile mind of James J. Hill. In the census of 1880, Colorado numbered 194,327 persons, while Montana's population was only 39,159.[9]

Another set of significant figures on cattle companies are those giving the amount of the capitalization of individual corporations. In the 1880–1900 era, New Mexico contained 48 companies with capitalization of $50,000 or less; only 17 had $1,000,000 or over. Colorado, because of its economy of small landholders, had 159 companies with a capitalization of $50,000 or under and only 19

[7] J. Evetts Haley: *The XIT Ranch of Texas*, and Lewis Nordyke: *Cattle Empire, The Fabulous Story of the 3,000,000 Acre XIT* (New York: W. Morrow; 1949) are both adequate histories of their subject, though this writer prefers the former. An excellent history of the Matador is W. M. Pearce: *The Matador Land and Cattle Company* (Norman: University of Oklahoma Press; 1964). The Continental Land and Cattle Company has yet to have a historian. However, their records in the main office in Denver, Colorado, are a rich source, though erratic in extensiveness.

[8] Joseph Nimmo, Jr.: "The Range Cattle and Ranch Business," *Executive Document 267*. House of Representatives, 48th Congress, 2nd Session (Washington: 1884), 55.

[9] *Tenth Census of the United States*, House Miscellaneous, 42, 47th Congress, 2nd Session (Washington: 1883), 250.

with $1,000,000 or over. Wyoming had 77 companies of $50,000 or under and 18 of $1,000,000 or over. Montana had 79 of $50,000 or under and 7 of $1,000,000 or over.[1]

Undoubtedly, the promotion by flamboyant soothsayers like Wilson Waddingham of New Mexico and Alexander Swan[2] in Wyoming affected the force of investment flow. However, much more decisive factors lay in the fundamental differences in the economies of the territories, the sparse settlement, the low economic development, and the small freehold emphasis. Admittedly, the entire region can come under the classification of "underdeveloped," but this is obviously a matter of degree.

To say categorically that there was a cyclic trend in the cattle market in a thirty-year period stretches the bounds of credibility. However, that there were peaks and depressions in response to market conditions, investor enthusiasm, and an overall national

[1] Incorporation records. Western Range Cattle Industry Collection, State Historical Society of Colorado, Denver.

[2] John Clay recalled a hostile though vivid caricature of Alexander Swan. "At that time [early 1880's] Swan was about fifty years of age. He stood about six feet and an inch, and wherever he went he made an imposing figure. His face was close shaven, he had a keen eye, a Duke of Wellington nose, and gold teeth. While his manner was casual it was magnetic and he had a great following. At Cheyenne groups of men sat around him in his office and worshipped at his feet. In Chicago he was courted by bankers, commission men, breeders of fine cattle; in fact, all classes of people in the livestock business. The mercantile agencies rated him at a million, while I doubt, so far as the range is concerned, if he ever owned an honest dollar." *My Life on the Range* (Chicago: 1924), p. 49. The Secretary of the Swan Land and Cattle Company had a kindlier recollection of Swan, though he was amazed at the nonchalant manner Swan took toward his business schemes. Lafrentz told how he first heard of the half-million-dollar South Omaha enterprise. "Mr. Swan and I were sitting on a baggage truck in the Union Pacific Depot at Omaha one evening waiting for the train to pull in over the bridge from Council Bluffs, when he said to me in a casual way: 'I have authorized my brother-in-law, Lem Anderson, to obtain options on about 2,000 acres of land south of Omaha,' and in answer to my 'What for?' he replied: 'I am going to start a town there, to be known as South Omaha.' Well, shortly thereafter the options were in and titles transferred to a corporation formed to take over. The land was plotted and the lots put on the market. The venture was successful from the very start. We persuaded William A. Paxton to remove his stockyards from Council Bluffs to this new location. The Railroads which served the two terminals of Council Bluffs and Omaha laid tracks to it as soon as the Chicago Packing Houses concluded to establish branches in the new town." F. W. Lafrentz Collection, Western History Research Center, University of Wyoming.

economic conditions can be completely substantiated. An enumer-
ation of the cattle companies formed and their accumulative
capitalization reveals the fluctuating pattern of the cattle investment. From 1882 to 1886 there were 93 cattle companies incorporated in Wyoming with a total capitalization of $51,232,000;
in Montana, 66 corporations with a capitalization of $19,509,000;
in New Mexico, 104 companies with a capitalization of $23,935,-
000; in Colorado, 176 with a capitalization of $74,296,000.[3] A
glance at these totals together with the figures of the aggregate
capitalization for 1880–1900 verifies the fact that this was the
major period of investment.

The 1882–5 years have traditionally been cast as the boom era
in the Western range cattle industry. What has been less well
recognized is the fact that many corporations continued after
the market crash of 1886–7 and that there were other periods
of sporadic growth in cattle company investments. Although they
were of shorter duration, these peaks in capital investment are a
discernible trend throughout the range country. In 1889–91
there was a brief but keen investment interest in the cattle industry.[4] This was due to several factors: a recovery from the
cattle market collapse, which had cut back the number of cattle
to a point substantially below market demand; an upswing in
exports; and, perhaps most of all, the gradual overall economic
growth in the West. One ranch manager, sounding out the shrewd
John Clay, asked, "Talk is everywhere that we have passed the
slump and that the market will be strong this year, what is your
opinion?"[5] Rumors were strong but many cattlemen and investors
alike remained wary.

The panic of 1893 quickly shut off the modest recovery. During
fall shipping time in 1892, Joseph C. Lea, aware of his own precarious situation, sensed financial trouble brewing. Sitting in

[3] Incorporation records. Western Range Cattle Industry Collection, State
Historical Society of Colorado, Denver.
[4] Henry Weare telegraphed his son in fall of 1889, "Prices are increasing
daily, whole market on the upsurge, ship your cattle!" Henry Weare to
George Weare. Jack Nason Collection, Spearfish, South Dakota.
[5] James T. Craig to John Clay, May 28, 1891. James T. Craig Collection,
Western History Research Center, University of Wyoming.

Hotel Hagerman in Eddy, New Mexico, Lea admonished his wife:

> I see where Francis Smith & Co. are selling out land and cattle in Southern Texas and I am afraid of our Kentucky stockholders and Dallas ones . . . who would like our valuable property. The jealous hearted would be so pleased to see us in trouble. We *all* owe too much money, watch your expenses carefully.[6]

For Lea and his fellow ranchmen, the improvement in their financial situation seemed agonizingly slow. The southern plains suffered an extreme drought from 1892 through 1894. The national panic hit Western banks hard, because there was little elasticity in their credit. By 1895, according to the editor of the St. Louis *Globe-Democrat*, the market appeared stronger, although he was forced to admit that this was owing to the bankruptcy of many firms and the spread of drought throughout the Southwest.[7]

A redemption for the cattlemen was in view in 1898; for the next three years, more cattle corporations were formed than had been initiated since the flush years of 1882–6. The aggregate capitalization of the newly organized corporations in these three years totaled $13,280,000, compared with the interim of 1887–98, when there was a total of $45,797,400 in Montana, Wyoming, Colorado, and New Mexico.[8]

A new wave of publicity about the profitability of Western ranches on the Northern range began reaching banking and financial circles in the East as early as 1896. John Gates, the superlative salesman of barbed wire and a founder of Texaco, remarked to Ellwood: "Real estate mortgages and the ranching situation in general is rapidly improving in the West. If you wish I will send you some good propositions in a few days."[9] Two weeks later, whether to whet Ellwood's appetite as an investor or merely as

[6] Joseph C. Lea to Mabel Lea, September 17, 1892. James T. Padgitt Collection, San Antonio, Texas.

[7] St. Louis *Globe-Democrat*, April 14, 1895.

[8] Incorporation records. Western Range Cattle Industry Collection, State Historical Society of Colorado, Denver.

[9] John Gates to Isaac Ellwood, June 20, 1896. Ellwood Collection, Western History Research Center, University of Wyoming.

information, Gates noted: "The mortgages I mentioned are all gone, sorry."[1]

One self-styled agricultural economist noted that in the ten years after 1892, the price of beef steers had doubled. This author was convinced that the improved market came from adherence to the time-honored motto: "Retain your heifers, sell your steer calves."[2] This monistic analysis of ranching economics hardly explains the radically improved situation of the range at the end of the 1890's.

An economist of the Department of Agriculture came much closer to the truth when he attributed the advance in beef prices to increased productivity in the national economy. He spoke particularly of the increased industrialization, the 20 per cent rise in population in the decade of the nineties, the demand for exports, and the scarcity of corn, which forced up the price of feeder cattle.[3] What most on-the-scene commentators failed to note was that after the collapse of 1886–7, both the Western manager and the Eastern investor had learned at least a modicum of economics of a cattle company. Expenses were closely scrutinized and curtailed, dividends were postponed, and an improved procedure of operation was adopted. Only when these business procedures were followed did the cattle corporation show a profit.[4]

In summation, the intense activity from 1882 to 1885 was the high point of investment in the range cattle industry; the nadir came in 1886–8, with a short period of recovery in 1888–9 and a much stronger resurgence in 1898–1901. After 1900 the cattle industry on the plains underwent a radical metamorphosis. Ranching increasingly became a locally contained business, with its financing centered in the community or the regional banking

[1] John Gates to Isaac Ellwood, July 6, 1896. Ibid.

[2] Robert M. Barker: "The Economics of Cattle-Ranching in the Southwest," *The American Monthly Review of Reviews*, XXIV (September 1901), 307.

[3] Fred C. Croxton: "Beef Prices," *The Journal of Political Economy*, XIII (March 1905), 201–16.

[4] The lessons learned are in part outlined in John T. McNelly: "The Cattle Industry of Colorado, Wyoming and Nevada and the Sheep Industry of Colorado in 1897," *Fifteenth Annual Report of the Bureau of Animal Industry for the Year, 1898*, 55th Congress, Document 307 (Washington: 1899), 377–82.

institution. The Eastern millionaire who came West in the twentieth century desired a "retreat" with glossy white-painted fences and well-groomed Hereford cattle contentedly grazing on green manicured hillsides. His last concern was profit making; in fact, for income tax purposes it was often highly desirable that the "ranch" should show a loss.

Whether in prosperity or adversity, the cattle company of the 1880's and 1890's supposedly kept its stockholders "informed" by means of the annual report.[5] In the heyday of the cattle industry, this cleverly contrived document was a masterpiece of understatement, innuendo, and distortion, crammed with prognostications of rich future dividends which were described in phrases calculated to lull the apprehensive stockholder. The omissions in annual reports frequently were more significant than the inclusions, especially for the young corporation which had issued only two or three reports. But after the market collapse of 1886–7, investors' skepticism, hardened by the lack of dividends, transformed the annual report into a remarkably calm and dull document in comparison with the effusions of former days.

Very few annual reports ever achieved the bluntness of those issued by the Teschemacher and deBillier Cattle Company. After months of "soul searching," Hubert Teschemacher decided that he might as well tell the stockholders the worst. In his report for 1887, he wrote:

> Since our last annual meeting the range cattle business has passed through the worst year in its history. A winter of unusual severity in Montana and northern Wyoming caused a heavy loss on the range. This was followed by a very hot and

[5] Archives the country over house a plethora of annual reports, both published and in manuscript. Among representative ones used in this study are: Red Bank Cattle Company: *Annual Statement*, Western History Research Center; The Capitol Freehold Land and Investment Company: *Annual Report*, 1885, 1886, 1887, 1888, and 1892, Panhandle Plains Museum; The Suffolk Cattle Company: *Annual Report*, 1885, 1886, Western History Research Center; The Brush Creek Livestock and Dairy Company: *Annual Report*, 1887, Western Range Cattle Industry Collection; Oasis Land and Cattle Company: *Annual Report*, 1887, 1888, and 1889, Western History Research Center; Holt Livestock Company: *Annual Report*, 1881, 1883, 1888, 1889, and 1892, Western Range Cattle Industry Collection; and Pioneer Cattle Company: *Annual Report*, 1884, Montana Historical Society.

dry summer in the central western States, causing farmers to ship to market everything that could go thus preventing any rise in beef during the Fall. . . .

There is very little doubt in mind that there will be an advance in the price of beef next year and with this will come an advance in value of range cattle, but I am still of the opinion that the company should dispose of their cattle as soon as practicable, and shall use every opportunity to effect the sale of the herd or any part of it.[6]

Much more restrained and more typical were the annual statements of the XIT Ranch. With the initial statement: "The condition of the ranch is in all respects most satisfactory,"[7] the report would then go into climate, condition of the range, new improvements, and the overall financial condition. The XIT reports issued during the difficult period 1885–93 continued their conservative optimism: "The Directors . . . have the pleasure in stating the affairs of the company continue to be in a satisfactory condition."[8] By 1892, the XIT reports followed the pattern of stating that in spite of poor regional and national economic conditions, the company had surmounted its difficulties (by implication, through the adroitness of the management) and would pay a respectable if not munificent dividend.[9]

Very like the annual reports in form, content, and tone were the minutes of cattle corporations. Major decisions were arrived at, sometimes covertly, sometimes overtly recorded by the secretaries in a "suitable and uniform style," as one director put it.[1] Neither the annual report nor the minutes offered much comfort or elucidation to the Eastern stockholder who did not hold an office in the company. If he desired enlightenment, he carried on a correspondence with the manager, or more astutely, made

[6] Teschemacher and deBillier Cattle Company: *Annual Report*, 1887. Teschemacher and deBillier Collection, Western History Research Center, University of Wyoming.

[7] The Capitol Freehold Land and Investment Company: *Annual Report*, 1887. Panhandle Plains Museum, Canyon, Texas.

[8] Ibid., 1888.

[9] Ibid., 1892.

[1] Henry Weare to George Weare, March 28, 1889. Nason Collection, Spearfish, South Dakota.

unannounced visits to the ranch. As Louis G. Stoddard of New Haven, Connecticut, observed in a letter to his manager Charles O'Donel: "It is always good to get to New Mexico to see our land; to me it is worth ten letters."[2] Stockholders in general shared Stoddard's opinion; however, in many cases, whether their fear for their investment would have been allayed by a visit is a moot question.

[2] Louis Stoddard to Charles O'Donel, June 9, 1901. Bell Ranch Collection, University of New Mexico Library.

V

"I have the greatest confidence in you..."

THE MANAGER

⅄ <u>B</u> CY ⵔ ND ⊥ ꙅ
ᓄ ᗅ ⵚ ⴹ ᓄ
ⵏ ⵔ ⵔ
ⵕ

Just after the turn of the twentieth century, Senator Francis E. Warren of Wyoming sat in his Washington office one bright June day mulling over a recent request from the editor of the *Breeder's Gazette* for his reminiscences of the range. Warren, who combined a strong Puritan sense of his calling with an even stronger devotion to the value of the dollar, had memories of life in Cheyenne twenty years before which were far from pleasant. He recalled:

All this time the large stockmen were inviting disaster upon themselves. Expensive establishments were maintained in town and on the ranch. Salaries were paid which would make the stockholders' hair curl. The assortment of drinkables on many of the ranches would do credit to a Broadway bar. In the heyday of prosperity, only a few men pretended to look after their stock interests personally. The practical work was left to hired foremen. The owners, stockholders, or managers, showed up in the roundups annually in gorgeous array, to the amazement and envy of all beholders. Only a small percentage knew anything practically about the business, but all talked learnedly about it theoretically. . . . To the managers, money was free as water, the entire operation rested on their shoulders.[1]

That the fortunes of any firm rested with the manager was uncomfortably recognized by most stockholders. Abner Taylor, urging John Farwell to take over the heavy responsibility of the XIT, wrote: "You know as well as I do, John, the necessity of having a good manager, who will watch our interests. Isn't it better to have a manager who is one of us and has our interests at heart?"[2] Farwell, who may have been only coy and waiting to be coaxed, yielded to the pleadings of Taylor and became manager-director of the XIT. A. D. Ferris, who sold Theodore Roosevelt on the merits of a ranching career in the Dakota Badlands, also emphasized the desirability of having a good manager.[3] Thomas Hord, a stockholder in the Lance Creek Cattle Company and a manager for a short interval, complained to Charles Smillie, a Brooklyn stockholder, that the reasons for their sad financial return of the past season could be laid "solely at the door of our manager. It is hard to see how he could have made more mistakes, if he would have been in partnership with the devil. The sooner we do something about this situation, the better off we will be."[4]

[1] Warren Collection, Western History Research Center, University of Wyoming.

[2] A. Taylor to John V. Farwell, July 9, 1883. XIT Collection, Panhandle Plains Museum, Canyon, Texas.

[3] Ray H. Mattison: *Roosevelt's Dakota Ranches* (Bismarck: Bismarck Tribune; 1958), and Mattison: "Roosevelt and the Stockmen's Association," *North Dakota History*, XVII (April 1950), 3–50.

[4] Thomas B. Hord to Charles F. Smillie, December 4, 1889. Hord Collection, Western History Research Center, University of Wyoming.

Smillie accepted Hord's advice; a new manager took over at the Lance Creek Cattle Company the next year. The calm, diligent, and shrewd William Hughes, owner (with John Simpson and others) of the Continental Land and Cattle Company, wrote his major partners: "We have finally secured a manager who I believe will work out; if he doesn't I am at my wit's end."[5] Simpson knew that in reality Hughes made most of the crucial managerial decisions, politely but firmly overruling his manager when occasion arose.

Similar comments could be multiplied ad infinitum. The value of a good manager was undeniably appreciated and the performance of a poor manager forever deplored. The eternal query was, where could a good maanger be found? Like Bordeaux wines, they were a rare commodity in the range country. Because of their scarcity, Horace Thurber, partner of the Arbuckles in Arbuckle Coffee, thought that the only answer was to send West "one of our clerks for the office work, who at least are slightly acquainted with business procedures."[6] However, a New York countinghouse clerk's adaption to the customs of the range country might be as unsuccessful as the ill-fitting habit he donned upon arriving in his new environment. From generation to generation in the West, tales of some Eastern dude's ludicrous actions or classic predicaments are repeated with undiluted zest. Once he alighted from the stage or Pullman car, the dude was fair game for the mimicry of clusters of cowboys. To many wide-eyed dudes, venturing West was an intoxicating experience. The most famous dude of all was Owen Wister, who with his usual zest for Western atmosphere, jotted down his observations as he tried to balance his notebook on his knees in a jostling stagecoach. Many Western stories about dudes were undoubtedly apocryphal, yet adjusting to the social and cultural life of the frontier was not a gentle process for many an Easterner. He felt ill at ease both on Sunday afternoon in the Victorian furnished parlors of

5 William E. Hughes to John Simpson, April 30, 1886. Hughes Collection, Denver, Colorado.

6 H. K. Thurber to Joseph C. Lea, January 14, 1885. Padgitt Collection, San Antonio, Texas.

the local community, and during working hours when he was trying to deal with the local banker or leading politician. Finally, the business principles of the Eastern mercantile company did not transfer *quid pro quo* to the ranching ledgers.

The scarcity of managers was reflected in many comments in the press. The *Field and Farm* noted in 1883: "Any man who can work with a few cowboys has a job. J. L. Brush [a prominent Colorado cattleman] came into our office last evening to complain about the scarcity of good men."[7] The San Marcial *Reporter* was more caustic in its observation: "Rumors are that the cause of so many poor showings by cattlemen this year is due to the lack of attention to the business by the cattlemen themselves. Tis for certain some companies have acted like they were headless and maybe they were."[8] The Socorro *Bullion* said in one of its news columns: "R. G. Head passed through last night . . . and we learned he has had nine offers recently to manage cattle companies. . . . So unusual a call from so wide an area of the country is, under the circumstances, a flattering compliment to the man."[9] As past manager of the Prairie Cattle Company, Head was reputed to be one of the ablest managers in range country, though some of his contemporaries thought him unbearably egotistic.[1] In any case, his leadership was widely conceded; among other positions, he served as president of the International Range Association formed in 1887.

Not all managers, of course, had the stature of Head, yet all contemporary indications are that Head was not alone in being courted by stockholders. Managers of almost any character were in constant demand. True, if they did not perform, they found themselves looking for other employment opportunities. A good part of the difficulty of finding managers can be ascribed to the

[7] *Field and Farm*, June 12, 1883.

[8] San Marcial *Reporter*, November 19, 1887.

[9] Socorro *Bullion*, January 23, 1885.

[1] With his usual stiletto deftness, Clay dissected R. G. Head's character: "Head was known as the $20,000 beauty in cowman's parlance. . . . He was honest and competent, but exceedingly vain and his promotion to this position, manager of Prairie, gave him a very bad attack of the swelled head. His aspiration was to be the Napoleon of the Western cattle business." John Clay: *My Life on the Range* (Chicago: 1924), 132.

fact that investors expected their managers to be paragons of virtue. The leading salesman of barbed wire in Texas, Henry Sanborn, minced no words when he told Isaac Ellwood about the difficulty he was having turning up a manager for Ellwood's Frying Pan Ranch "who will cover all your expectations and hopes."[2] After he had seen Ellwood's list of requirements for this mythical man, Sanborn pointed out that they were not finding the person of Ellwood's dreams because such a manager was not of this earth. "I want a man," wrote Ellwood, "who knows something of land and water problems, can make a good bargain in cattle sales and is able to manage cow hands."[3] In sum, Ellwood sought a suave, diplomatic, astute businessman and a shrewd broker. Sanborn advised Ellwood to settle for someone "who can get along with your men and is reasonably honest. If you receive this he will be worth his pay."[4] Ellwood may never have located his ideal manager, but he seemed reasonably well satisfied with both his managers and his foremen.

The majority of Eastern investors were also hunting for the perfect manager, and were just as often disappointed. The fact was that the intrinsic difficulties in investor-manager relations precluded an easy solution. The investor expected a manager adept at handling all the demands that would be made on him in running a half-million-dollar business with infrequent communication, insufficient capital, and modest recompense. John Bratt, Nebraska cattleman, presented the manager's side of the investor-manager problem.

It was not an easy job to handle two hundred or more cowboys with nearly a dozen different outfits and one thousand to twelve hundred horses keeping the work moving intelligently, finding camping places for each outfit and see that all, even the lone representative, had equal share and a square deal, but I had the reputation for doing it.[5]

[2] Henry Sanborn to Isaac Ellwood, January 24, 1886. Ellwood Collection, Western History Research Center, University of Wyoming.
[3] Isaac Ellwood to Henry Sanborn, February 17, 1886. Ibid.
[4] Henry Sanborn to Isaac Ellwood, January 24, 1886. Ibid.
[5] John Bratt: Trails of Yesterday (Lincoln, Neb.: University Publishing Co.; 1921).

One could not accuse Bratt of modesty, but he did indicate the heavy demands made on the manager.

A substantial reason for investor-manager quagmire was simply infrequent or inadequate communication. The manager, weary of scurrilous reprimands from his investor, seldom told all in his missives to the East. As Henry Weare noted to his father: "I am damn tired of trying to inform our stockholders of conditions out here, only to receive hell for my efforts."[6] Resigned to the fact that no matter what he did or said, it would be received unsympathetically Weare lapsed into two months' long silence, a pout which only increased the investors' wrath.

J. Coolidge Coffin, a native of Pembroke, Maine, had the same problem as the Weare stockholders in Chicago. He valiantly tried for three months to prod his manager John Thomas into responding to his letters. The break in the long silence brought the laconic remark from Coffin: "Evidently somebody has been getting away with the letters I have written you the last few weeks."[7] As a rule, investors did not go in for courteous subtleties in reminding their managers to write. Abner Taylor of the Chicago office of the XIT spewed forth to his Texas managers: "Are you dead, we begin to think so as we get no letters from you. If you are not dead will you take the time to write? We would like to know how the work is going."[8]

Two years later, Taylor had the opposite vexation when his loquacious manager, Colonel B. H. Campbell, dispatched letter after letter to the Chicago office giving the most mundane details of the XIT's operation. Finally, the frustrated Taylor called a halt.

Dear Sir, Your favor of Dec. 31st. received. Life is too short to read such long letters. So we turned it over to a man who had more leisure and he informs us this morning that among other things you want directions as to whether you should buy cattle.

[6] Henry Weare to George Weare, March 3, 1887. Nason Collection, Spearfish, South Dakota.
[7] J. Coolidge Coffin to John B. Thomas, January 12, 1878. Dunder Collection, Western History Research Center, University of Wyoming.
[8] A. Taylor to A. G. Boyce, January 9, 1887. XIT Collection, Panhandle Plains Museum, Canyon, Texas.

In the language of the doctor to the guide with Mark Twain in Paris, I intended to tell you to use your own judgment in purchasing those cattle, but I suppose I forgot it so I will tell you that we want you to use your own judgment and make such arrangements as your judgment shall dictate. . . . Now please go out and buy some cattle and stop writing such long letters.[9]

Campbell did buy the cattle, but he ignored Taylor's admonition on verbosity.

Isaac Ellwood's similarly long-winded manager, W. T. Carpenter, habitually began his weekly report with the phrase: "I thought that I would write you a few lines to let you know how . . ."[1] For Ellwood, Carpenter's loquacity presented a minor dilemma, for above all, Ellwood insisted on being kept informed on details of life on the ranch. Yet as he wrote his son: "I do not need to know every time one of our cattle switches his tail in the pasture, or takes a drink."[2] Later he again wrote his son: "Can't you encourage Carpenter to condense his reports?"[3] Ellwood's son attempted to tell Carpenter diplomatically to be brief, but to no avail. Until Carpenter was succeeded by D. N. Arnett, Ellwood continued to receive long, involved communications.

The distance, the inherent suspicion between manager and investor, and the lack of comprehension by each of the problems of the other, created barriers which few investor-managers ever completely surmounted. Most managers simply made their daily decisions and then hoped for approval from the Eastern capitalists, although unqualified approval was rarely forthcoming.

The manager was caught between the facts of local conditions and the demands of the investor two thousand miles distant, and his solutions were often unpopular. One of his enduring problems was the task of obtaining reliable cowboys. The Eastern investor, accustomed to less nomadic workers and a plentiful supply of labor, had difficulty fathoming the workings of the Western labor market. When W. T. Carpenter criticized the "lazy, slovenly

[9] A. Taylor to B. H. Campbell, May 11, 1889. Ibid.
[1] W. T. Carpenter to Isaac Ellwood, December 12, 1889. Ellwood Collection, Western History Research Center, University of Wyoming.
[2] Isaac Ellwood to William Ellwood, January 28, 1890. Ibid.
[3] Ibid., May 29, 1890.

cowhands"[4] to Isaac Ellwood, he received a sharp note back. "Rid yourself of the dead wood, the quicker the better."[5] This was fine advice, but not for a man faced with finishing several miles of fence or rounding up a herd for fall shipping time, when every pair of hands counted. Colonel William Hughes wrote his partner, John Simpson: "It is becoming increasingly difficult to get good hands, do you know of any that we could get here by August?"[6]

The trusted Eastern confidant who was suddenly removed from Broadway and Wall in New York to Thurber Avenue in Roswell, New Mexico, and told to take charge of a motley crew of cowboys soon yearned for the days when he had stood at the bar in Delmonico's. John Clay exuberantly painted these cow-boys as

> . . . real simon pure, devil-may-care, roystering, gambling, im-moral, revolver-heeled, brazen, light-fingered lot and yet a dash of bravado among them that was attractive to the stronger. They had no respect for a man and little for a woman. Yet they were good workers.[7]

The scenario writers of the twentieth century cannot alone be held accountable for the folk image of the cowboy. After the years had passed, many a cattleman's reminiscences became filled with drivel about the former golden days.

When a friend of Clarence King, Edgar Beecher Bronson, was met by King's partner N. R. Davis at the Union Pacific station in Cheyenne, Bronson, according to his own description, looked "better to hold down a hospital cot than to fork a cayuse."[8] Yet he was there to manage the ranch, and after an initial breaking-in period, Bronson was put in charge of a group of cowboys and

[4] W. T. Carpenter to Isaac Ellwood, November 6, 1889. Ellwood Collection, Western History Research Center, University of Wyoming.

[5] Isaac Ellwood to W. T. Carpenter, November 30, 1889. Ibid.

[6] William E. Hughes to John Simpson, February 7, 1886. Hughes Collection, Denver, Colorado.

[7] Clay: My Life on the Range, 123.

[8] Edgar B. Bronson: Reminiscences of a Ranchman (Chicago: McClurg; 1910), 25.

fifteen hundred cattle. The cowhands "as if by concerted agreement" decided to test the mettle of this "blue-bellied Yankee kid
tenderfoot." One morning, they openly disobeyed his orders and
spent the entire day jeering and idling through their work.[9]
Bronson's solution was to undertake a four-day journey to the
nearest town, Laramie, to hire a new outfit, leaving the herd in
charge of two loyal men. When he returned, not a beef "was
missing from the 1,506 left in their custody. It was remarkable."

There were many labor strikes on the range, and they were not
usually handled as easily as Bronson's trouble. John Clay recalled
with some bitterness the cowhand strikes which erupted in
Wyoming during the spring roundup of 1884, the largest roundup
that ever took place on the northern plains and one of the biggest
ever to occur in the West. "The cowpunchers led by Jack Flagg
[leader of the homesteader element in the Johnson County War]
and men of his stripe, struck for higher wages. . . . The foremen
did the work and they, after some show of resistance, lay down
and granted the demands of the boys."[1] Ever after, the name of
Flagg left a taste of persimmon in Clay's mouth.[2] Clay's concern
was not the higher wages that the cowboys had won, but the
way in which the wages were exacted. To Clay, as well as to
most nineteenth-century capitalists, strikes were unlawful, im-
moral, and economically wasteful.

The most famous, or infamous, strike by cowboys took place
in April 1883 in the panhandle of Texas, led by the foremen of
three large ranches, the LTT, the LX, and the LS. The cowboys'
grievances reputedly arose from the rigid control by the Panhandle Cattlemen's Association of the branding of mavericks, plus
the Association's unyielding opposition to any cowboy taking up

[9] Ibid., 93–106.
[1] Clay: My Life on the Range, 123.
[2] The taste was not gone when another strike in central Wyoming occurred in the summer of 1886. This strike did not last as long, though it
aroused the Wyoming Stock Growers Association. Horace Plunkett to
Thomas Sturgis, June 27, 1886; Wyoming Stock Growers Association
Collection, Western History Research Center, University of Wyoming.
Thomas Sturgis to Thomas Adams, June 21, 1886; ibid.: Field and Farm,
May 29, 1886.

small parcels of the public domain.[3] The latter policy was radically altered in later years when cattlemen were struggling for control of water rights. However, if the strike was based on these "injustices," it is strange that the cowboys' ultimatum to the "cattle barons" omitted any reference to them. Instead, the strikers asked for an increase in wages for cowboys, foremen, and "good" cooks. Outside of the slight allusion to culinary skill, these requests reflected only the perpetual clamor for higher wages.[4] If the cowboys were aroused about mavericks and the land question, they obviously did not feel strongly enough to incorporate them into their petition.[5]

The ranch managers and owners reacted with customary thoroughness to this strike. A month before it began, they had heard rumors of unrest and they immediately moved to counteract the menace. The aggressive Jot Gunter, whose brokerage firm of Gunter and Munson took over the sale of much of the land in the Texas panhandle, formed a plan. In a letter to the Governor's office in Austin, Gunter outlined the problem and answer:

> We have advice from our Ranch . . . that the cowboys throughout the Pan Handle have all combined and agreed to strike [sic] on April 1st for an increase to Fifty Dollars per month. . . . Should they carry out their programme, they will turn loose upon that country 250 to 500 reckless well armed men and may result in the loss of many lives and much property.
>
> We wish Gv. Ireland and Adjut. General in the event of trouble to send a force of Rangers to protect the property and lives of the Ranchmen. We do not wish our names to go out as moving on this matter as the cowboys if specially mad at us could ruin us by burning our range. . . .[6]

After a series of incidents, the cowboy strike collapsed rapidly. A show of strength by the owners was all that was necessary to

[3] A fairly complete account of this episode is in John L. McCarty: *Maverick Town, the Story of Old Tascosa* (Norman: University of Oklahoma Press; 1946), 107–14.

[4] "Cowboy Proclamation," Panhandle Plains Museum, Canyon, Texas.

[5] Jack Potter: *Lead Steer and Other Tales* (Clayton, N. Mex.: 1939), 34–40.

[6] Jot Gunter to A. L. Matlock, March 15, 1883. Gunter and Munson Collection, Southwest Collection, Texas Technological College.

wilt the pugnacity of the cowhands, but resentment lingered for years.

Whether the cowboys resorted to revolt or not, their crude and rough ways evoked constant complaint in the Western press. The Las Vegas *Optic* noted in the spring of 1885: "We are informed that some of the cowboys at Springer behaved outrageously yesterday. They swilled up on cowboy's delight and fired their revolvers promiscuously. . . . The revolver in the hands of the drunken cowboy must go."[7] The editor of the *Optic* went on to point out that the Northern New Mexico Stock Growers Association, meeting in Springer recently, had adopted "a plank in their rules" that no man who "habitually" carried a gun would be employed on the range this season. No later comment appeared in the paper as to how effective this action was. What angered the managers more than the cowboy antics was the way the cowboys handled the cattle. The Colorado, Texas, and Wyoming newspapers editorialized from time to time on the theme of cruelty on the range.

> The cattlemen of Colorado are agitating the subject of preventing the unnecessary cruelty and rough usage to which cattle on the range are subjected by the ordinary cowboy. . . . Most of the cowboys at roundups are hired, and they have no further interest than to whither the next camp is to be and to be there as soon as possible. . . . Such handling is destructive to the breeding interests of the country to an alarming extent, and one of the greatest reasons why the calf crop is short. Still owners in the East are asleep to all of this.[8]

His labor relations were the Achilles' heel of more than one manager. John Clay assured Thomas Adams, the secretary of the Wyoming Stock Growers Association, that their new manager on the Sweetwater would fully follow "the policies of our association." In addition, Clay commented that he hoped "Andrews [the new manager] will be able to get along with the cowboys. You know Pearce never succeeded in managing them." According to Clay, the former manager had had one revolt after another

[7] Las Vegas *Daily Optic*, April 8, 1885.
[8] Las Vegas *Daily Optic*, August 29, 1885.

on his hands. "This will have to cease or we will be in worse shape than the cattlemen in Johnson County."[9]

Sentimentality was not Clay's forte in the 1880's, particularly when it came to cowboys, but he did possess a Scotsman's stringent business sense; any policy or action which threatened dividends was anathema to him. What Clay discerned was that the poor financial returns of the Pratt-Ferris Cattle Company were solely the responsibility of Colonel J. H. Pratt. "He was unpopular on the range and the boys had it in for him. I made an appeal personally to the above gentleman [Pratt] but he was like a dog to his vomit."[1] Actually, the Pratt-Ferris Cattle Company, whether it had good public relations or not, was one of the more successful firms.

⨯ The dominant themes in investor-manager correspondence centered, understandably, on finance, especially on land acquisition and the purchase and sale of cattle. As the Eastern farmers filtered West onto the range, the cattlemen were forced to acquire more and more land outright and then to secure control of the water rights. The luxury of grazing one's herds on the free and luxuriant grasses of the national domain was rapidly passing. Competitive buying created a crisis in company finances, a pinch which was evident in the shaky economic era of 1886–9. Even such successful entrepreneurs as Colonel William Hughes thought his company's exchequer was depleted by an "over-extended range." J. D. Dilworth pleaded with his directors to buy more land or suffer the consequences. "In a few years, we will be cut off entirely from creeks and other water supplies. But also we will lose much of our grazing land, we must buy and now."[2] Managers scattered across the West echoed Dilworth's sentiments. W. T. Carpenter, with the Ellwood millions to draw on, urged his De Kalb entrepreneur to "buy quickly as much land as you believe you will need."[3] Ellwood had the resources and the desire

[9] John Clay to Thomas Adams, July 15, 1884. Wyoming Stock Growers Collection, Western History Research Center, University of Wyoming.

[1] Clay: My Life on the Range, 250.

[2] J. D. Dilworth to J. W. Wilson, September 27, 1890. Tolman Collection, Western History Research Center, University of Wyoming.

[3] W. T. Carpenter to Isaac Ellwood, October 29, 1890. Ellwood Collection, Western History Research Center, University of Wyoming.

to comply. For the beleaguered investor who had not seen a dividend check in five years, the paramount necessity of securing more land seemed questionable, if not ridiculous. Even Thomas Catron, who achieved the distinction of being the largest land-owner in New Mexico, called a halt when his manager, Charles Elmendorf, insisted: "We should have more land than the water rights proposal will give us."[4]

✗ Some investors reluctantly complied with their managers' pleas and authorized the purchase of more land. Senator Francis E. Warren so extended himself in land acquisition that he was in serious financial trouble for several years around the turn of the century. He wrote to his manager, W. W. Gleason: "What appeared to be a wise move in Colorado five years ago now seems foolhardy. We must economize everywhere we can until things ease a bit."[5] When Warren demanded economy, this was precisely what he meant. As owner of the Cheyenne Electric Company, it was his habit to go over the books to see why some customers were not consuming the "proper standard" of electricity! The inspirational message of the Puritan ethic was not missed on the senator from Wyoming. According to the allegations of a government investigator, although they were never proven, Warren engaged in another favorite sport of the day: enclosing government land. But if he did, there was certainly nothing unusual about the practice.[6] Bartlett Richards, a very successful cattleman of the sandhills of Nebraska, kept his fences around government land long after the custom had gone out of style.[7] His persistence won him a term in prison.

✗ The problem of land acquisition, made acute by the encroachment of small cattlemen and farmers on the range, was not easily resolved. Seeing the range vanishing day by day, the managers knew that something must be done—and quickly. Yet their ef-

[4] Charles Elmendorf to Thomas Catron, May 21, 1900. Catron Collection, University of New Mexico Library.
[5] Francis E. Warren to W. W. Gleason, January 17, 1899. Warren Collection, Western History Research Center, University of Wyoming.
[6] Warren Letterbook, 3. Ibid.
[7] Richards Scrapbook. Wightman Collection, Western History Research. Center, University of Wyoming.

forts to impress their investors with this fact usually met with failure. Brooding over the red ink on his cattle firm's book, a financier in New York, Boston, or Cleveland was far from convinced that a company bordering on bankruptcy should have a far-sighted land policy. The result was inevitable: the manager, positive that no future existed for their company unless land was purchased, and the investor, just as certain that no future existed if they did purchase, were locked in disagreement. Some compromise policy, often unsatisfactory to both parties, was usually reached. But all through the nineties, land acquisition was a prime irritant in manager-investor relations.[8]

Layer upon layer of folklore has been varnished onto the conflict between homesteaders and large cattlemen in the American West. Heroes with feet of clay have been created, and myths have been authenticated as reality and retold from generation to generation, always with plenty enthusiasm calculated to dispel all disbelievers. The Johnson County War and the Lincoln County War have been magnified as *causes célèbres* for Lilliputian nesters against the Brobdingnagian cattle corporations. Although the tales bring skeptical smiles to the countenances of the second generation, the third generation excitedly picks up the torch of imagined family honor. This three-generation cycle from rumor to skepticism to full acceptance of family folklore might be worth systematic critical appraisal.[9]

[8] The complex history of the land policy in the United States is still buried in the land office records. The following will be helpful as introductory works to this vast subject: Fred A. Shannon: *The Farmer's Last Frontier* (New York: Farrar & Rinehart; 1945); Paul Gates: *Fifty Million Acres: Conflicts over Kansas Land Policy, 1854-1890* (Ithaca: Cornell University Press; 1954); Charles L. Green: *The Administration of the Public Domain in South Dakota* (Pierre, S.D.: 1940); Walter P. Webb: *The Great Plains* (Boston: Ginn and Co.; 1931); Roy M. Robbins: *Our Landed Heritage* (Princeton: Princeton University Press; 1942); Addison E. Sheldon: *Land Systems and Land Policies in Nebraska* (Lincoln: The Society; 1936); Allan Bogue: *Money at Interest* . . . (Ithaca: Cornell University Press; 1955).

[9] Earl Pomeroy: *In Search of the Golden West* (New York: Knopf; 1957); F. E. Emery: "Psychological Effects of the Western Film: A Study in Television Viewing," *Human Relations*, XII (1959), 195-213; Loy O. Banks: "The Credible Literary West," *Colorado Quarterly*, VIII (Summer 1959), 28-50.

Taken in context of this literature, it would seem historical heresy to suggest that underneath this fiction, a closer approximation of the truth could be reached.

The facts were that the large cattleman or corporation, faced with declining profits (in some instances the company had never shown a return) and confronted with a reduction of its range, was forced either to buy land to protect the capital already invested or to go out of business. There is no glossing over the fact that there were many instances of illegality and ruthlessness on the part of cattle corporations which cannot be condoned by economic need or even by the argument that ethics in the nineteenth century were radically different from those of the twentieth. The *modus operandi* may have been significantly divergent in the business world of seventy-five years ago, but the ethical standards were not so dissimilar as to be unrecognizable, as some apologists suggest. But neither does one have to surrender to economic determinism to acknowledge that the acquisitive spirit of cattlemen toward the public domain was induced in large part by economic necessity.

As previously indicated, many Eastern investors showed extreme reluctance to acknowledge that the success of their company depended on land titles. Accustomed to the open and free range, the Easterners' adjustment to the radically changed land conditions demanded a level of entrepreneurial decision which some investors were either incapable of or not imaginative enough to discern. The cattlemen and investors, whether they liked it or not, were faced with either procuring a fenced-in range or liquidating the firm. The fact that this was quite obvious in the days of transition was all too often ignored by both their contemporary critics and later commentators.

Land, labor, capital, and cattle: all were preoccupations of the manager, whose success depended as often on his articulate communication with his investor as it did on mastering the details of his ranch. Obviously a major concern for any manager was the purchase, raising, and marketing of cattle. The correspondence of manager to investor is crammed with comments on the condition of cattle: "The cattle are doing well, though

some of the grazing in the Renchebrook pasture is poor."[1]
"There are several men in this county who have lost their cattle
from fever. We are going to move north soon."[2] The ferocity
of winter brought comments such as: "The herd looks more
like a mountain of bones, Mr. Rose, than I have ever seen it.[3]

Most of all, however, this correspondence shows a tremendous
obsession with the market, either forecast or rumored. Few
letters exchanged between investor and cattleman from mid-
May to November 1 did not contain some opinion or question
regarding the market outlook. Embarrassment was common
after the good prices which the manager had predicted did not
materialize when the fall shipping was completed, and the manager usually said lamely that "the commission man" had misled
him. E. C. Converse wrote John Thomas in July 1888: "I trust
the Chicago market will be as favorable next month as you anticipated last year. If so, we ought all receive a nice dividend,
though I am not spending it yet."[4] Cattle prices were somewhat
stronger in 1888, but not enough to put a bounce in Converse's
step as he walked down Wall Street. Thomas did manage to
send his investors a small dividend check; and with Converse's
he wrote a note: "Due to past heavy losses we thought we should
go easy on dividends this year."[5] Since this was the first dividend
in four years, Converse must have enjoyed that sentence.

Thomas had endured low prices long enough to be philosophical. His neighbor, Richard Trimble, was less sanguine when
discussing his fortunes. He wrote his father in 1886 describing
the exasperating experience he had recently had in both Chicago
and Omaha:

Since I wrote from Omaha I have been a day at Atlantic [Iowa]
two days at Gilmore [Nebraska] and three days in Omaha

[1] W. T. Carpenter to Isaac Ellwood, July 9, 1890. Ellwood Collection,
Western History Research Center, University of Wyoming.
[2] G. A. Lambert to B. A. Sheidley, October 20, 1880. Sheidley Collection,
Western History Research Center, University of Wyoming.
[3] James Norris to J. A. Rose, April 29, 1887. Western Range Cattle Industry
Collection, State Historical Society of Colorado, Denver, Colorado.
[4] E. C. Converse to John B. Thomas, July 7, 1888. Dunder Collection,
Western History Research Center, University of Wyoming.
[5] John B. Thomas to E. C. Converse, December 18, 1888. Ibid.

casting about for some better scheme to send our cattle direct to Chicago and give them away. The market has been a little stronger for the last few days but ten days ago it was simply ridiculous. Our class of cattle bringing from $2.80 to $3.00 per cwt. Many men think this was caused by a combination of reasons—labor troubles and failure of grass in Texas and short pasturage and no rain in several states making shipment very heavy—being the chief. These men expect a big market next year, but I look for no improvement until I see it. I really think that beef is just about where it should be in proportion to other staples.[6]

When managers were not grappling with market, land, or labor problems, they were fighting each other. While there might be a strong fraternal feeling in stock growers' meetings, there was no accord when competing companies were after the same section of land. Successful managers found it prudent to stay close to their range the year round. The manager of the Keystone Cattle Company, J. W. Rose, returned from a sojourn in Minneapolis in June 1885 to find his cattle scattered and his range usurped. Rose bitterly harangued Thomas Sturgis, the secretary of the Wyoming Stock Growers Association:

> In response to your request to fill out blanks as to no. of cattle under my control. Would say that on returning from Minn. I find reason of being "blackballed" by some of our neighboring syndicates, our business is so demoralized that it is impossible to state how many cattle we have, there being "pilgrims" last season suppose them now widely scattered. The occasion for us being singled out is beyond my comprehension. . . . I am making no noise about it hoping that this unjust and wicked prosecution fit only to be met out to a condemned criminal will pass soon.[7]

If Rose's intentions were to make no noise, he did not keep to them; over the next six months he screamed to anybody who

[6] Richard Trimble to Merritt Trimble, September 14, 1886. Trimble Collection, Western History Research Center, University of Wyoming.

[7] J. W. Rose to Thomas Sturgis June 20, 1885. Wyoming Stock Growers Association Collection, Western History Research Center, University of Wyoming.

would listen. Thomas Sturgis sent a diplomatic reply offering assurances that his trouble would melt away "soon."[8] Since Sturgis had previously received a spiteful letter from Harry Oelrichs's manager-director of the Anglo-American Cattle Company, words were about all he could offer the troubled Rose.[9] As a member of the executive committee of the Wyoming Stock Growers Association, Oelrichs had access to a political power which eclipsed any that Rose could bring to bear.

Even more distasteful to managers than becoming entangled in disputes with adjoining managers was being asked to join in arguments between stockholders or neighboring owners. In early December 1902, without previous warning, Isaac Ellwood opened a cryptic letter from G. G. Wright, attorney for C. C. Slaughter, whose ranch bordered on the Ellwoods' range. "On account of some of your cattle that had ticks on them being turned out of pasture '49' and into our pasture, Colonel Slaughter lost cattle valued at $5,577.50. . . . Would you please satisfy this claim?"[1] Not being overly fond of Slaughter, Ellwood ignored Wright's letter and sent a note off to his manager asking for "the full particulars."[2] Arnett told Ellwood that their cattle were free from ticks, but that ironically, "Slaughter's cattle have had outbreaks from time to time for the past two years."[3] On receiving this intelligence, Ellwood thought the matter should be completely "pushed aside." Highly disturbed, C. C. Slaughter personally wrote to Ellwood, arguing: "I am living in Texas, some 300 miles from where the trouble arose. I am satisfied that you must depend on your men for your news." That being the case, Slaughter went on to say, he had "sent my attorney to visit the ranch and learn the *facts*. He has a sworn statement of individuals who state your cattle had ticks." What did Slaughter intend to do with this information? "I am the last man that wants to go to courts, but

[8] Thomas Sturgis to J. W. Rose, August 2, 1885. Ibid.
[9] Harry Oelrichs to Thomas Sturgis, June 24, 1885. Ibid.
[1] G. G. Wright to Isaac Ellwood, November 20, 1902. Ellwood Collection, Western History Research Center, University of Wyoming.
[2] Isaac Ellwood to D. N. Arnett, December 9, 1902. Ibid.
[3] D. N. Arnett to Isaac Ellwood, January 7, 1903. Ibid.

I will unless you make up my loss. If you wish a disinterested person to arbitrate this problem, I would consent to this."[4]

Slaughter's letter infuriated Ellwood, who sent a wire to his manager: "Say nothing to any of Slaughter's men. Sending Fisk [Ellwood's lawyer]."[5] The dispute continued for over a year, with Slaughter and Ellwood exchanging insults personally and through their lawyers, managers, and even employees. The quarrel was finally resolved by each owner yielding some of his position. Ellwood paid $750, much to his disgust, but he admitted to his lawyer that it was good to be "relieved of this nuisance."[6]

The less wealthy managers often fell into the bad habit of asking for personal loans from their Eastern investors. Tempted by the thought of the rewards from making a quick sale of feeder cattle, or from a successful real estate venture, the manager would appeal to his investor for insignificant loans. At the convivial start of their ranching enterprise, most investors complied with these requests; but as the debts mounted and the dividends continued nonexistent, investors came to feel that their managers should suffer in mutuality. Many Eastern investors sympathized with John Bigelow when he icily announced that the only improvement in the Teschemacher and deBillier cattle statement for the past year had been the managerial stipend.[7]

Few stockholders were inclined to admit it, but substantial blame for the manager's financial predicament rested with them. Investors had, or pretended to have, utmost difficulty realizing that the managerial qualifications they expected could reasonably be filled by only a small number of men. Further, these managers were in great demand and well compensated for their services, whereas managerial salaries for the most part were meager. A well-known, highly experience, and successful manager like R. G. Head of the Prairie Land and Cattle Company received $2,000 a month for his

4 C. C. Slaughter to Isaac Ellwood, December 11, 1902. Ibid.
5 Isaac Ellwood to D. N. Arnett, December 23, 1902. Ibid.
6 Memorandum from Isaac Ellwood to A. W. Fisk, January 9, 1904. Ibid.
7 John Bigelow to H. E. Teschemacher, February 21, 1889. Teschemacher and deBillier Collection, Western History Research Center, University of Wyoming.

expertise.[8] Murdo MacKenzie, the shrewd Scot who was so successful in running the Matador Land and Cattle Company, lived in the style of his employers, sent some of his children to college, traveled in Europe, and enjoyed fine homes in Trinidad and Denver.[9] William Hughes of the Continental Land and Cattle Company paid his manager well; this was particularly generous, since Hughes made most of the managerial decisions himself.[1]

These highly paid managers were the exceptions, not the rule. James H. Pratt expected business talent, long hours, and abstinence from "libationous spirits" for $90 a month.[2] Isaac Ellwood dismissed the Arnetts' entreaties for raises with the succinct observation: "Everything in Texas has cost me more than I anticipated, just can't afford more now."[3] The Arnetts, father and son, were receiving $100 and $75 a month respectively, and Ellwood saw no reason to go above the average rate. John Clay believed that his manager of Western Ranches, Ltd., in South Dakota should rejoice on a salary of $95 a month. He wrote his friend and associate, James T. Craig: "We should watch our labor expense for once it gets up, it is difficult to lower."[4] Again, one could concede that there was some rationale to Clay's judgment. Since he had just fought to unscramble the tangled finances of the Swan Land and Cattle Company, "luxuries" of any nature were passé. However, most investors simply refused to admit the connection between adequate recompense and managerial quality. Jay L. Torrey told his brother in no uncertain terms: "We must cut expense, and wages are a good beginning place."[5] When Torrey's manager Amos Van Blair protested the slash in his salary, he received no solace from Colonel Torrey. "If you are convinced that your

[8] Las Vegas *Daily Optic*, June 12, 1885.
[9] W. M. Pearce: *The Matador Land and Cattle Company* (Norman: University of Oklahoma Press; 1964).
[1] William E. Hughes: *The Journal of a Grandfather* (St. Louis: 1912).
[2] J. H. Pratt to George Millhouse, April 18, 1887. Pratt Collection, Nebraska State Historical Society.
[3] Isaac Ellwood to D. N. Arnett, November 6, 1898. Ellwood Collection, Western History Research Center, University of Wyoming.
[4] John Clay to James T. Craig, May 21, 1896. Craig Collection, Western History Research Center, University of Wyoming.
[5] Jay L. Torrey to Richard Torrey, January 12, 1883. Torrey Collection, Western History Research Center, University of Wyoming.

worth is more than we are paying you then you are perfectly free
to seek employment in other pastures."[6]

The substantial disagreement on salaries derived as much as
anything else from the difference in managerial and investor
philosophies. The managers, being very appreciative of the personal wealth of their stockholders, found the economy-minded
wage policies incomprehensible. Managers made annual pilgrimages
back East and were entertained in elegant style on the Ellwood
estate in De Kalb, Illinois, or the Stoddard estate in New Haven,
Connecticut. A. J. Van Duzee's manager voiced a prevalent
opinion when he informed the Dubuque capitalist: "You expect
us to spend nights on the range, using sod as a bed, drinking
brackish water, while you enjoy the good food and soft bed, all
for the smallest of money."[7] The manager went on asking at some
length whether Van Duzee felt that this policy was "fair or just."
Van Duzee kept his temper and his manager for another few years,
but finally decided that the continual haranguing about salary and
other matters was not worth the expenditure of nerves and energy.

The manager's struggle to attain a more affluent position in
Western society left no alternative except to appeal for loans
where his security (usually his word) sufficed. Why not? The
Eastern financier who could pour thousands of dollars into creating "the finest ranch in Texas" ought to be able to spare a few
thousand for his loyal manager. The investor in turn felt caught.
If he complied with these continual requests for loans, to all intents
and purposes he was taking a risk which in the routine of his
business affairs in the East he would most assuredly avoid. If he
did not grant a loan, then he gambled the ill will of his manager
against the future prosperity of his company. The Eastern
financier, with a continent between him and his property, felt that
he was crippled enough without hazarding his manager's enmity.

H. K. Thurber, the New York coffee magnate, became so bound
up in the financial problems of his New Mexico partner, J. C. Lea,
that that he spent hours writing letters which repeated the same

6 Jay L. Torrey to Amos Van Blair, October 26, 1883. Ibid.
7 John Gailreath to A. J. Van Duzee, January 27, 1884. Van Duzee Collection, Aurora, Illinois.

points in a crisp, unmistakable language. "Now, if you think so highly of your land and cattle," wrote Thurber, in a typical letter in the fall of 1890, ". . . I will take a portion at a time and, as I have said before, only take the money that I have advanced and the interest on it."[8] The Lea-Thurber financial stalemate remained as the years dragged on. Thurber eventually lost interest as well as hope that his investment in New Mexico would ever pay dividends. J. F. Norfleet, the manager of Ellwood's Spade Ranch in Hale County, Texas, had better luck than Lea. After describing, in the most optimistic and glowing words, the prospects of wonderful range conditions and high cattle prices, Norfleet, in a by-the-way manner, asked for $2,000 to buy two hundred yearlings. Ellwood advanced the money, but with the warning: "I expect you to be as interested in my cattle as your own."[9]

Occasionally, loans were negotiated with ease and high spirits on the part of everyone involved. Richard Norris, a Boston hardware merchant, assured John Painter that as soon as "your beef gather [roundup] is over I will instruct you about the loan."[1] A month passed and Painter received the "joyous" news of a $10,000 loan with Norris's bubbling comment: "There is more good fortune in our guardian stars than this eh, Johnny boy!"[2] Norris was convinced that he had come into possession of a money tree—a pleasant feeling that faded away within two years.

More typical than the congenial exchange between Norris and Painter was the fencing of John Thomas, president of the Suffolk Cattle Company of Wyoming, and John Storrie, one of his managers. During his winter isolation at Hat Creek Ranch, Storrie sent two letters to Thomas, then living in Boston, asking "the favor of a loan," although the amount was unspecified. Thomas ignored the first "hint" for assistance and made a noncommital reply to Storrie's more "specific" suggestion. At last, his patience

[8] H. K. Thurber to Joseph C. Lea, November 6, 1890. Padgitt Collection, San Antonio, Texas.
[9] Isaac Ellwood to J. F. Norfleet, January 26, 1891. Ellwood Collection, Western History Research Center, University of Wyoming.
[1] Richard Norris to John Painter, July 11, 1889. Painter Collection, Greeley, Colorado.
[2] Ibid., August 18, 1889.

wearing thin, Storrie bluntly outlined his predicament. "At the risk of boring you, I will give you a few reasons why I want this money."[3] His "few reasons" took three pages to state and consisted mainly of the fact that he had overextended his credit, and now the holders of his mortgages threatened to foreclose. Another motivation was "my continual thought about matrimony with a nice girl in Crawford [Nebraska]." Storrie rested his case with the summation: "As I told you, I do not know where to turn for help, so if you will only have confidence in me, I will be very grateful and do all I can to merit it." Storrie's literate and smoothly phrased letter fell like a cold sponge on Thomas, who already felt plagued by having to "rob Peter to pay Paul." However, he did lend Storrie $4,000—after a long series of sermonizing letters. Thomas vividly depicted the horrors of bankruptcy: "No one will dare trust you after this experience"; the need for prudent management: "Watch your affairs, spend for only those items which will be certain to improve your situation"; and the folly of marrying without money: "How can you support two if you can not support one?"[4] Storrie, with money in hand, received the letters in good humor. He rebutted only one point, noting that Thomas's bachelorhood hardly qualified him "to speak on the subject of matrimony."[5]

The only managers who consistently avoided financial embarrassment were those who held stock in their companies. As managing directors, their dividends were welcome supplements to their salaries, and their Jekyll-Hyde position gave them freer access to their company treasuries as well as wider latitude in implementing company policy. T. B. Hord reminded his board of directors: "Managers ought to be considered more than foremen, though from your address I understand they are not."[6] Hord, as manager and stockholder in the Lance Creek Cattle Company, maintained running quarrels with several officers who insisted that he was

3 John Storrie to John B. Thomas, January 15, 1886. Dunder Collection, Western History Research Center, University of Wyoming.
4 John B. Thomas to John Storrie, February 20, 1886. Ibid.
5 John Storrie to John B. Thomas, March 17, 1886, Ibid.
6 T. B. Hord to Charles F. Smillie, April 12, 1888. Hord Collection, Western History Research Center, University of Wyoming.

far too dictatorial. Hord did not hesitate to make corporate
decisions without consultation, but as he told Charles Smillie,
president of the Lance Creek Cattle Company: "Someone should
decide what should be done in this outfit."[7] The Lance Creek
Company was hobbled from its inception by confusion of policy.

Yet the Lance Creek directors' protests were also common on
other boards of directors. The managing director, in the twin role
of owner and employee, had a partial immunity to criticism.
Other directors were sometimes reluctant to attack a member
of their club, especially since the managing director was better
informed on range matters than the director residing in Manhattan. Superior knowledge, though, was no substitute for a lucrative return, as John Thomas was firmly reminded by his friend
Joseph Ames.

Even if the Eastern directors decided to dismiss the manager,
it was embarrassing to have an ex-manager on their board of
trustees as a voting stockholder. The only totally satisfactory
solution was to purchase the manager's stock, and this could be
an expensive operation. Investors naturally wondered about the
advisability of buying a stock at par when they had bundles of
their own which were worth half par or less. When Thomas
Sturgis wrote Henry L. Higginson that he wanted to resign as
president of the Union Cattle Company and sell his stock to the
other officers, Higginson put the problem neatly in his reply:
"Give us one reason why we would be better off by buying your
shares? We already feel foolish enough holding a security with so
little negotiability."[8] Higginson described the dispirited character
of their board meetings and the disgruntled resolutions, concluding: "Who else would we get to take over our affairs at this
stage?" This point, which many directors made to their managers
when the managers became irritated or disconsolate, may have
reassured the managers, but it was most unsettling to the directors.
When investors lacked confidence in their manager but realized

[7] Ibid., August 4, 1888.
[8] Henry L. Higginson to Thomas Sturgis, June 22, 1888. Higginson Collection, Baker Library, Harvard University.

that they could not replace him, their feeling was not one of exuberance.

Another of the Eastern investor's worries was expressed by Isaac Ellwood when he warned his manager to take as much interest in Ellwood's herd as he did in his own. Cattlemen in the West were extremely reluctant to allow their foremen to own cattle and graze them on the range with the company's herds. There was always the unstated suspicion that at branding time, the foreman's brand might wander onto the hides of the company calves. The prohibition against owning cattle was an unwritten rule so strong in some localities that a cowboy who ran his own herd on the same range or nearby was automatically, if silently, suspected of rustling.

Only the most naïve would assume that the foreign corporation or the Eastern-based company was not taken advantage of both by its own employees and by neighboring cattlemen. It was a phenomenon of the range that Eastern companies inevitably had the highest proportion of mavericks and the lowest production of calves. Somehow their heifers were amazingly unfertile. After a few years' experience, the Eastern investor was not completely oblivious to the reasons for his poor calf crop, but he felt helpless to deal with the situation.

There were a number of tales floating around the billiard rooms of the Union League clubs which lacerated the sensibilities of every investor. One perennial[9] was attributed by Miguel Otero, Governor of New Mexico, to J. W. Lynch: "I recall one evening, at the Montezuma Club [Santa Fe] we were all relating some of our experiences, and Mr. Lynch began telling the boys how he started in the cattle business." This had been a most enchanting beginning, according to Lynch. "I worked for an outfit in Texas whose registered herd was, 'I.O.U.' I saw my opportunity. . . . I got very busy adding the figure '2' after the 'U' and right there I registered my own brand as 'I.O.U.2.'!" Lynch claimed that busi-

[9] The same story that so horrified and amused Otero was current in the Big Horn basin of Wyoming in the same period. Charles Lindsay: *The Big Horn Basin* (Lincoln, Neb.: 1932), 115.

ness thrived from the start. Since this contemporary tale had as many versions as storytellers, Lynch was undoubtedly kidding his listeners. Either he was a spellbinder or his audience was most gullible, for Otero was convinced that "J. W. Lynch was nobody's fool. He was as smart a they make them . . . but as unscrupulous as could be. . . . He broke every Englishman who trusted him."[1]

It would be as great a distortion to highlight the dishonesty of the managers as to ignore managerial improprieties and strange bookkeeping procedures. The wonder is that the managers were not more corrupt, considering their recompense and their opportunities. The manager-investor relationship was a bedeviled one from the first: each, extremely dependent upon the other, childishly sought ways to assert his independence. A few manager-investor teams, such as the Ellwood-Arnett and Stoddard-O'Donel pairs, carried on a more mature association which lasted for years. These instances of mutual cooperation were as rare as the number of astute managers.

Because of the heavy responsibility and inadequate pay, finding men who would measure up as managers was a continual talent hunt devoid of prizes. Investors tried numerous avenues in their search for the "right" man, only to be frustrated in their choice. Desiring the personification of a diplomat, businessman, and cattleman, they settled, with poor grace, for considerably less. They always had the gnawing suspicion that their manager withheld the truth (which he often did). The manager, on the other hand, believed that in any decision he made, he would be damned if he did and damned if he didn't (and this was often true too). The distance, the lack of able managers, and the ignorance of investors concerning range conditions left little room for manager-investor compatibility.

[1] Miguel Otero: *My Life on the Frontier, 1882–1897* (Albuquerque: University of New Mexico Press; 1939), II, 36.

VI

"You must stop drawing on me"

FINANCING THE COMPANY

Once a new manager walked across the threshold of his office, a glance at his books was enough to inform him that his first duty was to write his directors for more capital. Supplication after supplication from range managers dropped into the mail slots of Wall Street offices. Thomas B. Adams, secretary of the Lance Creek Cattle Company, pleaded with Charles Smillie: "It is absolutely impossible for me to get along without funds. Foreman's orders for labor and provision presented every day and account overdrawn. Immediate action of some kind must be taken."[1] Smillie, by this time inured to all emotional messages, telegraphed

[1] Thomas B. Adams to Charles F. Smillie, November 27, 1887. Hord Collection, Western History Research Center, University of Wyoming.

back: "No funds here, or likely to be had in near future, reduce expenses. Wait for cattle sales."[2]

Many a director cursed the day he had subscribed to stock in a cattle company when he discovered that initial capitalization seldom lasted more than the first year. In the early years of the range cattle industry, relatives and friends received the first appeals and gave the most rewarding responses. After dividends failed to materialize, loans consistently defaulted, and interest payments lagged, relatives lost their warm appreciation of cattle investment. Having just returned from a trip East, Captain Lea of New Mexico lamented to an acquaintance: "New York was a more friendly place three years ago. Now all I hear back there is questions as to what we are doing with our money, why the calf crop isn't better and when will we again be able to pay our notes." Captain Lea went on: "As you know . . . I am afraid my answer didn't satisfy their questions."[3]

When friends snapped their purses shut, directors sought out banks and commission firms. From corporate inception, bankers frequently looked over the shoulders of directors at company ledgers, yet they became the favored recourse for long-term financing only after relatives and friends declined to assist. Undoubtedly, this reluctance of directors to turn to the banks can in part be ascribed to the necessity of paying higher interest rates. But more crucial, it was far easier for a director who was defaulting on a note to write to "Cousin Joe" or the father of a Harvard classmate, describe his plight in soul-rending terms, and then wait and hope for understanding, if not empathy.

Bankers, along with the rest of the business community, accepted short-term cattle loans with little discrimination until the mid-1880's, when the shaky financial foundation of many corporations sent tremors through Eastern financial circles. Financiers' references to cattle investment then declined through stages of diminishing favor to disdain and sarcasm. One story, related in so many versions and attributed to so many separate individuals

[2] Charles F. Smillie to Thomas B. Adams, December 17, 1887. Ibid.
[3] Joseph Lea to John DeLany, May 9, 1887. Padgitt Collection, San Antonio, Texas.

as to confirm its apocryphal nature, was told by Charles Guernsey, an eastern Wyoming cattleman who succeeded in interesting Marshall Field and R. M. Fair in copper mines as well as cattle. C. L. Briggs (so the Guernsey version goes), a member of the Wyoming legislature, made a pilgrimage to Boston to obtain a loan on his cattle.[4] Briggs gushed to a Boston banker about the wonderful free grass, the wide vistas of open range, and the sleek cattle grazing thereon. During the onrush of the vivid monologue, the banker sat in silence. The Wyoming cowman attributed this quietness to the very favorable impression he was creating until, out of breath, he paused enough for the banker to interject: "Well, sir, I'd as quick make a loan on a school of mackerel off Cape Cod as to you on your cattle in Wyoming." Guernsey concluded that "Briggsie from Laramie, as he was called at the old Cheyenne Club, had to reach in his other pocket for horse car fare to his hotel that night."[5]

A few farsighted Eastern bankers may have foreseen the general downswing in the business cycle of the middle eighties and the accompanying decline in the cattle market, but there is little evidence to suggest that Eastern bankers in general were any more knowing than others in the financial community.[6] Cattle paper was not prominent in the total aggregation of loans in Eastern banks, so that bankers liquidated cattle loans with alacrity if conditions warranted it. Western bankers, who did not have such enviable diversity, were often too involved with cattlemen to foreclose when economic conditions indicated the wisdom of a tighter loan policy. These lax loan practices proved fatal to many Western banking institutions in the collapse of 1886–7 and again in 1892–3. Intensely personal in their business relationship, bankers in Western towns made loans to cattlemen who were not only friends, but more often than not, directors of their banks.

[4] Charles A. Guernsey: *Wyoming Cowboy Days* (New York: G. P. Putnam's Sons; 1936), 34.

[5] William French, an English rancher in New Mexico, related a similar story in *Some Recollections of a Western Ranchman* (London: Methuen; 1927), 190.

[6] For an enlightening discussion of the cyclic response of business to overall economic situations, see Rendigs Fels: *American Business Cycles, 1865–1897* (Chapel Hill: University of North Carolina Press; 1959), 128–54.

As in any society, in the East, West, North, or South, cattlemen split into groups not only on a social basis, but also in their business affairs. John Clay, reminiscing about the Cheyenne that he knew in the 1880's, recalled significant factions. "A crowd worshipped at the shrine of Swan; another lot looked to Tom Sturgis for inspiration. The Swan coterie mostly did business at the First National Bank; the other crowd supported the Stock Growers National Bank."[7] The Swan Land and Cattle Company failure in the spring of 1887 brought down the First National Bank with such a crash that it never recovered. On the other hand, the Stock Growers National Bank was reorganized, and Wyoming cattlemen still bank there today.

However potent personal contacts were in Western banking, it would be ridiculous to point to "friendship" as the principal destroyer of financial institutions in the West.[8] Reasons abound for the predicament of many Western banks: the lack of quantity or quality in collateral; the informality of business arrangements; the monolithic nature of loans, which centered on the cattle industry (admittedly, this reflected the lack of diversity in the Western economy); and the inadequate ratio between reserves and outstanding loans. All these elements disposed a bank to collapse at the slightest hint of an economic downturn.

M. E. Post, Cheyenne, Deadwood, and Leadville banker, wrote an anguished letter to his wife from South Dakota in 1887:

> I found conditions here much the same as in Cheyenne. We just trusted these people too far. The assets of most of them will not begin to pay off their indebtedness. . . . What or how though does one go about foreclosing an entire community? I am straightening out the mess the best I can.[9]

[7] John Clay: *My Life on the Range* (Chicago: 1924), 66.
[8] On bankers and cattlemen, useful accounts are Paul F. Walter: "New Mexico's Pioneer Bank and Bankers," *New Mexico Historical Review*, XXI (July 1946), 209–25; James T. Padgitt: "The Millers and Early Day Banking in Belton," *West Texas Historical Association Yearbook*, XXXII (October 1956), 103–21; Herbert P. White: "Conrad Kohrs, Cattleman," *Denver Westerners Brand Book* (Denver: 1960), 333–53; Monroe Cockrell: *After Sundown* (Chicago: 1962).
[9] Morton E. Post to Amelia Post, May 23, 1887. Post Collection, Western History Research Center, University of Wyoming.

Eventually, Post moved to California, made more money there, and repaid his Wyoming creditors. Post's stockholders were among the fortunate few; many people who owned stock in banks fell in the class of *miserables*—lost it all. Occasionally stockholders and bank officials cooperated during bad times not only for their own welfare, but also for their communities. In the panic of 1893, Edson Dayton, a large stock grower in North Dakota, returned from a trip East to find that his local bank at Dickinson was in difficulty. Dayton volunteered: " 'How would it do if I turned over half my account?' 'That would help,' he [the banker] answered. 'All I [Dayton] care to do is to meet current expenses.' To that he gave me a remarkable piece of advice. 'I wouldn't do that, no one is paying us.' "[1] Novel is the only accurate description for this exchange. Through Dayton's cooperation the bank froze assets until cattle sales receipts came in during the autumn. Payments were met and the Dickinson bank was again able to extend credit in a modest degree. Although this case was not unique in Western metropolises, it was rare enough. More often, bankers and businessmen floundered helplessly, devoid of the resources to work out their salvation.

Whether shaky or sound, solvent or in debt, cattlemen all too often found themselves obligated to their bankers a brief time after the sealing wax was dry on their papers of incorporation. A perusal of dozens of ledgers and hundreds of letters between bankers and cattlemen leads to the inescapable conclusion that the Western range cattle industry during the last two decades of the nineteenth century was operated basically on borrowed capital.[2] This dependence is hardly astonishing, as most industrial growth in the Victorian era blossomed on inflated stock issues and borrowed capital. More irritating to cattlemen was their long-term dependence on loans: year to year, the dreamed-about surplus never materialized, or was never large enough to enable the cattleman to free himself from interest payments.

[1] Edson C. Dayton: *Dakota Days* (Hartford, Conn.: 1937), 45.
[2] Lest his nephew forget from whence all blessing flowed, Henry Seligman needled: "Where would you be if suddenly our funds dried up?" Henry Seligman to A. J. Seligman, October 8, 1885. Seligman Collection, Baker Library, Harvard University.

Was the intrinsic cost of raising cattle so high as to prevent a profit? Soothsayers Latham, Strahorn, and Brisbin had a ready answer: the cost of rearing a steer on free grass was infinitesimal. After making several tours of the West, the government statistician Joseph Nimmo estimated that a steer could be raised for an average outlay of 75 cents to $1.25 per year.[3] But George Weare, on looking over his son's balance sheet, shuddered and wrote: "Do you realize it has cost us two dollars and thirty cents annually for every animal we have eventually sent to market? Can't this be reduced? I expect an affirmative answer."[4]

A good manager, frugal with the company's funds, could and would show a profit. Good managers, though, were scarce. Richard Trimble's father saw "no earthly" reason for the Teschemacher and deBillier Cattle Company to maintain two offices; couldn't these be joined?[5] On visiting the Swan Land and Cattle Company in 1888, John Clay was horrified to discover that it was still running in the plush fashion of 1883, indulging not only in dual offices, but in surplus employees.[6] Clay's methods of slashing overhead did not increase his popularity, but after several years of rigid economy the Swan Land and Cattle Company began sending out dividend checks again.

Because of unknown factors such as land values, it is impossible to give an accurate cost estimate per steer. Upon surveying numerous ledgers, however, one can arrive at approximations. Ellwood's records for the twelve-year period 1889–1901 reveal that his average annual cost for marketed cattle was $1.65.[7] Considering that Ellwood, in the early stages of his ranch, was more extravagant than he was in later cost-conscious years, this was an adequate showing. Ellwood was blessed by being able to finance his com-

[3] Joseph Nimmo, Jr.: *Report in Regard to the Range and Ranch Cattle Business of the United States* (Washington: 1885), 20–1.

[4] George Weare to Henry Weare, January 12, 1890. Jack Nason Collection, Spearfish, South Dakota.

[5] Merritt Trimble to Richard Trimble, June 23, 1885. Trimble Collection, Western History Research Center, University of Wyoming.

[6] Clay: *My Life on the Range*, 209–29.

[7] Ellwood Collection, Western History Research Center, University of Wyoming.

pany without resorting to long-term loans, thereby removing high interest rates from his debit columns.

Several approximate cost figures can be deduced for shorter periods. The Boston Livestock Company ledgers indicate that for 1882–4 their cost per marketed steer was $1.55 annually.[8] For the period 1897–1900, the Red Buttes Land and Cattle Company estimated its expense at 2.55 per steer.[9] A floating debt and consequent interest charges made it virtually impossible for the Red Buttes Company to show a profit. George McClellan, a cattleman in the Big Horn region of Wyoming, broke his expenses down and arrived at the figure of $1.85 as the average steer cost for 1890–1897.[1] The Pratt-Ferris Cattle Company, a much more profitable operation in the 1890's than in the 1880's, claimed that its expenses for 1889–96 averaged $2.05 per steer.[2]

Although the cost of raising a steer is not easy to determine, the obvious point is that for over a decade after 1885, cattlemen had difficulty in keeping red figures out of their final balance. An unstable market and rising costs made it necessary to have financial agility, an imaginative policy, and a good deal of luck in order to produce a profit.

Regardless of the cost of raising cattle, acquiring "stockers" was the heaviest outlay in any cattle company. Davis, Hauser and Company felt fortunate in 1879–81 to buy the higher-grade Oregon cattle for an average of $17.50 per head, with aggregate expenditures amounting to $112,652.04.[3] The price of stock cattle, of course, fluctuated with the overall financial gyrations of the cattle industry. In 1884, A. H. Arnett was amazed when his trail bosses bought eight hundred Oregon cattle for the bargain price of $13 per head.[4] The leaner Texas cattle were consistently lower in price

[8] Western Range Cattle Industry Collection, State Historical Society of Colorado.

[9] Arnold Collection, Western History Research Center, University of Wyoming.

[1] McClellan Collection, Western History Research Center, University of Wyoming.

[2] Pratt-Ferris Collection, Nebraska State Historical Society.

[3] Hauser Collection, Historical Society of Montana.

[4] Western Range Cattle Industry Collection, State Historical Society of Colorado.

than the Oregon "natives." Henry G. Hay boasted to his partner, I. W. Whipple, in 1880 that H. N. Dolan sold him "his trail herd for six dollars each. A bargain, I understand, as May Goldschmitt paid seven dollars and fifty cents last month."[5] In the late 1880's and 1890's, the price of stockers continued to bounce around erratically. Arnett, so proud of his Oregon purchase in 1884, was chagrined in 1888 to have to pay $15 apiece for his Texas cattle, even if they were two-year-olds and delivered to Dickinson, North Dakota. "How do you make anything on a contract like this?" Arnett moaned. "They say the drought is making these high prices, hell, Texas has always been dry!"[6] The manager of the Laramie River Cattle Company in 1892 vociferously complained to James Converse: "The price of [stock] cattle not even accounting for our expenses would not show a profit this year. . . . Don't you have a job for me in Boston?"[7]

The nature of the financial squeeze which caused many managers to feel that they had committed a serious *faux pas* in their choice of a profession is not obscure. If a cattleman purchased an Oregon yearling for $15 in 1884, fed it for two years at an estimated cost of $2.00 per year, paid interest, freight, labor, capital outlay, and commission charges, and then sold this 1,200-pound three-year-old on the Chicago market in 1887 for $2.90 per hundred weight, there is no mystery as to why he became apoplectic in discussing his profit. His company was probably already heavily in debt, and he had no chance for recouping his losses until the following fall.

Cattle companies arriving on the Western scene in the late 1870's and early 1880's grasped their range wherever they could find it. From time to time they might be forced by competing firms to purchase water rights or land adjacent to a stream, but seldom did they invest in acres of sagebrush. However, when barbed wire started tumbling out of the Ellwood wire works in De Kalb,

[5] Henry Hay to I. W. Whipple, March 24, 1880. Wyoming Stock Growers Association Collection, Western History Research Center, University of Wyoming.

[6] A. H. Arnett to Robert Oldham, April 18, 1888. Western Range Cattle Industry Collection, State Historical Society of Colorado.

[7] Arthur Mangus to James Converse, August 17, 1892. Converse Collection, Baker Library, Harvard University.

Illinois, in 1875,[8] the land system which had been free and easy (for some) underwent a catastrophic change causing a radical depletion of companies' exchequers. Forced to bid against homesteaders, small ranchers, and other cattle companies for land, the larger Eastern-financed concern either had to make a huge capital outlay for the domain or go into a feeding operation. Either gamble began grimly, with finances already strained to the breaking point.

George Weare outlined the common plight when he told a friend about the trouble his son was in after buying land which had passed into the estate of the now-deceased Dickey brothers.

> I think I mentioned to you the matter of the Dickey pasture that Henry bought in 1887 (after the hard winter). It was necessary for us to secure it in the condition of the country at that time and prevent Clay getting it and surrounding us as was his intention to do. It commands the Little Missouri range, where most of our cattle are. . . . It is the only hay land in that country and we can't allow it to fall into other hands without jeopardizing our vital interests as you readily see, if we are to continue our cattle business in that country especially since the railroad is coming on the south of us. When Henry gave his notes for the land $10,000 with 7% it was expected the Dickeys would be able to continue in the country and need the pasture and the trade was considered only temporary, but you know the history of those young men, both dead—Henry's notes went into the estate and must be paid.[9]

Caught in a contract born of expediency, the Weares faced unpleasant alternatives: They could either borrow to pay off their agreement or they could let their option lapse, thereby allowing John Clay to absorb their range. After wearisome debate, they finally went to Lyman Gage, president of the First National Bank of Chicago, secured a loan, and became the none-too-proud possessors of more land along the Little Missouri.

Competition, the most consistent motive for land expansion, was

---

[8] Ellwood started manufacturing in 1874; very little production occurred until 1875. Ellwood Collection, Western History Research Center, University of Wyoming.

[9] George Weare to R. M. Fair, September 14, 1891. Jack Nason Collection, Spearfish, South Dakota.

not the only factor. Senators Francis E. Warren of Wyoming and Thomas Catron of New Mexico are examples of the landlords who succumbed to a mania for swallowing up huge sections of the domain. Both senators eventually became financially overextended around the turn of the century; the Warren Land and Livestock Company went into receivership in 1897,[1] and without the timely assistance of Stephen Elkins, Catron's affairs would have been embroiled in 1901.[2] But the Warrens and Catrons were the exception, not the rule. The majority of cattlemen had no insatiable desire to become land barons, for the disposal of land, as the owners of the XIT discovered, was far more vexatious than ranching. The cattleman's land hunger usually abated when his water rights were protected and he had enough room to accommodate the periodic fluctuations of his herd.

Another expenditure subject to more rigorous scrutiny from the East than land speculation was labor charges. Studying ledgers, directors found this an item that could easily be fastened on, so that the manager was often placed on the defensive not only about the number and size of employee remunerations, but even his own salary! Thus John Bigelow, diplomat, author, and founder of the New York Public Library, sarcastically observed to Hubert Teschemacher: "The lone item that has improved in your financial statement since last year is your salary! Don't you think you could suffer along with the rest of us?"[3] Bigelow's caustic remarks were not altogether unjust. Teschemacher's scale of living, plus his father's reluctance to continue to maintain him in the style to which he was accustomed, had led to a personal embarrassment; and as one solution, he and his partner Fred deBillier had voted themselves handsome salary increments in a period when the company could ill afford them.[4]

The trials and tribulations of the Teschemacher and deBillier

[1] F. E. Warren to S. B. Tuttle, May 11, 1897. Warren Collection, Western History Research Center, University of Wyoming.

[2] Thomas Catron to Stephen Elkins, February 7, 1901. Catron Collection, University of New Mexico Library.

[3] John Bigelow to Hubert Teschemacher, January 22, 1886. Teschemacher and deBillier Collection, Western History Research Center, University of Wyoming.

[4] Teschemacher and deBillier Ledgers, 1884, 1885, and 1886. Ibid.

Cattle Company aside, an appraisal of the wages column in most cattlemen's ledgers shows little reason for criticism. The number of men employed, as well as the wages paid them, was kept as small as possible by most managers. J. F. Norfleet was fond of reminding Isaac Ellwood: "I have been very careful of the men I hired. With only four men, we have not wasted your funds."[5] Norfleet did not mention the quadrupled labor force he employed during fall shipping time, although of course this was a common occurrence at most ranches.

For an amazingly long period, the wage scale for cowboys hovered in the $25- to $40-per-month bracket, with room and board included. Foremen received from $50 to $100 monthly. As a rule of thumb, the manager argued that the number of employees essential to an operation was one ranch hand per every 600 to 1,000 cattle. In actuality, even prosperous ranches seldom reached this ideal ratio of men to beasts.

An expense less within the cattlemen's control than labor, and more important to their solvency, was the freight rate. Before the arrival of the railroad in a locality, cattlemen, in common with all Westerners, looked toward it as an economic savior. To a nineteenth-century American a rail connection was a promise of economic predestination. If he ever forgot this elemental fact, all he needed to remind him was to glance around the landscape, which was strewn with ghost towns. Everywhere he could see communities which had once dreamed of becoming trade centers, only to have their hopes become as empty as their false-front stores when the railroad bypassed them.

Frontier editors had an impassioned way of addressing clarion calls to legislative representatives and to the general citizenry concerning railroad rights-of-way.[6] The editor of the Big Horn *Sentinel* used the front-page banner: "Railroad Planned Soon—

[5] J. F. Norfleet to Isaac Ellwood, July 8, 1892. Ellwood Collection, Western History Research Center, University of Wyoming.

[6] Examples of the editorial hyperbole are evident during the decades of the 1870's and 1880's in such newspapers as the Laramie *Boomerang*, 1886–90; Dodge City *Times*, 1876–82; Las Vegas *Optic*, 1884–6; Cheyenne *Leader*, 1882–8; Kansas City *Livestock Indicator*, 1884–90; St. Louis *Globe Democrat*, 1882–90; San Marcial *Reporter*, 1878–86; Northwestern *Livestock Journal*, 1885–7.

Big Horn to Rival Sheridan."[7] The editor pointed out that for
Big Horn this would be a "resurrection"—an earthly version, it
was to be assumed. Frontier journalism was studded with such
references to the glorious advantages of the "two ribbons of iron."

Eastern investors, although they were less demonstrative, sometimes also looked to the railroad to repair their fortunes. H. K.
Thurber, New York financier, hurried off a letter to J. C. Lea:

> I do really hope that the town property will make a great
> deal of money, but Captain, as soon as I could sell off and while
> the excitement is on, I would sell, so as to reduce our holdings.
> The time to sell in a town is when the railroad is building; the
> moment it goes through the moment excitement dies away some
> other town comes up in its stead. It would be a great thing, if
> you could get the repair works and the car works at your town.[8]

The railroad arrived in the guise of a redeemer; all too often it
soon became the devil incarnate. The railroad protest movements
typified by the granger-alliance organizations were far from restricted to the Midwest. Western merchants, mining magnates, and
livestock men pealed out unceasing complaints about the evils of
railroad rates. Senator Warren, responding to. a constituent's
letters, resignedly agreed that "railroad rates are exorbitant, they
always have been and I suppose will always be."[9]

Although they damned the railroads vigorously, Western cattlemen were also the first to ask them for favors. Warren and Catron
were adroit in wheedling passes for family, relatives, friends, and
on occasion, political entourages attending the next state Republican convention. They were not the only freeloaders: the files of
the Wyoming Stock Growers Association are crammed with
requests to the secretary for passes. Ephraim Tillotson wrote
Thomas Sturgis: "I find that if you will intercede with the U. P.
for me, I have much better success."[1] J. R. Withrow, livestock

[7] Big Horn *Sentinel*, October 21, 1900.
[8] H. K. Thurber to Joseph C. Lea, December 20, 1888. Padgitt Collection,
San Antonio, Texas.
[9] Francis E. Warren to Melville Dunning, May 28, 1896. Warren Collection, Western History Research Center, University of Wyoming.
[1] Ephraim Tillotson to Thomas Sturgis, September 22, 1885. Wyoming
Stock Growers Association Collection, Western History Research Center,
University of Wyoming.

commission agent for the Union Pacific Railroad, wrote Thomas Sturgis:

It has been agreed by the lines in the Western Freight organization to make half-rates for shippers and their families, as well as members of your organization. Would you kindly pass the word along, as I have not the time to respond to all these letters.[2]

Understandably the railroad officials, after bestowing these favors, became ruffled when the delegates who rode their trains to the convention halls there proceeded to vilify railroad policies and rates.

The next year, Sturgis asked W. N. Babcock, passenger agent for the Union Pacific, about the policy on passes. Babcock replied tartly: "We will probably again issue them though you might inform your members we would appreciate a little more courtesy in their treatment at the convention."[3] Babcock might as well have shouted across the Nebraska prairies. The stock growers knew from the way they were wooed by Union Pacific officialdom (a wooing which grew more ardent in direct proportion to the Western track laying of the Chicago, Burlington and Quincy) that their pass privileges would not be discontinued no matter what they said about the railroad.

Were freight rates excessive? Yes, according to the vapid oratory against railroads by state and national stock associations; and yet there is striking evidence of the hollowness of these charges. In 1885, a government statistician, Joseph Nimmo, observed that the cost per head from Chicago to New York was $4.80, or the equivalent of 53 cents per hundred miles. The Northern Pacific Railroad charges of $6.65 per head from Miles City, or 56 cents per hundred miles, were a comparable rate. Further, since the Chicago-to-New York route was highly competitive whereas the Plains-to-Chicago route was relatively noncompetitive, it is difficult to believe that the railroads were "charging what the traffic would bear."[4] From the viewpoint of the railroads,

[2] J. R. Withrow to Thomas Sturgis, October 19, 1885. Ibid.
[3] W. N. Babcock to Thomas Sturgis, September 8, 1886. Ibid.
[4] Joseph Nimmo, Jr.: "The Range Cattle and Ranch Business," *Executive*

their freight policies only made economic good sense. As the New York and Chicago broker John F. Harris expressed it to Isaac Ellwood: "The Atchison Road has in the past and will in the future do all it can to foster the cattle interests, why would it follow any other policy?"[5] This was a rhetorical question yielding a pragmatic answer—it would not. His personal views to the contrary, the De Kalb manufacturer had to admit "there is considerable truth in what you say."[6] The Union Pacific Western division freight structure was far from stagnant. In 1885, charges were reduced by a quarter of a cent per pound. Two years later they were again reduced the same amount.

Yet cattlemen and railroad officials were bound to quarrel. Cattlemen grumbled about the destruction of their cattle by the "reckless engineers" on the way to markets, and they bewailed losses of steers that wandered on the track to be killed by those "belching fire engines." Surrendering to frustration, Babcock told Sturgis: "Your members have piled up claims on my desk of cattle killed by our trains until the number is almost half of the total assessed cattle along our rightway. Isn't this ridiculous?"[7] Sturgis was forced to concede that cattlemen had a propensity for seeing mirages of slaughtered cattle. Mutually dependent, the railroads and cattlemen remained mutually antagonistic into the twentieth century.

Railroad charges could at least be computed, but the weather was a perpetual gamble, since losses ran high during a severe winter. In an attempt both to minimize risk and to satisfy Eastern market demands for a better grade of cattle, managers in the 1890's turned to establishing feeding stations for their cattle. The discerning Western manager had recognized the portents of change in the range economy for some time. The West Las Animas *Leader* in December 1882 quoted an interview with an anonymous

Document 267, House of Representatives, 48th Congress, 2nd Session (Washington: 1884), 155.

[5] John Harris to Isaac Ellwood, February 14, 1894. Ellwood Collection, Western History Research Center, University of Wyoming.

[6] Isaac Ellwood to John Harris, March 5, 1894. Ibid.

[7] W. N. Babcock to Thomas Sturgis, July 9, 1886. Wyoming Stock Growers Association Collection, Western History Research Center, University of Wyoming.

manager: "The demand for feeders is increasing every season, for more corn and fewer cattle are being raised in those sections [Midwest] . . . they must look to the range and should plan our actions accordingly."[8]

After the terrible winter of 1886–7, the attention of Eastern investors was easily captured by the prospects of reducing losses by cattle feeding. But although an owner like William Hughes reacted favorably at first when his manager suggested that they establish a feeder ranch in Missouri for their Texas cattle, his fascination turned to skepticism after he had calculated the cost.[9] Friends of Hughes ignored his warnings and did establish their own feeding stations in Kansas, Missouri, and Illinois. Louis Stoddard questioned his manager, Charles O'Donel, about the possibility of the Bell Ranch purchasing feeding "farms" in Illinois. O'Donel cautiously opined that "perhaps we ought to go into the matter in some detail next season."[1] "Next season" never arrived as O'Donel procrastinated, developing one excuse after another until Stoddard finally took the hint and ceased writing on the subject.

Cattle-feeding operations achieved great popularity with cattlemen of the plains in the late 1880's and 1890's. Joseph Ames sent John Thomas a letter with the comment that some of "your friends have discussed the financial mess we are in."[2] On the third page, Ames finally arrived at his solution for the company's ills: "From talking with other friends who have been out there recently, everyone is discussing the rearing of feeder cattle, what do you think?" Thomas responded: "I have more than a few doubts about your proposal, but have sent [E. H.] Warner [his foreman] East to look over possible sites."[3] Warner toured the Midwestern countryside throughout the autumn of 1887 and finally became strongly attracted to Storm Lake, Iowa, "a very

[8] West Las Animas *Leader*, December 10, 1882.

[9] William E. Hughes to Joe Bragdon, June 8, 1892. Hughes Collection, Denver, Colorado.

[1] Charles O'Donel to Louis Stoddard, August 3, 1898. Bell Ranch Collection, University of New Mexico Library.

[2] Joseph Ames to John B. Thomas, June 29, 1887. Dunder Collection, Western History Research Center, University of Wyoming.

[3] John B. Thomas to Joseph Ames, July 17, 1887. Ibid.

pretty town of 2,500 inhabitants and a summer resort."[4] The tract
of land that Warner proposed purchasing contained 1,280 acres,
strategically situated with excellent railroad connections. Warner
wrote Thomas enumerating all the prominent and successful
cattle feeders in the Storm Lake vicinity, concluding: "They are
all *very* rich, I feel we will be like them in a short time, if you
will follow my advice."[5] Warner rambled on, sketching the fine
points of his plan for getting rich:

> I see nothing to prevent me from "going out and doing like-
> wise." I have found nature helps you far ahead of winter, and
> cattle will take in fat quicker with less expense, *they* helping
> you than you doing all the work, my theory being the nearer
> you treat animals as nature designed, the faster they improve,
> grass, warm weather, good water, a certain freedom, with corn
> and linseed cake ground and salt as nature bids them take it. . . .[6]

Then, using a technique of Brisbin's, Warner outlined the profits
from a "typical feeder" placed on the "verdant" grasses of an
Iowa "homestead." Charging off corn, linseed cake, and labor,
plus the initial cost of thirty dollars, Warner came up with a 58
per cent profit in six months of feeding. Letting nature take its
course, Warner insisted, steers would develop into sleek, portly
creatures at the rate of three pounds per day. "Now, John,"
finished Warner, "what do you think of our future?"

Wearied by the task of balancing his books for the past five
years, John Thomas remained skeptical. Instead of fat, dark red
Herefords, Thomas could only envision bright red figures on his
ledger page. Thomas sent a copy of Warner's letter to Ames, with
the note: "Warner tends to overstatement, but I suppose that the
reasoning he has done is fairly sound. I still have my doubts."[7]
The Suffolk Cattle Company's disastrous experiment in the feeding business justified Thomas's fears, for by 1889 the Suffolk debit
reached $57,000, primarily owing to the Iowa operation.[8]

[4] E. H. Warner to John B. Thomas, October 30, 1887. Ibid.
[5] Ibid.
[6] Ibid.
[7] John B. Thomas to Joseph Ames, November 14, 1887. Ibid.
[8] Suffolk Cattle Company Ledger, 1889, p. 16. Ibid.

What Ames and his investor acquaintances blithely ignored was the fact that cattle feeding could be as much of a speculative excursion as grazing the cattle on the open range. Dependent on the price of grain, the cattle feeder could easily slip into the vise of a rising grain market and a falling cattle market. The editor of the Laramie *Boomerang* summed up the situation in an essay euphoniously entitled "Gold in Wyoming Grass."[9] The editor pointed to the recent winter as a lesson to ranchmen, since hay had been $7.50 per ton immediately after the harvest and $20 a ton by November. The heavy snow, combined with the depleted crop of 1898, exhausted the surplus accumulated over the previous five years, and one merchant, August Trabing, was quoted as saying: "I was receiving telegrams from almost every station along the line of the Union Pacific, the burden of which was, 'Ship us hay at any price.' At one time I had orders for twenty-five cars and was unable to fill more than five cars."

The fluctuating valuation of feeders was a financial harassment year after year for numerous cattlemen. With only a limited time in which the cattle could be purchased, fed, and marketed, the cattle feeder was sometimes in the uncoveted stance of being forced to buy cattle on a rising market and to hope for high enough prices in six months to save him. When a cattle company's finances were already unstable, grafting on another business frequently gave the *coup de grâce* to the whole corporation. As Thomas pungently reminded Ames: "You thought our finances were in a horrible shape a year ago, you should see our books now!"[1] Ames replied: "We are all but ready to write the whole damn business off . . . all I can offer is my sympathy, you already have my money!"[2] Unquestionably cattle feeding could be a profitable enterprise; T. B. Hord amassed a fortune in grain and feeding businesses in Nebraska after the failure of the Lance Creek Cattle Company and the American Cattle Trust. The fact remained that unless they had magnanimous backers, the majority

[9] Laramie *Boomerang*, July 29, 1899.
[1] John B. Thomas to Joseph Ames, September 11, 1888. Dunder Collection, Western History Research Center, University of Wyoming.
[2] Joseph Ames to John B. Thomas, October 6, 1888. Ibid.

of cattle concerns could ill afford to take a flyer in cattle feeding during the transitional period of the nineties.

Speculative as it was, cattle feeding did not have the disastrous effects on a corporation that persistent range stocking did. Managers, at times with investors' support, would purchase huge herds even though the company was deeply in debt, on the assumption that the only way to rectify their financial state was to gamble all their fortunes on a hoped-for market rise. Portus Weare, on discovering that his nephew had purchased a herd of 3,000 cattle, had tremendous difficulty in controlling his temper. "Don't you think it would be better to rest a couple of seasons rather than dig our deep grave deeper?"[3] Fortunately for Weare and Company, and most of all for Henry, the nephew, cattle sales the next year proved so profitable as to liquidate a large portion of their entire indebtedness. "Something we can all be grateful for,"[4] Henry Weare undoubtedly wrote his uncle with genuine feeling.

Although fortified by the tremendous resources of Marshall Field and Levi Leiter, Colonel J. H. Pratt still winced at the advice of his partner and manager J. S. Collins to buy stock cattle "as quickly as we can" in 1893.[5] Never a man for subtlety, Pratt disagreed bluntly: "We could not justify an expenditure of this amount at this time, no matter how good it looks."[6] Collins stubbornly insisted: "You do not make any money in this business unless you are willing to invest in good times as well as bad . . . I disagree strongly with your argument."[7] Dissent Collins might, but Pratt stayed firm, and for the first time in three years, the Pratt-Ferris Cattle Company paid a dividend.

Two years later an acquaintance of Pratt's, Bartlett Richards, faced the same decision. A partner in the Spade Ranch in Nebraska, Richards was so successful in the cattle business that his operations attracted attention from the sandhills of Nebraska to

[3] Portus Weare to Henry Weare, May 17, 1893. Nason Collection, Spearfish, South Dakota.
[4] Henry Weare to Portus Weare, November 22, 1894. Ibid.
[5] J. S. Collins to J. H. Pratt, February 9, 1893. Pratt Collection, Nebraska State Historical Society.
[6] J. H. Pratt to J. S. Collins, February 21, 1893. Ibid.
[7] J. S. Collins to J. H. Pratt, March 6, 1893. Ibid.

Washington, D.C. Bennett Irwin, one of Richards's foremen, sent a letter in 1895 to Richards in Omaha outlining an opportunity to acquire 1,400 steers at "a ridiculously low figure."[8] At first Richards demurred on the basis of "unsettled" market conditions, but under Irwin's continuous appeals, he reconsidered and capitulated. Two years later, when he received his check from the commission house, he congenially confessed to Irwin: "That bargain was one of the best I ever made."[9] Unhappily, many Eastern investors and cattlemen did not receive such lucrative returns, and their correspondence exudes a nervousness bordering on panic. Caught in the overall economic downswing, and specifically the cyclic decline in the cattle market, many managers beseeched their investors to put up enough capital to increase their range stock.[1] Charles Elmendorf, who was reorganizing the American Valley Company, exerted all his influence with Thomas Catron and Stephen B. Elkins to restock the range.[2] Catron, settling his great bulk in an overburdened chair, wrote Elmendorf: "I wish you would straighten out the claims against the AV [American Valley] before you decide to make us millionaires . . . we will be lucky to stay afloat, let alone be affluent!"[3] As the involved affairs of the American Valley Company resisted solution, Catron's arguments were confirmed.

J. H. Barron, president of the New Hampshire Cattle Company, which merged with the Lance Creek Company, pleaded with Charles Smillie that their retrenchment policy was both unwise and unsound. Barron needled Smillie by pointing out that even taking into account the low market, the Lance Creek Company had not sent sufficient cattle to market for the past two years to meet expenses if they had received a munificent price. Sarcastically, Barron commented: "I thought we were in the cattle business to make money, how can we except to make our expenses

[8] Bennett Irwin to Bartlett Richards, March 22, 1895. Wightman Collection, Alliance, Nebraska.
[9] Bartlett Richards to Bennett Irwin, June 11, 1897. Ibid.
[1] Fels: *American Business Cycles, 1865-1897*, 189-94.
[2] Charles Elmendorf to Thomas Catron, September 11, 1899. Catron Collection, University of New Mexico Library.
[3] Thomas Catron to Charles Elmendorf, October 26, 1899. Ibid.

if we do not raise cattle?"⁴ Smillie cynically reminded Barron
that the New Hampshire Company had contributed much advice
but little capital to their merger. Further, the money situation
was extremely tight in the East, so that even if he agreed with
Barron's position (which he did not), the financial community
would have to be in a hypnotic trance before it could be induced
to "invest in a place they have already lost so much."⁵

The Barron-Smillie positions mirrored the diverse attitudes of
many investors and cattlemen. These questions became omnipresent during the 1890's when companies were debating whether
to liquidate or to gamble on the future by stocking cattle. If the
manager sold at the high tide of the market, he became a prophet
in the eyes of the investors, whereas if he sent the cattle to Chicago
at the bottom of the curve, his services were dispensable.

Together with range stocking and feeding, interest payments
absorbed a large proportion of a cattle company's returns. Myths
abound concerning the interest rates paid; and with currency
scarce, it is true that Western banks charged excessively high
interest—some as much as 2 or 3 per cent per month.⁶ Miguel
Otero, later governor of New Mexico, recounted how a cattleman might go to a bank to borrow $10,000 for six months and
have to pay 18 per cent interest "from maturity," the interest
of $900, plus 10 per cent commission, then being deducted in
advance. The commission charge, the borrower would be informed, came from rediscounting the note in the East. At this
point, the borrower could only sigh with relief to see the figure
of $8,100 neatly inscribed in his bank book. The well-worn note

⁴ J. H. Barron to Charles F. Smillie, January 21, 1887. Hord Collection,
Western History Research Center, University of Wyoming. Worried by
debts and frustrated in his managerial duties, Barron later committed suicide.
⁵ Charles F. Smillie to J. H. Barron, February 15, 1887. Ibid.
⁶ C. F. Coffee, a Texas and Wyoming cattleman, recalled: "We [A. H.
Webb, Coffee's partner] bought a herd of cattle, about 1,500 head, paid for
part of them and gave notes for the balance. We made for Cheyenne in
the summer of 1873. It being a poor year, we could not sell for as much
profit as I wanted to, so I had the cattle and wrote back to find out if
they would hold our paper for another year. I was favorably answered—
that they would if we would pay 2% per month or 24% per year. That
almost tickled us to death as we were paying 3% per month for what we
were getting at Cheyenne banks." *Letters from Old Friends and Members
of the Wyoming Stock Growers Association* (Cheyenne: 1923), 27.

was quickly dispatched to the East to be rediscounted at 4 per cent.[7]

What is commonly overlooked in discussions of exorbitant interest charges by Western banks is that except for short-term notes, the cattle industry was not financed by Western loans but by *Eastern* ones. Why pay even 1 per cent a month in the West, if you could get Eastern bankers to loan to you for 6 or 8 per cent annually? Should the Western cattleman have no "Cousin Joe" to write to at Newport, he became adept at ferreting out Eastern financial connections in order to take advantage of the low interest charges. At the height of the cattle expansion in the early 1880's, 8 per cent per year was a common Eastern charge for loans. William Tyler, president of the bank at Vincennes, Indiana, telegraphed Hay and Thomas in the spring of 1880: "We will charge you 8% which is 'rock bottom' here, we are having a large demand for money."[8] Henry Hay strained his friendly relations with Tyler by telegraphing back: "Your Shylock rates accepted!"[9] In the summer of 1879, A. W. Davis of Helena, Montana, inveigled $20,000 at 6 per cent for the Pioneer Cattle Company from capitalists in St. Louis. Davis joyfully reported to his partner Samuel Hauser that these were "the very best terms we could get."[1] Hauser must have smiled at Davis's naïveté, since the St. Louis financiers were old friends of Hauser and had promised him the loan six months before.

Reflecting national economic trends, interest rates vacillated throughout the 1880's and 1890's. J. P. Dilworth, cattleman of Southern Montana and Northern Wyoming, told his uncle in muddled syntax: "I can or could borrow $5,000 from the first National Bank of Billings for 12%, but can you do better?"[2] His uncle, J. R. Wilson, replied from Marion, Ohio, that he could

[7] Miguel Otero: *My Life on the Frontier*, 2 vols. (New York: Press of the Pioneers; 1935), 235.

[8] William Tyler to Henry Hay, April 17, 1880. Dunder Collection, Western History Research Center, University of Wyoming.

[9] Henry Hay to William Tyler, April 18, 1880. Ibid.

[1] A. W. Davis to Samuel Hauser, July 24, 1879. Hauser Collection, State Historical Society of Montana.

[2] J. P. Dilworth to J. R. Wilson, September 12, 1889. Tolman Collection, Clark, Wyoming.

indeed do better: "The funds will be forthcoming in the near future, though I am unsure of the rate it will be better than twelve per cent. We can't keep up with the money situation here as J. E. Stahl [the local banker] switches his advice weekly."[3] Henry Seligman kept his nephew in Montana informed on the money rate on Wall Street, writing in 1887: "I have discounted your note at six and five tenths per cent, the rate is stiff, but it was the best I could do at the present."[4]

Inspection of company ledgers indicates that the average interest paid for the decade of the 1880's came to approximately 8½ per cent for all loans, regardless of the duration of the loan.[5] During the 1890's the average sagged slightly to 8 per cent. For a given company or group of companies, it would be a game of fantasy to claim these figures were an impeccable guide. However, the sampling was geographically wide enough, the representation of both borrowers and lenders was diverse enough, and the time sequence was broad enough to make these averages useful as a general index.

Whatever expenses plagued manager and investor, the techniques and procedures for enticing funds varied but slightly. The theme was remarkably consistent; only the refrain changed from time to time. A popular device resorted to by company trustees was to issue bonds and then use these as security for loans. In the beginning when enthusiasm was high and confidence unlimited, many of these bond issues were debenture bonds, without security behind them. Unacceptable in sophisticated banking circles, debenture bonds were sacrificed at a discount and frequently absorbed by the trustees themselves, or by their friends if friends could be lured. In effect, the investor was subscribing additional stock (or becoming a stockholder) in the company,

---

[3] J. R. Wilson to J. P. Dilworth, October 8, 1889. Ibid.

[4] Henry Seligman to Albert Seligman, June 6, 1887. Seligman Collection, Baker Library, Harvard University.

[5] The companies whose ledgers were surveyed for the era 1880 to 1900 were Pratt-Ferris, Isaac Ellwood, Red Buttes Land and Cattle, Bell Ranch, Hay and Thomas, Lance Creek, Thomas and Page, N. R. Davis, Capitol Freehold, Pioneer Cattle, New Mexico Land and Livestock, Teschemacher and deBillier, Converse Cattle, Continental Land and Cattle, Weare Land and Livestock, Oasis Land and Cattle, Laramie Cattle, and Snyder Brothers.

because debenture bonds could be and frequently were converted into stock. As dividends waned, investors became skittish and debenture bonds had fewer and fewer purchasers. The Boston broker Henry Rice cleverly deduced: "What we are being asked to do is lend against loans for that is all that is behind these bonds, doesn't this strike you as a bit humorous?"[6] His partner George Denny, rooted in stern New England business practices, failed to see the comedy in the situation, although he did admit that it was fantastic. Debenture bonds lasted only as long as the dividends and the finances of the company appeared to merit the unsecured confidence; investors very quickly dropped these bonds and insisted on collateral bonds.

The disenchantment with debenture bonds coincided with the diminished enthusiasm for the cattle industry as an investment. The individual stockholder's misgivings increased in proportion to the absence of dividends. "When," wrote John Bigelow in his usually expressive manner, "do we see something come off your range instead of going onto it?"[7] Henry Seligman warned his nephew: "Your friends or mine are not going to trust you or me unless we start paying some of our indebtedness."[8]

Investors too ensnared to back out continued to put up capital, in the belief that the most logical way to salvage their original investment was to attempt to keep the company in the black. Entangled in the mesh of company finances, investors had little reticence about accusing everyone in sight of poor management. The manager came in for the most abuse, but investors also quarreled among themselves. The Boston banker Henry L. Higginson told James Converse that "the only thing we can do is appeal to the banks as I have suggested before. I am not inclined, if the rest of you are, to continue advancing Sturgis funds. He is perfectly reliable, but the cattle situation is getting worse in-

[6] Henry Rice to George Denny, February 2, 1886. Dunder Collection, Western History Research Center, University of Wyoming.

[7] John Bigelow to H. E. Teschemacher, July 29, 1885. Teschemacher and deBillier Collection, Western History Research Center, University of Wyoming.

[8] Henry Seligman to Albert Seligman, September 9, 1885. Henry Seligman Collection, Baker Library, Harvard University.

stead of improving. I do not like the risks we have been taking.
. . . I will be glad, if you wish, to help out with the banks."[9]
Converse, with some relish, relinquished the reorganization, and
eventually the affairs of liquidation, to Higginson.

Debentures were replaced by bonds backed by company assets,
but these bonds, while more acceptable, were still suspect. Lyman
Gage, former president of the First National Bank of Chicago,
remarked in a letter to Colonel Pratt: "The financial people here
are not interested anymore in accepting cattle of an undeter-
mined value and number, as collateral for your loans."[1] Gage's
sensitivity about the presence of cattle on the range was sharpened
by his experience with the Swan Land and Cattle Company debacle.[2] Gage's impressions of the financial climate were exaggerated,
however; bonds remained a common security for loans until the
commission houses and packers began dominating the cattle loan
market in the 1890's. Even then some commission firms accepted
bonds. Before the enclosure movement in the American West, cattle constituted the main collateral, but a succession of hard winters,
drought, and poor markets dampened the Eastern bank's willingness to take bovines as security. Instead, bankers began insisting
on real estate as backing for their loans. This change brought some
obvious problems for the cattlemen. Before the enclosure, companies held no more land than was necessary to keep water rights.
And even if a company had extensive landholdings, the cumulative value at two dollars an acre or less required an acreage of
XIT magnitude to be sufficient backing for a loan.

The application of Eastern real estate patterns to Western conditions led to more than one ludicrous miscomprehension. A. J.
Van Duzee, the manager of the Dubuque Cattle Company of
New Mexico, was astonished to receive a letter from his Mus-
catine, Iowa, banker: "We can not consider your note, since

[9] Henry L. Higginson to James Converse, January 24, 1888. Higginson
Collection, Baker Library, Harvard University.

[1] Lyman Gage to J. H. Pratt, April 2, 1889. Pratt Collection, Nebraska
State Historical Society.

[2] As president of the First National Bank of Chicago, Gage participated
in the organization and financing of a number of cattle corporations. With
the exception of the Weare Land and Cattle Company and Pratt-Ferris,
most of these ventures were, as Gage put it, "horrible trials."

you have no house or other substantial building on your land."[3]
That the appraisal of these "buildings" came to less than $3,000
Van Duzee had omitted. As he wrote to explain, however, ranch
residences in proximity to a community were frequently modest
abodes, because the managers and directors stayed in "town during the winter in more pretentious homes."[4] Isolated ranches had
more permanent residences, often as sumptuous as those in town.

During the 1885–90 era of financial adjustment, the trustees of
cattle corporations, unable to convince bankers of their solvency,
were left with no alternative but to advance their own capital
and feign loyalty to their friends' investments. A New York
broker, L. C. Iselin, answered George Colbourn's plea: "Between
now and the last of this week, I hope to scratch together $4,000
for you. I do not see at the moment where it is coming from.
I must look around and find one friend I have *not* called lately.
No cards!"[5] At least a certain credit could be given Iselin for
concocting an ingenious, if unbelievable, excuse.

Relations between managers and investors became increasingly
inflammable. Unable to satisfy their creditors with security of low-
value real estate and cattle whose worth would not be determined
until the fall sales, a seemingly inescapable predicament developed
for both parties. Arguments and disputes smoldered for months,
occasionally for years. Exasperated by the flow of counsel from
Augustus Gurnee, Hubert Teschemacher finally agreed that his
loans could be discounted at 5 per cent. "Take into consideration
the great difference in the ways of doing business East and West,
also the well known principle that if you get a good trade and also
a small concession and one can keep the other side good natured,
it is well to concede."[6] While Teschemacher's doubts were trans-
parent in the letter, he could invent no other path out of his

[3] Lewis Crandall to A. J. Van Duzee, August 14, 1885. Van Duzee Collection, Aurora, Illinois.

[4] A. J. Van Duzee to Lewis Crandall, September 7, 1885. Ibid.

[5] L. C. Iselin to George Colbourn, November 12, 1888. Iselin Collection,
Western Range Cattle Industry Collection, State Historical Society of
Colorado.

[6] H. E. Teschemacher to Augustus Gurnee, May 8, 1887. Teschemacher
and deBillier Collection, Western History Research Center, University of
Wyoming.

financial maze. A year later, when his notes went begging in spite of a 10 per cent discount offering, he looked back on this transaction as a highly opportune one.

In an effort to raise more capital, George Weare informed his brother Portus: "We could buy 2,000, 3,000 or 4,000 cattle of all ages and on a capital of $200,000 eventually work off our debts and hope to forget in a measure that we were once stockholders in a great company of $850,000."[7] Portus Weare could not forget or forgive his entanglement in a "great company of $850,000." Reluctantly he consented to go along with his brother, not from conviction but from desperation. On his personal obligation, the Continental Bank of Chicago loaned the Weare Land and Livestock Company $42,500 to purchase cattle;[8] and after a decade had passed, Portus Weare admitted that the decision had been a wise one, because the Weare Company paid dividends to cover his original investment.

Weare's personal endorsement of a corporation note, with other of his assets offered as collateral, was a typical approach to securing loans. Francis E. Warren mortgaged a sizable holding of Cheyenne real estate to save the Warren Land and Livestock Company.[9] Horace K. Thurber borrowed funds against his Arbuckle Coffee Company holdings for the Lea Cattle Company.[1] E. M. McGillin mortgaged his Cleveland dry-goods company to save his cattle firms, only to lose both the department store and his cattle investments.[2] Herman Oelrichs sighed and signed several notes for his brothers Charles and Harry.

In general, Eastern investors never resolved the dilemma in which they found themselves. Faced with substantial losses, the question perpetually arose: Why risk more? Their managers' arguments, regardless of eloquence, did not banish their fears.

[7] George Weare to Portus Weare, December 16, 1889. Nason Collection, Spearfish, South Dakota.
[8] Portus Weare to George Weare, January 18, 1890. Ibid.
[9] Francis E. Warren to W. W. Gleason, April 10, 1898. Warren Collection, Western History Research Center, University of Wyoming.
[1] H. K. Thurber to Joseph C. Lea, January 26, 1890. Padgitt Collection, San Antonio, Texas.
[2] See Gene M. Gressley: "The American Cattle Trust: A Study in Protest," *Pacific Historical Review*, XXX (February 1961), 61–77.

Joseph Ames commented to Thomas: "All strings I set up snapped this year, perhaps next year we can work them. But I do not have much faith myself, why or how can I convince our creditors?"[3]

Henry Hay, who later became assistant secretary of the United States Steel Company, nervously sought the advice of Thomas Sturgis in the winter of 1887: "I see no way but put up my Stock Growers Bank stock as collateral . . . see what you can raise in Boston . . . I would make almost any sacrifice in price to avoid going into debt further this year."[4] Sturgis found a Boston banker who would loan the capital for refinancing, but only with the stipulation that all unexpended funds in the fall, whether accrued from the loan or surplus from the cattle sales, would revert to a trusteeship of Boston financiers. Although Hay might consent to take a loss, he was not willing to sacrifice all pride or power; the envisioned consequences of the banker's requirement horrified him. "We might as well go into bankruptcy as to give over the management to those fools."[5] Five years later, exhausted mentally and physically, Hay exchanged the sagebrush of Wyoming for the sidewalks of New York.

John B. Thomas confessed to his Boston friend and associate, Joseph Ames, that the only collateral he had to offer was the Atlas Block in Cheyenne: "I can do very little myself, but I can talk pretty well yet and that is of some use to me. I *can* still sign my name, but that will soon be a useless operation."[6] If Thomas and his friends did not have sufficient collateral, they, like many of their investor acquaintances in the late 1880's, were forced to liquidate or to suffer a fate considered only slightly better— seeking a commission firm loan. Such a loan might ultimately find its way into the hands of packing firms, which one cattleman referred to as "a pack of gentle thieves."[7]

[3] Joseph Ames to John B. Thomas, June 30, 1887. Dunder Collection, Western History Research Center, University of Wyoming.

[4] Henry Hay to Thomas Sturgis, November 21, 1887. Wyoming Stock Growers Association Collection, Western History Research Center, University of Wyoming.

[5] Henry Hay to Thomas Sturgis, March 5, 1888. Ibid.

[6] John B. Thomas to Joseph Ames, June 21, 1889. Dunder Collection, Western History Research Center, University of Wyoming.

[7] John Walden to C. H. McIntire, April 8, 1879. Western Range Cattle Industry Collection, State Historical Society of Colorado.

Again and again one fact about cattle financing comes to the fore: in the early era of the industry, it was a matter of personal relationship. Organized with the bank accounts of Eastern friends or relatives, the corporation from its inception relied heavily on their continued good will. When the time arrived to refinance, which in some cases came embarrassingly soon after incorporation, the company was "thrown" on the generosity of its stockholders and their friends. If the corporation had the extreme good fortune to be supported by a Portus Weare, Marshall Field, H. J. Tilford, or Isaac Ellwood, its problem of access to capital was immeasurably lessened, though by no means solved. If the owner was forced into the unpleasant mission of visiting a banker or broker, the friendship of an H. L. Higginson, a Lyman Gage, or an A. J. Seligman became a crucial factor in economic deliverance. Obviously, a favorable interest rate, an acceptance of security, or the obtaining of a loan in the absence of collateral frequently hinged on the presence of a prominent financier on one's board of directors.[8] Not that personal relationships in the nineteenth century (or for that matter, the twentieth) were novel in corporate enterprises; rather, it is the degree to which cattle concerns were dependent on friendly assistance that should be noted. A marginal operation—highly speculative for most investors, with returns constantly in doubt—forced investors to operate on faith as to their ultimate reward. This was true not only as concerned future dividends, but also in regard to their trust in the policies of their managers two thousand miles distant. Faced with juggling interest, labor expenses, and cattle buying and feeding, the manager dangled on the good will of his investors to bail him out of his financial morass.

In macrocosm, cattle financing formed a well-structured pattern. In microcosm, the individual solutions reveal an imaginativeness that defies compartmentalization. The financial histories of three firms, the Lea Cattle Company, the Day Cattle Company, and the Lance Creek Company, illustrate a few of the highly

[8] The prospectus file of the Western Range Cattle Industry Collection is crammed with prospectuses listing blue-blood names such as Marshall Field, Lyman Gage, Herman Oelrichs, John Clay, John Arbuckle, James H. Ford, and Trenor W. Park.

original responses which cattlemen made to the challenges of cattle financing.

Captain Joseph Lea was born in Tennessee in 1841, served in the Confederate Army, and came to New Mexico in 1876.[9] Attracted by the nutritious grasses in Colfax County, Lea decided to raise sheep and cattle. He gained inspiration from the activities of his neighbor, John Chisum, whose success in ruling the Land of Enchantment has become part of Western folklore. Lea soon began casting about for a partner with the means to finance his ideas. He did not have to look far before he found Horace K. Thurber, partner in the Thurber-Arbuckle wholesale grocery house of New York and the United States Steamship Lines, who had journeyed West to Fort Stanton in 1883.[1] Stimulated by the land of the Chisums, Slaughters, and Waddinghams, Thurber had begun by purchasing a few sections of land. In association with John DeLany, post trader at Fort Stanton, he expanded his holdings: on April 23, 1885, the New York grocer and DeLany incorporated the El Capitan Land and Cattle Company for $300,000 paid-up capital.[2]

In the meantime, Captain Lea had contacted Thurber and outlined his own proposition in forceful language. A month after Thurber and DeLany had filed the El Capitan papers, Thurber and Lea incorporated the Lea Cattle Company with $1,000,000 capital stock.[3] Thurber, displaying all the symptoms of cattle fever syndrome, completed his investments that summer with a $250,000 stock subscription in the Arbuckle Post Percheon Ranch north of Cheyenne[4] and a $10,000 investment in the Teschemacher and deBillier Cattle Company.[5]

[9] Biographical data on Captain Lea is based on the Mesilla News, June 15, 1876; James C. Padgitt: "Captain Joseph C. Lea, the Father of Roswell," West Texas Historical Association Yearbook, XXXV (October 1959), 50–65; Sophie A. Poe: Buckboard Days (Caldwell, Idaho: Caxton Printers; 1936), 123–58; Field and Farm, May 18, 1889.

[1] Las Vegas Daily Optic, January 26, 1886.

[2] Incorporation records, New Mexico. Western Range Cattle Industry Collection, State Historical Society of Colorado.

[3] Ibid.

[4] PO Ranch Ledger, p. 53. Boice Collection, Western History Research Center, University of Wyoming.

[5] Teschemacher and deBillier Ledger, 1885–6. Teschemacher and deBillier Collection, Western History Research Center, University of Wyoming.

Under the Lea Cattle Company agreement, Lea sold 9,000 cattle to the company[6] for $250,000, and Thurber agreed to invest another $500,000 in cattle and $250,000 in obtaining water rights, land, and surplus for operating capital. Captain Lea's aggressiveness in procuring water rights was tattled to everyone by the Las Vegas *Optic*: "Captain Lea controls fifty miles of river frontage and numerous springs in Lincoln County."[7] With Thurber's blessing, Lea spent company funds at top speed for digging irrigation ditches, planting grain, laying out the town of Roswell, and stocking more cattle. The unending flow of Thurber gold and Lea initiative were to create, as the *Optic* mellifluously termed it: "a Garden of Eden in what was already paradise."[8]

Two years elapsed before Thurber attempted to call a halt to Lea's profligacy, although from the first year the drought combined with the sad cattle market put the Lea Cattle Company in a precarious state. Lea had a fundamentalist faith in the inexhaustibility of the Thurber millions; he deftly ignored the New York merchandiser's hair-raising communications to stop his drafts. In December 1886, Thurber fretted:

> Those cattle notes have got to be paid when due, and the heavy drafts you have been making on me have, as I fully explained to you before, taken all the money that I am willing to invest in Lincoln County, and I want to begin to get some of it back at as early a date as is possible.[9]

Annoyed and unrepentant, Lea volunteered to resign, but Thurber backed down, shaken by the thought of trying to run a cattle company from New York. Four days before Christmas in 1888, he was still speaking softly: "Captain, I have the greatest confidence in you—in your energy, honesty and earnestness, and I wish it were in my power to do all you ask of me."[1] But upon

[6] Las Vegas *Daily Optic*, May 8, 1885.

[7] Las Vegas *Daily Optic*, September 8, 1885.

[8] Ibid.

[9] H. K. Thurber to Joseph C. Lea, December 15, 1886. Padgitt Collection, San Antonio, Texas.

[1] H. K. Thurber to Joseph C. Lea, December 21, 1888. Ibid.

receiving Lea's latest group of drafts a few days later, Thurber's confidence melted: "Won't you please tell me the cost you have in regard to your cattle. . . . The reason I want this is, I wish to compare your expenses with those of other ranches, I have met so many people here who are in my situation."[2]

If Thurber's blunt tactics were devised to shock Captain Lea into recognizing the benefits of economy, it did not succeed. A more tempestuous exchange than the Thurber-Lea correspondence of 1888–9 would be difficult to imagine. Thurber had realized only two years of dividends on his entire investment in the New Mexico cattle industry.[3] Sitting in New York watching draft after draft fall on his desk, irritated beyond coherent expression, Thurber erupted with a stringent series of letters. On June 19, 1889, he said:

Now, my dear Captain, it is simply impossible; I cannot stand your drafts. I have told you over and over again that I have got to limit where I could go. I have told you that it was not a question of desire, but it was a question of necessity. I have advanced there to you about $800.00 in cash, and it simply is impossible for me to go any further. You tell me that a portion of this work is to be charged to you; suppose it is, that don't help me a bit. There is a large amount of back interest due me from you which I have not asked for, because I knew you could not pay it.

Captain, you have gone against my wishes, and simply draw on me, and I have paid and paid until I can go no further; and now I must request you peremptorily to stop all improvements and stop at once, unless you want your drafts returned to you and you be obliged to raise the money there at one enormous rate of interest. . . .

Now my dear Captain, don't think that this is pleasant for me to say to you, but it is necessary for you will certainly have

[2] H. K. Thurber to Joseph C. Lea, December 29, 1888. Ibid.

[3] The writer is deeply indebted to Colonel James T. Padgitt of San Antonio for providing access to the Thurber letters in his possession. The writer is also in debt to the Padgitts' hospitality, which he experienced in the Padgitt home in the winter of 1957 and the summer of 1962.

to get along on your own resources there. I must confess to my great disappointment at your going ahead as you have, when I told you for months past that there was a limit beyond which I could not go.[4]

Whether Lea was constitutionally unable to curtail expenses or whether he was too committed to be able to retreat is unknown. In any case, Thurber was far from satisfied. In late summer he sent Lea another letter, this time one of mixed sentiments.

Now, Captain, I want to reiterate, and I want you to believe that I am fully in accord with you and I firmly believe that you have done the best you could. The very large amount of money that I have put down there and so much that I didn't intend to, has put me in such shape that I can't get away. I have simply got to stay here and keep things going so as to pay the money that I have had to pay on those ranches.[5]

Part of the Lea Cattle Company's financial difficulty was caused by Captain Lea's inveterate habit of undertaking gigantic improvements. *Field and Farm* carried an article in November 1889 describing the construction of a six-mile flume conveying water to the desert on the Lea ranch.[6] The irrigated land was to be planted with alfalfa; the cost was reputed to be near $50,000. Earlier in the year, the same newspaper had given space to the Lea Cattle Company's extensive new ditching program which included the novel use of huge V-type scrapers, made to order in Denver.[7] Each scraper, powered by fourteen horses, was to displace "several tons of dirt a day." Considering the magnitude of these expenditures, one can read Thurber's letters with some sympathy. Having already advanced well over three quarters of a million dollars, Thurber lacked rapport with Lea's ambition of "making this the best ranch in New Mexico."[8]

The Christmas season of 1889 did not soften Thurber; on De-

[4] H. K. Thurber to Joseph C. Lea, July 19, 1889. Padgitt Collection, San Antonio, Texas.
[5] H. K. Thurber to Joseph C. Lea, August 27, 1889. Ibid.
[6] *Field and Farm*, November 30, 1889.
[7] Ibid., January 5, 1889.
[8] Joseph C. Lea to H. K. Thurber, October 25, 1888. Dow Collection, Roswell, New Mexico.

cember 22 he sat behind his ornately carved walnut desk and wearily composed another letter.

I have your letter with bill of Messrs. Poe, Lea & Cosgrove, and it just astonished me. My dear Captain, you keep telling me that you will stop drawing and stop these big expenses and yet they keep coming, and I have to pay so much money that I do not know where to get it; and it simply must stop, Captain.

Mind you, Captain, I am not blaming you, but I am only trying to impress it upon you that when you are getting $7 or $8 a head for calves a year old, you can't have the same expenses as when you got high prices for cattle.

I would like to know to what account to charge these groceries. I would be very glad not to complain, but I simply can't meet your demands, and your improvements have got to go; you have got to let them go by, and I have written you this so many times and I am almost ashamed to write it again.

Now, Captain, to go back to one thing: you are paying the same prices you formerly paid for help and you are paying the same prices for groceries, now when cattle are down in price, that you did when they were high, and it would seem to me that some of you must come to grief (as I have said before), going on that kind of a scale; and either you have got to run your cattle at a lower rate of expense or else there is no profit in it; and it seems to me that all of you men will have to get together and simply put the price of wages down and have less average expense—and that is only a necessity.[9]

Tired of Thurber's acrimonious letters, Lea insisted throughout the 1890's that the only solution was for Thurber to buy his interests. Thurber just as stubbornly refused to do so, on to the ill-founded logic that putting up with a spendthrift Lea was better than having a headless operation or than attempting to train a new manager. "In regard to buying you out, Captain, I haven't the slightest wish to do anything of the kind. How could I get along with that great big property?"[1]

The official end of the Thurber interests in New Mexico came with the drought of 1898, although the New York merchant had

[9] H. K. Thurber to Joseph C. Lea, December 23, 1889. Ibid.
[1] Ibid.

lost all personal concern five years before, when he gave up the idea that he would ever recoup the fortune he had sunk in New Mexico. Since he refused to replenish the company's treasuries, both the El Capitan and Lea Cattle Companies limped along. Finally in 1898 the Lea Cattle Company went into liquidation; a year later El Capitan closed its books, and the Thurber name vanished from the shadow of El Capitan Mountain. Few men had sustained greater losses in the range cattle industry. Investing at the peak of the boom and having a prodigal partner-manager who was himself ignorant of the risks involved, Thurber was foredoomed to financial disaster. Of all his investments, only the Arbuckle PO Ranch near Cheyenne proved really profitable; there he recouped his investment and got a handsome dividend.

In May 1889, Captain Joseph Lea married Mrs. Mabel Day, the "Cattle Queen" of Coleman County, Texas.[2] The Captain's bride was an amazingly resourceful young woman. The tale of her struggle to keep the Day estate intact after the death of her first husband in 1881 is unequaled for melodrama in the history of the cattle industry. The husband, W. H. Day, died intestate, leaving his widow and his year-old daughter a large but encumbered inheritance consisting of 77,550 acres enclosed by barbed wire; $33,000 worth of cattle on the trail contracted to his brother, James Munroe Day; and $2,000 in an Austin bank. Against these assets, Mabel Day soon discovered that there were liabilities— first, debts of $35,000 and then, after a year when all the claims had drifted in, of $117,500—an astronomical figure to the widow. The chief debts consisted of sections in the Day pasture which were enclosed but not paid for, and claims of other cattlemen against the estate.[3]

Unfortunately, Mabel Day had not only to contend with pressing claims of her creditors, but also with the rapacity of her brother-in-law and her husband's former business associates. The

[2] Again the writer is deeply in debt to Colonel Padgitt for providing his manuscript on the unique career of his grandmother, Mrs. Mabel Day. The following account is based heavily on this manuscript and on interviews and conversations with Colonel Padgitt in 1957, 1962, and 1965.

[3] Padgitt manuscript, 53–6.

first year and a half of her fight against these Texas cattlemen reads like a Victorian melodrama complete with Simon Legree villains in tooled boots and a beautiful heroine resplendent in a black lace dress.[4] The astonishing fact is that the melodrama so closely corresponded to reality.

One of the first issues facing Mabel Day was an agreement for the sale of 1,800 yearlings which the administrator of her husband's estate, Mr. Driskill, made with her brother-in-law, James Munroe Day. If this contract was accepted, she stood to lose $9,300, the difference between a higher bid and that of her brother-in-law.[5] After her vigorous protests were ignored, she resolved to borrow the money to pay off Driskill and have the court appoint her executrix of the estate in his stead. Neither step was easily accomplished. A James Taylor willingly consented to loan her the money, but in return he demanded a half interest in the Day cattle when all the claims against the estate were settled. Only after Mabel Day agreed to post a bond of $150,000 did the court appoint her administratrix, and this left her in charge of her own destiny but of little else. She owed money on the estate to the predatory Texas cattlemen, and somehow she had to pay for the large amount of unpurchased land in the Day enclosure.

After weeks of mulling the problem over, Mrs. Day decided that the only way out was to sell her cattle. But to whom? Certainly not to the Texas gentlemen, who had plagued her at every step; in all her experience with them, she had always had the worst of the bargain. Finally she recalled the wealthy distillers in the bluegrass region of Kentucky, where as a girl she had attended the female academy, Hocker College, at Lexington. She wrote her former professor, J. M. Hocker, frankly stating her problem and requesting his help. Hocker, as he was now in the omnibus business, had obviously exchanged grooming young ladies for horses, a perfectly reasonable switch in Kentucky. In a long and garrulous reply, he predicted that he could and would

[4] The Padgitt Collection contains many ardent testimonials from a wide range of suitors.
[5] Padgitt manuscripts, 57.

assist her. Soon afterward, Hocker and a William Tarr, a prominent distiller of Lexington, visited the Day ranch. In spite of the
drought conditions, the Lexington distiller was impressed with
what he saw. At the end of his visit Tarr told Mabel Day that
he would have to discuss the matter with his associates, Ephraim
Sayre, president of the First National Bank of Lexington, and
George White, a fellow distiller. Upon his return to Lexington,
Tarr wired Mrs. Day to come immediately to Kentucky to close
the negotiations.

The three gentlemen agreed to organize the Day Ranch Company with a capitalization of $200,000. They consented to give
Mrs. Day $75,000 immediately to settle the claims against the
cattle, on her promise that when she gave title to the cattle they
would be absolutely free of any obligations. Mr. Sayre had commented: "We don't want to buy ourselves any law suits."[6] The
agreement was struck, and the Lexington businessmen sent a
lawyer to Austin to investigate the legal difficulties involved in
settling the cattle claims. But these proved so severe that Judge
Hunt, the Lexington attorney, did not believe Mabel Day could
turn over the title to her cattle without the threat of a lawsuit.
Consequently he advised his clients in Kentucky to void the
contract. Faced with this new development, Mabel Day composed
a diplomatic letter to Mr. Hocker, pleading for time to resolve
her debts and asking his assistance in reopening the negotiations.
She concluded: "My notes become due the 4th of August, five
days off. Well, the darkest hour is just before the day."[7]

Unable to find anyone willing to loan her the needed money,
she left for New York City. On September 27, Mrs. Day exult-
antly reported to an old friend, Colonel Booth, a radical change
in her circumstances: "I returned from New York with some
money and succeeded in getting Mr. Taylor to settle for $41,915
cash. In doing that, the money I had gotten as an advance on my
trade [the $75,000 from the Lexington associates] became avail-
able to me and I have succeeded in settling those large debts

[6] Ibid., 77.
[7] Ibid., 84.

against my husband's estate and in closing the trade in Kentucky . . . first made."[8]

Mabel Day did not have long to enjoy her triumph, for in Texas a fence war broke out in which large cattle corporations, especially foreign and Northern companies (one and the same in the eyes of many Texans) had miles of their fences torn up.[9] Exasperated by her newest trouble, Mrs. Day told Colonel Booth, "I own all the land within its enclosure and if I want to let 'Northern capitalists' come and make fortunes in a few months or years, it is my affair—not Governor Ireland's."[1] The fence-cutting war subsided in 1884, leaving Mabel Day with miles of fence to repair at a cost which, together with her personal obligations, totaled $29,000. She also owed final payments to the state of Texas for lands in the Day pasture. A newspaper reporter had summed up her previous successes with the phrase: "She emerges triumphantly, a free, independent and happy woman"; but reviewing her debts, Mrs. Day could only lament: "I still owe better than $66,000 . . . that's a long way from being free and independent."[2] She never achieved her elusive goal of emancipation from debt, although she always did manage to liquidate her most pressing obligations. Looking over her business affairs at the end of the fence war, she summarized her situation to Colonel Booth: "I hope you will not suffer uneasiness, for I am bound to succeed. I will think of nothing else. I will go to the ranch and be so economical till I get out of debt."[3] For the next twenty years she fought to retain her ranch, and at her death she left sizable holdings to her daughter and grandson.

A much shorter-lived operation than Mrs. Day's was the Lance Creek Cattle Company, organized in 1886[4] and liquidated in 1891. At its genesis, the Wyoming company was a grafting of mal-

[8] Ibid., 87.
[9] A historical account of the fence war is available in Wayne Gard: "The Fence Cutters," *Southwestern Quarterly*, LI (1947).
[1] Padgitt manuscript, 87–8.
[2] Ibid., 117.
[3] Ibid.
[4] Incorporation records. Western Range Cattle Industry Collection, State Historical Society of Colorado.

formed limbs. It listed a capitalization of $10,000,000, which was largely an exercise in mythology, as the assets amounted to $210,033.21.[5] The leading entrepreneurs in the firm were T. B. Hord, who contributed his cattle ranch and feeding operations near Central City, Nebraska; Thomas B. Adams, who brought his North American Cattle Company into the Lance Creek concern; and Charles F. Smillie, a New York importer associated with several cattle enterprises in the Cheyenne vicinity. Throughout the short unhappy life of the Lance Creek Company, Adams and Smillie were the operational heads. Both in his position as secretary of the Wyoming Stock Growers Association and as resident manager-investor in the Lance Creek Company, Adams occupied a key position from which to assess the Western economic climate. Smillie, a shrewd judge of talent and money, possessed an uncanny ability to borrow with small collateral. One of the chief "hidden" assets of the Lance Creek firm consisted of the Adams-Smillie relationship; though it was often inflammatory, the two men acted together to pull the company through crisis after crisis which would have sunk many more substantial firms.

The first year of the Lance Creek Company was spent in solving organizational problems innate in the merging of several companies. But at the year's end, anyone casually glancing at the Lance Creek books could perceive that consolidation had not remedied their economic ills. Responding to Adams's distracted memorandum of late November 1887 for funds, Smillie calmly replied: "Tell me our total indebtedness as of *now*, and I will see what can be done."[6] A month passed and Smillie reassured Hord that funds would be deposited in the Stock Growers Bank to cover interest on the notes and pay off the principal of some. The New York broker added the postscript, "We must see what else we can think up to cut expenses."[7]

Whether in response to this injunction or as his own attempt at a cure for the company's troubles, Adams decided that expenses

[5] *Field and Farm*, March 6, 1886. Lance Creek Letterbook, 168. Western History Research Center University of Wyoming.
[6] Charles F. Smillie to Thomas Adams, November 28, 1887. Hord Collection, Western History Research Center, University of Wyoming.
[7] Charles F. Smillie to Thomas Adams, January 2, 1888. Ibid.

might be reduced by, one, joining the American Cattle Trust, and two, consolidating herds with yet another cattle firm, the New Hampshire Cattle Company. Unfortunately, neither solution proved fortunate. The American Cattle Trust, instead of being a source of economy, became an exasperating debit, while the manager and president of the New Hampshire Cattle Company, J. H. Barron, was an unruly business partner. Adams sent a letter to Hord in which he insisted on "the management of the combined herds being *under your control*, and having the 'financing' of the companies done through our office. I have not much faith in Mr. Barron's practical knowledge of the cattle business."[8] Two months later, Barron complained that he was receiving very little cooperation from anyone in the Lance Creek office: "Can't you do something about this?"[9] Adams not only refused to assist Barron; by now he had also come to distrust Hord's business acumen. One of the major defects of their business, he wrote Smillie, was that "It is simply impossible for me to get any satisfaction from Mr. Hord. He is not a business man, has not the slightest idea of the value of keeping track of little details, especially in financial matters."[1]

With managerial discord rife, it is not surprising that difficulty arose as to the efficiency of the operation. Smillie compulsively pressed Adams for a more exact forecast of expenses, "so that I may plan better at this end."[2] Nettled, Adams replied: "In regard to the amount of necessary money for running expenses on the range, I beg to say that expenses are likely to be around $500 per month."[3] Smillie, hoping beyond hope for a $29,000 profit from their feeding businesses at Central City, Nebraska, which could then be applied to their indebtedness, was highly distressed when the profit fell $11,000 short of the anticipated goal. Adams admitted disappointment too, noting: "The only point where we miscarried was the cost of feeding. It would be a very wise man that could possibly estimate the price of corn and hay . . . six

[8] Thomas Adams to T. B. Hord, March 12, 1888. Ibid.
[9] J. H. Barron to Thomas Adams, May 19, 1888. Ibid.
[1] Thomas Adams to Charles F. Smillie, May 23, 1888. Ibid.
[2] Charles F. Smillie to Thomas Adams, June 5, 1888. Ibid.
[3] Thomas Adams to Charles F. Smillie, June 26, 1888. Ibid.

months before the feeders are put on the market."[4] Smillie acknowledged that no person should shoulder the blame; nevertheless, he was at a loss as to where to turn to coax funds for running their company another year.

Beset by criticisms from Hord, Barron, and Smillie, Adams developed an intense case of nervous frustration. In answer to an attack from T. B. Hord, he fired back a letter which summed up the affairs of the Lance Creek Company:

> As regards feeding for the coming seasons, I have decided that it is impracticable. We cannot feed without a large outlay of money. We have two sources from which to obtain this commodity. One is our bondholders, who are already our creditors, and who are in a violent frame of mind, and would not advance us a dollar for any purpose. The other source is the western banks, and I have every reason to believe that if we were to borrow any money from them for any purpose, our present bondholder creditors would object and stop us. With the present range beef market, I do not believe that it would be justifiable to feed anyway....
>
> I am disgusted at the way in which things are going at sixes and sevens in the management of our business as no one seems to know exactly what he has authority and what he has not authority to do. So far as I am concerned, I do not propose to remain longer in this position unless we can get along more smoothly, and have some system agreed upon for the conduct of our business.[5]

Adams's spirits revived when six months later a higher market enabled the company to obtain a greater return. The respite was all too brief, however, for by another year the prospects looked as poor as ever. The gain for 1889 came to only $13,806.69,[6] not enough to keep up their interest payments and retire their debts, let alone pay any dividends. Adams told Smillie in a "My dear Charlie" letter that he had written the directors outlining the company's precarious position. "I do not expect they will get much encouragement from my communication, but the situation

[4] Thomas Adams to Charles F. Smillie, August 13, 1888. Ibid.
[5] Thomas Adams to T. B. Hord, August 29, 1888. Ibid.
[6] Lance Creek Company Letterbook II, 163. Ibid.

is unavoidable and they must grin and bear it."[7] Adams attributed the poor showing to low prices and to the failure of the corn crop, which resulted in a loss in their feeding operations. Then he made a basic admission: "Our resources are just too slim to weather continued crises." Adams could have applied the same generalization to the situation of eighty or ninety per cent of his fellow investors in the cattle industry.

The directors were discouraged by their losses, the managers were divided by dissension, and the cattle market was down (although it was soon to have an upswing); in light of these facts, the directors, on February 27, 1891, instructed Adams to liquidate, as Smillie said, "with as little pain but as fast as possible."[8] Adams carried out his instructions with relief, and the Lance Creek Cattle Company was no more.

Although they were highly individual and creative in their responses to challenges in company financing, the Lea, Day, and Lance Creek companies had many problems in common with other range corporations. All were concerned with high overhead caused by factors such as interest rates, the price of stockers, feeding operations, and the necessity of acquiring land. At one stage in their corporate existence, most were dependent on the generosity, or depending on your outlook, charity, of the Eastern investor. Indeed, the Lance Creek and Lea Cattle Companies were mere skeletons without the fat of Eastern dollars. With the high interest rates and the even higher skepticism of Western bankers after 1885, the cattle corporations had little choice than to search for financiers living in the East. Crucial to their success in Wall Street, Federal Square, or State Street was the personal relationship. In both East and West, family groups, investment cliques, and Union League Club associates smoothed the path along which the gold was dropped.

[7] Thomas Adams to Charles F. Smillie, August 16, 1890. Ibid.
[8] Charles F. Smillie to Thomas Adams, February 27, 1891. Ibid.

VII

"Dear friend, I have a business proposition to lay before you"

THE COMMISSION FIRM & THE BANKS

In the walnut-paneled parlor of his mansion in De Kalb, Illinois, in 1885, Isaac Ellwood pondered a letter from a new Kansas City acquaintance. On a recent trip there Ellwood had visited several commission agents, heard numerous proposals, and rejected all offers. Now he turned over in his mind a fresh overture from a commission man, J. P. Warner:

I have a business proposition to lay before you that promises a rich reward for anyone who can command means at the present time. . . . I do not want you to think I am visionary nor please don't pass this thing by lightly, its no speculation its uterly [sic] true and brought by the force of circumstances & when the conditions are changed we will never see the like again. Its our opportunity to make some quick & easy money . . .[1]

But Ellwood passed up the promise of a "rich reward"; a full two years went by before he decided to enter the ranching business in a major way. Many of his business associates, however, were seduced by the ingenious propositions of these commission agents. To many cattlemen, the commission agent was as big a villain as the railroad, but regardless of his contemporary reputation, he played an integral role in the range cattle industry. As a broker, adviser, and banker, the commission firm multiplied its functions as the nineteenth century advanced. Whatever the specific need—the sale of cattle in the Chicago stockyards, the purchase of land in the Texas panhandle, or the assumption of a loan for a cattle company in northern Montana—there was a commission firm eager, for a price, to provide the service.

In the formative years of the range cattle industry, the commission agent's activities pivoted around the brokerage of buying and selling cattle and land. As the capital requirements of the industry mushroomed, the commission firm assumed a vital function in quickly providing needed cash, for the Western bankers were either skittish or, in many cases, not even available for negotiating short loans. Thus the titles of prominent commission firms rolled off the lips of Western cattlemen as smoothly as the names of Arbuckle's Coffee or Sloan's Liniment.

The success of a commission firm depended on the popularity of its agent.[2] John Clay, who merited the description "canny" if ever a Scot did, had a paramount influence in the Wyoming Stock Growers Association for over three decades, and even served a hectic term as its president during the Johnson County War. In the natural course of events, Wyoming cattlemen fa-

[1] J. P. Warner to Isaac Ellwood, August 18, 1885. Ellwood Collection, Western History Research Center, University of Wyoming.

[2] Newspaper summaries of stock growers conventions invariably mentioned the names of commission agents attending.

vored the commission firm of this popular Scot. Thomas Sturgis urged his friend W. C. Lane to continue to send his cattle in care of the Clay firm, "as they have always done better by us than others."[3] Lane's inclination was toward spreading his business over several firms, but Sturgis's words carried the force of apostolic truth.

Joseph Rosenbaum, a highly successful Chicago competitor of John Clay, provided the financially teetering Montana cattlemen with a generous advance in credit after the collapse of 1886–7. The tale of Rosenbaum's financial rescue has become a classic still related, with embellishments, in the Treasure State. Learning of the disastrous collapse, Joseph Rosenbaum boarded the Northern Pacific for Helena. Upon arrival, he called together all the Montana cattlemen who were in debt to Rosenbaum and Company. The debtors came, though reluctantly and with considerable uneasiness, expecting to hear a sermon on the necessity of foreclosure. There was a hush as Rosenbaum rose to give his short speech, and when he sat down, the cattlemen were speechless. Instead of giving a scriptural message on liquidation, he had volunteered to lend them a million dollars to assist in recouping their losses. The generous offer was accepted and eventually entirely repaid. Twenty years later, when Rosenbaum's sons faced ruin because of a collapse in the Chicago Grain Exchange, Montana cattlemen amassed a million-dollar credit for them. This timely assistance enabled the Rosenbaums not only to regain their losses, but also to reap a handsome profit.[4]

The Clays and Rosenbaums centered their commission businesses in Chicago, and another group of firms clustered around Kansas City. There Frank L. Underwood[5] played host to visit-

[3] Thomas Sturgis to W. C. Lane, September 16, 1883. Wyoming Stock Growers Association Collection, Western History Research Center, University of Wyoming.

[4] Charles W. Towne and Edward N. Wentworth: *Cattle and Men* (Norman: University of Oklahoma Press; 1955), 268–9.

[5] For the Underwood–Prairie Cattle Company relationship, see Maurice Frink, W. Turrentine Jackson, and Agnes Wright Spring: *When Grass Was King* (Boulder: University of Colorado Press; 1956), 200–4. Other pieces of the Prairie history can be garnered from Albert W. Thompson: "The Great Prairie Cattle Company, Ltd.," *Colorado Magazine*, XXII (March

ing Scotch and British capitalists, charming them into leaving their capital and their affairs in his "trustworthy" hands. Andrew Snider,[6] who had the vision to carve up huge sections of un-occupied territory in the Texas panhandle and Cherokee strip, exemplified the commission agent who practiced what he preached. Throughout 1882, the Kansas City *Livestock Indicator* sandwiched references to Andrew Snider's most recent "bar-gain" in its columns.[7] Albert G. Evans of the flourishing partner-ship of Hunter and Evans adroitly guided his firm in and out of successive ranching operations. In many ways, the Hunter and Evans alliance typified the successful commission firm that had no hesitation in following the advice it so freely offered its clients. They purchased and organized a host of cattle companies, until their brands at one time stretched from the forty-sixth to the thirty-first parallel. Hunter lived in St. Louis, "the gateway to the West," and Evans in Kansas City, ideally situated at the geographic bottom of the trade funnel of the Southwest.[8]

1945), 76–83; *Red River Chronicle*, November 3, 1883; Cimmaron *News and Press*, October 24, 1881; Las Vegas *Daily Optic*, February 21, 1885; *Field and Farm*, June 19, 1886; Kansas City *Livestock Indicator*, December 12, 1889.

[6] The Kansas City *Livestock Indicator* referred to Andrew J. Snider as "a genial, courteous, six-foot high, horny-handed cattleman." Snider was born in Fairfield County, Ohio, on March 3, 1833. At the age of eleven, Snider "was thrown on his own resources." Over the next nine years, he worked, in peripatetic manner, as a cattle driver, plasterer, seaman, and stage driver. In 1857, he landed in Denver, Colorado. He developed a lucra-tive freighting business between Denver and the Virginia City region of Montana. In 1870, he again changed vocations by moving to Kansas City and establishing a commission business. Nine years later, he sold his business to James H. Campbell and joined his son in a commission firm. By 1884, this firm was handling 40 per cent of the total receipts in Kansas City. Snider died in 1893. Kansas City *Livestock Indicator*, August 16, 1885; J. W. Freeman (ed.): *Prose and Poetry of the Livestock Industry* (Kansas City, Mo.: 1905), 747; *Field and Farm*, January 16, 1886, May 7, 1892, August 3, 1889.

[7] Kansas City *Livestock Indicator*, September 28, 1882; January 27, 1882; November 11, 1882.

[8] A characteristic of commission organizations was the constant divorce and regrouping that went on between partners. The Hunter and Evans concern is a prime illustration. In 1883, the firm first appeared in St. Louis as Hunter and Evans. In 1888, M. P. Buel joined, and "Company" was added to the title. By 1892, Buel's name was given free billing. Evans died and Hunter then retired, and A. J. Snider, Jr., decided to ally himself with the firm. The new name became Snider and Buel. (St. Louis Public Library to Gene M. Gressley, February 3, 1957.)

In December 1874, John Chisum of New Mexico sold one of his ranches to Hunter for $319,940. If the estimated 30,000 head of cattle was an actual count rather than a book count, Hunter had reason to be pleased with the deal. As an illustration of the seriousness with which Hunter took his ranch, the Mesilla *News* reported that Colonel Hunter had "on the way . . . 221 fine bulls from Kentucky to place on his new ranch."[9] Few cattlemen as early as 1875 were doing anything to upgrade the quality of their stock, let alone importing bulls in this fantastic proportion.

Five years later, Hunter and Evans turned their attention east from New Mexico to Texas by assuming the debts of, and one-third interest in, the Driskill Ranch in the Cherokee strip for $225,000.[1] Although "Uncle Jess" Driskill supposedly possessed 54,000 cattle, this figure was based on book count, so that Hunter must have known they were purchasing as much wind, sand, and stars as they did cattle. The Hunter-Evans lawyers were again busy in 1883 organizing the Comanche Land and Cattle Company for $1,000,000[2] These papers had no more than come to rest on the desk of the secretary of state before Hunter and Evans were incorporating the Running Water Land and Cattle Company with an announced capitalization of $1,500,000. A month later, the busy partners filed the incorporation papers of the Hunter and Evans Land and Cattle Company in St. Claire, Illinois, this time listing a capitalization of $2,000,000.[3] Colonel Hunter was not bluffing when he advised his clients "to go and do likewise."

The Kansas City *Livestock Indicator* informed its readers that the Hunter-Evans combination "has been rumored to have over six million in cattle companies."[4] Nor were these partners alone among commission agents in assuming the role of cattle kings; other firms, although they did not assemble empires comparable to Evans and Hunter's, also acquired significant range holdings. John Clay

9 The Mesilla *News*, December 4, 1874.
1 Kansas City *Livestock Indicator*, July 27, 1882.
2 Ibid., March 8, 1883.
3 Ibid., June 6 and 25, 1885.
4 Ibid., August 9, 1885.

not only directed the affairs of the Swan Land and Cattle Company and Western Ranches, Ltd., but his firm held stock in both concerns. Frank L. Underwood absorbed a small amount of the stock in both the Prairie Cattle and the Palo Blanco Companies. Frequently the commission firm bought stock at the behest of its clients, for it was somehow comforting to investors if their agents volunteered in the sink-or-swim-together spirit.

The mechanics involved in the commission operation of taking a consignment of cattle and negotiating with a buyer at the stockyards followed a rigid pattern year after year. Each spring the commission houses sent their salesmen West to drum up business for the fall; in "Round about the Town" columns, Western newspapers reported their arrival at "The Inter-Ocean," "Briar Inn," or other splendid hostelries. Usually, the agreement between rancher and commission agent was reached in a civilized fashion at the "Buffalo Bar" or some other popular emporium such as the Cheyenne Club.

When the commission firm or cattleman wanted to assure the receipt of a specified number of cattle, a formal document was drawn up. This agreement stipulated the number of cattle: "not more than ——— nor less than ———"; specified the age and grade: "all native raised"; and the delivery date: "between September 10th and September 30th, 1898." It also specified that all cattle were to be in good health and that the shipment would contain no runts, scrubs, blind animals, or diseased ones, and that all cattle which could be classed as Mexican or which were "yellow, black brindle or buckskin collars" were to be cut out prior to delivery.[5] The price was left to the market conditions prevailing whenever the cattle arrived at the stockyards. Although there were occasions when both the firm and the cattleman would gamble and set a price for delivery six months in advance, this practice became common only with the more stable market conditions at the close of the nineteenth century.

[5] This paragraph is a composite of several agreements, but especially one between F. S. Scott, Willcox, Arizona, and Clay and Forrest, Chicago, Illinois, April 11, 1899. John Clay and Company, Denver, Colorado.

Once the cattle had been consigned, the commission firm tacitly adopted the role of banker for the cattle corporation. If a cattle company discovered a shortage of funds in mid-July, an appeal immediately went out to the commission firm for an advance on anticipated receipts in the autumn. A. J. Davis of the Pioneer Cattle Company of Montana asked the Rosenbaum firm for $15,000 in August of 1884: "We are in a temporarily tight situation which should be better in a few months."[6] Rosenbaum quickly responded that they would be "pleased to loan the money, but we do expect all your cattle this year."[7] Then, to soften the impression: "We know you are usually good customers." Davis, not to be intimidated, shrewdly remarked to Rosenbaum: "You will receive our best intentions if we receive yours."[8] The implication could not be missed: if the loan and interest were advantageous, the Rosenbaums could expect their consideration. This exchange was fairly typical; there was perpetual sparring between commission firms and cattle companies over consignment of business in response to favorable action on a loan. In the early years of the range industry, cattle corporations on principle disliked committing their fortunes to the hands of a single commission firm. In part, this was due to the pervasive rumors, season after season, of collusion between packers and commission firms. The gossip was never proved or disproved; whether true or false, it lingered on.

Whether or not a cattle company required more money at midsummer, it was customary to draw on the commission firm for an advance as fall marketing time approached. This practice, plus the high cost of feeding and the dehydration of cattle, usually precipitated a quick sale by the commission agent, once the cattle limped out of the stock cars. The early-morning scene at the stockyards was a memorable one, with cattle bawling, agents loudly huckstering, and the omnipresent stench. The day's end was signaled "by common consent . . . at 3 o'clock p.m., at which

6 A. J. Davis to the Rosenbaum Brothers, August 4, 1884. Hauser Collection, Historical Society of Montana.
7 Rosenbaum Brothers to A. J. Davis, August 23, 1884. Ibid.
8 A. J. Davis to the Rosenbaum Brothers, September 5, 1884. Ibid.

time a whistle on the engine-house near the water tank is blown."[9] Chaos retreated, even if the odor remained.

Discord sprang from the intrinsic nature of the commission firm–cattleman relationship. The cattleman, loading his animals in stock cars to be unloaded a thousand miles distant and surrendered them to the whims of a capricious market, was uneasy from the moment the train disappeared. If the price received meant disaster for his company—and for many owners, this was a constant possibility after 1885—he immediately vented his displeasure on the most obvious straw man, the commission agent. Attacking railroads and commission firms was a popular pastime. The files of stock associations and cattle companies are stuffed with ulcer-forming correspondence among cattlemen, investors, and commission firms.

The Wood Brothers, in response to a purple-prose letter from Thomas and Page, offered a stereotyped and unoriginal analysis of the low market: "The run of cattle for the past few days—in fact for two weeks, has been heavy and there has been a marked decline in values—especially anything not strictly fat."[1] Clay, Robinson, and Company, baffled by the recalcitrant attitude of John Brush, a Greeley, Colorado, cattleman, wrote: "We have always tried to do our best by our customers. You received better prices than many and yet you complain most . . . if you still are not satisfied we will be happy to recommend your business to one of our friends."[2] Evidently Brush refused to accept the hint, for the following year he was again engaged in the lively sport of debating with the Clay organization.

The fluid character of the cattle market was reflected in the Rosenbaum Company's letter of "explanation" to the Weares in the fall of 1888:

[9] Edward W. Perry: "Livestock and Meat Traffic of Chicago," *House Miscellaneous Document 25*, 48th Congress, 2nd Session, Vol. II, 1884–5, 10. Perry provides a vivid description of the Chicago stockyards in this selection.

[1] Wood Brothers to John B. Thomas, October 21, 1882. Dunder Collection, Western History Research Center, University of Wyoming.

[2] John Clay to John Brush, November 17, 1887. Western Range Cattle Industry Collection, State Historical Society of Colorado.

We have made it a point during the last ten days to sell every afternoon and it has saved thousands of dollars to our clients. Every salesman who has carried over has suffered by it: we may change our policy of course next week, meantime this is the course we have pursued . . . 14,000 cattle today again and there will be no improvement this week. I am sorry personally your cattle came on such a bad market but we cannot help it.[3]

Because of the Weares' personal involvement in a commission business, they were more sympathetic than most cattlemen with the problems plaguing the Rosenbaums.

A favored device used by the commission firm to turn the wrath of a disappointed shipper was to blame another agency—especially the railroads, since these were already on the cattleman's list of bogeymen. Thus the Wood Brothers lamented to Isaac Ellwood: "Had these cattle arrived yesterday morning, when they were due here, we could have had no difficulty in realizing, at least 10¢ more for them, and perhaps 15¢."[4] The Wood letter ended with a proposed remedy: "The railroad company is responsible for the delay on Wednesday. . . . We believe they should make those losses good to you. Thank you for your continued remembrance and confidence."

Whether Ellwood accepted the commission firm's analysis is unknown; however, if he followed the practice of his fellow cattlemen, he lodged a protest with the railroad and then forgot about it. Railroads commonly accepted a percentage of claims for cattle killed or maimed in shipment, but they were less ready to reimburse for delayed shipments. As the freight agent of the Northern Pacific wrote Samuel Hauser: "There are too many things which we cannot control to take your accusation [delayed freight] seriously. Were you in our place you would agree."[5] The point was, of course, that Hauser was not in their place and he did not agree.

[3] Rosenbaum Brothers to Henry Weare, November 12, 1888. Nason Collection, Spearfish, South Dakota.
[4] Wood Brothers to Isaac Ellwood, September 23, 1898. Ellwood Collection, Western History Research Center, University of Wyoming.
[5] Edward Dowley to Samuel T. Hauser, October 23, 1884. Hauser Collection, Historical Society of Montana.

The letter of J. N. Tolman of the Dilworth Cattle Company, although more emphatic than most, exemplifies the complaints which commission agents faced when they walked into their offices to begin the day. Tolman, discovering that a neighbor's cattle had brought better prices on the market than his own shipment, began a letter to Rosenbaum with an effort to be calm, dispassionate, and totally logical, but halfway through it, his emotions conquered.

I can not understand why the Murphy cattle—which were *gathered at the same time,* off the *same* range, where they have been running together for years and shipped the *same* day— from the same point and in the *same* kind of *cars,* should have sold *very* much better than the Dilworth cattle. . . . There is no possible doubt that the Dilworth cattle were as good as the Murphy cattle. And yet the Murphy cattle sold better than the Dilworth cattle, can you explain this?[6]

The Rosenbaums evidently did not succeed in enlightening Tolman to his satisfaction, for the next year he sent his cattle in care of Clay, Robinson and Company.

Yet when the eccentric ways of the cattle market perplexed even the commission concerns who were on the scene, how could a commission firm successfully defend itself against an irate shipper? How were they to explain to a distraught cattleman 1,300 miles distant why the prices had been so low on the day his cattle were sold? Always hopeful, the firm would attempt a propitiatory answer to these explosive letters, but the cattlemen naturally refused to be mollified when several thousand dollars were involved. What is less reasonable is that both cattlemen and investors wailed to their commission agents year after year, when it was obvious to all that the market was sluggish. Eastern investors, as uneducated in the mystique of the cattle market as their managers, fumbled for an explanation at their leisure. Levi Leiter, one of the more sophisticated and analytical of investors, went out to the stock-yards himself in order, as he remarked to Colonel James H. Pratt, "to see what is going on out there. I concluded that anyone who

[6] J. N. Tolman to Rosenbaum Brothers, October 1, 1891. Tolman Collection, Clark, Wyoming.

dabbled in the cattle market is probably a fool."⁷ Yet Leiter retained his investments in the Pratt-Ferris Cattle Company for twenty years, and the dividend checks that he received hardly made him look like a fool.

Through the mid-nineties, the Clays, Rosenbaums, and Woods assisted in financing cattle corporations by advancing funds on anticipated sales, or else by extending loans. Later, when faced with competition from the cattle loan companies backed by the packing industry, some commission firms accepted longer loans.

While the Clays and Rosenbaums did own stock in cattle enterprises, their primary interest was in the commission side of the cattle business. Another group of commission brokers emphasized the acquisition of real estate, and these firms provided longer-term loans as well as assuming the financial management of cattle corporations for absentee owners. During the decade of the eighties, Frank L. Underwood, W. A. Clark, A. J. Snider, and Francis Smith attracted and channeled sizable amounts of Eastern and foreign capital into the West. Underwood and Clark preferred concentrating on pure brokerage rather than becoming entangled in the managerial end, although in response to demand from foreign investors they did perform this service.

One of the most successful firms, which deserved the confidence its investors gave it, was Francis Smith and Company, whose offices were in Indianapolis, Memphis, and San Antonio. Smith's initiation into brokerage for American insurance companies came in 1872 when the Equitable Trust Company of New York appointed him its agent in Indianapolis.⁸ Success must have been rapid, for he was soon a large stockholder in the company. Three years after this

⁷ Levi Leiter to J. H. Pratt, September 17, 1880. Pratt Collection, Nebraska State Historical Society.
⁸ Francis Smith was born near St. Albans, England, "in the South front bedroom . . . overlooking Watling road," on May 28, 1834. William Smith, Francis's father, realizing that without "strong family influence" there would be little opportunity for a family of boys "to get on," decided to emigrate to America in 1847. The Smith family first settled in Toronto, Canada, where William Smith manufactured tallow candles. The business collapsed, so in 1850 the Smiths moved to Canandaigua, New York, where William Smith died in 1866. Francis Smith: "My Family." Carlile Bolton-Smith Collection, Washington, D.C.

appointment, Smith went abroad, visited several investment companies in Great Britain, and thereby became the agent for the Scottish-American Mortgage Company and the Dundee Mortgage and Trust Investment Company.

The New England life insurance companies proved stiff competition for the foreign concerns; by 1879, the rates in farm loans slid from 10 to 8 per cent. The death knell to foreign investment in Indiana was administered by the state legislature when it passed a bill withdrawing the protection of the courts from nonresident corporations.[9] Disgusted and angered by this discrimination, British companies decided to shift their capital to Canada, but Smith convinced them that the American South was a greater investment field than Canada. So accurate was Smith's prognostication that by 1884, over twenty British companies had established offices below the Mason-Dixon line and were "investing tens of millions of dollars."[1]

In the early 1880's Francis Smith and his partners, who included his son Bolton Smith, A. S. Caldwell, and John M. Judah, opened a branch office in San Antonio, Texas. The first area that attracted

[9] Francis Smith: "The Revival of the South, due to Foreign Money," 3. Ibid.
[1] On the problems, difficulties, and variations in cultural patterns between investing in the North and the South, Francis Smith wrote an amusing commentary: "Instead of a quiet, plodding farmer of the North, who with his family did all of his own work upon fifty to two hundred acres of land, the Southern planter was found to be a sensitive, high-spirited gentleman, who would not soil his hands with labor. He was frequently a general, a colonel or major, whose farming was done in gloves and on horseback and by negroes under his overseer. . . . It was not an unusual thing for the owner of a large plantation to come into the office and announce that he owned so much land in such a county, throw his deeds upon the counter and demand the sum of money he required forthwith, to take home with him by the next train or steamboat, and he became very angry if his demand was refused. It required time to educate the people from this, the old condition of things, to the new and necessary one. . . ." Nevertheless, for all the trials and tribulations of being a broker in the South, Francis Smith believed he had made a viable contribution to the economic resurrection of the South, for he concluded, "Much has been said and written about the 'revival of the South.' Many magazine articles have eloquently attributed it to various causes—to all but the right one. The real cause of the revival of the South was the introduction of cheap foreign money, which ignored all political conditions and gave a money value to the land by considering it a safe collateral to loan money upon." Ibid.

Smith's eye was the southern counties of the Lone Star State along the lower Rio Grande. Smith had been ill, and since his doctor had prescribed plenty of fresh air, he decided to combine business with his physician's advice and tour Texas.[2] With an interpreter he traveled over much of the Rio Grande and Brazos River areas, eventually wandering up into the panhandle. Smith was impressed and excited by the country: here were possibilities for profit that exceeded his investments in Southern plantations. His enthusiasm was evidently contagious, for soon his British and American clients were sending him capital to be put into Western real estate.

In the winter of 1887, Francis Smith, Caldwell and Company dissolved. Francis Smith retained the San Antonio office and the ranch business,[3] A. S. Caldwell and Bolton Smith returned to Memphis and plantation investments, and John M. Judah retired, although he stayed with Francis Smith as a private investor. On January 1, 1890, Francis Smith again added "company" to his corporate title by bringing into the firm H. P. Drought, a young lawyer who previously had been associated with another loan agency, Ballantyne, Patterson, and Scudder. Drought, an aggressive, bright, and astute businessman, was, like Smith, an "instinctive broker." He had the uncanny ability to estimate at once the promise of a borrower and the generosity of a lender. Precisely a decade later, on January 1, 1900, Francis Smith retired and the firm at 108 Yturri Street became H. P. Drought and Company.[4]

While most of Francis Smith and Company's investors were from the British Isles, whether he was negotiating for one of them or for an American client his procedure followed the same well-organized pattern. His British clients might demand more information on the gyrations of American politics, the newest tax and alien laws, or a recent judicial decision, but the mechanics of loaning capital, whether pounds or dollars, were basically the same.

When one investor had the temerity to question a recent Smith-

[2] "Historical Memorandum." Smith Collection, H. P. Drought and Company, San Antonio, Texas.
[3] Ibid.
[4] Ibid. (The firm he established is carried on in San Antonio in the mid-twentieth century by his grandson, Thomas Drought).

approved loan, the San Antonio commission agent succinctly stated his lending philosophy:

It is only those [loans] that we consider strictly first class in all respects, viz. character and location of the security and character of the borrower, that we accept. To get these loans upon our books we often have to make some concessions and promises as to right of pre-payment, etc., all of which are more or less demanded by the best borrowers and we want none other.[5]

On another occasion when Smith was challenged, he gave his reasons for preferring "range" loans to "farm" loans. He claimed that not only was the farmer more at the mercy of the elements than a rancher, but his labor supply fluctuated more and was more undependable. Furthermore, Smith reasoned: "The owner of a pasture is a man of broader mind and broader means than that of a small agriculturist." As proof, he stated: "This is illustrated by the fact that while the cattle man has generally good credit in banks anywhere in Texas, the men who are strictly farmers have scarcely any credit whatever with the banks."[6] Also, the loans per acre were much smaller on pasture than on a farm, and the titles were safer and far easier to abstract, thus reducing transferral costs. What Smith neglected to explain was that the ease with which cattlemen could get credit was due to the fact that they owned the banks! It also is doubtful that the weather dealt more harshly with the farmer than the rancher in the big droughts of 1890 to 1894.[7] Whether Smith's reasoning was fallacious or not, the twenty-page letter in which he stated it satisfied the curiosity of the correspondent, for in the next communication this client suggested that in the future their letter style should tend toward "brevity."

[5] Francis Smith to Northern Counties Investment Trust, April 18, 1893. Letterbook 3. Ibid.

[6] Francis Smith to Canadian-American Mortgage and Trust Company, January 23, 1890. Letterbook 5. Ibid.

[7] On the droughts in the Southwest, see Roy Sylvan Dunn: "Drought in West Texas, 1890–1894," *West Texas Historical Association Year Book*, XXXVII (October 1961), 121–36; W. C. Holden: *The Spur Ranch* (Boston: Christopher Publ. House; 1934), 44–50; W. C. Holden: "West Texas Drought," *Southwestern Historical Quarterly*, XXXII (October 1928), 103–23.

The daily routine of conducting a commission business, of course, brought more problems than those involved in selecting the "right" borrowers, though in the long run a lack of judgment in this matter could ruin a commission firm. As Francis Smith told one customer: "We know by experience that one bad loan can give us more trouble than 500 good ones."[8] Another vexing problem for Smith was how to reduce or eliminate overhead on the local agent, or as Joseph Lea described him, "the double middleman."[9] Smith was incensed with competitors who circularized every county attorney advising that he would receive "plush commissions" by sending applications to their firm instead of to Smith's. "It is bad enough to maintain an effective agency without being liberal in this regard."[1]

Most local agents would receive a 1 per cent commission for securing a loan, or as high as 2 per cent when good loans were scarce. The difficulty with this, both for the lender and for the commission house, is evident. If a loan was negotiated at 8 per cent, then the local agent absorbed 1 per cent, Francis Smith appropriated another 2 per cent, and the client was left with a 5 per cent return on his investment. This much overhead seemed unreasonable to many investors. With annoying frequency, letters delivered to 108 Yturri Street, San Antonio, complained about the amount "you make on us for taking our money." To these correspondents, Francis Smith Company had a consistent, if stale, answer: "We are operating on the narrowest margin commensurate with good service . . . our competitors are having twice the number of losses."[2] In effect, Smith suggested that they were free to wander across the street, but if they did, they could expect to suffer even more than they were now.

The American insurance companies appreciated Francis Smith's

[8] Francis Smith to Canadian-American Mortgage and Trust Company, January 23, 1890. Letterbook 5, Smith Collection, H. P. Drought and Company, San Antonio, Texas.

[9] Joseph C. Lea to H. K. Thurber, February 12, 1887. Padgitt Collection, San Antonio, Texas.

[1] Francis Smith to Massachusetts Life Insurance Company, October 8, 1899. Letterbook 5, Smith Collection, H. P. Drought and Company, San Antonio, Texas.

[2] Francis Smith and Company to William McKenzie, May 28, 1899. Ibid.

argument, for, as one executive noted: "You have had a much smaller rate of loss than any broker we know. How do you do it?"[3] In letter after letter to his customers, Francis Smith explained various segments of his loan policy. Taken as a whole, his correspondence gives a clear picture of his business philosophy. Foremost, he emphasized the necessity for meticulous attention to detail: "You can not conduct a mortgage business as you would a banking business because scarcely a day passes that borrowers do not want to know something. . . ."[4] Incessant correspondence with investors regarding their land titles, value of their acreage, interest, and collateral releases, was a heavy drain on a broker's time. Hours and even days were further dissipated by the requests of some lenders for a step-by-step account of individual loans. But no question, sarcastic or polite, was ever ignored. Smith stressed to his subordinates that the success of the business depended "heavily on all of us answering all questions, no matter how silly, from our customers."[5] The Smith files provide exhaustive testimony that he followed his creed.

In response to a contract from Massachusetts Mutual Life Insurance Company in the fall of 1899, Smith defined the services of his firm in precise language. He would be able to secure first mortgages[6] "on productive real estate worth from two to three times the amount of the loan." Further, his company would take care of title defects and security, and would pay the taxes and insurance until the debt was liquidated. For this brokerage, Smith proposed to absorb either 1½ per cent of the interest on the loan or 2½ per cent of the gross amount of the loan. As additional inducement for Yankee investors, Smith assured them that all their money would be placed in Texas or in the Southwest.[7]

[3] Connecticut General Life Insurance to Francis Smith, January 23, 1890. Bolton-Smith Collection, Washington, D.C.
[4] Francis Smith and Company to William McKenzie, May 28, 1899. Ibid.
[5] "Memorandum," February 8, 1889. Ibid.
[6] Francis Smith and Company had a cardinal rule of never accepting chattel mortgages as collateral. Interview with Carlile Bolton-Smith, November 12, 1963, Washington, D.C.
[7] Francis Smith to Massachusetts Life Insurance Company, October 8, 1899. Letterbook 1, Smith Collection, H. P. Drought and Company, San Antonio, Texas.

Persistent devotion to detail infused every transaction, but this was only one facet of the systematic loan policy that Smith fashioned over his years of lending on Southern plantations and Western ranches. If the loan requested was to be used partially to liquidate an existing obligation, then "the utmost diligence and the greatest care to preserve the evidence of the use of the money we advance . . . is taken."[8] In spite of intensive vigilance, occasionally a loan was approved which had a heavy lien on the collateral. This disclosure inevitably caused a loss for Francis Smith and Company, because they immediately informed the lender of their findings and offered restitution.

In May 1897, a cattleman in Duvall County, Texas, received a $10,000 loan with collateral consisting of several sections of his land. Shortly after the transaction, Smith discovered a vendor's lien on the property, and he immediately sent letters to the borrower and the local agent that they would have difficulty forgetting. Integrity, as well as devotion to detail, was a quality Smith expected from all business associates. More than one customer received a scathing letter because he "overlooked" a financial obligation or defaulted on a loan.

The San Antonio commission agent offered some intriguing justifications for his partiality to land south of the thirty-sixth parallel. "We consider Texas the best loaning field in the United States!" Why? The heavy increase in land values for the past decade, the "immense" spread of railroad trackage, the increased immigration, a rich agricultural base and finally, if litigation had to be resorted to, "the action of the courts . . . will be prompt and impartial." If investors still had doubts after this résumé of the advantages of investing in Texas through Francis Smith and Company, they were referred to John Easton and Company of 52 William Street or to Brown Brothers, 50 Wall Street, New York City, who "can tell you all you want to know about us."[9]

Francis Smith's exposé of Texas and his company's attributes was in no sense an exaggeration. Though before the denouement of many a loan, few would have envied Smith's commission. All

[8] Ibid.
[9] Francis Smith to William McKenzie, August 17, 1899. Letterbook 6. Ibid.

collateral offered by a prospective borrower was carefully scrutinized for liens on the title.

The resolution of a dispute on collateral completed only the first
stage in broker-borrower negotiations; the fencing then turned to
interest rates. Prospective clients frequently played off one commission firm against another in their attempt to inveigle the most
advantageous rate. In retaliation, Francis Smith would refuse to
carry the discussion further unless the borrower showed "complete sincerity," although this was a threat that carried conviction
only in periods of a tight money market. Smith explained this
problem to a restless investment house demanding to know why
its money was not being invested: the "rough fact is that a borrower could make little use of the money . . . and most loans
that are made are for the purposes of speculation."[1] As encouragement, however, Smith added:

> The cattlemen have made a great deal of money and many
> people are now going into the business who looked upon it
> with disfavor a few years ago when the price of cattle was low.
> These people require money to buy cattle, and many of them
> will have to borrow.

One potent psychological advantage a commission firm could
exploit was the fanatic desire of some borrowers for secrecy.
Smith, in analyzing the mentality of the borrower, became convinced that borrowers were especially reluctant to have their
business acquaintances know that they were paying a heavy rate
of interest. The main reason was that if the borrower desired to
dispose of his property, a lower interest rate would be far more
attractive to a prospective purchaser. In lieu of paying a higher
rate, borrowers would often consent to an extra assessment of
1½ per cent cash commission.[2]

Francis Smith, caught between demands for increased interest
from lenders and reduced interest from borrowers, developed a
sophisticated answer for both. To the lender he would state: "The
condition of the loan business in Texas now is . . . so demoralized

[1] Francis Smith to Guild and Shepherd, November 3, 1898. Letterbook
4. Ibid.
[2] Francis Smith to Investors Mortgage, September 10, 1897. Ibid.

that we find it necessary to take good loans regardless of whether they bear 8, 9 or 10%."[3] If this did not satisfy, Smith would argue: "The last two years have been to the cattle raiser as bad as has been known for a quarter of a century."[4] Or to an especially recalcitrant investor, Smith would emphasize: "The loan business is on a safer and better foundation than for several years."[5] Thus even if the interest is only 8 per cent, the loans made "are as secure as your balance in the Bank of England."[6]

For borrowers he also had palatable words: interest rates had now sunk as low as they "have been for over a decade. Why not take advantage?"[7] Or he comforted a distraught borrower: "In light of past disasters, it is amazing that anyone sees wisdom in investing in the West."[8] Again, "The length of the loan is extraordinary for these times."[9] The fluctuating financial conditions during the 1880's and 1890's provided a convincing background for Smith's appeasing words. The fact that these arguments were diplomatically and cleverly rephrased over and over was not attributable to Smith's deviousness but to the irascibility of a particular client. Through his long business career, Smith continued to receive fierce attacks on his loan policy structure. Always firm and courteous, Smith maintained an amazing equanimity toward this harassment. The sagacity of his approach was verified at the end of the 1890's, when letters came to San Antonio from both foreign and American investors full of praise for his efforts.

The bulk of daily business that crossed the threshold of Francis Smith and Company was handled in a routine manner, but there were many individual transactions that required original responses. One of the largest single business deals that Smith participated in began in 1899 and was completed after he left the

[3] Francis Smith to Connecticut General Life Insurance Company, January 22, 1891. Bolton-Smith Collection, Washington, D.C.
[4] Francis Smith to E. E. Chalmers, October 11, 1890. Ibid.
[5] Francis Smith to A. Dean, May 12, 1895. Ibid.
[6] Francis Smith to Gresham Life Insurance Company, October 16, 1899. Letterbook 5, Smith Collection, H. P. Drought and Company, San Antonio, Texas.
[7] Francis Smith to L. A. Nares, June 12, 1896. Bolton-Smith Collection, Washington, D.C.
[8] Francis Smith to A. E. Downing, July 19, 1898. Ibid.
[9] Ibid.

firm. A Mr. Edward C. Lasater applied that March for a loan of $200,000, to be used to pay off contractual debts and to expand his 220,000-acre ranch.[1] Among the most pressing of his liabilities was an obligation to Mrs. Richard King of the enormous King Ranch. H. P. Drought, conjecturing on Lasater's motives, commented: "It may be our insinuating that Mrs. King would be exceedingly glad to get the land on which she has a mortgage that made him feel that he would like to have the loan in the hands of someone else."[2]

Among the major challenges confronting Francis Smith and Company from its first flirtations with an investor was the task of making a prospective loan inviting enough to catch his interest, and yet cause it to sound snugly conservative, as if it were being placed by the House of Morgan. In their attempts to achieve this finely balanced mixture of speculative enthusiasm and high-collar security, the letters from Francis Smith's company could seesaw strangely. The Lasater loan taxed their ingenuity to the utmost. In a six-page single-spaced letter, Drought described the soundness of the loan and the business acumen of Lasater with subdued ardor. Lasater, wrote Drought, had consented to assume a five-year $200,000 loan paying 8 per cent interest. As security, he had 220,000 acres of fee-simple land and 66,000 acres of adjoining leased land. "The soil is everything it should be for cultivation . . . of course for grass, for there is not sufficient rainfall to make agriculture profitable."[3] As additional collateral, Lasater had cattle worth $230,000, "ripe" for market, plus another 16,000 head. Warming up, Drought related Lasater's conviction that "he will never lose a calf or animal from the lack of grass or water, and that his percentage of increase will always be large; so large that it would not be much increase if he had a very much larger herd." A guarantee against drought, infertility, and the cattle market was surety indeed! It is doubtful whether Francis Smith and Company or the United States Mortgage Company, recipient

[1] Francis Smith to William McKenzie, May 18, 1899. Letterbook 6, Smith Collection, H. P. Drought and Company, San Antonio, Texas.
[2] H. P. Drought to William McKenzie, March 21, 1910. Ibid.
[3] Ibid.

of the letter, took Lasater's sentiments literally, yet there seemed little harm in quoting them.

A sleek herd and lush grazing land were the tangible assets in the loan to Lasater; an intangible advantage was the business finesse of the owner. In Drought's description Lasater became the archetype of the Puritan ethic: "Of Mr. Lasater . . . we cannot speak too highly; hard working, industrious, frugal, thoroughly versed in his business, and in every respect a man worthy of confidence and credit." After this aria on the merits of the loan to Lasater, Drought conceded: "We see but one defect in the loan, and that is that Lasater will not take it for five years." In spite of or because of Drought's letter, the Lasater loan was transacted.

The loan to Lasater fell into a common category of business handled by Francis Smith. If a ranchman wished to exchange creditors or to consolidate or extend his loan, this was motivation enough to walk through the doors of 108 Yturri Street. Another class of loan for which Eastern investors provided funds came from the cattlemen's need for operating money after one of the recurring droughts. As the grass burned and withered before a blast-furnace wind, cattlemen rounded up everything on four legs and jammed them into cattle cars, sending them off with a prayer on their lips for the compassion of the Kansas City, Omaha, or Chicago markets. Scarcely had the last cattle car disappeared when the cattlemen began planning how to restock their range. Usually the receipts from a glutted drought market were only enough to start a nucleus of a herd. The ranchers then turned to banks and commission houses, or, after the turn of the century, to the packer-financed cattle loan companies. The most forcible argument for restocking the range was that, in reality, cattlemen had no other alternative. As Francis Smith pointed out: "It is a well known fact that owners of ranches cannot get as a rental from them one-half what can be made by stocking them."[4]

In 1896 Smith reported a typical case, that of Seaton Keith, "who through bad financiering and . . . dry weather now has no

[4] Francis Smith to Northern Colonies Investment Trust, June 12, 1896. Ibid.

cattle, but plenty of grass."[5] If Keith could obtain a $7,000 to $10,000 loan, he could purchase 1,000 head of cattle, "which would," as he said, "allow me to start anew." Smith sketched the terms of the loan: a new company would be incorporated which would have title to all cattle, all the profits from natural increase of the herd would go to Keith, and he in turn would pay 10 per cent to the investor.

These terms, which appeared time and again in Smith's correspondence, held much appeal for both lender and borrower. Establishing a new company which held title to the cattle gave the lender a strong legal case if there was a default in payments on the loan. Even more attractive to the lender was the high interest rate, because these loans were usually negotiated in a tight money market and the risk on the transaction was seen as greater than normal. From the borrower's viewpoint, any reasonable device that allowed him to make a new start was a happy event, for frequently all he possessed was his own hands and his land.

After the loan had received the approval of both parties, the "mission" of Francis Smith and Company, as they were fond of explaining, had only begun. Now they became confessor and counselor to all, advising on the payment of taxes, making innumerable trips to the legislature to lobby for favorable bills, mediating disputes between lender and borrower, advising on cattle purchases and even on shipping dates. All these duties were performed with professional aplomb, requiring, as H. P. Drought reminded one investor, "infinite patience."

In one side of their business, Francis Smith and Company were unique—they had a positive loathing of foreclosure. When a client defaulted in a loan payment, they went to excruciating lengths to pacify the lender, to provide extra money for the borrower and, above all, to give advice on how to remedy the situation which caused the lapse in payment. Their motive for carrying borrowers as long as they could was simple: it was just better business. As Francis Smith told a highly distraught investor: "You ask why we have not started foreclosure proceedings against Shipley. Principally because we believe Shipley can run his ranch

[5] Ibid.

better than we can . . . his difficulty at this moment is not due to poor management but to the avidity of his creditors."[6] In another letter later that year, Smith again set forth his philosophy: "Our low losses, if no other reason, justif[y] our hesitation to fore-close."[7]

To a British customer on Commercial Street in Dundee, or an American insurance executive on Broad Street in New York, the "eminent saneness of this policy" escaped perception. As one overwrought investor noted: "It is fine if you want your money to sink out of sight, but we do not want ours to follow."[8] As the mid-nineties approached, however, the investors found less and less reason, either imagined or real, to put Francis Smith on the defensive. In 1896 he recalled for one client that in the past several years his firm had not lost a penny—a phenomenal record for this era.

Owing to the absence of some records and the inadequacy of others, it is impossible to estimate the total amount of capital Francis Smith and Company handled. In a bouyant letter to the Massachusetts Mutual Life Insurance Company in 1899, Smith reminded them that he had placed $9,000,000 for investors since 1881 with infinitesimal losses,[9] and further, that he had not had to take over any real estate. Yet when he referred to nine million, was he speaking of both British and American capital? In another letter four years before, Smith had told William McKenzie of Dundee that he was pleased to "have assisted you in placing half a million pounds." The best conclusion, based on fragmentary ledger sheets and letterbooks, is that from 1880 to 1900, Francis Smith and Company managed between $12,000,000 and $14,000,000 for their clients, both British and Yankee. This figure can be compared with estimates by Professor Rippy that the British in-

[6] Francis Smith to Connecticut General Life Insurance Company, April 18, 1893. Ibid.

[7] Francis Smith to James A. Donald, May 21, 1890. Bolton-Smith Collection, Washington, D.C.

[8] Samuel Blassingham to Francis Smith, August 30, 1893. Smith Collection, H. P. Drought and Company, San Antonio, Texas.

[9] Francis Smith to Massachusetts Mutual Life Insurance Company, October 8, 1899. Ibid.

vested $25,000,000 in Texas livestock[1] and by W. Turrentine Jackson that British investments in the livestock industry in the American West may have reached $45,000,000.[2]

Regardless of the total amount invested, the clients of Francis Smith had reason to be grateful that if the rewards over two decades had been erratic, the losses had been negligible. Other Dundee and London investors, who saw their money vanish in Swan Land and Cattle Company stock or in the Prairie Cattle Company could well envy those who discovered and remained with Francis Smith and Company.

Through cajoling, plain logic, and devoted service, Francis Smith was able to keep both lender and borrower appeased, if not cheerful. Other commission firms were not so fortunate. As early as the middle 1880's, commission agents found themselves increasingly lumped with railroads and packers as objects of scorn to cattlemen and investors. The Laramie *Boomerang*, commenting on the Chicago reaction to the resolution of the Wyoming Stock Growers Association against the "exorbitant" rates of stock "parks" and commission men, rambled: "They are, in their blind eagerness to make their business profitable as possible, doing just what will diminish and perhaps destroy it. This is not the first public protest. . . ." Haranguing on a wide range of grievances, the editor went on to say that if the stockyard officials were deaf, the commission agents were blind, for "interviews with prominent commission men show that they have no intention of taking any action in regard to the matter. They all seem firm in the belief that Wyoming cattle can not be diverted from Chicago."[3]

In reality, the commission firms were not so sanguine as the *Boomerang* led its readers to believe. The Wyoming Stock Growers Association passed resolutions protesting the high stockyard and commission rates in 1885, 1886, and 1887.[4] After the 1887

[1] J. Fred Rippy: "British Investments in Texas Lands and Livestock," *Southwestern Historical Quarterly*, LVIII (January 1955), 331-41.
[2] Frink, Jackson, and Spring: *When Grass Was King*, 223.
[3] Laramie *Boomerang*, April 11, 1884.
[4] "Minutes," 1885, 1886, 1887. Wyoming Stock Growers Association Collection, Western History Research Center, University of Wyoming.

convention, an irritated John Wood wrote to Thomas Adams, secretary of the Wyoming Stock Growers, suggesting that someone from the firm come out to discuss "our mutual problems."[5] Adams referred the letter to Joseph M. Carey, president of the Wyoming Stock Growers, with the note scribbled across the top, "Our Omaha shipments have been noticed."

Montana stock growers were as perturbed as their Wyoming neighbors by the tariff of commission firms. Their association's resolution, passed in 1888, stated that the rates were "unfair, unjust and against the best interests of the industry."[6] The specific grievance of the Montana cattlemen was the commission firms' practice of levying a fixed charge of fifty cents per head. The Montana resolution said: "The commission salesmen are requested to remedy this great evil by changing the present method . . . to one per cent of the gross sales."[7]

The accumulated resolutions began to jolt the commission firms out of their lethargy. In 1890, John Wood wrote to the secretary of the Wyoming Stock Growers Association, remonstrating: "For the past few years, there has been too much time occupied by stock growers gatherings in legislating against the general commission trade . . . this is a mistake. We are employed by you and supported by your production then why are not our interests mutual?" He concluded with the plea: "There are greater evils existing than the Chicago commission man. . . ."[8]

Not so, George B. Loving would have argued. A Fort Worth cattleman and banker, Loving in 1899 conceived the idea of organizing a $35,000,000 corporation which would include a number of the largest ranches in Texas and New Mexico. Loving may have derived his idea from the earlier unsuccessful American Cattle Trust, in which he was a participant. In any case, his effort represents one of the last major undertakings of a gigantic cattle scheme.

[5] John Wood to Thomas Adams, May 8, 1887. Ibid.
[6] Russell B. Harrison to Thomas Sturgis, May 24, 1888. Ibid.
[7] Ibid.
[8] John Wood to Thomas Adams, May 28, 1890. Ibid.

In letters to Isaac L. Ellwood, Loving outlined his plan.[9] The proposed company would be managed by "practical and successful cattlemen," namely C. C. Slaughter of Dallas; J. C. Loving, secretary of the Texas Cattle Raisers Association; Charles Goodnight, founder of the famous JA Ranch in the Texas panhandle; and George Loving. The board of directors would be comprised of influential Easterners—Colonel Abner Taylor and John V. Farwell, organizers of the XIT Ranch—and politicians—Senators Donald Cameron of Pennsylvania and Shelby Collom of Illinois. In addition, many prominent Eastern bankers would be asked to serve, for "as you know, bankers like their say."[1]

Loving assured Ellwood that his company was not a nebulous plan—he already had options on 800,000 cattle, 17,000,000 acres of land, and 10,000 horses. This solid base, managed by practical cattlemen and directed by an influential board of directors, ensured the payment of a "handsome dividend promptly and regularly to the stockholders."[2] Unfortunately for Loving, the bankers did have their say. Reporting to Ellwood on his recent visit to New York's financial district, Loving described the bankers as saying that the proposal had merit but that the scattered locations of the ranches would prevent efficient management. Loving assessed this reason, probably correctly, as a "put-off."

Although Loving had a frigid reception on Wall Street, not all New York financiers felt the same way about Texas and the West. On May 28, 1907, William Ellwood, Isaac's son, listened to an address by James F. Allen, president of the Oriental Bank of New York City, which was so glowing that upon returning to De Kalb, Illinois, Ellwood scribbled a note to Allen asking for a copy. The tenor of the speech, more rhetorical than substantive, was a plea for rapprochement between East and West.

There was a time when the Bankers of the East and their brother bankers of the West seldom saw each other, but the

[9] George B. Loving to Isaac Ellwood, September 20, 1899. Ellwood Collection, Western History Research Center, University of Wyoming.
[1] Ibid., February 17, 1900.
[2] Ibid., April 6, 1900.

personal equation now largely enters into it and we realize to the fullest that the passage of Scripture which tells us that we "be brethren." . . . Capital stands like a timid maiden on the threshold of your State waiting to be invited in. Many miles of railways await to be stretched across your prairies. Will you keep them out? I hope not. Make good laws and enforce them. . . . Texas banks have written a glorious record in the past, and they will write a still more glorious record in the days to come. Could I but lift the veil that hides the future from us and see the Texas to be I verily believe I would see a "Wonderland."[3]

Regardless of the success of Loving's plan, the cattleman, after long and prayerful meditation, might have admitted that there were greater evils, but certainly the commission firm occupied a prominent place in his high court of devils. In spite of fumbling attempts at improving their public image, the commission agents remained in the Western mentality as exploiters along with the railroads and packers. Members of the American Cattle Trust, although chiefly occupied with the wrongs done them by the packers, also sought relief from the "middleman."[4] Sporadically, groups of cattlemen would band together to sell their cattle direct from the range to the packing house, but inevitably low prices and poor discipline would drive them back to the commission agents.

One of the more sustained of the ranchers' efforts, reminiscent of the grand scheme of George Loving, came in 1907 when the Co-operative Livestock Commission was organized. The leading figures in this enterprise were Murdo MacKenzie of the Matador Cattle Company, W. J. Tod of the Prairie Company, and Charles O'Donel of the Bell Ranch. The Co-operative Livestock Commission Company was dedicated to twin goals: first, to instigate suits against monopolistic practices of their competitors, and second, to market cattle for members at "drastically reduced fees." It failed in both, but in achieving defeat, it had a lively time.

Kansas City became the center of the legal attack on the

[3] James F. Allen: "Texas as Viewed from New York" (Corpus Christi, May 28, 1907). Ellwood Collection, Western History Research Center, University of Wyoming.
[4] A discussion of the viscissitudes of the American Cattle Trust is given in Chapter 9.

monopoly. Because of a strong antitrust law that had been passed by the Missouri legislature, together with a precedent-setting court decision in Kansas, "the hub of the Southwest cattle trade" appeared to offer a favorable legal and economic climate. All through the autumn of 1907, the case against the Kansas City Exchange and the Traders Exchange was systematically researched and testimony was taken from disgruntled cattle shippers. T. W. Tomlinson, secretary of the Co-operative Livestock Commission Company, had high hopes for a test case "that will make the situation so warm at Kansas City that firms will also settle at Chicago."[5]

On the first anniversary of the Co-operative Livestock Commission, Tomlinson dictated a caustic report to the members. There were 1,738 stockholders scattered through nineteen states, holding 5,120 shares of stock at par value of ten dollars each. The expenses for the commission houses located at St. Joseph, St. Louis, Chicago, and Kansas City were $97,792.37, the receipts $89,531.03, and the loss $8,261.34. What caused the deficit? In blunt language Tomlinson gave a single answer: "The losses during 1907 are entirely charged to the lack of support on the part of your stockholders."[6] Tomlinson went on to point out that over the past year, not even 50 per cent of the stockholders had shipped their cattle to the Co-operative; the majority of receipts had been from "outsiders." The secretary berated the members: "We have every reason to expect your loyalty. This company was organized to protect the interests of the producers . . . the only way to remedy abuses is to establish an independent company such as this one!"

Tomlinson's annual report did not disturb the deep indifference of the members. The reasons for this lethargic reaction and the eventual failure of the Co-operative firm are not difficult to uncover. In the first place, the organization belied its name, as Tomlinson had noted, for it did not receive the cooperation of its members. A barrage of criticism from other commission firms exploited a major weakness—that the Co-operative members were receiving

[5] T. W. Tomlinson to Charles O'Donel, September 5, 1907. Bell Ranch Collection, University of New Mexico Library.
[6] Ibid., March 11, 1908.

less than others for their cattle in the market. The Co-operative officials, of course, realized the potency of this attack and tried to fend it off with counter-propaganda. A. L. Ames, president of the Co-operative, told O'Donel: "The extreme pressures brought to bear by the Exchange, has made the country feel we are unable to secure market values. . . . If you could arrange to have several public meetings in your part of the country, I believe it would be effective to counteract these lies."[7]

Meetings were held, but effective they were not. Another year brought only more division in the Co-operative ranks; even Ames was rumored to be considering establishing a rival commission firm.[8] By October 1908, the directors decided to shut down the offices at Kansas City and St. Joseph. Tomlinson thundered: "This is the direct outcome of the boycotting and secret warfare waged against this company by the other commission firms and the feeder speculators."[9] The termination of the Co-operative Livestock Commission Company was solely a matter of time; in the summer of 1908, the two remaining offices closed. Lying in the pile of unfinished business were fourteen suits against other commission concerns for $96,000.

As a protest movement, the Co-operative Livestock Commission had much in common with other livestock protests of this era: it was full of sound and fury, but achieved little concrete progress. The grounds for failure were there from the inception in the inadequate financing, vicious attacks from competitors, and dissent and disunion among the members. Above all, the suspicion—and at times proof—that your neighbor was receiving more for his cattle than you were for yours led to extremely low morale. The unlacquered truth was that cattlemen and investors alike were not willing to forgo immediate profits for promises of great rewards in the millennium. As Tomlinson put it: "Principles do not seem to cut very much ice with our members."[1] It was easy to be an agnostic if you thought you would lose several thousand

[7] A. L. Ames to Charles O'Donel, September 12, 1907. Bell Ranch Collection, University of New Mexico Library.
[8] T. W. Tomlinson to Charles O'Donel, September 8, 1908. Ibid.
[9] Ibid., October 1, 1908.
[1] Ibid., September 10, 1908.

by becoming a convert. The failure of the Co-operative Livestock Company did not mean that the ranchers capitulated to "exploitation"; instead, cattlemen and investors switched from economic to political means to remedy their economic grievances.

As the nineteenth century waned and the twentieth dawned the commission firm's function underwent a metamorphosis. Instead of serving as banker, manager, and counselor, the commission agent narrowed his duties to the brokerage side of his business. The hallowed names of John Clay and Company, H. P. Drought and Company, and Rosenbaum Brothers continued to sparkle on the enameled calendars into the mid-twentieth century. The names, the tradition, and the pride were there, but the days had passed when a commission company's refusal of a loan meant disaster for the debtor.

Yet for the era 1880 to 1900, the commission firm had been a decisive factor in the economic development of the range cattle industry—first as a steward for Eastern and foreign investors, then as a banker. Most impressive of all was the contribution made by the commission firms after the depression of the middle eighties. With the diminished inputs of Eastern and foreign capital, the skittish attitude of Eastern bankers toward cattle paper, and the inadequate resources of Western banks, the commission firm suddenly assumed the role of prime risk taker. The commission agent was far from being at ease in his role as the main buttress of the range economy. The promoter genre—the Underwoods, Clarks, and Waddinghams—vanished from the scene; the Clays, Sniders, and Smiths, well grounded in Western economics, remained. If the resurgence of the cattle industry in 1888–90 and from 1894 on can be attributed to many factors, certainly the commission firm was the catalyst.

After 1900, Western economic growth reached the state where regional banking institutions such as the Kountzes' and the Cosgriffs' absorbed more and more cattle notes. In the first two decades of the twentieth century a new financing agency, the livestock loan company backed by various packing interests, forced many commission firms out of the loan business. The Chicago Livestock Loan Company, owned by Chicago stockyard interests; the Spokane Cattle Loan Company, owned by Armour's; and the Portland Cattle Loan Company, owned by Swift, were but a few names that replaced the Clays and the Rosenbaums in Western consciousness.[2] The depression of the 1920's wiped out many loan companies,[3] and livestock financing then was transposed to the War Finance Corporation, which was followed in the 1930's by the Regional Agricultural Credit Corporation and the Livestock Producer Credit Association.[4]

[2] J. L. Driscoll to Edward N. Wentworth, June 6, 1941. Wentworth Collection, Western History Research Center, University of Wyoming.
[3] J. W. Jasper to Edward N. Wentworth, May 29, 1941. Ibid.
[4] An enlightening résumé of cattle financing in the twentieth century is in Monroe F. Cockrell: *After Sundown* (Chicago: 1962).

VIII

"I think it is necessary
that we secure the removal of...

POLITICS

Financial involvement in the West meant political commitment: once the Eastern investor signed over his dollars, he inevitably became involved in territorial or state politics. His political interest freely roamed from the local sheriff's appointment to the passage of a bill on pleuropneumonia in the legislature, national or state. He plagued Washington officials with delegation after delegation and put personal pressure, with varying effectiveness, on presidents from Rutherford B. Hayes through Theodore Roose-

velt. No political matter was too minute or Gargantuan for his attention, should it remotely border on his vested interests.

In the spring of 1885, Thomas Sturgis found on his desk a letter
from W. H. Parker, a New Hampshire investor. Not one for
obliqueness, Parker stated his business at the start: "I think it very
necessary that we secure the removal of Hugh J. Campbell,
United States Attorney of the Dakota Territory. . . . He is a dis-
honest man and should be removed."[1] What was Campbell's
perfidy? He had refused to prosecute in spite of a "proven" case
of rustling. Furthermore, Parker was confident that he could
dispose of the United States Attorney with ease.

> I am satisfied that I can secure his removal by visiting Wash-
> ington. He was the first appointed by Hayes in recognition of
> services rendered to the famous Returning Board in Louisiana
> in 1876 . . . and may be fairly presumed of coming within scope
> of Cleveland's definition of "offensive partisan."

Whether because of Parker's animosity or the slow grinding of
Cleveland's patronage machine, United States Attorney Campbell
did later step down to become plain Attorney Campbell.

Parker's plans to induce Campbell's political eclipse were far
from an isolated case, and investors often found themselves
exhilaratingly successful in their political projects. Stock growers'
associations, in consultation with governors and legislators, found
eager receptiveness to their endorsements. Governor William Hale
wrote Thomas Sturgis that "without delay on receipt of your
favor I appointed Mr. Lindsey to County Treasurer."[2] Nor was the
investor's influence confined to appointments. A member of
the firm of Francis Smith and Company, in attempting to explain
the ways of the Texas legislature to a British friend, finally blurted:
"It is astonishing how much you can do with the legislature if
you go about it in the right way. Of course, it takes time and
money, but if the object you are after is important enough to
warrant the expenditure of time and trouble you can usually ac-

---

[1] William H. Parker to Thomas Sturgis, May 26, 1885. Wyoming Stock
Growers Association Collection, Western Research Center, University of
Wyoming.
[2] William Hale to Thomas Sturgis, June 27, 1884. Ibid.

complish your object." Bribery was not implied; only that efficient management of a legislature required the lobbyist to make a
special kind of educational effort. "We know that the great defect
in our legislature is the lack of knowledge, the blank ignorance of
the great majority of members."[3] Yet the commission agent maintained that enlightenment usually dawned for the lawmakers
when individuals took the time to point out the specific evils
in legislation. These concluding moral sentiments could be para-
phrased in Shakespearean overtones, "The fault dear Brutus . . ."

Occasionally, instead of influencing a legislature, an Eastern investor discovered that it was he who had been manipulated. John
V. Farwell, Chicago capitalist and one of those "possessed" by
the monstrous XIT Ranch, explained to a friend that a primary
reason for floating their bonds in England rather than the United
States was the fear of political censorship by "demagogue politicians" who "would herald it from one end of the state to the
other—that we were getting 30 million dollars' worth of property
for building their State House which ought really go into the
Treasury of the State—the larger part of it. We could not convert
the statement as to real value."[4]

To their perpetual embarrassment, a few politicians found themselves currying favors. Senator George Vest of Missouri beseeched
Samuel Hauser, mining magnate of Montana, for a "frank" opinion of the safety of investing in one of Hauser's smelters. "I
haven't much money as you know, and ten thousand is a little
fortune to me. . . . If it is all right, I mean a sure thing, I will
put my ten thousand in cheerfully."[5] Hauser's soothing reply
evidently set Vest's mind at ease, as he authorized Hauser to take
stock in his name.

Some Eastern investors retained their enthusiasm for Western
politics over two decades; others flitted in and out of the political
scene in response to their own fears and preoccupations or those

[3] Francis Smith and Company to William McKenzie, March 6, 1901.
Letterbook 3, Drought Collection, San Antonio, Texas.
[4] John V. Farwell to W. C. Prescott, October 31, 1885. XIT Collection,
Panhandle Plains Museum, Canyon, Texas.
[5] George Vest to Samuel Hauser, June 24, 1888. Hauser Collection,
Historical Society of Montana.

of their managers. For length and intimacy of association, as well as for its record of accomplishment, the relationship between Senator Stephen Elkins and Thomas Catron was unique. When Elkins departed from New Mexico in 1876, he left in spirit only; behind remained his extensive investments in lands, livestock, banks, and mines, a fortune which continued to multiply. In long gossipy letters, Catron kept Elkins, who was by then a senator from West Virginia, up to date on New Mexico politics and on their mutual investments. Sometimes the gossip was savored with accusations, for Catron had a fixation that Elkins could do more for their interests in Washington circles than he seemed to be accomplishing. Elkins in turn thought Catron downright unappreciative. In one reply to reproachful comments from Catron, Elkins riled: "Ingratitude is a sin. I am not going to try to answer your letter in detail." Then he proceeded to do so point by point, reminding Catron that in previous years, when "your enemies were fighting you both in Washington and New Mexico, I let every other matter drop and directed myself to your defense," although the price had been high. "In this defense, I incurred obligations that to this day I am discharging."[6]

Catron's response is unknown, but certainly this resentful letter did not restrict the number or the length of Catron's communications to Elkins. Almost until Elkin's death, Catron sent letter after letter to Washington asking for favor after favor. No matter was too small for Catron to ask Elkins's advice or assistance on. Lieutenant Plummer, assistant quartermaster at Santa Fe, desired to rent a storeroom "22 x 86 feet" from Catron. Would Elkins contact the War Department to obtain permission for Lieutenant Plummer to take up this rental?[7] Later, Catron berated the national Republican party for "not taking more interest in New Mexico." Catron assured the West Virginia senator "that without doubt this territory is Republican, if properly managed."[8]

As the years passed, the Catron-Elkins correspondence showed

[6] Stephen B. Elkins to Thomas B. Catron, August 15, 1879. Elkins Collection, West Virginia University Library.
[7] Thomas B. Catron to Stephen B. Elkins, February 23, 1892. Ibid.
[8] Ibid.

little abatement, although it did become more formal and cold, and the "Dear Steve" changed into "Dear Elkins." However, not only did Catron diligently keep Elkins apprised of their investments, but his letters exhaustively reported the political scene from the town plaza to the territorial mansion. Undoubtedly, few Eastern senators in Washington had access to much intimate knowledge of Western economic and political conditions as Stephen B. Elkins. On the other hand, there were few Western politicians who asked for and received as many favors from Washington as Thomas Catron. As late as 1900, Catron hounded Elkins on the subject of his appointment to United States Attorney, embodying the forthright injunction: "I hope you will insist upon McKinley appointing me to that office. Do not ever overlook it or neglect it."[9]

As Catron's political power in the territory declined, his missives to Washington increased in irascibility. He moaned to Elkins in 1901: "The degree of corruption, rascality, outrage and wrong now prevalent in this territory under Otero's administration and through his gang is fearful." There was only one remedy: "I gave Captain Muller a letter to you; he is a special friend of Roosevelt; he is honest and true; he ought to be made Governor. I ask you to do everything to help him while there you must see that Otero is not reappointed." To leave no doubt of his sincerity, Catron added: "If we are to have him [Otero], I will sell my property for what I can and leave town. I mean business by this letter."[1] But in spite of Catron's threats and apoplectic opinions, Roosevelt reappointed Manuel Otero for another term.[2] Catron's

[9] Thomas B. Catron to Stephen B. Elkins, March 29, 1900. Catron Collection, University of New Mexico Library.
[1] Ibid., November 11, 1901.
[2] Onetime governor of New Mexico, George Curry, recalled the strategic position of the Catron law firm in New Mexico politics in his autobiography: "At that time [1880's] the law firm of Catron, Thornton, Clancy and Cockrell enjoyed the unusual situation of having in its membership the leaders of both the Democratic and Republican parties in the territory. Thomas B. Catron was the acknowledged leader of the Republican party, while Judge W. T. Thornton was regarded as the Democratic party leader, although his leadership was disputed by J. H. Crist, Democratic party chairman and a smooth political manipulator. Junior members of the Catron-Thornton firm were Frank W. Clancy and Frank Cockrell, a

influence in 1900 was not what it had been in the past. As with most politicos who have tasted power, Catron was slow to perceive that his political magnetism was atrophying. On reflection, Catron could have been well satisfied with his life in New Mexico. Few partisan partnerships in Western territorial politics had operated longer or more effectively than the Elkins-Catron alliance.

Another East-West alliance, that between Joseph C. Lea and his New York partner H. K. Thurber, was more representative of cattlemen's politicking. Thurber offered his partner a seemingly unending stream of advice on cattle economics and Western politics, all with the confident authority of years of success in Wall Street. When the problem arose of how to lure a railroad through their land, Lea received minute advice on the direction the bill should take through the territorial legislature.[3] The fact that Thurber was two thousand miles from the political cross-currents of New Mexico in no way diminished his confidence in his political perception. In one respect, this was a reflection of Thurber's Eastern conservatism; as far as he was concerned, there were few buoys to which one could tie in any political sea. First of all, possibly skeptical of Lea's affiliation, he urged his manager to adhere to "those honest and great Republican principles. It is only fair to say that the Republicans are the ones that are progressive, rightminded people who want to see our country progress and prosper. All the way through the Democrats are a bad set of Bourbons."[4] Moreover, Thurber explained, even if you dissented

son of the U. S. Senator Francis N. Cockrell of Missouri. Senators Cockrell and Vest of Missouri were then among the influential members of the Senate. It was known that in event of election of a Democratic President, they would be influential in the selection of men for federal appointments in New Mexico, major posts being the governor, United States marshal and Secretary of the Territory. It appeared that the Catron law firm might dictate these appointments, whichever way the national election might go." H. B. Hening (ed.): *George Curry, 1861–1947* (Albuquerque: University of New Mexico Press; 1958). Otero's viewpoint on the Catron-Otero feud is hammered out in M. A. Otero: *My Life on the Frontier* (Albuquerque: University of New Mexico Press; 1939), II, *passim.*

[3] H. K. Thurber to Joseph C. Lea, February 22, 1888. Padgitt Collection, San Antonio, Texas.

[4] Ibid., December 10, 1888.

from Republican principles, they were the party in power and
it was to your definite advantage to espouse their platform.

Regardless of what Lea thought of Republican ideals, he showed
little hesitation in requesting patronage. Thurber usually gave
these petitions prompt attention. When Lea wanted a friend
retained as postmaster of Roswell, all he did was write to New
York, and Thurber's political magic soon functioned: "You may
rest easy there at Roswell, Mr. Cosgrove will remain postmaster.
I have it all fixed and if there is any other place where having a
postmaster will do the Republican party any good, I can fix it, if
I know about it soon."[5] Not wishing to miss the knock of opportunity, Lea responded with a list of six communities.

When Lea learned that a friend was having trouble securing a
clerkship, Thurber assured him: "This matter will be taken care
of in due course, I am planning on going to Washington next
week."[6] And soon the message drifted to Roswell from Washington that the friend had received the appointment. On another of
his Washington trips, Thurber conferred with Benjamin Harrison
regarding the appointment of one L. C. Fort of Las Vegas as the
Fifth Judicial District Judge.[7] Harrison complied. It is a reasonable conjecture that Thurber's contributions to the Republican
exchequer were not small.

President Harrison had a broader knowledge of the West than
many of his predecessors, for his son Russell Harrison served as
secretary of the Montana Stock Growers Association for over a
decade, and was an influential cattleman and newspaper publisher
as well. Harrison also had the advantage of experience gained when
he was chairman of the Senate Committee on Territories.

In Elkins's negotiations for the assets of the Pioneer Cattle
Company—negotiations in which Russell Harrison was the go-
between—Russell's father, then Senator Harrison, could give him
excellent advice, since he was a good friend of the West Virginia
senator.[8] In turn, Russell described the paramount cattle issues of

[5] Ibid., January 2, 1890.
[6] Ibid., June 12, 1889.
[7] H. K. Thurber to Benjamin Harrison, June 25, 1890. Ibid.
[8] The Harrison-Elkins negotiations are described in Chapter 3.

the day—pleuropneumonia, the national cattle trail, and the leasing system—from the viewpoint of Montana for Washington ears. He also took note of Washington's reaction to these viewpoints, when he candidly commented to Thomas Sturgis:

> The St. Louis convention did the ranch interests of the West a great deal of injury by attracting the attention of the East and Congress to the privileges they enjoy. Through my father, who is chairman of the senate committee on territories, I have unusual facilities for ascertaining the feelings of the members of Congress on the subject of the ranch industry, and it seems to me if the subject is not handled with great care and judgment at both St. Louis and Chicago conventions this fall, we will be taxed so much a head by an act of Congress for the privilege of running our stock upon the unfenced public domain.[9]

All in all, perhaps the astonishing thing is that so little came from all this firsthand information and influence. Except for the passing of the Animal Industry Bill, which occurred while Harrison sat in the gentlemen's club of the United States Senate, there is little evidence that Harrison's administration favored cattlemen. He did respond to pressures during the Johnson County War in Wyoming to proclaim martial law and send federal troops to extract the cattlemen from the "nester" beehive.[1] However, his delay in

---

[9] Russell B. Harrison to Benjamin Harrison, October 24, 1885. Wyoming Stock Growers Association Collection, Western History Research Center, University of Wyoming.

[1] The Johnson County War was the culmination of the economic unrest of the late 1880's in northern Wyoming. For a decade, the large cattlemen had suffered extensive losses from "rustling." Finally, as much from frustration as anything else, a group of cattlemen from southern Wyoming, accompanied by hired Texas gunmen, invaded Johnson County with the implied purpose of killing some of the more notorious thieves. A skirmish took place a few miles south of Buffalo, Wyoming, in which the "invaders" were completely outnumbered and surrounded by the irate residents of Johnson County. The United States troops from neighboring Fort McKinney had been ordered to the scene by the Secretary of War at the explicit request of the governor and senators from Wyoming. The military took the cattlemen into custody and they were removed to Cheyenne, where they were eventually released. As with many vigilante activities in the West, it is extremely dubious whether there was any beneficial outcome. The bitterness remains today in the second and third generations. For accounts of varying reliability and viewpoint, see A. S. Mercer: *Banditti of the Plains* (Cheyenne: A. S. Mercer; 1894); R. B. David:

doing so lost him as many Western friends as his action gained.[2] The negative thesis could be advanced that Harrison was not so inimical to cattle interests as Cleveland nor so partisan as Theodore Roosevelt.

The Harrisons, Elkinses, Roosevelts, Stoddards, Leiters, and Eastern investors in general were more influential on specific issues in territorial or state politics in the West than they were when questions of national importance arose concerning the range. When such larger topics loomed, the Eastern investor frequently turned to the national or state stock growers' associations to air his views. Whatever the issue—railroad rates, land legislation, or cattle disease—Eastern investors, either in person or through their managers, made certain that their principles were given thorough hearings at stock conventions.

In view of the diminutive economic returns in the cattle industry, the political power exercised by the stock growers' conventions has been regarded as remarkable. The influence of the Wyoming Stock Growers in the territorial legislatures through 1886, its subsequent decline, and its resurgence after 1900, are legendary.[3] Some detractors claim that few bills passed in the

---

Malcolm Campbell, Sheriff (Casper, Wyoming: Wyomingana, Inc.; 1932); John Clay: *My Life on the Range* (Chicago: 1924); William Walker: *The Longest Rope* (Caldwell, Idaho: Caxton Printers; 1940).

[2] In a famous letter from Senator Francis E. Warren to W. C. Irvine, prominent Wyoming cattleman and later president of the Wyoming Stock Growers Association, Warren reminded his friend: "Notwithstanding your sentiment that the men of the cattle party are martyrs; that they were justified in what they did; and notwithstanding I may agree with you perfectly; yet law and order, officers of the law and people outside of the range of a perfect knowledge of all the ins and outs of the Wyoming matter, look upon the cattlemen as the invading party and the first law breakers so far as loss of life and burning of property is concerned." Francis E. Warren to W. C. Irvine, July 23, 1892. Warren Collection, Western History Research Center, University of Wyoming.

[3] The political influence and rise and decline of the Wyoming Stock Growers Association are well outlined in W. Turrentine Jackson: "The Wyoming Stock Growers Association: Political Power in Wyoming Territory, 1873–1890," *Mississippi Valley Historical Review*, XXXIII (March 1947), 571–94; "The Wyoming Stock Growers Association, Its Year of Temporary Decline, 1886–1890," *Agricultural History*, XXII (October 1948), 260–70; "Administration of Thomas Moonlight, 1887–1889," *Annals of Wyoming*, XVII (July 1946), 139–62; "Railroad Relations of the Wyoming Stock Growers Association, 1873–1890," *Annals of Wyoming*, XIX (January 1947), 3–23.

Magic City of the Plains which did not have the brand of approval: W.S.G.A. When investment returns declined after 1886,
and W.S.G.A. political influence shriveled in direct proportion,
one Eastern stockholder offered his eulogy:

> I look upon the sum we pay you as the most profitable ex-
> pense we have. . . .
> New England stockholders would be uneasy if they knew the
> protection of the W.S.G. assn. was in danger of being withheld
> from their property. I have not hesitated to say that so far as
> stealing is concerned, your association has rendered our cattle as
> safe as though they were "hobbled" in one of our N.[ew]
> H.[ampshire] barns.[4]

These sentiments were not shared by stock growers in all parts
of Wyoming. Thomas B. Adams received a member's complaints:
"We have a case of rustling on hand at present which the Association ought to investigate but you know how effective our
present efforts have been in that direction."[5] Adams reminded the
member that "even in more prosperous days, we have never
guaranteed the safety of every single head."[6] Adams's argument
had a reasonable air: why should he apologize for an association in
trouble?

Even more perplexing than its touted power has been the historical evaluation of the Wyoming Stock Growers Association. The
growth and influence of the Association has been regarded by
many historians as a capricious occurrence; and yet when one
looks at the Association's power against the backdrop of the
Equality State's economic structure, there seems little reason for
mystification. Wyoming's territorial economy through the 1890's
rested on two trestles: the Union Pacific Railroad and the range
cattle industry. Politically (and economically, though this thought
made both parties uncomfortable) these two groups were mutually
interdependent, and they voted that way. Territorial Wyoming
had no "richest hole on earth" to rival Bingham, Utah, or

[4] J. H. Barron to Thomas Sturgis, January 6, 1887. Wyoming Stock
Growers Association Collection, Western History Research Center, University of Wyoming.
[5] John David to Thomas Adams, December 7, 1888. Ibid.
[6] Thomas Adams to John David, January 10, 1889. Ibid.

Anaconda, Montana; no "richest square mile on earth" to compete
with Gilpin County, Colorado, or Silver City, New Mexico; no
granger element rivaling Nebraska's or the bonanza farmers' of
the Dakotas. Wyoming's economy was undiversified and under-
developed, and the Union Pacific Railroad and the range cattle
industry, the two partially mature economic agents, directed the
political life of the territory, and any other result would have
required an explanation.

Of course, other stock growers' associations, such as those of
Colorado, Montana, Texas, and Nebraska, were also potent political forces in their respective states.[7] However, their political influence was in direct ratio to their economic importance. John
McShane, owner of the Omaha stockyards, boasted: "Our livestock bill was considered in the lower house yesterday and will be
passed tomorrow. I know, for it has cost me sleepless nights and
mortgaged several other bills I wanted."[8] In a nostalgic mood, a
Colorado cattleman, John L. Brush, brought up a similar experience to a friend: "Do you recall when we had to trade with all
those hard rock counties? I do not want to do that again."[9]

It was seldom that the Eastern investor could make his annual
visit coincide with the territorial stock growers' conventions, so
that he had to depend on his managers to present his views. Even

[7] For the influence wielded by stock associations, the following tomes
are helpful. Ora B. Peake: *The Colorado Range Cattle Industry* (Glendale,
Calif.: A. H. Clark Company; 1937); Louis Pelzer: *The Cattlemen's
Frontier* (Glendale, Calif.: A. H. Clark Company; 1936); Robert Fletcher:
Free Grass to Fences, the Montana Cattle Range Story (New York: Uni-
versity Publishers; 1960); Lewis Nordyke: *Great Roundup, the Story of
Texas and Southwestern Cowmen* (New York: Morrow, 1955); Maurice
Frink: *Cow Country Cavalcade: . . .* (Denver: Old West Publ. Co.; 1954);
Agnes Wright Spring: *Seventy Years. A Panoramic History of the Wyom-
ing Stock Growers Association, Interwoven with Data Relative to the
Cattle Industry in Wyoming* (Gillette, Wyo.: Wyoming Stock Growers
Association; 1942); Robert D. Burleigh: "Range Cattle Industry in
Nebraska to 1890" (unpublished master's thesis, University of Nebraska,
1937); Clifford P. Westermier: "The Legal Status of the Colorado Cattle-
men, 1867–1887," *Colorado Magazine*, XXV (May 1948), 109–18.

[8] John A. McShane to Thomas Sturgis, February 13, 1885. Wyoming
Stock Growers Association Collection, Western History Research Center,
University of Wyoming.

[9] John L. Brush to A. G. Thatcher, January 12, 1888. Western Range
Cattle Industry Collection, State Historical Society of Colorado.

if "in his chair," an Eastern "guest's" political adroitness in un-familiar surroundings is dubious! However, Eastern investors did try to attend the national cattle conventions that met from 1883 on. Enunciating the motives for having a second national conven-tion in 1884, John Clay told a manager: "When it is held in Chicago, one advantage I observed last year was that your in-vestors obtained an eye witness view of your problems."[1] Clay also said that among the Chicago financial community who had attended the 1884 St. Louis meeting, he found much more sympathy toward range problems after the convention adjourned than before it met. The implication was that the investor might be suspicious of his own manager's scripture and verse on Western conditions, but when managers as a whole bespoke the same tidings, disbelief crumbled.

In the early years, the investor found the national stock con-ventions useful platforms for expressing his opinions, especially since he hoped that the extra publicity would lend them additional weight when they filtered back to his congressman. Like many special-interest groups, Eastern investors found it a perpetual battle to give the impression that there was a solidarity of Western opinion. Congressmen, receiving a host of conflicting letters, were unlikely to be impressed by one particular viewpoint.

The first national convention of cattlemen was held at Chicago on November 15 and 16, 1883.[2] The idea had originated with the commissioner of agriculture, George Loring. Since his appoint-ment in 1881, Loring had advocated legislative action on the problem of cattle disease, primarily pleuropneumonia. In a circular he urged cattlemen to assemble as soon as possible to consider the geographic extent of the disease, its transmission, methods for its eradication, and the necessary legislation. Loring's appeal focused on sentiment that already abounded in the Western wind. As early as 1880, N. R. Davis, in a letter to Clarence King crammed with

[1] John Clay to Thomas Sturgis, February 21, 1884. Wyoming Stock Growers Association Collection, Western History Research Center, Uni-versity of Wyoming.
[2] A brief summary of the convention is in Ernest S. Osgood: *The Day of the Cattleman* (Minneapolis: University of Minnesota Press; 1929), 169–70.

prophecy and optimism, mentioned the value of a national association of cattlemen.[3] D. W. Smith, an affluent Hereford breeder in Illinois, extolled the merits of such an organization to Thomas Sturgis.[4] The commission agent R. G. Hunter of St. Louis spoke of the "tremendous help it would be for all of us if we would only join together."[5] Levi Leiter queried James Pratt why "you people in the West do not cooperate more and bicker less."[6] Actually, the answer to this was simple: most managers and investors—including Pratt and Leiter—were far too occupied with their own affairs to worry about cooperating with other cattlemen. State and territorial associations were an evolution of the late seventies, in response to the demands for protection and clarification of ownership. But vexations over cattle disease, national cattle trails, and legislation could not compete with the problems of wresting one's livelihood from a raw land. Cattlemen were aware of these larger issues, but they were not worried enough to act upon them.

However, by 1883 enough pressure had built up until in both East and West Loring's motion offered an escape valve. Furthermore, Loring's issue of pleuropneumonia was of vital interest to every livestock man, East or West, for all definitely held an opinion on pleuropneumonia. Recognized as a disease since Colonial days, it had first attracted wide attention in Massachusetts in 1862, when a state commission made strenuous though unsuccessful efforts to eradicate it.[7] By the 1880's, livestock men over the nation were concerned over the spread of the disease, and petitions from Westerners, Midwesterners, and Easterners fell like ticker tape on the desks of congressmen. The blow that snapped

[3] N. R. Davis to Clarence King, June 23, 1880. Thorp Collection, Western History Research Center, University of Wyoming.

[4] D. W. Smith to Thomas Sturgis, January 11, 1882. Wyoming Stock Growers Association Collection, Western History Research Center, University of Wyoming.

[5] A. G. Hunter to Thomas Sturgis, May 8, 1882. Ibid.

[6] Levi Leiter to James Pratt, October 6, 1884. Pratt Collection, Nebraska State Historical Society.

[7] U. G. Houck: *The Bureau of Animal Industry of the United States Department of Agriculture: Its Establishment, Achievements and Current Activities* (Washington, D.C.: 1924), 3.

lethargic congressmen to action came in the winter of 1880–1, when the British government, for all practical intents, slapped an embargo on American cattle. In a feeble attempt to soothe the hue and cry that thundered from the cattle interests, Congress appropriated $15,000 for an investigation of pleuropneumonia and raised it to $100,000 in the next session. The Treasury Cattle Commission, which was assigned the inquiry, issued its verbose report in 1882, saying at length that any effective regulation of cattle diseases depended on federal rather than local authority.[8]

The motley collection of cattlemen who braced themselves against the frigid winds blowing off Lake Michigan in mid-November 1883 had the Treasury Report as a basis on which to disagree. The mobilization of grass-roots reaction had been one of the prime motives behind Loring's activities. If he was waiting for an expression of stockmen's opinion, he received it, and it was not antiphonal.

A majority of commission firms and several packing houses vehemently opposed federal regulation, although in making their public protests they were astoundingly inept. Thomas Sturgis labeled the opposition "petty, spiteful and greedy men." Their petition, he observed, "began with a confession of ignorance and ended with the childish plea that the measure was introduced by men who wished offices under it."[9] The fervent pleas of commission firms were brushed aside by the majority of one hundred and seventy delegates; if anything, the firms' antagonism only strengthened the resolve of cattlemen and their investors. By the second and final day of the convention, four resolutions had been debated and passed: One, that pleuropneumonia was a potent threat from the Atlantic Seaboard to the Rockies. Two, that the only successful eradication depended on the cooperation between state and "general government." Three, that a committee should be "forthwith" appointed to go to Washington to "prepare a bill [for the establishment of a Bureau in the Department of Agricul-

[8] Osgood: *The Day of the Cattleman*, 168.
[9] Thomas Sturgis: "Address to the National Cattle Growers Association" (Chicago: 1885), 2. Wyoming Stock Growers Association Collection, Western History Research Center, University of Wyoming.

ture] and work towards its passage." Four, that another convention should be called for November 1884 at Chicago.[1]

The cessation of convention oratory did not drown debate;
quite the contrary, it merely whetted appetites. Soon, antagonism
toward the proposed Animal Industry Bill began to come from
the Southwest as Texas cattlemen, who had been inadequately
represented at the Chicago convention, feared a federal quarantine
that might seal off their Northern markets. As the winter wore on,
the voices against the bill grew louder. The commission firms,
afraid that all competition between Northern and Southern cattle
would be eliminated when Southern cattle were quarantined, be-
sieged the Illinois congressional delegation with petitions and
personal visits. In their blind wrath they became childish, stating
in one entreaty that "no contagious disease was known West of
the Alleghenies." Further, they warned, if the proposed legislation
were enacted "hordes of horse doctors" would invade the countryside, poking and jabbing at anything "with four legs and a tail."[2]

The political maneuvering which went on during the winter
and spring of 1884 remains obscured in the limbo of history, since
Commissioner Loring's files as well as much of the Department of
Agriculture's records were destroyed years ago.[3] However, the
correspondence of Thomas Sturgis, secretary of the National
Cattle Growers Convention of 1883 and also of the committee
sent to Washington, reveals many of the machinations in the
legislative fight. In December 1883, the committee of twenty met
with Commissioner Loring to map strategy for the ensuing struggle in Congress.[4] A day later they had "a very cordial meeting"

[1] J. B. Grinnell: "Address to the Wyoming Stock Growers Association"
(Cheyenne: 1885). Ibid.

[2] Edward Price to Thomas Sturgis, March 18, 1884. Ibid.

[3] The papers of William C. LeDuc, Commissioner of Agriculture, 1877–
81, are in the Minnesota Historical Society; in his autobiography, a strange
document full of mysticism, LeDuc inaccurately recalled: "Hog cholera,
pleuropneumonia and Texas fever were prevalent among our stock and
affecting our trade at home and abroad. I established a bureau of animal
industry and employed a competent veterinary surgeon to inspect the
herds." William G. LeDuc: "Autobiography" (unpublished manuscript,
Hastings, Minnesota, 1911). LeDuc Collection, Minnesota Historical
Society.

[4] The size of the committee is open to question. Clay remembered it

with the chairmen of the Senate and House agriculture committees.[5]

When Grinnell and Sturgis climbed into their grimy railroad
cars to return home for Christmas in 1883, they had reason for
celebration, since not only were they assured of the full cooperation of the chairman of both agriculture committees, but also
Representative Hatch suggested that they draft a proposed bill for
introduction in January. The bill was composed, after, as Grinnell
put it, "a full study of foreign legislation, United States Court
decrees and the temper of our lawmakers."[6]

If Grinnell and Sturgis had visions of quick passage for their
bill, they soon learned what politics was like. Recalling the
legislative maneuvering, Grinnell told a group of enthusiastic
Wyoming cattlemen: "Time would fail me to mention the
perils in passage, to recount the votes on adroit amendments, re-
commendations and particularly acts, coupled with sleepless genius
of obstruction for three long months."[7] The opposition to the
bill developed quickly, forcibly, but unfathomably. Elmer Wash-
burn, president of the Stockyards National Bank in Chicago, and
Nelson Morris, a Chicago packer and member of the commission
firm of Gregory Cooley and Company, rented a suite in the
Willard Hotel as a base for their legislative lobbying. Here they
were host to Senators Richard Coke of Texas and John Morgan
of Alabama, "the verbose and violent opposition." The objections
conceived and reiterated with unceasing monotony by the opponents of the Animal Industry Bill revolved around several well-
worn points: One, the proposed bill was a direct and insidious
violation of states' rights. Two, "horse doctors" would visit one's
ranch and willfully slaughter one's cattle. Three, pleuropneumonia
was not a contagious disease notwithstanding all commissions to

---

as eight in number. Grinnell, who was in Washington during the winter
of 1883–4, spoke of the "unmanageable twenty." From all deductions,
after the first part of November, the delegation did not exceed six individuals.

[5] J. B. Grinnell: "Address to the Wyoming Stock Growers Association"
(Cheyenne: 1885). Wyoming Stock Growers Association Collection,
Western History Research Center, University of Wyoming.

[6] Ibid.

[7] Ibid.

the contrary, so that the whole debate was "fanning the air in a cave of the winds."[8]

The unstated motives of the opposition were as personal as their filibustering was spurious. Nelson Morris, a heavy investor in cattle feeders, was frightened by any confession that cattle disease existed. Morris went into paroxysms of consternation at the very thought of cessation of the lucrative export trade to Great Britain, and he felt that all this talk about cattle disease could only increase British uneasiness. Although Morris was the most excited, he had the sympathy of all packers and commission men who shook before the specter of having only cattle from the Northern plains available for sale. One emotional commission agent exploded to the maverick John Clay: "You would have us paying the prices they [cattlemen] ask, instead of the fair market price. What are you trying to do, ruin us?"[9] Clay, however, continued to argue that if pleuropneumonia were not checked, the nation's entire livestock industry was seriously threatened.

In countering Morris and his allies, Sturgis, Grinnell, and Clay devised a many-pronged attack. First, Sturgis sent out a circular to Eastern investors, leaving nothing to the imagination concerning the horrors of the pleuropneumonia awaiting everyone's cattle.[1] The remarkable response to this appeal can only be ascribed to the investors' vision of the plains dotted with the decayed carcasses of their animals. This crusade for dollars all investors could understand. To support Sturgis in his campaign, G. W. Simpson, trustee of the Bay State Cattle Company of Boston, made four trips to Washington in the spring of 1884. He told Sturgis: "I will be happy to go again, should you wish me to. The next time I suppose I had better visit our enemies as well as our friends."[2] The courtly Abram S. Hewitt offered to drop over to Washington "if you think you need me."[3] W. V. Johnson of Louisville suggested to Sturgis that he "pester" his own congressman. After a few months Johnson

[8] G. Cooley and Company to Thomas Sturgis, March 6, 1884. Ibid.
[9] J. Bartlett to John Clay, February 20, 1884. Ibid.
[1] Thomas Sturgis: "Circular on Cattle Disease, 'What Should Be Done'" (unpublished manuscript, 1883). Ibid.
[2] G. W. Simpson to Thomas Sturgis, April 19, 1884. Ibid.
[3] Abram S. Hewitt to Thomas Sturgis, March 24, 1884. Ibid.

sent Sturgis a note that he had assurances from the Kentucky delegation "that they will vote with us." He had also contacted tannery owners over the Midwest and East to enlist them "in furthering our case."[4] In response to Sturgis's circular John Arbuckle agreed to take a train to Washington "as often as I can be of service and it is convenient."[5] Edmund Converse, at the instigation of Hubert Teschemacher, "buttonholed" many of the New York and Massachusetts officeholders.

The Eastern investor did not confine his assistance to visits to the nation's capital; he also opened his purse. In the latter part of January and throughout February, John Clay was soliciting funds from his Chicago friends, for as he told Sturgis, "If we are to keep up our work in Washington, more money is needed and now!"[6] By the end of March, Clay had enriched their cash fund by $5,670. In one of his periodic trips back East, Sturgis extracted another $3,000 from his friends to "aid our cause."[7] Apparently expenses did not rise to meet income, for, with the consent of the donors, Clay later transferred $2,600 to the treasury of the National Cattle Growers Association.[8]

Sturgis and Clay courted the support of investors; they also flooded congressmen with "grass-roots" circulars and petitions throughout the spring of 1884. Its supporters kept close watch on the week-to-week progress of the bill and deluged Clay and Sturgis with advice.[9] The bill's detractors, while not as organized as the sponsors, nevertheless were successful in rounding up the congressmen from Texas, Alabama, Georgia, and Florida, so that for a short interval during the end of April and the beginning of May, the rumors on Capitol Hill were that the bill was doomed. G. W. Simpson harassed Thomas Sturgis with daily communications entreating him to advise their supporters to compromise "or all will be lost." Simpson said: "I ought not criticize the action of our friends, senators and investors, but it certainly is injudicious, to

[4] W. V. Johnson to Thomas Sturgis, March 18, 1884. Ibid.
[5] John Arbuckle to Thomas Sturgis, April 5, 1884. Ibid.
[6] John Clay to Thomas Sturgis, April 17, 1884. Ibid.
[7] Thomas Sturgis to John Clay, April 28, 1884. Ibid.
[8] John Clay to Thomas Sturgis, August 7, 1884. Ibid.
[9] These reports were most frequently written by J. B. Grinnell.

say the least, to not grant some concessions."[1] That same week, a letter arrived from Senator D. C. Plumb of Kansas informing Sturgis: "All will be in good order in a few more weeks."[2] Vacillating between the advice of Plumb and Simpson, Sturgis wired one of his lobbyists, Henry Metcalf, asking his opinion. Metcalf, who replied that all "that can be done has been done," held the view that the bill's fate now rested with Senators Plumb of Kansas and Vest of Missouri.[3] Sturgis, more from the absence of an alternative than anything else, sat tight, and finally on May 29, 1884, a bill to establish a Bureau of Animal Industry was passed and later approved by the President. Thus ended a five-year struggle.[4]

Reading the bill, one can see that it was a child of compromise; significant alterations were made in it between the first and second sessions of the Forty-seventh Congress.[5] Dissatisfied with its provisions, Grinnell later lamented that "our enemies should be publicly blamed for our failure."[6] In spite of Grinnell's lamentations, Thomas Sturgis was full of optimism as he rode over his Goshen Hole ranch on a brilliant day in June 1884. As he jogged along, he reviewed the events of the past year and thought, as he later wrote to a friend: "We have every reason to be satisfied with our accomplishments in this struggle."[7] Never before and never again would the Eastern investors and the Western cattlemen unify with such a single-minded legislative purpose. Sturgis was

[1] G. W. Simpson to Thomas Sturgis, April 29, 1884. Wyoming Stock Growers Association Collection, Western History Research Center, University of Wyoming.

[2] D. C. Plumb to Thomas Sturgis, April 28, 1884. Ibid.

[3] Henry Metcalf to Thomas Sturgis, May 3, 1884. Ibid.

[4] John Clay's *My Life on the Range* is without peer as a window through which to glimpse the managerial side of the cattle industry. Yet Clay's memory could fail him on specifics. He recalled the Bureau of Animal Industry as having been established after the meeting of 1887 at Kansas City. He also gave credit for the passage of the Animal Industry Bill to D. W. Smith and Major W. A. Towers, among others. Smith and Towers may have been active in the struggle, but there is little to indicate this conclusion in Sturgis's correspondence.

[5] *Congressional Record*, 47th Congress, Session I (1881-2), 5112-6; 6827-31.

[6] Grinnell: "Address to the Wyoming Stock Growers Association." Wyoming Stock Growers Association Collection, Western History Research Center, University of Wyoming.

[7] Thomas Sturgis to Azel Ames, June 19, 1884. Ibid.

the first to concede that much of the credit belonged to his friends in Federal Square and Wall Street. He wrote G. W. Simpson: "Without your help, Hewitt's, Converse's, and Leiter's, we would have floundered time and again. Is there any way that we now can help you?"[8] Simpson replied that his and his friends' efforts on behalf of the cattle-disease legislation were not altruism, "but plain dollars and cents."[9] He had worked for the bill in order to ensure his investment first; any philanthropic motives were secondary.

The last resolution of the 1883 Chicago convention scheduled another convention for November 1884. While innocent-sounding, this resolution caused an uproar from the spring through the summer of 1884. The St. Louis commission firms and Southwestern cattlemen, jealous of their Chicago competitors and fearing the influence of Northwestern cattlemen, determined to organize a rival meeting. Under the leadership of Hunter and Evans, this group announced a convention "which will be truly representative of all cattle interests"[1] to be held in St. Louis in mid-November, the same time as the Chicago meeting. The Chicago livestock men quickly accepted the challenge. All through the spring and summer, letters crisscrossed the country in a paper war full of accusations and counter-accusations.

John Clay wrote his good friend Sturgis: "There are but two cities fitted for our associations' headquarters, Chicago and Kansas City, not St. Louis! We must work through thick and thin for Chicago."[2] As secretary of the 1883 convention, Sturgis received periodic communications from Chicago urging him to send out more circulars advertising the 1884 Chicago meeting. The editor of the *Breeder's Gazette*, A. H. Sanders, said: "We are intent on having a convention of not ranch-men merely, but one which shall speak for the cattle raising interests of our whole country." Then in a swipe at St. Louis planners: "The time chosen for the St. Louis convention makes it impossible for the best at-

[8] Thomas Sturgis to G. W. Simpson, July 9, 1884. Ibid.
[9] G. W. Simpson to Thomas Sturgis, July 24, 1884. Ibid.
[1] "Circular Letter," January 18, 1884. Ibid.
[2] John Clay to Thomas Sturgis, June 23, 1884. Ibid.

tendance should they even desire to do so. The situation is one that requires . . . the greatest consideration."[3]

The president of the 1883 convention, the Chicagoan E. W. Perry, was blunt: "It is the apparent plan of the St. Louis people to checkmate the cattlemen of the North and West. . . . We then must go ahead and organize for what good can come of yielding to the St. Louis clique?"[4] Initially, the St. Louis interests rebutted the Chicago argument by insisting that Chicago's 1883 convention had not been representative, nor would it be so in the future. A. T. Atwater of the Hunter-Evans firm exploded to Sturgis: "The bonafide cattlemen and raisers who signed the call for the St. Louis convention decided that some action should show Chicago that she had trod upon the toes of the entire cattle raising district West of the Mississippi River."[5]

As the muggy summer wore on, the supporters of the St. Louis convention decided to assume a sophisticated pose. Pretending to ignore Chicago, they wrote to individual cattlemen depicting the profits and delights of a convention held in the autumn in the city which since the fur trade era had been regarded as "the Gateway to the West." The inevitable occurred; since neither the "Windy City" nor the "Gateway City" would bow out, both conventions took place. The one in Chicago began first, attracting a moderate attendance of Northwest and Midwest stockmen, breeders, and a sprinkling of holdovers from the annual fat stock show. The languid discussion spent itself on the age-old issues of railroads, commission firms, leasing the domain, and cattle disease. After a spiritless three days, the Chicago meeting adjourned, and a delegation boarded the Illinois Central for St. Louis.

John Clay recalled their reception: "We went down from the Chicago meeting innocently thinking that the Southern men who were back of this meeting were going to discuss the cattle problems of the day."[6] Then with feigned astonishment, Clay recalled how they had been taken in. Imagine—not the main cattle ques-

---

[3] A. H. Sanders to Thomas Sturgis, August 28, 1884. Ibid.
[4] E. W. Perry to Thomas Sturgis, August 21, 1884. Ibid.
[5] A. T. Atwater to Thomas Stugis, August 22, 1884. Ibid.
[6] Clay: *My Life on the Range,* 118–19.

tions of the day, but the national cattle trail preoccupied the minds of the Southwestern cattlemen! Clay's contemporaries, reading his account years later, must have smiled at his mock amazement, for the men who traveled from Chicago to St. Louis were neither as naïve nor as imposed on as Clay implied. All summer, correspondence among the Chicago livestock men had been referring to the national cattle trail as a prime motive for the St. Louis convention. It is strange indeed if Clay was not aware of this issue, as the trail had been a Southern obsession for some years.

Northern cattlemen must have been mortified that the St. Louis meeting was by far the largest-attended convention up to that time (it also held the record for years to come). An estimated 2,500 cattlemen and hangers-on elbowed their way into the Exposition Hall, gaily streaming with banners and decorated with huge "horned vases" flowers.[7] In a celebrated attempt at making everyone a participant, almost everyone was put on a committee. Eight investors and cattlemen sat on the resolutions committee.[8] By day investors mingled with their managers and friends on the convention floor; by night they crowded into the hotel bars. Of the men most active in the proceedings, Edmund and James Converse, B. W. Crowinshield, George Blanchard, F. E. Moreland, Henry M. Rogers, and Joseph Ames arrived from Boston; E. M. McGillin came from Cleveland; and William A. Clark and Levi Leiter represented Chicago financial circles. John G. Baker came alone from Wilmington, Delaware.

Debate on the cattle trail did not occupy the entire convention —there was a multitude of other issues on which cattlemen could violently disagree. The quarantine laws were subject to warm dispute; the absorption of Indian reservations into the public domain "was crucified and buried," according to Clay; debate on the exportation of cattle to Great Britain forced tempers high. Actually organizing the convention occupied two days while Southwestern

[7] James Cox: *Historical and Biographical Record of the Cattle Industry and the Cattlemen of Texas and Adjacent Territory* (St. Louis: 1895), 103–4.

[8] Mrs. Augustus Wilson (compiler): *Parsons Memorial and Historical Library Magazine* (St. Louis: 1885), 303.

and Northwestern cattlemen maneuvered for political advantage.[9]
The "neutral" John L. Routt of Colorado was elected chairman,
A. T. Atwater of St. Louis secretary, and General N. M. Curtis of
New York vice-president. It was a slate "which would satisfy
no one, but which few would object to," in the jaundiced opinion
of one delegate.[1]

The issue which the Northern cattlemen forced on the convention, and the one on which any semblance of unity disappeared,
was the subject of leasing the public domain. The ramifications
of leasing land had been hotly debated for years, both inside
and outside Congress. Frederick V. Coville, an inspector for the
Department of Agriculture, summarized the advantages most often
cited by the proponents: stockmen could depend on specific
pasture, they had incentive to conserve the grass, certain pasture
could be regarded as under forage, the percentage increase in
breeding would be higher, cattle rustling would be reduced, and
the use of supplementary feeding would be encouraged.[2]

Coville's fascination with the leasing system was not shared by
many of his contemporaries, including some in government
agencies. Statistician Joseph Nimmo, whose analysis of the range
cattle industry has now achieved the status of a classic, strongly
dissented.[3] First, Nimmo parroted the old threat that if the public
domain were leased, the settlers would be compelled to abandon
their homes, sell their land at ruinous prices, and "in various ways,
be at the mercy of the great herdsmen." In case his audience's
emotions were unstirred by this image of the Simon Legree cattle
baron versus the homesteader, Nimmo pointed out that the leasing
system violated all precedent in public land policy. Furthermore,
by leasing to large "range monopolists," one would shut out all
competition. Nimmo also discerned the shadowy figure of corrup-

[9] Ibid., 291–308.
[1] Joseph M. Carey to Thomas Sturgis, December 12, 1884. Wyoming
Stock Growers Association Collection, Western History Research Center,
University of Wyoming.
[2] Frederick V. Coville: "Report on Systems of Leasing Large Areas of
Grazing Land," 58th Congress, 3rd Session, (1904–5), *Senate Document 189*.
[3] Joseph Nimmo, Jr.: "The Range Cattle and Ranch Business", House of
Representatives, 48th Congress, 2nd Session, *Executive Document 267*.

tion hovering over public domain transactions. Indeed, as far as immorality was concerned, Nimmo implied that the entire leasing operation might exceed the "Indian problem." In conclusion Nimmo observed: "It will be much more promotive of the public interests if the lands now held by the Government shall be dedicated to the rearing of men rather than cattle."[4]

The Coville-Nimmo dispute neatly mirrored the juxtaposition of the advocates and the adversaries of the leasing system. The complexities, the legal intricacies, and the almost Oriental confusion of land policy are outside this topic. One scholar, in a recent thorough investigation of the New Mexico domain, reached the exasperated conclusion: "Given a sensible system, sensible people would have largely followed it. Given an impossible system, even sensible people rebelled against it."[5]

To concede that legislation pertaining to the public domain was ineptly conceived and even more inadequately executed is not to say that Congress ignored the rangeland beyond the 100th meridian. Congressional hearings designed to probe into the land questions were held in 1879, 1885, and 1904.[6] The testimony of cattlemen in 1879 was, not surprisingly, unanimous in its emphasis that the domain should be parceled out to them either by leasing or by outright sale. Interlaced through the testimony were the answers to the critics: arid land was suitable only for grazing, the cattlemen had an "inherent" right to the land on a first-come-first-serve basis, over-grazing already threatened the existence of the cattlemen, and furrows through the prairie would make them a vanishing species.

These arguments, stale from repetition, also flavored the testimony given in 1885 and 1904. One variation on the old tune in 1885 was the emphasis placed on unlawful enclosure of public land and the menace of alien ownership. By 1904, however, the situa-

[4] Ibid., 48.

[5] Victor Westphall: "The Public Domain in New Mexico, 1854–1891," *New Mexico Historical Review*, XXXIII (April 1958), 143.

[6] Reports of Committees of the House of Representatives for the First Session of the 49th Congress (1885–6), Vol. II (Washington: 1886); 46th Congress, 2nd Session, (1879–80), *Executive Document 46–51*; 58th Congress, 3rd Session, (1904–5), *Senate Document 158–92*.

tion had changed radically, and the land was now occupied to a degree which would have caused the cattleman of two decades before to shudder. The cattleman's cry then became "Let Us Alone!" The committee's report said: "There is an expression of opinion from some sections that range matters will adjust themselves by the natural change brought about in the gradual settlement of the country." Yet it conceded the age-old fear that "under any system of control the larger owners and corporations would secure a monopoly in the use of the pasture land."[7]

In retrospect, scanning twenty years of committee hearings, hundreds of pages of testimony, and the Record's account of hours of sleep-inducing oratory on the floor of Congress, one can hardly be astonished that the cattlemen's 1884 meeting in St. Louis failed to resolve the land question. What is surprising, the discussion reached such an acrimonious pitch that the Eastern investors and their managers walked out of the convention. Why, among a group of cattlemen, should the upheaval have been so violent on the leasing issue? The answer lies half-hidden among the sound and fury of the oratory: The number of cattlemen at the convention who had merely "princely" holdings was far greater than the number who had the "baronial" holdings of the corporation and cattle king. Thus, those with smaller domains had a claustrophobic fear of arising some morning and finding themselves completely in the shadow of a huge Eastern or foreign-financed firm. In the leasing system the smaller cattleman perceived the ideal ploy for the expropriation of his range by his corporate neighbor. What would happen to his water rights? His access to rail points?[8] These and dozens of other fears came flooding in on him as he sat in the St. Louis Exposition Hall listening to the eloquent speeches of Thomas Sturgis, Ernest Nagel, Joseph M. Carey, and Azel Ames, with their ingeniously contrived logic on "the basic advantages of leasing our land." The cattlemen with moderate or small holdings were the culprits who jammed the watered-down leasing resolution through the convention, leaving the Northwestern cattlemen

[7] 58th Congress, 3rd Session, (1904-5), Senate Document 189, 18.
[8] A Texas manifestation of the leasing furor is in J. Evetts Haley: "The Grass Lease Fight and Attempted Impeachment of the First Panhandle Judge," Southwestern Historical Quarterly, XXXVIII (July 1934), 1-27.

so disgusted that they bolted the convention two days before adjournment.[9]

Copious verbiage has been expended on the conflicts between sheepman and cattleman, and homesteader and cattleman; these are portrayed as the irreconcilables who caused so much strife across the West. A far more credible cinematic picture could be made from the struggle between the cattlemen who owned ten to twenty thousand acres and their neighbors who lorded it over sixty to seventy-five thousand acres. The Las Vegas *Optic* expressed a common sentiment: "The cattlemen here have made good out of their property. There are no great cattle monopolies such as oppress the small cattle growers in other parts of New Mexico. Most of the cattlemen have less than 10,000 head and there is excellent range for more."[1]

But Western morality plays are so much more satisfying when depicting a suntanned, muscled homesteader, shovel in hand, as a David gazing up at a grizzled Goliath of a cattleman armed to the teeth astride a snorting horse. Undeniably there was a struggle on the range for land and water between "honyockers" and cattlemen, but it was as much a contest between the "have somes" and the "have mores" as between the haves and the have-nots.

One reporter at the St. Louis convention of 1884 summarized the feelings of many: "But it was a notable fact that only the representatives of great capitalists, syndicates and large firms already in practical possession of immense areas of the public domain, were found advocating the scheme."[2] Besides being called a greedy scheme, the leasing plan was labeled downright un-American.[3] One delegate "loudly declared [that] to make Uncle Sam assume the attitude of an Irish or English landlord and to collect rents and perform all the odious duties and acts of a landlord was re-

[9] The meaningless resolution concluded: "That it is the sense of this convention that it should be for the best interests of the stock growers located upon this arid region, and to the entire country, to lease these lands for pre-emption laws. . . ." Joseph Nimmo, Jr.: *The Range and Ranch Cattle Business*, House of Representatives, 48th Congress, 2nd Session, *Executive Document 267*, 46.

[1] Las Vegas *Daily Optic*, November 5, 1884.

[2] Wilson: *Parsons Memorial and Historical Library Magazine*, 304.

[3] St. Louis *Globe-Democrat*, November 19, 1884.

pugnant to American institutions."⁴ Patriotism then was upheld with the exit of the traitorous proponents of leasing.

The National Cattle Growers and Horse Association met in the fall of 1885, but as John Clay cryptically commented: "It was as great a failure as the other was a success."⁵ Seeking strength in numbers, the Chicago and St. Louis organizations merged their assets and their differences in the winter of 1886 into an amorphous group called the Consolidated Cattle Growers. They held their annual meeting in Kansas City in 1887, but sparse attendance dampened everyone's enthusiasm. The sole contribution of the Consolidated Cattle Growers consisted of sending delegates to Congress to testify on pertinent legislation. After the Kansas City meeting, the Consolidated Cattle Growers faded away.

Concurrently with the formation of the Consolidated Cattle Growers, another group of cattlemen on the high plains gathered at Denver⁶ and organized the International Range Association.⁷ John Clay quickly assessed and dismissed this movement with the comment: "It was a very milk and water concern, neutral in its efforts."⁸ As to concrete results, Clay's verdict was accurate, but the convention was far livelier than he represents. The 1887 meeting in Denver attracted cattlemen from British Columbia to Mexico, and the proceedings were made dramatic by long and sharp exchanges on the merits of the American Cattle Trust. E. M. McGillin of Cleveland, Ohio, a heavy investor in the cattle

---

⁴ Wilson: *Parsons Memorial and Historical Library Magazine*, 304.

⁵ Clay: *My Life on the Range*, 120.

⁶ *Rocky Mountain Daily News*, February 10, 1887.

⁷ In the circular that went out in 1886, the new organization went under the name of "International Range Cattle and Horse Growers Association." The circular emphasized that there was no incompatability between the new organization and the Consolidated Cattle Growers Association. "In the conduct of range matters there are numerous questions of common interest to all stockmen of the plains in which our eastern brethren have and take not interest. By the union of rangemen in strong working organization they will be prepared to give crystalized views to the representatives of the Consolidated Cattle Growers Association to meet in Chicago next fall, thus giving it aid and strength it could not otherwise have." "International Range Cattle and Horse Growers Association Circular." Wyoming Stock Growers Association Collection, Western History Research Center, University of Wyoming.

⁸ Clay: *My Life on the Range*, 127.

industry, persuaded the convention to espouse a fertile idea for a vast monopoly of cattle-producing interests. The scheme proved unworkable, however, and the last gasp of the International Range Association came in 1888, when the *Rocky Mountain News* wrote the terse obituary: "The meeting of the International Range Association at Denver does not appear to have amounted to much. No practical question affecting the range or cattle interest was brought under discussion."[9]

With the collapse of the International Range Association, no major effort to organize a national association of livestock men occurred for a decade. Then in January 1898, a cluster of Colorado stock growers, who had the promotional acumen of the Denver Chamber of Commerce and Board of Trade, invited those interested in an association of livestock men "to come to Denver."[1] Over a thousand delegates attended the first meeting, although almost half of these were from Colorado. The Eastern investors were conspicuous only by their absence, although some of them did send "observers." The new range fraternity took the name of the National Livestock Association. But the warm glow of cordiality so evident in the first gathering soon grew chilly; by 1901, the common pattern of dissension appeared. The smaller cattlemen, convinced they were being neglected, pulled off to form the rival Western Range Association, which later became the American National Cattle Growers Association. Being regarded as a second-rate citizen was evidently worse fate than being a junior partner, for in 1906, the National Livestock Association and the American Cattle Growers Association submerged their individuality in the American National Livestock Association.[2]

Over thirty years had passed since the first cattlemen had huddled together in Chicago. Failure, much more than success, had been the hallmark of national cattlemen's associations: one only needs to peruse the accounts of the proceedings to realize

[9] *Rocky Mountain Daily News*, April 16, 1888.
[1] *Proceedings of the National Stock Growers Convention* (Denver: 1898), 5–6.
[2] Alvin Steinel and D. W. Working: *History of Agriculture in Colorado* (Fort Collins: 1926), 154–66; Ora B. Peake: *The Colorado Range Cattle Industry* (Glendale: 1937), 156–68.

the continual ferment and dissension that ran rampant at these conventions. Foremost, cattlemen bred on individualism were fractured into several interest groups that defied amalgamation: Northwestern cattlemen versus Southwestern cattlemen and large corporations versus smaller ranchers. Everyone, of course, attacked the commission firm and packer. Superimpose over these conditions the incendiary issues of the national cattle trail, the leasing of the public domain, and cattle disease, and the wonder is that the divergent groups would even take chairs on the same convention floor. Fifteen years after the St. Louis convention, one commentator surgically dissected the convention malady: "But the truth compels us to record, as a matter of history, that the association proved a failure. . . . The unanimity between states and sections necessary to make an organization of cattlemen all-powerful was painfully lacking."[3]

Depleted treasuries usually forced these associations into an earlier demise than the normal process of disintegration. From 1884 through 1886, John Clay diligently assumed the malodorous task of seeking financing from state associations and individuals alike.[4] For a brief time, his efforts were successful, but as the financial crisis in the cattle industry grew after 1885, Clay's dunning letters began to be studiously ignored. Clay pleaded with Thomas Sturgis: "Do the best you can for us will you? I know money is scarce, but the cause is righteous."[5] If John Clay recalled these solicitations, they must have caused him later embarrassment, for in his autobiography he asserted: "The work, the aim of our various associations, from the St. Louis convention in 1884 to the present time have in the main been destructive, not constructive."[6]

The Eastern investor as a politico maneuvering at the national level was not a distinguished success. With the exception of the Animal Industry Bill, he produced little in the way of national legislation favorable to the cattleman. As a territorial or state po-

---

[3] Cox: *Historical and Biographical Record of the Cattle Industry*, 117.
[4] John Clay to Thomas Sturgis, December 22, 1885, April 19, 1886, and December 31, 1886. Wyoming Stock Growers Association Collection, Western History Research Center, University of Wyoming.
[5] Ibid., May 9, 1886.
[6] Clay: *My Life on the Range*, 198.

litical figure working through local stock growers' organizations, the investor's efforts were often outstandingly effective. But as his investment in the cattle industry shriveled, so did the attractiveness of Western politics. The American Cattle Trust represented the last drive in the nineteenth century to obtain economic concessions beneficial to the Western cattle interests through the organized efforts of Eastern investors. After the Trust's dismal failure, Eastern investors cheerfully abdicated the political reins to their Western managers and politicians. From now on, any anticipated political advantage would have to originate in the fertile mentalities of the Westerners, with only sporadic help from the Eastern investor.

IX

"I think I have lost
a pound of flesh a day"

DECLINE AND LIQUIDATION

ᴧᴡ B CY Ꙩ ND ⊥ ᵵ
ᐤ ᴧ ♉ ⅄ C ᐤ
ᴴ ᴏ ℞
Ꝗ

Spring came late in 1887. The winter had been so bitter that the
high plains cattlemen would never forget it.[1] In October, after

---

[1] Interpretations differ on the effect of the winter of 1886–7; see T. A.
Larson: "The Winter of 1886–1887 in Wyoming," *Annals of Wyoming*,
XIV (January 1942), 5–17; R. S. Fletcher: "The Hard Winter in Montana,
1886–1887," *Agricultural History*, IV (October 1930), 123–30; R. H. Mattison:
"The Hard Winter and the Range Cattle Business," *Montana Magazine of
History*, I (October 1951), 5–21; J. Orin Oliphant: "Winter Losses of Cattle
in the Oregon Country, 1847–1890," *Washington Historical Quarterly*, XXIII
(January 1932), 3–17.

an unusually dry summer,[2] the howling blizzards with their sting-
ing winds had descended upon the land and lasted for long months.
Consistently below-zero temperatures and heavy drifts of snow
immobilized both men and animals in this open land. A deceptive
thaw arrived in January, encasing the vegetation in an icy crust
which successfully defied the frenzied pawing of starving beasts.
Finally, flocks of buzzards, circling slowly over gulches filled with
decaying carcasses, heralded the end of the long white winter.

Life lost its appeal for many of the ranchers who had the heart
to ride over their range. Decades later, Granville Stuart, hardened
by years on the frontier, shuddered at the memory of the disaster.
"A business that had been fascinating to me before suddenly became distasteful. I wanted no more of it. I never wanted to own
again an animal that I could not feed and shelter."[3] The deep
gloom that settled over the cattle industry did not brighten with
the heavy spring rains and the luxuriant grass that blanketed the
range. When the losses were actually tallied, several behemoth
cattle corporations, already on the edge of bankruptcy, tumbled
over the brink.

When it was learned, in January 1887, that the $2,000,000
Dolores Land and Cattle Company of Texas had failed,[4] cattlemen became loath to pick up their newspapers. As one manager
wrote to the East: "The news is unbelievable and I hope un-
realized in New York."[5] The worst blow to the morale of the

2 The young English rancher William French wrote: "Many strange
things came to my notice during the drought. I had heard of cattle climbing
trees, but was disposed to regard it as an exaggeration till one day I saw
a great, lanky steer, five or six years old, standing on his hind legs, with
his forefeet resting on a cotton-wood limb, eight or nine feet in the air.
While in this position he was hooking down with his horn branches which
still held a few green leaves within his reach and devouring them." William
French: *Some Recollections of a Western Ranchman* (London: Methuen;
1927), 132. Other descriptions of the drought can be found in *Field and
Farm*, May 22, June 18, 1886; J. J. Wagoner: *History of the Cattle Industry
in Southern Arizona, 1540–1940* (Tucson: University of Arizona; 1952), 47;
Laramie *Daily Boomerang*, May 18, 1886.

3 Granville Stuart: *Forty Years on the Frontier* (Cleveland: A. H. Clark;
1925), II, 237.

4 Laramie *Boomerang*, January 4, 1887.

5 A. W. Hardesty to Abraham Hewitt, April 23, 1887. Thorp Collection,
Western History Research Center, University of Wyoming.

cattle industry came on May 16, 1887, when the Swan brothers of Cheyenne announced a reorganization. The Denver *Republican*'s first-page banner screamed: "A Huge Failure in Cattle."[6] The Cheyenne *Leader*, trying not to alarm its readers, headlined: "A firm's Suspension, Swan Brothers assign for the benefit of Creditors. Assets more than Sufficient to meet the liabilities."[7] The article itself was an imaginative attempt at comforting the Cheyenne community. Nevertheless, the editor was forced to concede that the gossip "created a decided sensation in this city yesterday morning and formed the main topic of conversation during the entire day." The failure of the Swan brothers meant far more than the decline of just one firm. Alec Swan, with his Duke of Wellington profile and his immaculate attire, had been a symbol of confidence that prosperity on the range was an eternal matter. As early as 1885, when a few prescient cattlemen thought that they foresaw trouble, Swan issued an unctuous statement calculated to tranquilize the doubting Thomases. His insolvency dealt a fatal blow to the optimists who mouthed platitudes concerning a silver-lined future.

Nor as the summer wore on and the autumn arrived was there any relief in the financial fog which settled over the range country. The Dickey brothers, Val and Will, whose dashing manner, socially and financially, had served as a topic of conversation for over a decade, surrendered to their creditors in October 1887.[8] Their finances were in such a hopeless state of confusion that it was months before their creditors could straighten out their books. At the same time, the Niobrara Land and Cattle Company went into bankruptcy.[9] According to contemporary accounts, the disintegration of the Niobrara took less than a year. In the fall of 1886 this Montana-Nebraska-based corporation claimed 39,000 cattle valued at over $1,000,000. A year later, they could discover only 9,000 head and their assets fell to $250,000, on

[6] Denver *Republican*, May 17, 1887.
[7] Cheyenne *Leader*, May 17, 1887.
[8] John Clay: *My Life on the Range* (Chicago: 1924), 94–5.
[9] *Field and Farm*, October 15, 1887.

which they would be fortunate "to garner fifty per cent."[1] Their liabilities stood at $350,000.

As the year 1888 began, cattlemen from Helena to Austin were seriously wondering if there would be any upturn in the cattle situation. The press occasionally carried a brave article full of hope that a "golden future will soon be here"; but just when a few cattlemen and a scattering of investors were about to swallow their own propaganda, the Union Cattle Company slid into receivership in January 1888.[2] The *Rocky Mountain Daily News* took a jocular tone: "The latest big collapse, the failure of the Union Cattle Company, came as a surprise to many people. What do you know about that!"[3] The usual scapegoats, the poor market and "shrinkage in herds," were blamed for the collapse in street-corner conversations in Cheyenne. Added to these causes was the more sinister one of the Union's heavy involvement in the American Cattle Trust. The Trust, shrouded in secrecy from the beginning, was the favorite object of cynical scrutiny by Western editors, and the fact that Thomas Sturgis held the dual offices of secretary of the American Cattle Trust and president of the Union Cattle Company lent credence to the opinion that the Union's downfall had been caused by the Trust. Actually, the talk, even if it was conjecture, was not ill-founded. Certainly the financial difficulties of the Trust had caught the Union Cattle Company in a period of financial readjustment; however, the Union failure was due to far more complex reasons than its tortuous connections with the Trust.

Both contemporary observation and later historical interpretation have resulted in a distorted portrayal of the era of liquidation in the cattle industry. The rise and fall of the range cattle business has commonly been described as a neat drama in three acts: The cattle industry began with a nomadic period, when herds grazed aimlessly over lush landscape. There followed a boom era, with wild speculation and huge returns; and this was succeeded by a decade of sharp contraction and an exodus of Eastern and foreign

---

[1] E. C. Abbott and Helena Huntington Smith: *We Pointed Them North* (New York: Farrar & Rinehart; 1939), 101–2.

[2] *Rocky Mountain Daily News*, January 18, 1888.

[3] Ibid., February 27, 1888.

capital. In a panoramic view, there is substantial accuracy in these generalizations, but considerable refinement is essential if reality is to be brought into sharper focus.

Eastern disenchantment with the range cattle industry did not suddenly erupt in 1887; many investors were skittish regarding their cattle paper as early as 1885. On the other hand, the frightening disaster of 1886–7 did not result in an immediate wholesale departure of Eastern capital. New investment after 1886–7 did decline to a trickle for more than five years, but while investors were reluctant to put fresh funds into the cattle industry, they frequently retained their original stock. Of the sample of 93 investors 48 held on to their cattle paper as late as 1895, and 29 of these financiers, or their families, still had their holdings after 1900. A hasty and enthusiastic commitment in the boom period did not necessarily change to a rapid departure in the transitional era. Speculators like the Swans, Waddinghams, and Hatches panicked and fled, but the Sturgises, Fields, and Clays—solid entrepreneurs with wide experience in investment—held on. Although the entrepreneurs might diversify their investments in the nineties, they left the gold-edged stock with the embossed popeyed steers in their portfolios.

However, both classes of investors—those who stayed and those who left—were given to excruciating introspection for months after "that year." In their analyses of the disaster they damned the extremes of both man and nature: overgrazing, overproduction, inflated stock subscription, and unusually inclement weather were the reasons reiterated to boredom in newspapers, on street corners, in the Cheyenne Club, or over cognac in the Union League Club. Occasionally, other factors came into the discussion, such as the invasion of "nesters," the general countrywide recession, and the lack of capital.

Another facet of the post-mortem seldom whispered on Carey Avenue but often proclaimed on Wall Street, was poor management. John Bigelow was typical of investors in petulant moods when he wrote asking his manager: "What have you been doing, if anything, for the past year?"[4] That the irritation of investors

4 John Bigelow to Hubert E. Teschemacher, May 11, 1886. Teschemacher

with their managers was not entirely unjust is demonstrated by the firms which managed to survive, such as the Warren Land and Livestock, the Matador, the Aztec Land and Cattle Company, the Bay State Cattle Company, and Pratt-Ferris, all of which had above-average managerial talent.

These firms also possessed adequate capital—another element essential for survival in a business world dominated by the ethics of Social Darwinism. Besides their actual bank accounts in their Eastern or regional institutions, investors like Marshall Field, Levi Leiter, William Rockefeller, and J. S. Case had only to nod gently at their bankers to assure a flow of money to their cattle companies. Henry Weare was not merely oozing sentimentality when he gushed to Uncle Portus: "Without your help, we would have gone under long ago. I realize how fortunate we have been when I ride along the Belle Fourche [River]."[5]

Three quarters of a century later, it is hardly a perilous occupation to perceive weaknesses in the economic structure of the range cattle industry. Both managers and investors must share the blame for the depression in the late eighties. Admittedly nature, in the hard winter of 1886-7 and the droughts on the southern plains beginning in 1885, was a contributing force. Specific losses are still open to debate; actual or imagined, however, they had the same psychological impact. Also leading to the debacle in the late eighties were the push of the "honyocker," driving his scraggly oxen before him and ripping up miles of sod; excessive interest rates and the inflexible credit system; overgrazing and the unrealistic land system; and overproduction and low cattle prices. Yet in some ultimate assessment, responsibility for the high mortality in cattle firms may rest heaviest on poor fiscal management both in the East and in the West. The truth was that many cattle companies were not run as businesses.

Infected with the optimism of the boom years, and enjoying the luxury of spending the unaudited funds of a group of investors a

and deBillier Collection, Western History Research Center, University of Wyoming.
[5] Henry Weare to Portus Weare, February 21, 1889. Nason Collection, Spearfish, South Dakota.

thousand or more miles distant, too many Western managers let the day-to-day managerial chores slide. They held a philosophical premise, wonderfully expressed by the young Harvard graduate Richard Trimble in answer to a querulous letter from his father:

I am sorry thee has so little confidence in my ability to judge whether it is for my advantage to stay on the ranch or in Cheyenne. There are two sides to the cattle business, the theory and the practice; one is learned better in Cheyenne where men congregate and the other on a ranch.[6]

One could sound expansive over a cranberry glass full of amber bourbon in Cheyenne or Roswell in convivial conversation with friends, with all thoughts of range problems dashed from one's head. Then came the autumn, when tallying brought the unwelcome realization that perhaps taking inspirational lessons in Cheyenne was less valuable than listening to the foreman's ungrammatical report out on the range. If managers were nonchalant, investors were often startlingly naive. In the delusion that investments multiplied with each calving in the spring, they were reluctant to give either the time or the sustained capital necessary to develop their Western enterprises. Cherishing their emancipation from reality, the investors were rudely jolted by the crash of the late eighties.

The painful necessity of liquidation was a challenge which elicited a variety of responses. Some managers, either fearing investors' reactions or hoping against hope for an upswing in the cattle market, delayed revealing the hopelessness of their financial plight. John B. Thomas, the manager-investor of the Suffolk Cattle Company, in a letter marked "confidential," confessed to a fellow Bostonian friend and investor: "We are in a horrible situation. I am not sure how long we will last, but *please* say nothing to C—— or the rest, they will know soon enough!"[7] Owing partly to the tenacity of its manager and partly to the wisdom of

6 Richard Trimble to Merritt Trimble, February 22, 1883. Trimble Collection, Western History Research Center, University of Wyoming.

7 John B. Thomas to Joseph Ames, December 8, 1887. Dunder Collection, Western History Research Center, University of Wyoming.

an investor committee, the Suffolk Cattle Company weathered its financial crisis.

Few corporations in the process of liquidation remained in that agonizing stage longer than the Teschemacher and deBillier Cattle Company. Incorporated on August 28, 1881, the company had three ranches, 2,000 head of cattle, an authorized capital of $250,-000, and a paid-up capital of $211,000.[8] After a year, the Harvard classmates Teschemacher and deBillier were even more confident that the rewards of a cattle enterprise were unlimited. While the dividend checks were a fresh memory, they polled their stockholders and requested authorization to increase their capitalization to $750,000. However, investors' subscriptions did not match investors' enthusiasm: the paid-up capital reached only $491,600.[9] Results of the augmented capital became apparent by 1883, when the Teschemacher and deBillier Company owned five ranches and 18,750 head of cattle with a marked valuation of $483,750.[1] Then trouble struck; the firm, which for three years had enjoyed high returns, was suddenly faced with a sharply reduced income when the price of range stock dropped to $2.50 per hundredweight in November 1884. This shaky situation prompted one stock journal to counsel: "If you have steers to shed, prepare to shed them now,"[2] advice that shook many a dozing investor to upright attention.

In 1884 and 1885 Teschemacher and deBillier stuck to their popular policy of paying dividends, but these dividend checks came from reserve capital, for the company borrowed $42,000 in the summer of 1884 to meet running expenses.[3] In 1885, Teschemacher reached the astounding conclusion that their range was

[8] "Incorporation of the Teschemacher and deBillier Cattle Company," *Record of Incorporations*, Secretary of State, Cheyenne, Wyoming (1881), I, 468. For more detailed delineation see Gene M. Gressley: "Teschemacher and deBillier Cattle Company," *Business History Review*, XXXIII (Summer 1959), 121–37.

[9] Teschemacher and deBillier Ledger, 1882, 19. Teschemacher and deBillier Collection, Western History Research Center, University of Wyoming.

[1] Ibid., 1883–5, 29.

[2] Louis Pelzer: *The Cattlemen's Frontier* (Glendale, Calif.: A. H. Clark Company; 1936), 139.

[3] Teschemacher and deBillier Ledger, 1883–5. Teschemacher and deBillier Collection, Western History Research Center, University of Wyoming.

inadequate for their herds. Perhaps the drop in the market had upset his equilibrium, because this revelation came less than sixteen months after he had assured his stockholders that the range would hold approximately 5,000 more head. Whatever his motive, several investors labeled the decision ridiculous. They were particularly piqued that the first time they learned of this move was in the annual report of 1885. John Bigelow commented:

> I now learn for the first time that the pasturage on our ranges was insufficient and that you were driving your stock into neighborhood states. I think this necessity and the occasion of it should have been communicated to the stockholders.
>
> I shall feel obliged to you for an explanation of this sudden default of our range, if that has made default, and if not, the reason for us boarding our stock in other states. . . .
>
> P.S. Would it not be better policy to take your stockholders in a little more of your confidence.[4]

The Teschemacher and deBillier Cattle Company came through the calamitous winter of 1886–7 in far better condition than many concerns: Teschemacher estimated that their company had losses totaling 10 per cent of their herd. Although the market for 1887 continued to drop, however, in a grand gesture at ignoring the winter's losses, plus the poor market a 4 per cent dividend was issued. This unalterable determination to declare dividends is not easily reconciled with the company's financial position. Teschemacher was forced to concede that dividend funds were available only after $36,000 was borrowed from the Stock Growers National Bank of Cheyenne.[5] Perhaps he regarded the dividend as an inevitable sop to the directors and of little permanent consequence if his policy of liquidation was adopted. For in his annual report for 1887, Teschemacher bluntly advised:

> There is very little doubt in my mind that there will be an advance in the price of beef next year and with this will come an advance in value of the range cattle, but I am still of the opinion that the company should dispose of their cattle as soon

[4] John Bigelow to H. E. Teschemacher, May 11, 1886. Ibid.
[5] *Annual Statement of the Teschemacher and deBillier Cattle Company,* 1887, 1. Ibid.

as practicable, and shall use every opportunity to effect the sale of their herd or any part of it.[6]

This recommendation to liquidate rounded off three years of expansion and two of hesitancy; but there would be five more years before the announced plans for liquidation were concluded. The amazingly long and tortuous winding-up period can be explained only by the reluctance of the managers to take their own advice. This may not have surprised the stockholders, however, since a chief reason for the muddled affairs of the Teschemacher and deBillier Cattle Company was the multi-administrative arrangement.[7] Until Richard Trimble returned East in 1885, he, H. E. Teschemacher, and Fred deBillier all shared the managerial duties, much to the confusion of their head foreman Jim Shaw, who was exasperated by the number of conflicting orders which came either from Cheyenne or from the ranch headquarters at Uva, Wyoming. Once Shaw wrote to Cheyenne from the Telegraph Ranch: "Somebody at Uva better come out here soon, if you fellows don't want a mess."[8]

The Teschemacher and deBillier Cattle Company could not seem to stay in or get out of the cattle business. But apparently this "first we are, now we aren't" predicament was no reason to forego the pleasure of dividends, since in 1889 a 3 per cent dividend was declared. The pestiferous John Bigelow, scanning the 1889 dividend check, sarcastically wrote:

I have been looking over your last statement today. . . . The expenses are manifestly disproportionate to earnings. I would feel greatly obliged if you would send me a list of the people employed on and for the ranch during the past year with their respective compensations and also a statement of the supplies and cost, neither of which appears in your report. I believe there must be some leakage in this department of the business which is worth looking after.[9]

[6] Ibid.
[7] Richard Trimble to Merritt Trimble, October 14, 1886. Trimble Collection, Western History Research Center, University of Wyoming.
[8] Jim Shaw to Fred deBillier, January 23, 1886. Teschemacher and deBillier Collection, Western History Research Center, University of Wyoming.
[9] John Bigelow to H. E. Teschemacher, February 21, 1889. Ibid.

Other stockholders had also protested that expenses bore little relation to earnings. This failure to reduce costs in ratio to earnings is inexplicable and inexcusable. Augustus Gurnee cryptically wrote: "The labor costs for 20,000 head are the same as for 12,000 head, why is this?"[1]—but Teschemacher left the letter unanswered. In 1890 and 1891, dividends of 1½ per cent were mailed out, together with a summary statement that progress was being made in winding up the company's accounts. The stockholders would have to take that statement on faith, for there was little evidence of "things seen." The number of cattle had held constant for two years; so how "progress" was defined is a mystery.

The Johnson County War between homesteaders and ranchers in 1892 helped to accomplish what the managers had been unable to do for five years:[2] Teschemacher and deBillier played active roles in this fiasco, and both left Wyoming soon after. DeBillier, suffering from a nervous breakdown, disappeared in the South for a time. Teschemacher, after hurriedly arranging for the sale of their herd to Senator Francis E. Warren,[3] departed for Central City, Nebraska, six days before Christmas in 1892. The affairs of the company were left in the hands of Henry G. Hay, president of the Stock Growers National Bank and later assistant secretary of the United States Steel Corporation, who succeeded in closing the books of Teschemacher and deBillier the following summer. Actually, the investors' losses were not staggering in comparison with those of other firms in the West. If the cause of this company's failure can be attributed to any single factor, it was poor management. Nowhere was this shortcoming more obvious than in the corporation's fumbling attempts at settling its business after a liquidation policy had been decided on. This ineptness exasperated the stockholders and frustrated the management.

When Teschemacher and deBillier first arrived in Wyoming in 1879, they developed a fast friendship with the Sturgis brothers,

[1] Augustus Gurnee to H. E. Teschemacher, March 22, 1889. Ibid.
[2] The issues of the Johnson County War are briefly outlined in Chapter 8.
[3] Henry G. Hay to F. E. Warren, April 20, 1893. Wyoming Stock Growers Association Collection, Western History Research Center, University of Wyoming.

Thomas and William. The Sturgises had emigrated to Wyoming from Missouri in 1873, and in partnership with William C. Lane and Gordon B. Goodell, had staked out three ranches in northeastern Wyoming and southwestern Dakota.[4] For a decade the business prospered, and the partners took a prominent place in the political and economic life of the territory. Thomas Sturgis, as a founder of the Wyoming Stock Growers Association, served as the first secretary; his brother William, as assistant secretary, became his alter ego. Thomas Sturgis also established the Stock Growers National Bank, serving as its first president. John Clay highlighted their influence in his autobiography:

> There were two factions in cattle circles at that time in Cheyenne. A crowd worshipped at the shrine of Swan; another lot looked to Tom Sturgis for inspiration. The Swan coterie mostly did business at the First National Bank; the other crowd supported the Stock Growers National Bank. On the surface everything was lovely, but when you got into the inside circle you soon found out that the lines of demarcation were plainly marked. Intellectually Sturgis was head and shoulders above them all.[5]

In 1883, caught up in the expansionist fever, Thomas Sturgis boarded the Union Pacific in Cheyenne and headed for Boston. Sturgis's name, well known in Boston for over a century, opened the black-enameled, gold-knobbed doors of Boston's financial elite, and his rounds on Beacon Hill met with excellent success, especially after the equally illustrious names of Alexander Agassiz, Henry L. Higginson, and Quincy Shaw were added to his board of directors. With the capital furnished by Boston subscribers, Sturgis formed a new concern—the Union Cattle Company—which absorbed the entire assets of Sturgis, Lane and Goodell.[6]

In a formal but nostalgic letter to Henry L. Higginson in Jan-

[4] Robber's Roost Historical Society: *Pioneering on the Cheyenne River* (Lusk, Wyo.: 1956), 5.
[5] Clay: *My Life on the Range*, 66.
[6] The Union Cattle Company was incorporated on February 27, 1883. Incorporation records, Western Range Cattle Industry Collection, State Historical Society of Colorado.

uary 1888, Thomas Sturgis reviewed its history.[7] It was his sad duty to advise, he said, that on January 17, 1888, the Wyoming court had appointed two receivers for the Union Cattle Company. Sturgis gave a strict account of the assets and liabilities for the preceding five years. The capitalization of $2,000,000 included the property of "sixty thousand head of cattle, with very complete outfit of horses, wagons, ranch buildings, corrals, as well as some eight thousand acres of land in fee, and grazing privileges over *four and a half million more*,"[8] all valued at $2,400,000. Set against these assets was a $600,000 chattel mortgage.

The "markedly prosperous and fertile years" of 1883 and 1884 had produced dividends of 8 per cent each. The first hint of financial trouble, Sturgis said, came in 1885: "It had been thought that the distance of your ranges from civilization precluded the possibility of any annoyance from immigrants who might settle for many years to come. But these expectations proved to be fallacious and the purchase of land became absolutely necessary." Then repeated the cascade of bad fortune which struck the Union Cattle Company. Beef prices fell, the grass "gradually grew thin," and expensive feeding operations became essential so that a feeding station was purchased at Gilmore, Nebraska, for a quarter-million dollars. In less than nineteen months the company's debt soared from $600,000 to $1,600,000, largely because of the tremendous acquisition of land and the feeding station at Gilmore. The interest on this debt alone threatened to engulf their operating budget. Sturgis said that "with the income of the company as of 1883 and 1884, the interest on our debt was not oppressive, but the situation having materially changed it was deemed wise to fund the debt if possible." Debenture bonds were marketed in the autumn of 1886 for $749,000, and the balance of the debt was carried on the books.

The original investors—Agassiz, Higginson, Shaw, and the Sturgis family—underwrote the largest percentage of the bond

[7] Thomas Sturgis to Henry L. Higginson, February 5, 1888. Higginson Collection, Baker Library, Harvard University.

[8] Italics are the author's.

offering, not in a spirit of fervent loyalty to the Union Cattle Company, but in awareness that selling bonds to anyone outside the company would be difficult to impossible.[9] From their correspondence with the Sturgises, it seems doubtful that the Boston investors were totally aware of the seriousness of the Union Cattle Company's predicament. At least, years later Higginson moaned that "we were in the dark." Whether or not this was remorse in retrospect or justification for past ignorance is difficult to discern.

Once the Union Cattle Company began a downhill slide, it gathered momentum with each passing month. When the firm decided to join the American Cattle Trust in the spring of 1887, a herd tally was taken. Although, according to Sturgis, "your officers thought they had 55,000 head of cattle on their range . . . the tally showed but 30,000 left."[1] In one sentence Sturgis summarized the Union Cattle Company's "frightful" dilemma: "Your beef cattle had shrunk in selling value from $60.00 per head in 1883 to $20.00 in 1887, and the value per head of the main body of the herd had decreased in nearly equal proportion." After this chilling explanation there was little left to be said. Sturgis concluded his painful letter with one meager consolation: "The ill fate that has pursued your company is not peculiar to it, but has been shared by all its neighbors, by many to a greater degree."

But the Boston investors were not comforted by this sentiment, and they tended to blame the Sturgises instead of fate. Although the receivers in Cheyenne collected the pieces of the company with dispatch, haggling went on among Sturgis and his Boston acquaintances from receivership in 1888 until 1893, when the company office doors were finally locked. Higginson and Shaw kept unrelenting pressure on the Sturgises for more funds. The Sturgises in turn thrashed about trying to find the capital to liquidate their debts. William Sturgis pleaded with J. B. Warner of Boston for funds to retain his life insurance policy: "Surely there must be men in Boston who would wish a six per cent investment on such security." He reminded Warner that the Sturgis family's

[9] F. K. Sturgis to Henry L. Higginson, undated. Higginson Collection, Baker Library, Harvard University.
[1] Thomas Sturgis to Henry L. Higginson, February 5, 1888. Ibid.

fortunes had not always been this low: "That name used to be well known on State Street when my old Uncle William Sturgis was alive."[2] They finally found Lyman Gage, a Chicago banker, who was willing to do what their Boston friends were not, namely, to extend their loans. Under the continued prodding of Henry L. Higginson, Thomas Sturgis exploded: "I am under moral obligation, which I full recognize, to do as I agreed and if I live and recover myself, financially, which last I assure you I am going to do, I will keep good my guarantee to Mr. Shaw. In the meantime, I must ask him to wait."[3]

Even in liquidation, bad luck pursued the Union Cattle Company. As Sturgis wrote Higginson, on July 31, 1890, at the Gilmore feeding station, "The whole plant went up in flames, I am heartsick."[4] At last Higginson assumed a more philosophical attitude and told Frederick Voorhees, one of the Cheyenne receivers: "Shaw and I have become resigned to the fact that most of our investment is gone. But we will do our best to save what we can."[5] He was not being facetious; over the next two years, Higginson used all his financial ingenuity to reduce the liabilities of the Union Cattle Company by first one means and then another. In October 1892, he finally told F. K. Sturgis, a relative of Thomas Sturgis: "The Union Cattle Company situation is hopeless, Shaw and I have decided to end the negotiation quickly."[6] Thus the firm came to an end in 1892, although the Sturgis family retained investments in and around Cheyenne through the First World War.[7]

During the nineties, the era of economic readjustment, speeches given at stock growers conventions were filled with fire and brimstone as orators denounced the full range of pet enemies—the Eastern monopolists, the government in Washington, the nesters, the railroads, ad infinitum. The editor of the *Northwestern Livestock Journal*, A. S. Mercer, felt profoundly moved by the warm

2 William Sturgis to J. B. Warner, October 13, 1888. Ibid.
3 Thomas Sturgis to Henry L. Higginson, February 11, 1889. Ibid.
4 Ibid., August 15, 1890.
5 H. L. Higginson to Fred P. Voorhees, September 17, 1890. Ibid.
6 H. L. Higginson to F. K. Sturgis, October 28, 1892. Ibid.
7 Mrs. Hebard Paine to Gene M. Gressley, May 20, 1958.

reception accorded him as a speaker at the Helena convention of
the Montana Stock Growers Association. The intoxicating ap-
plause moved him to switch from mundane matters of quarantine
to a free-swinging attack on the Eastern press:

> If we scuttle the ship, we go down together. Never in the
> history of the cattle business has there been a time when there
> was so much at stake with the cattlemen as today. Every Jim-
> crow paper from the city of New York to San Francisco is
> today making it its business to belittle and demean the cattle-
> man of the plains. Why? They don't know that situation. They
> have laid hold of a few garbled extracts—cowboy slanders, and
> all that sort of thing until they are warped in their ideas.[8]

As Mercer ran down and dinner time approached, he put forward
his unstartling solution: "The Western country has got to come
together and consolidate. We have all got to combine and leave
local prejudice outside . . . all pull together!"

Yet five years later, Mercer turned his editorial wrath against
the Wyoming Stock Growers Association in a bitter attack on
the Johnson County "invasion." From the day it came off the
press, Mercer's sensational book *The Banditti of the Plains* has
been one of the most-hunted volumes in Western history, both
for destruction and preservation, depending on one's motive. As
a *persona non grata* in Cheyenne, Mercer moved to the Bighorn
basin in northern Wyoming, where he lived the rest of his life.

Investors and their managers flitted in carrousel fashion from
solution to solution in search of a restorative for their economic
ills. Throughout the winter of 1886–7, rumors floated about that a
gigantic trust of all the cattle-producing interests in the country
was being formed.[9] The initial reaction was mixed; Major William
Shepherd, a British tourist who prided himself on having a more
sophisticated knowledge of the Western American than his fellow
countrymen, pontificated on the mixed feelings about monopoly
which he discerned in the Westerner.

[8] *Minute Books*, Montana Stock Growers Association, Historical Society
of Montana.

[9] *Rocky Mountain Daily News*, January 20, 1887; French: *Some Recollections of a Western Ranchman*, 142; Las Vegas *Daily Optic*, December 3,
1886.

There is nothing the Western man calls out against more than he does against monopolies. Yet five minutes after a tirade, in which excellent principles have been laid down, and the injury to the cowboy and its citizens dwelt upon from railway, holders of large land tracts, owners of bonanza mines, and millionaries generally, you find that this ardent Republican has either a quartz ledge or a water privilege which he is wailing for some Eastern monopolist to develop, or that he may be an arrant monopolist himself in a small way, have secured from the county the right to buy tools on a road which has not cost him twenty days labor, or he has fenced in some natural curiosity, or has enclosed the only water to be met along miles of road travelled years before he settled the district. In truth, everywhere the public good is sacrificed to the interest of individuals.[1]

Shepherd's observations were perceptive; the Westerner definitely had passed a schizophrenic view of the Easterner and monopoly. On the one hand, he recognized that Eastern capital was essential to the West's economic development, even survival; yet this very dependence made him rebellious.

The first substantive information that Westerners received about the Cattle Trust came early in 1887, when on a cold, blustery February 9th, Edward M. McGillin, a dry-goods entrepreneur of Cleveland, Ohio, and an extremely heavy investor in the range cattle industry, addressed the International Range Association meeting in Denver, Colorado.[2] His acid speech was directed at the meat-packers of the East who, he maintained, controlled the cattle markets. By this monopoly, they were bankrupting the cattle grower with ruinous prices.

The only sensible answer was to fight monopoly with monopoly, McGillin said, and quickly presented his plan for a huge trust, incorporated at one hundred million dollars. This corpora-

---

[1] William R. E. Shepherd: *Prairie Experiences in Handling Cattle and Sheep* (New York: O. Judd; 1885), 130.
[2] The discussion in this chapter follows Gene M. Gressley: "The American Cattle Trust: A Study in Protest," *Pacific Historical Review*, XXX (February 1961), 61–77. There have been a few significant changes on the basis of post-publication research in the Higginson Collection, Baker Library, Harvard University.

tion would "arrange, manage, sell every animal from the time it was dropped a calf until it was beef in the consumer's basket." How was the capital to be raised from investors and cattlemen? McGillin had a ready answer: subscribing cattlemen would mortgage their herds to the extent of $5 per head, and the sum would be payable in five annual installments subject to 6 per cent interest. These payments would be deducted from beef sales by the proposed monopoly. No cattle were to be sold outside the pool by members a. any price. Each state was responsible for electing its own directors, these directors would elect a president, and the various state presidents would be directors of the national company. McGillin concluded his oration with a blend of admonition and futuristic omen:

> Fail to organize the company I propose and inside of ten, more likely five years, there will be no such thing in this country as a ranchman, and not one-third of even the present depressed prices for such ranch property will be realized. Start my company on the basis I propose, and inside of ten years the stock of the company will be worth more than all your range properties, and this will be accomplished without putting up the price of beef to consumers one cent.[3]

McGillin's speech was politely applauded. The delegates' immediate reaction was calm, but during the next two days, corridors buzzed with talk of it. After the convention adjourned, the newspapers took up the debate, and for four months "correspondents from Santa Fe, Cheyenne, Omaha" appeared in the Western press arguing the pros and cons of the Trust.

The debate centered on the feasibility of McGillin's scheme—not on whether there should or should not be a trust. Monopoly was accepted, but the definition of it was far from unanimous. One of the most tenacious opponents of the Trust was Orzo A. Hadley, former governor of Arkansas and a New Mexico cattleman. Hadley's main objection to McGillin's idea was that it was far too complex and gigantic, so that if by some fortuitous cir-

[3] *Rocky Mountain Daily News*, February 10, 1887.

cumstance it should be born, it would collapse of its own weight.[4]
Hadley turned from this negative argument to a positive one. He
proposed that instead of attempting to cover all transactions related to the cattle industry, they should restrict the alliance to the
packing and transportation industries. Furthermore, no cattleman
should be compelled to sell to the Trust's packing company unless the price received was as high as the market price. R. G. Head,
manager of the Prairie Land and Cattle Company, immediately
denounced Hadley's proposal as "unworkable." Head insisted that
unless one took the commission agent, feeder, and other middle-
men into a trust, any attempt at monopoly would be foredoomed.[5]

All the debate became academic when on May 3, 1887, the
New York *Times* reported the formation of the American Cattle
Trust. Behind that announcement were three months of hard bargaining. Returning to Cleveland after his speech, McGillin had
renewed his contact with Thomas Sturgis and urged him to assume
the lead in getting the Trust under way. Sturgis agreed, after
discovering that Eastern investors were immediately receptive.
After all, this was the era of trusts; what was more natural than to
solve the economic sickness of the cattle industry by forming a
monopoly?

In organization, the American Cattle Trust was modeled directly
after the Standard Oil Trust. In early April, F. K. Sturgis bragged
to Henry L. Higginson: "We have (through influence) obtained
a copy of the Standard Oil Trust, a most difficult thing to do."[6]
Further, Sturgis trumpeted that they had managed to secure the
cooperation of the huge Chicago packer Nelson Morris. "It will
be the *salvation* of the ranch interests when I tell you that Morris
kills 1,000 steers daily and utilizes them in every part; you will
readily see the gain will be very great if the ranch interest can
share the *slaughtering profits*." Sturgis closed by predicting that

[4]*Northwestern Livestock Journal*, July 15, 1887; Denver *Republican*,
July 16, 1887.
[5] Ibid.
[6] F. K. Sturgis to Henry L. Higginson, April 7, 1887. Higginson Collection,
Baker Library, Harvard University.

soon the Cattle Trust certificates would be listed on the stock exchange: "I see no reason why they should not be as good, or better, than the cotton oil trust certificates."

But Higginson, already enmeshed in the financial intricacies of the Union Cattle Company, was querulous when he heard of the Trust's development. In a "My dear Henry" letter, Sturgis did his best to reassure the skeptical Boston investment broker: "I am not surprised that you ask if this cattle trust is safe."[7] If the cotton trust is safe, Sturgis argued, the cattle trust is safe—with more than a bit of flattery Sturgis added: "Safe, because you will be in the management"—safe because of Nelson Morris's solid knowledge and immense influence in the packing industry. Then Sturgis weakened his assurances of safety by explaining: "What I hope you can do is to say to a few of your rich people, 'here is a big gamble . . . let me buy your interest in it on the ground floor to make or lose.'" Sturgis appeared to be saying that if gambling is safe, then the American Cattle Trust is safe, but after consideration Higginson concluded that if the Union Cattle Company was going to subscribe to the Trust, he should become active in the monopoly for his own protection.

Gilded on the office door of the American Cattle Trust in New York, the names of the board of directors made an imposing roster. It reflected a judicious blend of leading cattlemen and Eastern financial figures: For the West, there were John L. Routt, governor of Colorado, R. G. Head of New Mexico, C. C. Slaughter and John T. Lytle of Texas, and Thomas Sturgis and Francis E. Warren of Wyoming; representing the East were Richard T. Wilson, Jr., broker, Samuel Thomas, ironmonger, Charles T. Smillie, importer, and Charles T. Leonhardt, stockbroker, of New York. The first—and last—officers of the Trust were Thomas Sturgis, chairman, Richard T. Wilson, vice-chairman, and Charles T. Leonhardt, secretary-treasurer. Assisting these officers were eleven state trustees who were charged with the direction of the Trust's affairs at a local level.[8]

The Trust was still in process of organization when there was

[7] Ibid., April 9, 1887.
[8] *American Cattle Trust Statement* (New York: 1890).

controversy over the inclusion of Nelson Morris as an adviser to the directors. Thomas and Smillie insisted that if the Trust desired to retain the confidence (and money) of investors, someone of Morris's experience and stature in the packing industry was essential.[9] This was especially true since the packing operation side of the Trust would require the heaviest slice of the initial capitalization. Warren fretted that if Morris's name were closely identified with the Trust, their enemies would immediately say that the Trust was in collusion with the packing industry.[1] His anxiety was well grounded; critics of the Trust harped on just this theme.

After its organization, the Trust rapidly developed. Morris's Chicago plant was bought for $2,000,000; feeding farms were purchased next to those of the Union Cattle Company at Gilmore, Nebraska;[2] contracts for canned beef were negotiated with the French and Belgian governments.[3] A hundred thousand cattle, so it was rumored, were necessary to fulfill the French contract alone. Sturgis had barely settled into his office chair before he had a host of applications from concerns asking for admission to the Trust.

Two thorny problems, never successfully resolved, were first, who would appraise the property of an applicant, and second, what type and what amount of credit would be extended to the affiliating company until the first cattle were sent to the stockyards.[4] Finally, as to appraisal, the solution was to have three appraisers, one chosen by the Trust, one by the applicant, and the third by both the Trust and the applicant. When the evaluation had been concluded, the new company's property was paid for in Trust certificates, valued at twenty-five cents on the dollar. The certificates were frankly conceded to be highly speculative. Fran-

[9] American Cattle Trust Letterbook, August 26, May 13, September 9, 1887. Western History Research Center, University of Wyoming.
[1] Francis E. Warren to Thomas Sturgis, August 12, 1887. American Cattle Trust Letterbook, Western History Research Center, University of Wyoming.
[2] *Northwestern Livestock Journal*, June 10, 1887.
[3] Denver *Republican*, June 6, 1887.
[4] Francis E. Warren to Charles Ferris, July 28, 1887. American Cattle Trust Letterbook, Western History Research Center, University of Wyoming.

cis Warren candidly wrote to the well-endowed banker and stockman of Lander, Wyoming, Eugene Amoretti:

> It is believed that these Certificates will largely increase in
> value the moment the turn comes in cattle, and even if no rise
> occurs in cattle we expect some advance in the Certificates. If
> a man takes the Certificates and holds for a rise, we believe the
> Certificates will rise faster than the cattle themselves, so that
> at a later date, if the Certificates are sold, more would be realized
> than by keeping cattle for the rise and then selling.[5]

Within six months after the first board meeting, there was dissension at every managerial level. The Eastern trustees, uninitiated
in the economics of the cattle business, held to the opinion that
solvency and profit depended on the sale of all marketable cattle
every shipping season.[6] The Western managers labeled this policy
ridiculous and advocated an increase in the capitalization so that
feeding operations could be expanded. They argued that the herds
could be held for the most advantageous price. The Eastern
trustees refused even to consider the possibility of increasing the
capital. By the spring of 1888, there was a stalemate concerning
the direction in which the Trust would move next.

The Western trustees carried on a running dispute—on the one
hand with their Eastern counterparts, and on the other hand with
the local managers. One trustee complained: "I am full up with
tiffs."[7] The amalgamation of the affiliating company herds led to
endless disagreement. Some managers claimed that they were assigned too many cattle to raise profitably on their allotted domain. Others protested that the geographical areas given to their
herds were parceled out without due regard to water rights,
settlers, or competing livestock interests.

In spite of the managerial upheaval by the spring of 1888, the
structure of the Trust had been completed. The total number of
cattle stood at 218,934, with a "conservative" valuation of $3,862,-
214.76. The total resources, including land, equipment, and the

---

[5] Francis E. Warren to Eugene Amoretti, September 6, 1887. Ibid.
[6] Francis E. Warren to Thomas Sturgis, October 2, 1887. Ibid.
[7] R. G. Head to Francis E. Warren, August 7, 1887. Warren Collection,
Western History Research Center, University of Wyoming.

packing plant, came to $7,959,071.61.[8] When these figures are compared with the number of cattle in Wyoming in 1888, which totaled 753,648 valued at $10,186,362.75,[9] any pretense the Trust made at having a monopoly of the cattle produced in the West, let alone in the rest of the country, was plainly ludicrous. In fact, 85 per cent of the members of the Trust lived in Texas, New Mexico, Colorado, and Wyoming.

The first glow of enthusiasm and interest in the Trust by applicants began to wane in the summer of 1888. Potential members became more and more reluctant to ally themselves with the Trust. Francis Warren shrewdly analyzed prospective candidates:

I find this about herds coming in: First, very many are not in condition financially to pay their expenses until fall or secure release of mortgages, or arrange for certificates to be taken in lieu of other security. . . .

Second, a class of men who can come in with their cattle are firm believers in a large rise in cattle in the near future and believe that the commodity itself will rise faster than the certificates representing them.

Third, another class are putting in their time either for salary, or with their own cattle, have ranches and wish to keep property under their own individual ownership as far as possible.

Then after the foregoing classes comes those who are afraid of change and stay out until they see; those who are suspicious of everything (and this is an exceedingly large number); and still others who are jealous because they were not first and failed to get prominent positions.[1]

The 1889 financial report revealed the dismal state of the Trust: The total herd count was now only 164,472, with an appraised

8 *American Cattle Trust Statement* (New York: 1890). For some inexplicable reason, calves and bulls were omitted from the Trust's calculations.
9 *Report of the Governor of Wyoming to the Secretary of the Interior, 1887* (Washington: 1888), 8–10, 657–9.
1 Francis E. Warren to Thomas Sturgis, July 24, 1887. American Cattle Trust Letterbook, Western History Research Center, University of Wyoming.

valuation of $2,911,286.18.[2] But the trustees cavalierly dismissed the decline in assets and declared a 3 per cent dividend, evidently because they felt that if the dividend was passed, it would only serve to reveal the true position of the Trust—namely, bankruptcy.

The year 1890 saw no improvement, although there was an increase in the Trust's afflictions. The slowly rising cattle market was more a harbinger of false hopes than of actual improvement. The homesteader continued his relentless push onto the range. The meat-packing-company subsidiary sustained a loss in 1889 and continued to lose in 1890. The drive for markets in the East resulted in a complete rout, because the Trust had neither the resources nor the ability to compete with Swift and Armour. The cost of feeding at the Gilmore farms exceeded the receipts for 1889.[3]

Although the trustees refused to face it, the dissolution of the Trust was obvious to all impartial observers by the spring of 1890.[4] The actual liquidation that began in the summer was done with ease, but not without pain. Since a high percentage of the liabilities of the Trust were carried in the pockets of the trustees, the erasure of the deficits was a bookkeeping procedure.[5]

Economically the Trust had been an unmitigated failure. As a protest movement, it was a significant indication of the temper of both the Western cattlemen and the Eastern investors, and from its wreckage both parties absorbed a lesson. With a couple of notable exceptions, such as the Co-operative Livestock Commission Company and George B. Loving's abortive monopoly plan in 1910, cattleman and investor now switched from economic to political means as a proper weapon to relieve their plight.

Over the decade following the passing of the Trust, many of its leaders found their way into politics: names such as Baxter, Slaughter, Head, Routt, Warren, and Hadley appeared with frequency on election ballots. These men were all in the forefront of the agitation against the packing industry. At the national level, the

[2] *Amermican Cattle Trust Statement* (New York: 1890).
[3] Denver *Republican*, June 20, 1888.
[4] *Rocky Mountain Daily News*, July 21, 1890.
[5] Cheyenne *Daily Sun*, August 24, 1890.

first political recognition of the cattlemen's attack came with the Vest Committee investigation of 1888–9.[6] Headed by Senator George Vest of Missouri, who could boast among his wide accomplishments the authorship of a famous eulogy to a dog, the committee took the testimony of 110 witnesses in seven different cities. As the committee moved from city to city, the Western and Eastern press gave wide and often caustic coverage to its hearings. After assimilating the laborious testimony of all witnesses, who insisted that they represented their phase of the livestock industry, the committee categorically affirmed that a combination indeed existed among the packers.

Fourteen years after the Vest Committee report came the next major investigation of the packing industry, when a representative from South Dakota, S. W. Martin, introduced a resolution to have an inquiry into livestock prices. The Martin resolution was a culmination of two years of public and legislative flagellation of the dress beef industry. The Commissioner of Corporations, J. R. Garfield, was assigned to lead this investigation, and his report in 1905 was decidedly unsettling to the critics of the dress beef industry. Garfield emphatically noted: "The investigation shows that the profit of the packer per head per hundred pounds of dress beef is relatively small and that it cannot exercise a very important influence either on the cattle raiser or on the consumer of beef."[7] The report dumbfounded cattlemen. Vehement accusations were hurled at the committee; but as with so much oratory, it was lively and spirited, but devoid of concrete results.

Another ten years elapsed before the pressure had built up for the third investigation. This time, a representative from Missouri, William P. Boland, introduced a resolution to probe the complaints of monopoly against the packers. A vitriolic debate killed the Boland resolution, and Boland and his friends tried another tack. They persuaded President Wilson to authorize the Federal

[6] "Testimony taken by the Select Committee of the United States Senate on the Transportation and Sale of Meat Products," 51st Congress, 1st Session, *Senate Report 829*.

[7] "Report of the Commissioner of Corporations on the Beef Industry," 58th Congress, 3rd Session, *House Document 382*, 268.

Trade Commission to inquire into the "alleged violation of the antitrust laws." The Trade Commission diligently, if not enthusiastically, uncovered evidence for over a year. At the conclusion of their search, they flatly announced that there was without any doubt "a definite and positive conspiracy for the purpose of regulation purchase of livestock and controlling the prices of meat.[8]

The opponents of the packing industry, better organized this time than during the previous investigations, seized on the findings of the commission and began a pestiferous legislative barrage. The most vigorous and tenacious leaders were Senators John B. Kendrick of Wyoming, William S. Kenyon of Iowa, and Asle Gronna of North Dakota, together with Representative Gilbert Haugen of Iowa. The final consequence of their legislative pressure was the Packers and Stockyards Act of 1921,[9] a much-watered-down version of the Gronna and Kenyon bills of the previous sessions. The passage of the Packers and Stockyards Act was full recognition that the cattlemen were cognizant of what the grangers had realized three decades before; a successful attack on a monopoly depended on a political and not an economic vehicle.

While the cattleman on the national scene was engaged in a struggle with the packers, back at the ranch he was occupied with a set of problems peculiar to a new era. The passing of the unfenced range did not go unnoticed in the Western press. In articles colored by romanticism and nostalgia and bordering on the maudlin, the "splendor" of the range days was described and redescribed. The Wyoming *Tribune* remembered "the cattle barons" as "waxing powerful and rich, their ambitions were unlimited and in some cases their greed startling."[1] *Field and Farm* saw the cattleman as the ghost of an almost forgotten past: "A more honorable set of men were never engaged in any busi-

[8] *Report* of the Federal Trade Commission on the Meat Packing Industry (Washington: 1919), Part I, 32.
[9] "Packers and Stockyards Act, 1921," *United States Statutes at Large,* 67th Congress, 1st Session, Vol. XLII, Part I, 159–70.
[1] Wyoming *Tribune,* March 30, 1904.

ness; they loved God and feared only the devil, they were liberal and just to their fellow men, hence their success. . . ."[2]

For those who whined about their present predicament, the experienced cattleman had nothing but disdain. R. G. Head told a reporter: "I hear a great deal of complaint about the low price of stock cattle these days. Men who have them to sell think they are going to be ruined." Head thought this was pure fantasy: "Why, when I was a young man down in Texas, a dollar and a half and two per head was all that was expected for yearlings and two year olds and yet we lived and paid our debts."[3] Some newspapers saw light in inky darkness; the editor of *Field and Farm* reminded his readers that in contrast to the past: "The business is now run on business principles and not as speculation."[4]

Whether one was emotionally attuned to the new age or not, there was no debate that transition was the era's keynote. The metamorphosis from an open range to a ranch economy became more accepted with each passing year. Feeding, an experimental device for range cattlemen in the eighties, became the standard procedure by the nineties. The fight to maintain the same level of profit on smaller herds forced cattlemen to upgrade their herds through selective breeding. The importation of pedigreed bulls, once regarded as a luxury and a fad, now became a necessity.

Eastern and foreign corporations, burdened with massive sections of the domain, now searched for profitable ways to shed their unproductive real estate. One of the favorite techniques was to carve the range into farms to supply the farmers' pressure for land, although some corporations came only reluctantly to this conclusion. Julius Day of New Mexico and New Haven, Connecticut, treasurer of the Bell Ranch, wrote his manager: "It looks as though we would at last have to admit . . . that we cannot afford to graze cattle on corn and wheat lands, but I think that if we still are to consider selling that great property,

---

[2] *Field and Farm*, March 6, 1897.
[3] Ibid., July 6, 1889.
[4] Ibid., October 31, 1891.

we should make up our mind the highest price that we can ask and then stand for it."[5]

Other cattlemen were much less hesitant about fencing off farms and then advertising their land widely for colonization. The once-hated nester now became the beloved farmer, the means to economic salvation. The man whom Francis Smith considered such a good loan risk in the 1890's, Edward Lasater, began colonizing his 300,000-acre "pasture" in south Texas shortly after the turn of the century.[6] A rash of subdividing occurred in the panhandle and west Texas ranches for two decades after the beginning of the twentieth century. The XIT Ranch, spurred by the need of capital and a ready market, sold off much of its land. The Bovina Cattle Company, once part of the three-million-acre XIT, created farms from its range.[7] The Snyder brothers staked farms over their land in a desperate attempt to stave off their financial collapse,[8] and the Muleshoe Ranch followed suit soon after. The Ellwoods, father and son, at first dismissed all thought of parceling their estate, but they began to weaken as they received more and more attractive offers.[9] Two of the best-managed and most successful colonization schemes were carried out by S. W. Swenson and Sons, who took over the Spur lands and the White Deer Company, which was a remnant of the gigantic Francklyn Land and Cattle Company.[1] The visionary C. W. Post saw west Texas as a mecca for the unemployed and established Post City, Texas, as the nucleus for his farming community. A Utopian philanthropist, Post did not fit the mold in Texas or Michigan.[2]

[5] Julius Day to Charles O'Donel, May 29, 1908. Bell Ranch Collection, University of New Mexico Library.

[6] J. Logan Jones: *The Individualist, An Autobiography* (Kansas City, Mo.: Brown-White-Lowell Press; 1942), 218.

[7] Thelma Walker Stevens: "History of Bailey County" (unpublished master's thesis, Texas Technological College, 1939), 24.

[8] Ibid., 32–4.

[9] Fred Horsborvan to W. L. Ellwood, March 14, November 24, 1911. Ellwood Collection, Western History Research Center, University of Wyoming.

[1] J. E. Ericson: "Colonization of the Spur Farm Lands," *West Texas Historical Association Yearbook*, XXXI (October 1955), 41–53.

[2] Charles D. Eaves and C. A. Hutchinson: *Post City, Texas* (Austin: Texas State Historical Association; 1952), *passim*. Nettie Leitch Major: *C. W.*

The cattleman's enemies, the railroads, eagerly cooperated with these projects, offering prospective settlers enticing rates to venture to the land of their dreams, sometimes even furnishing box lunches for the journey. Once at the point of debarkation, the "excursionists" eagerly seized the opportunity to scramble off their trains and unlimber. Usually they were met by long streams of assorted vehicles and quickly carted off to be given an en- thusiastic sales talk on the rewards of living in west Texas. One enterprising would-be settler asked a cowboy what the principal crop was, to which he received the disconcerting reply, "Suck- ers!"[3] Fortunately for this tourist, he had not committed himself irrevocably.

The commission firm of Gunter and Muson replied with unadulterated glee to one customer concerning the real estate values in Mineral City, Texas.

We have received many letters asking for the same informa- tion within the last five years, and take as much pleasure in answering them as reading them. There have been around hundreds and perhaps thousands of lots sold in Mineral City and there is big money in it—to those that sell the lots. But these lots in Mineral City have one great drawback—they are so hard to find. We have been living in this county for ten years and in spite of all our efforts we have never been able to find the place. . . . The finding of this mystic metropolis would dry away the tears from many a disappointed eye; and bring joy to those long drowned in despair. The founders of this city have seen fit to leave this country preferring to go to China as Missionaries, rather than gaze upon the walls of our penitentiary. . . . If you have lots in Mineral City we would advise you to sell them without delay and then take your chances of escaping arrest.[4]

Mineral City was not the only mirage the Eastern investor had chased since coming West. Psychologically prepared for high

---

Post: *The Hour and the Man* (Washington: Press of Judd and Detweiler; 1963), 124–33.

[3] Stevens: "History of Bailey County," 52.

[4] Gunter and Muson Letterbook, April 11, 1882. Southwest Collection, Texas Technological College.

returns on a low investment, the steep decline of his stock caught many an investor unaware. In many instances investors had only themselves to blame for this lack of financial perception, for the Eastern-financed cattle companies in the West were frequently not run as business operations. Muddled managerial direction compounded by the lack of communication between East and West effectively prevented the investor from keeping a tight rein on company affairs.

In the heyday of the trust, a few investors convinced themselves that the solution to their troubles would come with the formation of a cattle monopoly, but the American Cattle Trust faded away without ever achieving widespread popularity. The cattleman, finally realizing that a political cure must be sought, began a battle for legislation which lasted well into the twentieth century. While the legislative debate was echoing in the halls of Congress, the cattle companies in the West turned to colonization as the means to relieve their economic burden of thousands of acres of land uninhabited by either man or beast. The paradox of transition was complete when the once-despised homesteader became the courted settler. The West of the eighties, the West of the Eastern investor's dreams, if it had ever existed, had disappeared.

X

BALANCE SHEET

R. M. Allen, Harvard class of '74 and manager of the Standard Cattle Company, sat in his rambling white clapboard mansion in Ames, Nebraska, in 1893 and painfully composed an article on his "range experiences." Asked by his alma mater to assess the opportunities in the range cattle industry, Allen was quick to admit that the heyday of the college graduate was passing. "Nor do I think that in the future we shall see more college men, for I regret to say the experience of those who have already tried it has not been financially fortunate."[1]

[1] Richard M. Allen: "Harvard Men in the Range Cattle Business," *Harvard Graduates Magazine*, II (1894), 183–94.

Then Allen, perhaps with mist in his eyes, recalled how "the days are irrevocably passed when the hot and dusty rancher just in from a journey of three days to a week . . . could find seat at the Cheyenne Club with young men from New York, Boston and England. . . ." Allen suggested that should any Harvard graduate find the cattle industry irresistibly attractive, he might do well to join "some good concern" as a cowboy, because the expense of establishing a ranch was so high and the risk of loss so great as to be prohibitive. Besides, the only available range left was in Montana. Allen's advice to the Harvard generation of the 1890's was a far cry from the inspirational message of the promotional campaign which had been so effective with their fathers. Yet Allen's opinion would have been widely echoed in range country. The West, for cattlemen of the nineties, was most certainly not the land of opportunity of the seventies.

For the Eastern financier, had the cattle industry been a profitable investment? Regarding the majority of investors, the answer is a qualified no. As for the total investment in the range, the absence of detailed corporate records makes it impossible to arrive at any accurate estimate of average profit. We do know that while almost half of the 93 investors described in Chapter 3 retained their cattle company stock ten years after the boom, few of them realized high returns.

The very number of investors who vanished from the scene is evidence that cattle investments did not pay. Henry L. Higginson wrote off his whole adventure in cattle corporate finances as "an inopportune investment." E. M. McGillen lost his dry-goods business in Cleveland while trying to bolster his various ranch schemes. McGillen decided that southern California was the place to go for health and fortune, but fate decided otherwise, as he achieved neither in the land of oranges and sunshine. Joseph Glidden, whose invention of simplified barbed wire contributed so much to the transformation from a range to ranch economy, had a partnership with Henry Sanborn in a Texas panhandle ranch which ended in a dismal failure. H. J. Tilford, the Louisville distiller, got out of the cattle business and wrote John Brush: "I intend sticking to the making of bourbon, something I at least know a little about. You fellows that make money on the range deserve every nickel."[2] Herman Oelrichs remarked to Thomas Sturgis: "Fortunately I did not invest more in the Anglo-American, at last count my losses totalled $475,000 and Harry [his brother] believes they may go higher."[3] There was always a bright side for Herman Oelrichs; if his losses had reached a million, there might have been cause for complaint. Theodore Roosevelt came out of the Dakota Badlands hale and hearty in physique, but not in pocketbook. Godfrey Syndacker's association with Alexander Swan resulted in financial headaches of migraine proportions but in little financial profit.

The roll call of disappointed investors could run on. The obvious conclusion is that for a goodly proportion of investors, their great expectations remained just that—expectations, and no more. This is not to ignore the fact that a small percentage of companies showed excellent returns. Marshall Field and Levi Leiter reaped dividends averaging 11 per cent on their stock in the Pratt-Ferris Cattle Company over a ten-year period.[4] The Converses, during a comparable length of time, received annual dividends of 8 per cent from the Laramie River Cattle Company.[5] Robert Bacon, a partner in the House of Morgan, got dividends of 9 per cent from the Riverside Land and Cattle Company,[6] although his losses in the Teschemacher and deBillier Cattle Company neatly absorbed these gains.[7] Clarence King received returns as high as 50 per cent on his investment with his partner N. R. Davis.[8] The Seligman family shared in the cornucopia that poured

[2] H. J. Tilford to John Brush, May 7, 1894. Western Range Cattle Industry Collection, State Historical Society of Colorado.

[3] Herman Oelrichs to Thomas Sturgis, August 29, 1887. Wyoming Stock Growers Association, Western History Research Center, University of Wyoming.

[4] Ledger, November 30, 1898. Pratt Collection, Nebraska State Historical Society.

[5] Ledger, 1884–1911. Converse Collection, Baker Library, Harvard University.

[6] Ledgers, 1882–8. Riverside Land and Cattle Company Collection, Western History Research Center, University of Wyoming.

[7] Ledgers, 1881–90.Teschemacher and deBillier Collection, Western History Research Center, University of Wyoming.

[8] Thorp Collection, Western History Research Center, University of Wyoming.

from the coffers of the Pioneer Cattle Company, a phenomenal success from the beginning, which paid over half a million in dividends during a seven-year period.[9] The success of these firms distinguished them from the mass of corporate debacles, since most investors unfortunately never had the pleasure of seeing a dividend check.

When one computes the dividends on the few successful companies whose ledger sheets are available for the period 1882-6, he discovers that the average declared dividend was just over 8 percent. Thus few Eastern investors found a pot of gold in the West; the attitude of most was expressed by Isaac Ellwood when he said to his son: "If we break even on our money in the ranch, I will be content—but not for long!"[1] Ellwood, having invested over three quarters of a million with no profit in sight, began to see the gloomy side of all reports from Texas. Yet in the final assessment, Ellwood's fears never materialized, and his ranch proved such a good investment for his children that part of the holdings which he amassed in the nineties are still in the hands of his family.

What became of the Eastern investors' interests in these cattle companies? As previously noted, 48 of the 93 investors still held their stock in 1895, and 29 held it as late as 1900, although many were apathetic about their possessions. Thomas Adams, former president of the North American Cattle Company, conceded to a friend: "I thought the holdings of the North American [Cattle Company] had long since been liquidated."[2] A few investors often retained their cattle shares by default. H. K. Thurber, for example, would have been delighted to unload his stock five years before he finally resigned himself to turning over to his partner what assets remained of the Lea Cattle Company.

Other investors maintained a strong interest in their cattle

[9] "Beef Sales, Dividends." Hauser Collection, Historical Society of Montana.

[1] Isaac Ellwood to William Ellwood, January 19, 1890. Ellwood Collection, Western History Research Center, University of Wyoming.

[2] Thomas Adams to J. Howard Ford, October 22, 1888. Wyoming Stock Growers Association Collection, Western History Research Center, University of Wyoming.

investments. Marshall Field, while he depended heavily on the Pratt family to supervise the operation, still had a lively curiosity about Pratt-Ferris affairs. The Converses were a long time accumulating enough confidence in their managers to ignore the minutiae connected with their company. The Farwells and Taylors, both families who were listed among Chicago's four hundred, kept up with XIT affairs into the twentieth century.

The Oelrichses, with a dynasty built on seafaring, held on to South Dakota real estate long after they preferred to forget their strong ties with the Anglo-American Cattle Company. Robert Ingersoll, even when he had ceased to be closely associated with New Mexico, kept his interest in the Dorsey Ranch, a property he had received in the first place for his eloquence in defending Stephen W. Dorsey in the Star Route frauds. The Goodriches of Akron rubber fame held their domain in New Mexico for years after the boom era in ranching. Those investors identified with other segments of the livestock industry, such as the Cudahys, Armours, Clays, Rosenbaums, and Morrises, had reason to retain their ranches, if for nothing more than propaganda value. When talking with a group of booted stockmen, it was convenient to use an "I am one of you" tone, even though the stockmen were not deceived. The Seligman family of New York, heavy plungers in mines, railroads, and corporate finance in general before they amassed the huge Aztec Land and Cattle Company, retained their land as well as their steady flow of dividends long after the periods of boom and disaster had passed.

While for various reasons many investors clung to their holdings as late as 1900, the bulk of Eastern capital had flowed back to Wall Street by then. Into the vacuum of cattle financing came the cattle loan company and the regional bank, agencies which in turn gave way to government bureaus during the 1920's. John Clay, who had pioneered in the cattle loan business, did not hesitate to speak out against this transformation of the cattle industry. In 1922 he crisscrossed the country giving a speech with the homey title "Coming Back to the Wagon" in which he pleaded for a renewal of the imagined ideals of yesteryear. Today, Clay argued, intense devotion to business, careful management, and hard work were the only way out of the cattlemen's financial morass and the only alternative to government "interference." "It is back to the Wagon, back to the sheep wagon, back to work, back to the old bell mare, and the cook's unwelcome yell of 'Roll out boys.' That is why Jordan is here today [president of the Wyoming Stock Growers Association], that is why he is such a wealthy man—he stayed with the Wagon."[3]

For all his mawkishness, Clay's argument in the 1920's was substantially the same as range philosophy in the 1890's, for individualism has always been a range motto. Yet even as the stock growers vigorously applauded Clay in 1922, they were again influenced by the East, this time Washington instead of New York.

If the Eastern investor did not make his fortune in the West, the managing director-investor did gain experience that in many cases seasoned and steadied him. The young Harvard man with his well-groomed mustache and the Eastern remittance man sent West by his family for his "health" often returned to family fold and fortune. Disillusioned with the cattle business, Richard Trimble joined the House of Morgan and eventually became the first secretary-treasurer of U. S. Steel. His close friend and associate from his Western days, Henry Hay, became assistant secretary. J. Howard Ford, who could boast of being the best billiard player in the Cheyenne Club, returned to New York and founded the Meyer Rubber Company, which later merged with Goodyear.[4] Fred deBillier, after recovering from his nervous collapse brought on by the Johnson County War, joined the diplomatic corps[5] and spent the rest of his life in Foreign Service posts in Europe. After leaving Montana, Albert Seligman went into his family's investment company and participated in the social life of New York, although he found it tame.[6] Politics he also found dull, after

---

[3] John Clay: "Coming Back to the Wagon" (Cheyenne, 1922).

[4] Robber's Roost Historical Society: "Pioneering on the Cheyenne River" (Lusk: 1956), 11.

[5] Virginia Trenholm: *Footprints on the Frontier* (Douglas, Wyo.: Douglas Enterprise Co.; 1945), 176.

[6] *National Cyclopedia of American Biography* (New York: J. T. White; 1945), XXXII, 430.

having been in the middle of the roistering political life of the Butte and Helena "Copper Kings." Azel Ames found Boston's Back Bay more congenial than the frigid winters of Montana, but he kept up his friendships, as well as a small investment, in the Treasure State for years beyond the turn of the century.[7] After practicing law for a short time in Cheyenne, Henry M. Rogers joined his attorney friend Ames as one of the most distinguished members of the bar in the city of beans, cod, and Cabots.[8]

F. W. Lafrentz left Cheyenne for Ogden, Utah, when the Swan Company went through its reorganization, and a number of young men from the East joined Lafrentz, for Ogden was highly touted as a metropolis which would soon succeed Denver and Seattle as the entrepôt of the Northwest. When Ogden's promise failed to materialize, Lafrentz left for Wall Street, where he founded the F. W. Lafrentz Accounting Firm and became president of the American Surety Company. Lafrentz had such a strong emotional attachment to the West that in his ninetieth year, he brought his son West to accompany him over the Oregon Trail.[9]

Moreton E. Post, Cheyenne banker, reversed the eastward migration and left for California, where he soon made several fortunes in real estate, orchards, and utilities.[1] George W. Baxter, besides holding his extensive cattle interests, served as governor of the Wyoming Territory. Forced to resign by President Cleveland because of his enclosing of government land, Baxter left Cheyenne for Denver, where he carried on a career in real estate and ranching for eight years. Then he returned to Knoxville, Tennessee, and entered the insurance business with his father-in-law.

After spending eleven years in the West, Henry Blair left Wyoming for Chicago in 1893,[2] both amassed and married for-

[7] Biographical file, Historical Society of Montana.

[8] Henry M. Rogers: *Memories of Ninety Years* (Boston: Houghton Mifflin Co.; 1928).

[9] Biographical file, Western History Research Center, University of Wyoming.

[1] *Press Reference Library, Western Edition,* 2 vols. (New York: International News Service; 1913–15), 342.

[2] Chicago *Tribune,* February 25, 1932.

tunes there, and built the Chicago elevated railway system. Benjamin S. Miller left his ranch in the Indian Territory in 1898 and wrote an esoteric autobiographical account of his life in the West.[3] His later career was devoted to building up extensive real estate holdings in the vicinity of Binghamton, New York. Gordon B. Goodell, old friend and associate of the Sturgis brothers, left the liquidation of the Union Cattle Company in their hands and returned to Portland, Maine.[4] With capital borrowed from friends in New York, he went into the lumber business and made a "satisfactory" living. Goodell was one of the most popular men on or off the range, and one of the few in the cowboy strike of 1884 who had no trouble with his outfit.

R. C. Lake, who ran cattle from the Dakotas to Texas with his partners G. E. Lemmon and Richard Toomb, settled in Evanston, Illinois, when the partnership was sold out, founded a bank, and became a director in several corporations.[5] William Sturgis and his brother Thomas, having lived in the West for over twenty years,[6] opened offices in the financial district of New York in the mid-nineties. Thomas Sturgis became a contractor and fire commissioner of New York and played a very active role in Republican politics in company with his good friend, Theodore Roosevelt. William Sturgis chose a career in banking and investment, and his son became the president of the First National Bank of New York.

Thomas B. Adams, valiantly attempting to hold the Wyoming Stock Growers Association together through the era of depression and after the dynamic leadership of the Sturgises, finally gave up in disgust and returned to Brooklyn.[7] Two decades later, he said in an emotional letter to Alice Smith, secretary of the Stock

[3] Benjamin S. Miller: *Ranch Life in Southern Kansas and Indian Territory* (New York: Fless & Ridge Print.; 1896); Cornell Alumni Biographical file, Cornell University.
[4] Biographical file, Western History Research Center, University of Wyoming.
[5] J. W. Leonard: *Book of Chicagoans* (Chicago: Marquis; 1905), 345.
[6] Biographical file, Western History Research Center, University of Wyoming.
[7] Harry Crane (ed.): *Letters from Old Friends and Members of the Wyoming Stock Growers Association* (Cheyenne: 1923).

Growers: "If there was one decision I made in my life that was right, it was leaving Wyoming. That last three years there were perfect hell, no one knew how to pull us out of the mess though there was plenty of advice."[8] Adams became an executive of the North American Copper Company, and after retirement spent his time in philanthropy.

It is not astonishing that, coming from a wealthy background, these men found financial success upon backtracking to Wall Street or Federal Square. Many pushed their armchairs up to the board of directors table in their own family firm. Others secured positions with former friends in the West, as Henry Hay did with Richard Trimble at U. S. Steel and as J. Howard Ford did in receiving his start from Fred deBillier, friend and fellow investor. A few, such as F. W. Lafrentz, created their own careers, but not many could claim that they were self-made men.

Certainly the business experience that these manager-investors received in the West provided valuable help in their later careers, even if the lessons, as Hubert Teschemacher believed, were chiefly negative. Richard Trimble felt that his three years as secretary of the Teschemacher and deBillier Cattle Company had been well spent. He wrote his parents: "We have all learned from our last years in this business, though it has been expensive. I am going to return as there is little I can do here, there are too many managers as it is."[9] For Trimble, as for many young men who had followed Horace Greeley's dictum, living in the West had been a maturing process, if nothing else. Sometimes startling transformations took place after a sojourn in the West for these youths fresh from an Ivy League education. More than the physical maturing of a mustache fuzz to bristle or tinge of gray in the hair was involved. John Thomas, exhausted by his months of negotiation with his former partners, the Pages, confessed to Joseph Ames: "I came here five years ago full of life, I now believe I have aged

[8] Thomas Adams to Alice Smith, November 14, 1915. Wyoming Stock Growers Association Collection, Western History Research Center, University of Wyoming.

[9] Richard Trimble to Mrs. Merritt Trimble, November 9, 1884. Trimble Collection, Western History Research Center, University of Wyoming.

twenty years."[1] Ames attempted to console his friend with the idea that "some good must come from bitter experience."[2] It is doubtful if this Pollyannish sympathy was much of a balm for Thomas, as the logic of this moral must have missed him. But, in sum, many a young Eastern investor grew up in the West.

Although his cattle stocks did not commonly earn money, the Eastern financier found his Western experience helpful in making other investments in Western resources. While the Eastern financier lost his enthusiasm for the cattle industry, this did not mean at all that he neglected the rest of the opportunities beckoning to him in the West. Of the ninety-three men studied, thirty-nine invested in diversified areas in the West after they had ceased to be concerned about their stock in cattle companies.[3] August Busch invested heavily in railroads and land,[4] Jacob Haish, Ellwood's tenacious De Kalb competitor, in Western lumber.[5] Levi Leiter and Marshall Field expanded their Western investments to include farm mortgages and railroads, and for a short while, Leiter owned two silver mines in the Leadville, Colorado, area.[6]

[1] John B. Thomas to Joseph Ames, November 14, 1885. Dunder Collection, Western History Research Center, University of Wyoming.

[2] Joseph Ames to John B. Thomas, December 21, 1885. Ibid.

[3] The following are investors who invested in other aspects of the West after liquidating their cattle stock: *Farm mortgages*—John Arbuckle, George Kellogg, Levi Leiter, Marshall Field, Portus B. Weare, Joseph Rosenbaum, N. K. Fairbanks, R. M. Fair, Jack Casement, Jerome I. Case; *Railroads*—August Busch, Henry L. Higginson, Levi Leiter, Marshall Field, Edwin J. Marshall, Philetus Sawyer, Richard Trimble, William H. Vanderbilt, Portus B. Weare, John Haldane Flagler, George R. Blanchard, Henry A. Blair, Joseph Seligman, Joy Morton, Silas Reed Anthony, Edmund Seymour, N. K. Fairbanks, R. M. Fair, John Bigelow, William Rockefeller, Charlemagne Tower, Jack Casement; *Mining*—Robert Bacon, Levi Leiter, Marshall Field, Richard Trimble, Portus B. Weare, John Haldane Flagler, David M. Goodrich, Robert D. Evans, Joseph Seligman, Stephen B. Elkins, Augustus Gurnee, William C. Greene, William C. Whitney, William Rockefeller, Quincy Shaw, Charlemagne Tower, Jack Casement; *Urban Real Estate*—William Clark, Marshall Field, Stephen B. Elkins, Augustus Kountze, Charlemagne Tower; *Lumber*—George Kellogg, Philetus Sawyer; *Petroleum*—Edwin J. Marshall, Silas Reed Anthony, Edmund Seymour; *Banking*—Henry A. Blair, Joy Morton, Stephen B. Elkins, Augustus Kountze, Jerome I. Case; *Utilities* —Edwin J. Marshall, Silas Reed Anthony, and Edmund Seymour.

[4] *National Cyclopedia of American Biography*, V, 23.

[5] De Kalb *Daily Chronicle*, June 10, 1926.

[6] Biographical file, Western History Research Center, University of Wyoming.

After the Keystone Cattle Company was liquidated, E. C. Kellogg spread his interests in South Dakota to include mining and lumbering.[7] John McShane, who had been a heavy stockholder in the Bay State Cattle Company, switched his interests to Omaha Stockyards and the Cudahy Packing Company.[8] Portus B. Weare, although he insisted that his disenchantment with the West was complete after his "regretful experience" in the Weare Land and Livestock Company,[9] soon began erecting a string of elevators across the prairie in the Red River Valley. When the Klondike rush started, Weare shrewdly established a trading company between the Klondike and Seattle, and from this company he gained far more than any bonanza struck in the Yukon.

John Haldane Flagler of Boston, whose first wife was a member of the prolific Converse family, kept his broker busy buying Utah copper, Kansas Pacific, Union Pacific, and Dolores Mining stock long after he had withdrawn from the board of the Ames Cattle Company.[1] Quincy Shaw and his brother-in-law Alexander Agassiz appear to have invested in almost any Western enterprise that promised profits,[2] including the Union Pacific mines near Telluride, Colorado, farms in Colorado, and real estate in California. The cattle industry thus served to introduce many Eastern investors to a wide range of Western investment in a broad scope. This coincided with the Eastern investor's often having been attracted to the cattle industry from previous investments in other Western schemes. Even if the capitalist had only unsavory recollections of his short life as a "cattle baron," he by no means shunned the rest of the West. On the contrary, they might now be enticed into mining, railroads, or real estate, for opportunities appeared everywhere; just as they may have been originally attracted to the cattle industry by their other Western investments.

[7] Ibid.

[8] Arthur C. Wakeley: *Omaha: The Gate City, and Douglas County, Nebraska* (Chicago: S. J. Clarke; 1917), 130–3.

[9] *National Cyclopedia of American Biography*, X, 475.

[1] Biographical file, Western History Research Center, University of Wyoming.

[2] "Alexander Agassiz," *National Cyclopedia of American Biography*, III, 98–9; "Quincy A. Shaw," XXVII, 484–5.

An intriguing idea to speculate on is that the financier who was accustomed to worldwide fields of investment tended to send his money West more readily than his colleagues who usually invested near home. Undoubtedly the habit of thinking in terms of distant places on the globe made a man less apt to worry about the difficulties of communication and transportation to the West. A review of the financiers with global outlook gives mixed evidence on this point. The great shipping families—the Oelrichses, the Sturgises, and the Powpers—certainly did not dominate investment in cattle. Henry Hyde, with his Equitable agents abroad and his lawyers in Colorado, demonstrated that whether he was advising on a scheme in Vienna or a mining deal in Silver Plume, he gave wide latitude to his on-the-scene agents.[3] Hyde did insist on being kept informed, but he seldom felt the necessity of sending long, complex communications like John Bigelow or George Weare. The Arbuckles sent their manager to Cheyenne with the same admonition they gave their South American plantation overseers: "Make your decisions, but make the right ones." A parallel career to the Arbuckles was the Forbes family of Boston. Although, as far as is known, they never became stockholders in a cattle company, John Murray Forbes took the immense fortune garnered from the China trade and drove the Chicago, Burlington and Quincy across the land.[4] In sum, the evidence is too slight to do more than suggest that men engaged in trans-world trade invested more heavily in the West because of this global experience.

A large question, and one on which much more information exists, is whether the Eastern investors in the cattle industry were speculators. The answer is yes in the sense that any investment in the trans-Mississippi West was a speculation—as investment in underdeveloped regions always is. The real issue is the degree of speculation which was involved. Were the real estate maneuvers of the Leiters in Chicago and less risky than their dealing with the Pratt-Ferris Cattle Company? Levi Leiter, the patri-

[3] Hyde Collection, Baker Library, Harvard University.
[4] Richard C. Overton: *Burlington West* (Cambridge: Harvard University Press; 1941).

arch of the Leiter family, conjectured that the significant business
and industrial growth would be to the south of the Chicago Loop
and purchased accordingly. Marshall Field dissented and bought
his holdings to the north; both men, in the fullest sense, were
speculating. Did the Converses' stock in the Tidioute Oil Farm
Company in western Pennsylvania represent more of a gamble
than their stock in the Teschemacher and deBillier Cattle Company?

To some extent, any judgment regarding the degree of speculation is a subjective one.[5] Two criteria which are pertinent to

[5] A "speculator" defined is an elusive process. Paul Gates, whose work is
some of the most satisfactory, maintains that a land speculator was one who
withheld land from development with the anticipation of receiving a higher
price. This definition comes close to the heart of the subject. Allan and
Margaret Bogue favor the usage which was common to newspaper readers
during the nineteenth century, "where generally it denoted an individual
who purchased large acreages of unimproved land, intending to sell after
land values had risen sufficiently to make their sale remunerative and who
was not interested in working the land as a personal enterprise or in building up a long-term estate." The Bogues point out that though a settler and a
railroad entrepreneur have both been considered land speculators, they
would both be excluded under this definition. A speculator, for the Bogues,
is a "type of investor."

Paul Gates discerned types of investors, but the classification was much
more inclusive than that of the Bogues. Gates found four classes of speculators: one, the small farmer who purchased "more land than he could
reasonably hope to utilize"; two, the professional men such as bankers, editors, lawyers, politicians, who invested in land as an avocation; three, the
"professional speculator," who purchased large amounts of government land
through soldier warrants and script, then sold his land through promotion;
four, the genre of speculator who was an "eastern capitalist taking a flyer in
western lands."

Land speculation aside, what of the speculator in other ventures in the
West? Eastern investors who were buying stock in Western mining
corporations such as the Telluride mines in Colorado were taking high risks,
as the Livermores, Agassizes, and Shaws of Boston discovered to their
chagrin. Ernest Miller, Harold Williamson, Arnold Daum, and Paul Giddens
have all written with insight and amusement concerning the speculation in
"Pithole City" and other western Pennsylvania communities with less
glamorous names. The speculative craze in lumber has recently been described by Ralph Hidy, Frank Hill, and Allan Nevins in their excellent
history of the Weyerhauser Company. Speculation, obviously, was endemic
to the economy wherever there was a new natural resource to develop, or a
company stock to manipulate.

As the Bogues and others have commented, the best criterion to measure
a speculator is motivation. What was the speculator's "intent" when he invested in a specific stock or section of land? All well and good, but how
does one psychoanalyze investor's motives? If he were so indiscreet as to

the question are how long the Eastern investor retained his stock in a cattle company, and whether he expected a higher return from his cattle investment than from other shares he held in Eastern corporations. Certainly in the incipient stages of cattle investment, many a financier, lured by the fables of the promoters, expected to retire in luxury on his magnificent dividend checks. When these anticipations proved illusory, they revised

write self-revealing letters, or if his reputation left an easily recognized trail such as Jim Fisk or I. C. White, he can be classified by this method; but most investors' motives seem to have been schizophrenic. Jay Cooke scorned Pennsylvania oil stock as high-risk, yet he gave free rein to his speculative urges in the Northern Pacific. Richard Trimble who, as a Morgan partner, was the solid, true-blue image of a conservative financier, took disastrous flyers in ranching and mining in Mexico. Even Jay Gould has been unjustly maligned, if we are to accept the valiant efforts of his most recent biographer, Julius Grodinsky.

"Intent" without contradiction is an excellent guidepost to speculation, but it is also very treacherous to assess. Most investors were too clever and discreet to reveal their basic motives, and in the absence of an internal personality profile, the historian is thrown back on external judgments. How long did an investor retain his stock? What return did he expect? Also, if it is available, an investment portfolio can produce valuable revelations.

Finally, one added caveat, in the opinion of the writer, is that far too much attention has been given to the differentiation of speculative techniques in various segments of the economy. A speculator, whether he was taking risks in cattle, railroads, mining, land, or oil, was still gambling. Speculation is a reflection of a particular emotional pattern, regardless of the means or the final outcome.

Readers intrigued with this problem will find the following helpful: Allan and Margaret Bogue: "Profits and the Frontier Land Speculator," *Journal of Economic History*, XVII (March 1957), 1–24; Paul W. Gates: "The Role of the Land Speculator in Western Development," *Pennsylvania Magazine of History and Biography*, LXVI (1942), 314–33; Paul W. Gates: *The Farmer's Age* (New York: Holt, Rinehart and Winston; 1960); Paul W. Gates: *The Illinois Central Railroad and Its Colonization Work* (Cambridge: Harvard University Press; 1934); Harold F. Williamson and Arnold Daum: *The American Petroleum Industry; the Age of Illumination, 1859–1899* (Evanston: Northwestern University Press; 1959); Ernest C. Miller: *Oil Mania* (Philadelphia: Dorrance and Co.; 1941); Overton: *Burlington West;* Mary E. Young: *Redskins, Ruffleshirts and Rednecks* (Norman: University of Oklahoma Press; 1961); Mary W. Hargreaves: *Dry Farming in the Northern Great Plains, 1900–1925* (Cambridge: Harvard University Press; 1957); Ralph W. Hidy, Frank E. Hill, and Allan Nevins: *Timber and Men* (New York: Macmillan; 1963); Leslie E. Decker: *Railroads, Lands, and Politics* (Providence: Brown University Press; 1964); Allan G. Bogue: *Money At Interest* (Ithaca: Cornell University Press; 1955); Margaret B. Bogue: *Patterns from the Sod* (Springfield: Illinois State Historical Society; 1959); and William B. Gates: *Michigan Copper and Boston Dollars* (Cambridge: Harvard University Press; 1951).

their retirement schedules and expectations accordingly. Jay L. Torrey had pieced together his holdings in the Sunlight basin, in northwestern Wyoming, with the promise to his brother: "We will make far more in cattle than we could on farm land in Missouri."[6] Three years later he conceded that these were false hopes: "I will be content if we can only show a profit of ten per cent."[7] A year later he decided that even this target exceeded his ability; however, over a five-year period the Embar Cattle Company paid slightly more than 8 per cent in dividends. It was the same with other Western investments; Henry Hyde of Equitable was at first nonplused to discover that his Denver real estate produced only an 8 per cent profit, but he finally agreed with Henry Wolcott that "this is a very creditable showing."[8]

Francis Smith's clients, after receiving a few written lectures in which Smith made the distressing investment picture very clear, came to be well satisfied with an 8 to 10 per cent return on their capital. The Thurbers, not as easily mollified, wanted very much to realize 12 per cent on their Lea Cattle Company stock,[9] but before they finished with the Lea Cattle Company, they would have rejoiced to get back their investment without dividends. T. Jefferson Coolidge, the Boston capitalist who must have discovered opportunity beckoning on every hand since he invested so widely in Western ventures, judged a satisfactory dividend to be the highest he could reap. Coolidge was even forced to admit to Henry Higginson that his stock in Western railroads was paying "handsomely."[1] Stephen B. Elkins thought that Catron was unrealistic to insist on more than 10 per cent from the Bank of Santa Fe.[2]

There is little to substantiate the accusation that the nineteenth-

[6] Jay. L. Torrey to Richard Torrey, November 2, 1891. Torrey Collection, Western History Research Center, University of Wyoming.
[7] Ibid., July 27, 1894.
[8] Henry B. Hyde to Henry Wolcott, March 22, 1897. Hyde Collection, Baker Library, Harvard University.
[9] H. K. Thurber to Joseph C. Lea, May 11, 1889. Padgitt Collection, San Antonio, Texas.
[1] T. Jefferson Coolidge to Henry L. Higginson, June 4, 1898. Higginson Collection, Baker Library, Harvard University.
[2] Stephen B. Elkins to Thomas Catron, May 27, 1891. Elkins Collection, University of West Virginia Library.

century entrepreneur demanded higher returns from his Western investments than from his Eastern. Most investors appear to have regarded 10 per cent as a reputable dividend; although they would have enjoyed more, they did not anticipate it. As to the question of speculation in the West versus that in the East, what could have been more risky than the oil investments in western Pennsylvania in the 1860's?

Indeed, the gambling instincts of these western Pennsylvania petroleum promoters showed up in the West as a repetition of their business "philosophy" in the East. In August 1895, eight independent petroleum operators, mostly from Bradford, Pennsylvania, joined to form the Pennsylvania Oil and Gas Company. The announced purpose of their new organization was "mine drilling and operating for oil and other minerals and refining and storing and transporting same."[3] The scene of their operations was the Salt Creek Field in central Wyoming, over fifty miles from the nearest railroad. After seven years of litigation, sporadic drilling, and discovery of a modest amount of oil, the promoters returned to western Pennsylvania over $200,000 poorer for their efforts. If these speculators had been lucky enough to drill twenty miles further south, they would have hit a huge pool of oil— which they would then have had no means of transporting to market. Yet these were seasoned operators, many of whom had been exploring and producing petroleum for twenty years or more in Pennsylvania, and there is no reason to assume that they dramatically altered their business techniques when they looked West.

An accurate statement of the case might be that investing in the West was a high-risk affair by the standards of the most conservative entrepreneur. Nevertheless, numerous capitalists proved that the odds of gambling on the economic returns in an underdeveloped region could be greatly reduced. Names that became synonymous with Western investment, such as Leiter, Field, Ellwood, Tilford, Stoddard, Hill, and Forbes, demonstrate

[3] Pennsylvania Oil and Gas Minute Book, August 4, 1895. Midwest Oil Corporation Collection, Petroleum History and Research Center, University of Wyoming.

that one could both build solidly in the West and come out with a comfortable profit.

In sharp contrast to the promoters of the Pennsylvania Oil and Gas Company was John D. Archbold, president of the Standard Oil Company, who in 1899 sent three of his top executives, C. L. Lufkin, F. H. Oliphant, and J. E. Eckert, to survey the oil resources of the mid-continental and Rocky Mountain regions. They covered over forty actual or potential petroleum-producing areas in Wyoming, Colorado, and what was loosely described as "Indian" territory, using, as they sarcastically noted, "every conveyance known to man." In their report on the future of Wyoming oil, written from the Inter-Ocean Hotel in Cheyenne, the weary oil scouts admitted that several of the prospects they examined were potential, but their conclusion was that "there is no financial inducement" to proceed unless adequate transportation facilities were constructed. Furthermore, they advised Archbold that with such a limited local market, the costs of transportation might be prohibitive in any case. The Standard Oil Company must have adopted this advice, for it was years before the company invaded the Rockies.

If the length of time an investor holds a stock can be used to judge whether his intentions are speculative, certainly a substantial percentage of the Eastern investors did not look upon the cattle industry as an opportunity for pure gambling. Almost half of the 93 Eastern investors in the sample studied had their cattle stock ten years after purchase, while another 20 per cent were still stockholders after fifteen years. Promoters with no other desire than to cut and get out, as the expression goes in the lumber industry, would not bother to hold their stock for a decade or more. As for the motivation behind the cattle investors' retention of stock, some, quite naturally, assumed that there was little point in disposing of cattle company shares at a huge loss. Others, such as Levi Leiter, had a genuine attachment to land per se. As he wrote Colonel Pratt in 1893: "Even if the cattle market drops, we still have our land";[4] and he went to to say

[4] Levi Leiter to James H. Pratt, February 2, 1893. Pratt Collection, Nebraska State Historical Society.

that soil in any age or circumstance is a good investment. A good number of investors held their stock simply because they did not see the cattle industry as any more of a risk than some of the corporate enterprises in the East. Any Wall Street financier in the nineties could see his fellow capitalists losing heavily in the cotton trust, copper trust, or distilleries trust; risk in the cattle industry appeared to be fairly pale in comparison with these speculations.

In no instance did any of the 93 investors examined sell his stock in less than three years. William H. Vanderbilt liquidated his "charter" stock in his Hermosilla, Colorado, ranch in three years at a fine profit.[5] George Blanchard, Boston mercantilist, sold his shares in the North American Cattle Company in a short time; however, this was evidently due to disagreements over policy and not to any diminished fascination with the cattle industry, for within six months he was on the board of directors of the Western Union Beef Company, a chair he held for eight years.[6] J. I. Case modified his investment policy in South Dakota to include ranches as well as farm mortgages.[7] This variation was mainly due to his control of several local banks, which enmeshed him in financing ranches whether he favored it or not. That farms, rather than rangeland, should have dominated his thinking is hardly strange, considering his vocation. Rufus Hatch, by any definition a stock manipulator and speculator par excellence, toyed with his interest in cattle industry, confining most of his activities to brokerage in companies and lands, particularly during his "playful" activities with the Chicago and Northwestern Railroad.[8]

From any point of view, the cattle industry attracted many Eastern investors of a conservative nature. One such was Colonel Torrey. Although initially he may have expected a "full house," as he himself said, he was quickly brought down to reality, and thereafter he was content, if not joyous, when he reaped

[5] Denver *Tribune*, August 20, 1879.
[6] *Field and Farm*, February 3, 1894.
[7] M. Wilson Rankin: *Reminiscences of Frontier Days* (Denver: Smith-Brooks; 1935), 106; William L. Kuyenkendall: *Frontier Days* (Denver: 1917).
[8] Laramie *Daily Boomerang*, March 24, 1884; *Dictionary of American Biography*, VIII, 393-4.

an 8 or 10 per cent dividend on his cattle stock. Nor did he often seem anxious to sell out of the cattle company, once he had committed himself. He would vigorously protest what he discerned as mismanagement, extravagance, or poor judgment; but even when relations grew strained, he held on to his shares. And more important, even if the Eastern investor became disillusioned with the cattle industry, he continued making other investments in the West, from the "Blue Boy Mine," and the "Cactus Creek Oil Company" to the Great Northern Railroad.

Further, in the wild fluctuations of the business cycle that were the pattern in the late nineteenth century, the Eastern capitalist came to regard his cattle investment as no more risky than other stocks in his bank vault. The economic landscape was strewn with corporate disasters; why should the financier feel extraordinarily reckless when buying stock in a cattle company sold to him by a friend or relative? If he had given the matter studious consideration, he might have agreed that he was being unwise in investing in an underdeveloped region, even if it was full of immense natural resources. But he probably did not reflect extremely long, since anywhere he looked, up or down Wall Street, his friends and enemies were following the same path of investment.

Like all Easterners who came West, the investor brought with him a culture—"civilizing influences" which were veneered onto the West. Years after the last billiard ball had ricocheted off the table in the Cheyenne Club game room, cattlemen were still repeating tales of the "exploits" of members—how one inebriated soul, cussing the enormous painting of a fine specimen of a bull by Paul Potter, raised his shaky hand and brought the critter down with three erratic shots and a shout.[9] The great social affairs which revolved around the Club were more genteel than rowdy, however. Depending on one's opinion, Cheyenne was blessed or damned with a miliitary post, Fort D. A. Russell. Whatever other cultural contributions the post made to life in Cheyenne, the officers and an occasional officer's daughter gave variety to

[9] Agnes Wright Spring: *Cheyenne Club* (Kansas City: Don Ornduff; 1961).

the social whirl. One young daughter of an officer stationed at Fort D. A. Russell recalled an unforgettable ball of her youth at the Cheyenne Club.[1] The night of the affair, the champagne flowed like water, and every variety of rare and delicious food and wine could he had for the asking. The Club's rooms "were atristically and lavishly decorated. Smilax and roses were twined around the stairs and balconies." The atmosphere was set with "softly shaded light which cast a warm glow over the brocaded draperies . . . tall potted palms reflected in large, diamond-cut mirrors." The guests' attire matched the decor in richness. "Louise Swan [Alexander Swan's daughter] wore a lovely yellow satin dress with a large bustle and side panels that had just arrived by express from New York." The wide-eyed officer's daughter, Mary Jackson, was astounded to see that "the beautiful and expensive favors which each of us received that evening had also been purchased in New York and rushed to Cheyenne for the ball."

A Cheyenne Club affair symbolized the glitter of Eastern culture to the frontier, an importation which obviously was as alien to the West as the Japanese prints hanging in the Sturgis brothers' log cabin on the range. The Dutch fireplace tiles imported by Hiram Kelley for his mansion on Central Avenue in Cheyenne,[2] and the green elephant hide "papering" the walls of the Osgood mansion in Redstone, Colorado, were but touches of Eastern culture.[3] They represented a facade of civilization, but not more. The clash of effete Eastern culture with crude Western life, sometimes had its amusing consequences, as when a range foreman finishing a meal at the Denver Club in Denver, Colorado, was presented with an elaborate filigree finger bowl into which, after only a moment's perplexity, he plunged in his face. He then drank what liquid remained.[4]

Other "civilized" accouterments were acquired with considerable sacrifice and expense. Arthur Anderson, who had the good

[1] Mary Jackson English: "Army Girl: Experiences on the Frontier," *Brand Book of the Denver Westerners* (Denver: 1949), 135–45.

[2] A fascinating collection of frontier architecture of the elite of the "cattle kingdom" is in Laramie County Historical Society: *Early Cheyenne Homes, 1880–1890* (Cheyenne: 1962).

[3] Len Shoemaker: *Roaring Fork Valley* (Denver: Sage Books; 1958).

[4] Interview with Russell Thorp, August 10, 1959.

fortune to marry a Milbank heiress, came out to northwestern Wyoming from New York in the late 1890's in order to construct a "retreat." He quickly discovered that "to build a fireplace and chimney, which, as well as most of the house itself, is my own handiwork, forty-four horse wagon loads of stone had to be hauled four miles." As Anderson was flabbergasted to learn, "I could not even procure a nail without sending to Billings, one hundred fifty miles distant."[5]

In architecture, the impact of East on West was marked.[6] The fine old two-story white clapboard Victorian homes lining Thurber Avenue in Roswell, Last Chance Gulch in Helena, or Carey Avenue in Cheyenne reproduced the Midwest down to the iron grill gate swinging in front of the stone carriage block. The low-slung one-story ranch house was relegated to the range and seldom made its appearance in town. It would be two decades before a reverse trend would set in and West would conquer East, with the "ranch" house becoming the standard architecture in bedroom cities such as Elyria, Ohio, or Barrington, Illinois.

As early as 1886, Westerners suspected that they were beginning to submit to the pace setting of Eastern fashion. An editorial in *Field and Farm* chided its readers: "It is the rule of the men of the plains and particularly for cowboys to speak most contemptuously of Eastern fashion and Eastern dudes. But in fact, they themselves are as much the slave of this fashion as anyone." The editorial pointed out: "No man, who can possibly avoid it, engages in any part of the business of raising cattle . . . without first procuring a white felt hat . . . a pair of fancy chaperoos, or overalls and . . . higher french heels [boots] are indispensable."[7] The editor probably exaggerated his case to delineate his argument, but as Owen Wister observed, the cowboy at a Saturday night dance did don a strange assortment of styles and apparel for the benefit of an admiring glance from the scarce female population.

[5] A suggestive study of Eastern architecture transposed bric-a-brac by bric-a-brac to the West is Marion D. Ross: "Architecture in Oregon, 1845–1895," *Oregon Historical Quarterly*, LVII (October 1956), 33–4.

[6] *Field and Farm*, May 8, 1886.

[7] Ibid.

The Eastern investor often brought books in his baggage when coming West, and sometimes whole libraries were transported across the continent. Although the Duck Bar cowboys were highly amused to see their employer Hubert Teschemacher reading the paperback French classics which had been his at Harvard, this did not stop them from borrowing volumes in English. Teschemacher taught a few of his cowboys to read, and decades after he had left Wyoming, books with his bookplate in them appeared on the shelves of friends in central Wyoming.

The manager of the Bell Ranch, C. M. O'Donel, ordered East for that "compendium of all learning" the *Encyclopaedia Britannica*, "11th edition, India paper impression, full flexible sheepskin binding, together with double shelf mahogany book case."[8] In cattlemen's circles the Bancroft histories—in full leather binding and embossed with the name of the owner, if one were affluent enough and really wanted a show piece—were often prominently displayed in the "sitting room." This was as much a testimony to the shrewd and aggressive selling of the Bancroft salesmen as to the literary tastes of the rancher.[9] The Bancroft set, and the War of the Rebellion series doled out by grateful Congressmen to their constituents, incongrously reposed side by side in the local library, which more often than not was above the Silver Dollar Bar or in the back room of Hank's Barber Shop.

Some Eastern influence lacked a cultural flavor but did offer moral counsel. Thomas L. Page of Hat Creek, Wyoming, and Brooklyn, wrote to Thomas Adams in the Stock Growers office in Cheyenne: "I am very much pleased to note . . . that they have strung up 20 evil disposed persons, cattle thieves, in about the vicinity of Laramie city. . . . Hope the good work will go on." As a parting shot, Page concluded: "Other localities are in need of such Christian influence."[1]

[8] Charles O'Donel to Cambridge University Press, April 18, 1911. Bell Ranch Collection, University of New Mexico Library.

[9] For the salesmanship of Bancroft's hucksters, see John Caughey: *Hubert Howe Bancroft, Historian of the West* (Berkeley: University of California Press; 1946).

[1] James L. Page to Thomas Adams, December 9, 1888. Dunder Collection, Western History Research Center, University of Wyoming.

While the West that has been popularized is the West of Page's letter, this is only a caricature of a way of life which, although rough, had an integrity and an individuality which impressed Owen Wister as a new civilization. In this land the Eastern investor left behind the memories of a way of life that Western society would attempt to emulate from then on.

What, in the final analysis, were the economic benefits the Eastern investor brought to the West? First and foremost, he provided capital when it was desperately needed for an expanding industry; there is no question that the Western range cattle industry would have lagged for years without this financial transfusion. Historically, the industry has been dependent on credit to an abnormal degree, and in the void of regional financing, cattlemen in the nineteenth century had no alternative but to seek capital in the East or overseas. The significantly higher interest rates in the West cemented this financial bond between East and West long after the period of spectacular growth had passed.

Any current definitions of underdeveloped regions fit the West of the nineteenth century.[2] Insignificant industrialization, low per capita income, inadequate credit facilities, and scarcity of transportation all were characteristics of the American West. It was not until after 1900, for example, that a major packing company established plants in Texas.[3] Nevertheless, much of the West's economy was quite dynamic, most significantly its population growth. Economic propulsion, however, was primarily in the non-industrial sectors, and this fact, taken with the colonial base from which the West started, still placed that region in a position of tremendous inferiority to the East. The rate of population

[2] An analysis of the problems and implications of underdeveloped regions can be found in John M. Hunter: "A Case Study of the Economic Development of an Under-Developed Country: Cuba, 1899–1935," Ph.D. dissertation, Harvard University, 1950; Mohammad Zaki Hashem: "The Theory of Economic Development of Under-Developed Countries, with a Study of the Development of the Egyptian Economy, 1927–1947," Ph.D. dissertation, Harvard University, 1950; Henry Cramer Edison: "Denver as the Financial Center of the Eastern Rocky Mountain Region," Ph.D. dissertation ,University of Michigan, 1940.

[3] Troy J. Cauley: "Early Business Methods in Texas Cattle Industry," *Journal of Economics and Business History*, IV (May 1932), 516–86.

growth in the Mountain West from 1870–90 was the fastest in the nation, yet the total number of residents in 1890 reached only 1,213,935 out of a national total of 62,947,714.[4] With the exception of Idaho, the labor force which was engaged in transportation and communication showed the most dramatic increase, for by 1910 forty per cent of the people in the Mountain states listed these services as their occupation.[5] In a colonial economy the crucial role of a capital infusion such as the Eastern investors supplied is self-evident.

The importance of Eastern capital to the cattle industry is obvious from the doldrums of 1885–90, which marked the withdrawal of Eastern investment.[6] The precipitous decline in Eastern capital was not the only negative influence on the cattle industry, for the low market, the generally incompetent management, and national depressions all contributed to the long recession. But though cattlemen studiously ignored it, the distasteful truth was that local and commission financing was unable to cope with the credit needs of the cattle companies. Eastern capital had propped them up, and the exhaustion of this source froze the industry on a plateau which was too high for them to maintain.

As an economic pump primer for the West in general, not just the cattle industry, the Eastern financier's capital made a permanent contribution. When the investor in cattle deduced that his cattle company was not going to shower him with manna, he sought other avenues of profit—and his investments in minerals, transportation, and land provided the bridge over which capital flowed between East and West into the twentieth century.

The cattlemen, as much as any Westerner, has had his grudges —in part valid—about Eastern economic exploitation and political domination. Yet the Eastern investor who returned to his brownstone mansion also had grounds for resentment. Lured by sooth-

<hr>

[4] *Historical Statistics of the United States Colonial Times to 1957* (Washington, 1960), 12.

[5] Harvey S. Perloff, Edgar S. Dunn, Eric E. Lampard, and Richard F. Muth: *Regions, Resources, and Economic Growth* (Baltimore: Johns Hopkins Press; 1960), 181.

[6] Robert M. Barker: "The Economics of Cattle-Raising in the Southwest," *The American Monthly Review of Reviews*, XXIV (September 1901), 305–13.

sayers two decades before to expect incalculable good fortune from his cattle company stock, instead he harvested chiefly the atmosphere of bright blue sky, pure air for his consumptiveness and game trophies to decorate his den—in short, the very lure, which would draw his grandchildren out of megalopolis to the "frontier" seven decades later.

BIBLIOGRAPHY

Two striking characteristics of the literature of the range cattle industry are its phenomenal amount and erratic quality. We have pounds of "Fifty Years in the Saddle" cowhand reminiscences, but only a few John Clays who took the time to provide insight into the managerial side of the cattle industry. This is but one void: in addition, there is remarkably little primary literature on the packing industry; land brokerage in the West is a vast unknown field; the battles on cattle legislation are almost a complete vacuum; and for all the wordage on the homesteader-cattleman conflict, we have astonishingly little knowledge of the enclosure movement. Studies of the Paul Gates and Allan Bogue type on Western land problems would be of immense value.

Any historical work on the economics of the cattle industry must depend heavily on manuscript material. Unfortunately, only a fraction of this material is available, though one would have to concede that the cattle industry is better off in this respect than many phases of American history. The following is a selection of sources which had pertinency for this study. Those diligent researchers desiring a more extensive bibliography will find Ramon Adams's *The Rampaging Herd* a fruitful compendium.

Primary Sources

MANUSCRIPTS AND MANUSCRIPT COLLECTIONS

American National Livestock Association Records. Western History Research Center, University of Wyoming, Laramie, Wyoming.

Arnold (C. P.) Collection. Western History Research Center, University of Wyoming, Laramie, Wyoming.

Bell Ranch Collection. University of New Mexico Library, Albuquerque, New Mexico.

Blair (Henry) Collection. Western History Research Center, University of Wyoming, Laramie, Wyoming.

Boice (Edgar) Collection. Western History Research Center, University of Wyoming, Laramie, Wyoming.

Bolton-Smith (Carlile) Collection. Washington, D.C.

Carter (John J.) Collection. Humble Oil Corporation, Tulsa, Oklahoma.

Catron (Thomas) Collection. University of New Mexico Library, Albuquerque, New Mexico.

"Circulation on Cattle Disease, 'What Should Be Done'" (unpublished manuscript, 1883). Wyoming Stock Growers Association Collection. Western History Research Center, University of Wyoming, Laramie, Wyoming.

Clay (John) Collection. Clay and Company, Denver, Colorado.

Coffee (William) Collection. Western History Research Center, University of Wyoming, Laramie, Wyoming.

Converse (James) Collection. Baker Library, Harvard University, Cambridge, Massachusetts.

Cooke (Jay) Collection. Baker Library, Harvard University, Cambridge, Massachusetts.

Coolidge (T. Jefferson) Collection. Baker Library, Harvard University, Cambridge, Massachusetts.

Craig (James T.) Collection. Western History Research Center, University of Wyoming, Laramie, Wyoming.

Dodd (S. C. T.) Collection. Petroleum History and Research Center, University of Wyoming, Laramie, Wyoming.

Dow (Hiram) Collection. Roswell, New Mexico.

Drought (H. P.) Collection. San Antonio, Texas.

Dun and Bradstreet Collection. Baker Library, Harvard University, Cambridge, Massachusetts.

Dunder (Clarence) Collection. Western History Research Center, University of Wyoming, Laramie, Wyoming.

Elkins (Stephen B.) Collection. West Virginia University Library, Morgantown, West Virginia.

Ellwood (Isaac) Collection. Western History Research Center, University of Wyoming, Laramie, Wyoming.

Gunter and Munson Collection. Southwest Collection, Texas Technological College, Lubbock, Texas.

Gushurst (P. A.) Collection. Western History Research Center, University of Wyoming, Laramie, Wyoming.

Guthrie (William) Collection. Western History Research Center, University of Wyoming, Laramie, Wyoming.

Harrison (Russell B.) Collection. Eli Lilly Library, Indiana University. Bloomington, Indiana.

Hauser (Samuel) Collection. Historical Society of Montana, Helena, Montana.

Higginson (Henry L.) Collection. Baker Library, Harvard University, Cambridge, Massachusetts.

Hord (T. B.) Collection. Western History Research Center, University of Wyoming, Laramie, Wyoming.

Hughes (William E.) Collection. Hughes Estate, Denver, Colorado.

Hyde (Henry) Collection. Baker Library, Harvard University, Cambridge, Massachusetts.

King (Clarence) Collection. Princeton University Library, Princeton, New Jersey.

Lafrentz (F. W.) Collection. Western History Research Center, University of Wyoming, Laramie, Wyoming.

LeDuc (William G.) Collection. Minnesota State Historical Society, Minneapolis, Minnesota.

McClellan (George B.) Collection. Western History Research Center, University of Wyoming, Laramie, Wyoming.

Midwest Oil Corporation Collection. Petroleum History and Research Center, University of Wyoming, Laramie, Wyoming.

Montana Stock Growers Association Collection. Historical Society of Montana, Helena, Montana.

Nason (Jack) Collection. Spearfish, South Dakota.

Otero (Miguel) Collection. University of New Mexico Library, Albuquerque, New Mexico.

Padgitt (James T.) Collection. San Antonio, Texas.

Painter (John E.) Collection. Greeley, Colorado.

Pratt (J. C.) Collection. Nebraska State Historical Society, Lincoln, Nebraska.

Regennitter (E. L.) Collection. Western History Research Center, University of Wyoming, Laramie, Wyoming.

Riverside Land and Cattle Company Collection. Western History Research Center, University of Wyoming, Laramie, Wyoming.

Seligman (Henry) Collection. Baker Library, Harvard University, Cambridge, Massachusetts.

Sheidley (B. A.) Collection. Western History Research Center, University of Wyoming, Laramie, Wyoming.

Smith (Francis) Collection. H. P. Drought and Company, San Antonio, Texas.

Snyder (J. W., D. H., and T.) Collection. University of Texas Library, Austin, Texas.

Strahorn (Robert) Collection. College of Idaho, Caldwell, Idaho.

Teschemacher (H. E.) and deBillier (F.) Collection. Western History Research Center, University of Wyoming, Laramie, Wyoming.

Thorp (Russell) Collection. Western History Research Center, University of Wyoming, Laramie, Wyoming.

Tolman (Bronson) Collection. Clark, Wyoming.

Torrey (Jay L.) Collection. Western History Research Center, University of Wyoming, Laramie, Wyoming.

Trimble (Richard) Collection. Western History Research Center, University of Wyoming, Laramie, Wyoming.

Van Duzee (A. J.) Collection. Aurora, Illinois.

Warren (Francis E.) Collection. Western History Research Center, University of Wyoming, Laramie, Wyoming.

Wentworth (Edward N.) Collection. Western History Research Center, University of Wyoming, Laramie, Wyoming.

Western Range Cattle Industry Collection. State Historical Society of Colorado, Denver, Colorado.

Wightman (Nell) Collection. Alliance, Nebraska.

Wister (Owen) Collection. Western History Research Center, University of Wyoming, Laramie, Wyoming.

Wyoming Stock Growers Association Collection. Western History Research Center, University of Wyoming, Laramie, Wyoming.

XIT Collection. Panhandle Plains Museum, Canyon, Texas.

GOVERNMENT PUBLICATIONS AND DOCUMENTS

Barnes, William Croft: *The Story of the Range*. Washington; 1926.

Congressional Record. 47th Cong., 1st Sess. Washington; 1881–2.

Coville, Frederick V.: "Report on Systems of Leasing Large Areas of Grazing Land." *Senate Document 189.* 58th Cong., 3rd Sess. Washington; 1906.

Historical Statistics of the United States, Colonial Times to 1957. Washington; 1960.

McNelly, John T.: "The Cattle Industry of Colorado, Wyoming, and Nevada and the Sheep Industry of Colorado in 1897." *Fifteenth Annual Report of the Bureau of Animal Industry for the Year 1898. House Document 307.* 55th Cong., 3rd Sess. Washington; 1899.

Nimmo, Joseph, Jr.: *The Range and Ranch Cattle Business. Executive Document 267.* House of Representatives. 48th Cong., 2nd Sess. Washington; 1886.

"Packers and Stockyards Act, 1921." *U.S. Statutes at Large.* 67th Cong., 1st Sess. Washington; 1921.

Perry, Edward W.: "Livestock and Meat Traffic of Chicago." *House Miscellaneous Document 25.* 48th Cong., 2nd Sess. Washington; 1885.

"Report of the Commissioner of Corporations on the Beef Industry." *House Document 382.* 58th Cong., 3rd Sess. Washington; 1905.

Report of the Federal Trade Commission on Investigation of Maximum Profit Limitation on the Meat Packing Industry. Senate Document 15. 66th Cong., 1st Sess. Washington; 1919.

Report of the Governor of Wyoming to the Secretary of the Interior, 1887. 50th Cong., 1st Sess. Washington; 1888.

Reports of Committees of the House of Representatives for the 1st Sess. of the 46th Cong. Executive Document 46–51. 46th Cong., 2nd Sess. Washington; 1880.

Senate Document 189. 58th Cong., 3rd Sess. Washington; 1906.

Tenth Census of the United States. House Miscellaneous 42. 47th Cong., 2nd Sess. Washington; 1883.

"Testimony Taken by the Select Committee of the U. S. Senate on the Transportation and Sale of Meat Products." *Senate Report 829.* 51st Cong., 1st Sess. Washington; 1890.

PRINTED DIARIES, MEMOIRS AND PRIMARY SOURCES

Abbott, E. C., and Helena Huntington Smith: *We Pointed Them North.* New York: Farrar & Rinehart; 1939.

Adams, E. B.: *My Association with a Glamorous Man . . . Bulkeley Wells.* Grand Junction, Colo.: 1961.

Alder, Cyrus: *Jacob Henry Schiff: His Life and Letters.* 2 vols. Garden City, N.Y.: Doubleday, Doran and Co.; 1929.

Aldridge, Reginald: *Life on a Ranch.* New York: D. Appleton; 1884.

Baber, D. F.: *Injun Summer.* Caldwell, Idaho: Caxton Printers; 1952.

Baumann, John: *Old Man Crow's Boy.* New York: W. Morrow; 1948.

Benton, Frank: *Cowboy Life on the Sidetrack.* Denver, Colo.: Western Stories Syndicate; 1903.

Biggers, Don H.: *From Cattle Range to Cotton Patch.* Galveston, Tex.: 1908.

Bratt, John: *Trails of Yesterday.* Lincoln, Nebraska: University Publishing Co.; 1921.

Brisbin, James S.: *Beef Bonanza; or, How to Get Rich on the Plains.* Philadelphia: J. B. Lippincott; 1881.

Bronson, Edgar B.: *Reminiscences of a Ranchman.* Chicago: McClurg; 1910.

Brooks, Bryant Butler: *Memoirs of Bryant B. Brooks.* Glendale, Calif.: A. H. Clark; 1939.

Carnegie, Andrew: *The Gospel of Wealth and Other Timely Essays.* New York: Century Company; 1900.

Carpenter, Will Tom: *Lucky 7.* Austin: University of Texas Press; 1957.

Chatterton, Fenimore: *Yesterday's Wyoming.* Aurora, Colo.: Powder River Publ.; 1957.

Clay, John: *My Life on the Range.* Chicago: 1924.

Cockrell, Monroe: *After Sundown.* Chicago: 1962.

Coutant, C. G.: *Progressive Men of the State of Wyoming.* Chicago: 1900.

Cox, James: *Historical and Biographical Record of the Cattle Industry and the Cattlemen of Texas and Adjacent Territory.* St. Louis: Wordward & Tiernan Print.; 1895.

Culley, John Henry: *Cattle, Horses and Men of the Western Range.* Los Angeles: Ward Ritchie Press; 1940.

Dayton, Edson C.: *Dakota Days.* Hartford, Conn.: 1937.

Dodd, S. C. T.: *Memories of S. C. T. Dodd, Written for His Children and Friends, 1837–1907.* New York: 1907.

Driscoll, R. E.: *Seventy Years of Banking in the Black Hills.* Rapid City, S.D.: Gate City Guide; 1948.

Foster, James: *Outlines of History of the Territory of Dakota and Emigrant's Guide to the Free Lands of the Northwest.* Yankton, Dakota Territory: M'Intyre & Foster Printers; 1870.

Freeman, J. W. (ed.): *Prose and Poetry of the Livestock Industry.* Knasas City, Mo.: Franklin Hudson Publ. Co.; 1905.

French, William: *Some Recollections of a Western Ranchman.* London: Methuen; 1927; New York: Frederick A. Stokes; 1928.

Hall, Bert L.: *Roundup Years, Old Muddy to Black Hills.* Pierre, S.D.: The Reminder, Inc.; 1954.

Hastings, Frank Stewart: *A Ranchman's Recollections.* Chicago: Breeder's Gazette; 1921.

Hughes, William E.: *The Journal of a Grandfather*. St. Louis: 1912.

Jones, J. Logan: *The Individualist, An Autobiography*. Kansas City, Mo.: Brown-White-Lowell Press; 1942.

Kuykendall, William L.: *Frontier Days*. Denver: 1917.

Lang, Lincoln Alexander: *Ranching with Roosevelt*. Philadelphia: J. B. Lippincott; 1926.

Letters from Old Friends and Members of the Wyoming Stock Growers Association. Edited by Harry Crane. Cheyenne, Wyo.: 1923.

MacDonald, James: *Food from the Far West*. London: W. P. Nimmo; 1878.

Mercer, A. S.: *Banditti of the Plains*. Cheyenne, Wyo.: A. S. Mercer; 1894.

———: *Big Horn County, Wyoming, the Gem of the Rockies*. Hyattville, Wyo.: A. S. Mercer; 1906.

Miller, Benjamin S.: *Ranch Life in Southern Kansas and the Indian Territory*. New York: Fless & Ridge Print.; 1896.

Otero, Miguel: *My Life on the Frontier*. 2 vols. New York: The Press of the Pioneers, Inc.; 1935-9.

———: *My Life on the Frontier, 1882-1897*. 2 vols. Albuquerque: University of New Mexico Press; 1939.

Parsons Memorial and Historical Library Magazine. Compiled by Mrs. Augustus Wilson. St. Louis: 1885.

Poe, Sophie A.: *Buckboard Days*. Caldwell, Idaho: Caxton Printers; 1936.

Potter, Jack: *Lead Steer and Other Tales*. Clayton, N. Mex.: 1939.

Proceedings of the National Stock Growers Convention. Denver, Colo.: 1898.

Rankin, M. Wilson: *Reminiscences of Frontier Days*. Denver, Colo.: Smith-Brooks; 1935.

Resources and Attractions of the Idaho Territory. Boise, Idaho: 1881.

Resources of Dakota. Sioux Falls, Dakota: Argus-Leader Co.; 1887.

Sheedy, Dennis: *Autobiography of Dennis Sheedy*. Denver, Colo.: 1922.

Shepherd, William R. E.: *Prairie Experiences in Handling Cattle and Sheep*. New York: O. Judd; 1885.

Shiel, Roger R.: *Early to Bed and Early to Rise*. Indianapolis: Sleight Printing Co.; 1909.

Strahorn, Robert E.: *The Hand-Book of Wyoming and Guide to the Black Hills and Big Horn Regions, for Citizen, Emigrant and Tourist*. Cheyenne (Chicago: Knight & Leonard); 1877.

———: *To the Rockies and Beyond, or A Summer on the Union Pacific Railroad and Branches. Saunterings in the Popular*

Health, Pleasure, and Hunting Resorts of Nebraska, Dakota, Wyoming, Colorado, New Mexico, Utah, Montana, and Idaho. Omaha, Neb.: Omaha Republican Print.; 1878.

Stuart, Granville: *Forty Years on the Frontier.* 2 vols. Cleveland: A. H. Clark; 1925.

——: *Montana and the Northwest Territory: Review of Mercantile, Manufacturing, Mining, Milling, Agriculture, Stock Raising, and General Pursuits of Her Citizens.* Chicago: 1879.

Swanberg, W. A.: *Jim Fisk: The Career of an Improbable Rascal.* New York: Scribner; 1959.

Territory of Wyoming, Its History, Soil, Climate, Resources, Etc. Laramie City: Daily Sentinel Print.; 1874.

Texas As It Is: or, the Main Facts in a Nut-Shell. Containing more common sense and practical information about Texas for twenty-five cents than ordinarily gained for the same amount of dollars. . . . Weatherford, Tex.: 1876.

Thayer, William M.: *Marvels of the New West.* Norwich, Conn: Henry Bill Pub.; 1889.

Timmons, William: *Twilight on the Range.* Austin: University of Texas Press; 1962.

Vaughn, Robert: *Then and Now; or Thirty-Six Years in the Rockies.* Minneapolis, Minn.: Tribune Printing Co.; 1900.

Von Richtofen, Baron Walter: *Cattle-Raising on the Plains of North America.* New York: Appleton; 1885.

Walker, William: *The Longest Rope.* Edited by D. F. Baber. Caldwell, Idaho: Caxton Printers; 1940.

Warner, Amos G.: *American Charities.* New York: T. Y. Crowell; 1894.

Wister, Owen: *Owen Wister out West.* Edited by Fanny Kemble Wister Stokes. Chicago: University of Chicago Press; 1958.

NEWSPAPERS

Big Horn [Wyoming] *Sentinel.* 1899–1901.

Douglas [Wyoming] *Bill Barlow's Budget.* 1892.

Cheyenne [Wyoming] *Daily Sun.* 1890.

Cheyenne [Wyoming] *Leader.* 1870–94.

Cheyenne [Wyoming] *Northwestern Livestock Journal.* 1885–7.

Cheyenne [Wyoming] *Wyoming Tribune.* 1904.

Chicago [Illinois] *Tribune.* 1932.

Cimarron [New Mexico] *News and Press.* 1881–2.

Cleveland [Ohio] *Plain Dealer.* 1899–1920.

BIBLIOGRAPHY 307

De Kalb [Illinois] *Daily Chronicle.* 1926.
Denver [Colorado] *Daily Tribune.* 1879.
Denver [Colorado] *Field and Farm.* 1882–9.
Denver [Colorado] *Republican.* 1881–8.
Denver [Colorado] *Rocky Mountain Daily News.* 1873–90.
Denver [Colorado] *Times.* 1898.
Denver [Colorado] *Tribune.* 1879, 1882.
Dodge City [Kansas] *Times.* 1876–82.
Georgetown [Colorado] *Courier.* 1887.
Kansas City [Missouri] *Livestock Indicator.* 1882–90.
Laramie [Wyoming] *Boomerang.* 1884–99.
Laramie [Wyoming] *Daily Boomerang.* 1884, 1886–7.
Laramie [Wyoming] *Sentinel.* 1871–83.
Las Vegas [New Mexico] *Daily Optic.* 1880–6.
Los Angeles [California] *Times.* 1919.
Mesilla [New Mexico] *News.* 1875–6.
New York [New York] *Daily Graphic.* 1889.
New York [New York] *Evening Post.* 1905.
New York [New York] *Times.* 1892, 1912.
Pueblo [Colorado] *Colorado Chieftain.* 1869.
St. Louis [Missouri] *Globe-Democrat.* 1882–95.
San Antonio [Texas] *Daily Express.* 1884.
San Lorenzo [New Mexico] *Red River Chronicle.* 1883.
San Marcial [New Mexico] *Reporter.* 1878–88.
Socorro [New Mexico] *Bullion.* 1885.
West Las Animas [Colorado] *Leader.* 1882.

ARTICLES

Allen, Richard M.: "Harvard Men in the Range Cattle Industry." *Harvard Graduates Magazine,* II (1894), pp. 183–92.
Banks, Roy O.: "The Credible Literary West." *Colorado Quarterly,* VIII (Summer 1959), pp. 28–50.
Barker, Robert M.: "The Economics of Cattle-Ranching in the Southwest." *The American Monthly Review of Reviews,* XXIV (September 1901), pp. 305–13.
Bogue, Allan, and Margaret Bogue: "Profits and the Frontier Land Speculator." *Journal of Economic History,* XVII (March 1957), pp. 1–24.
Brown, Nancy Fillmore: "Girlhood Recollections of Laramie in 1870 and 1871." Wyoming Historical Society, *Quarterly Bulletin,* I (January 15, 1924), pp. 12–17.

Cauley, Troy Jesse: "Early Business Methods in Texas Cattle Industry." *Journal of Economics and Business History*, IV (May 1932), pp. 416–86.

——: "Early Meat Packing Plants in Texas." *Southwestern Political and Social Science Quarterly*, IX (March 1939), pp. 416–86.

Cochran, Thomas C.: "The Legend of the Robber Barons." *Pennsylvania Magazine of History and Biography*, LXXIV (July 1950), pp. 307–21.

Commercial and Financial Chronicle (1880–99).

Connally, Grace M.: "The Bar-S Ranch." *West Texas Historical Association Yearbook*, XXXIII (October 1957), pp. 94–104.

Curti, Merle: "The History of American Philanthropy as a Field of Research." *American Historical Review*, LXII (January 1957), pp. 352–63.

Croxton, Fred C.: "Beef Prices." *The Journal of Political Economy*, XIII (March 1905), pp. 201–16.

Destler, Chester McArthur: "Entrepreneurial Leadership among the 'Robber Barons': A Trial Balance." *Journal of Economic History*, Supplement (1946), pp. 28–49.

——: "The Opposition of American Business Men to Social Control during the 'Gilded Age.'" *Mississippi Valley Historical Review*, XXXIX (March 1953), pp. 641–72.

——: "Wealth Against Commonwealth, 1894–1944." *American Historical Review*, L (October 1944), pp. 49–69.

Dodd, S. C. T.: "The Present Legal Status of Trusts." *Harvard Law Review*, VII (November 1893), pp. 157–69.

Dunn, Roy Sylvan: "Drought in West Texas, 1890–1894." *West Texas Historical Association Yearbook*, XXXVII (October 1961), pp. 121–36.

——: "West Texas Droughts." *Southwestern Historical Quarterly*, XXXII (October 1958), pp. 103–23.

Emery, F. E.: "Psychological Effects of the Western Film: A Study in Television Viewing." *Human Relations*, XII (1959), pp. 195–213.

English, Mary Jackson: "Army Girl: Experiences on the Frontier." *1947 Brand Book of the Denver Westerners*, III (Denver, 1949), pp. 135–45.

Ericson, J. E.: "Colonization of the Spur Farm Lands." *West Texas Historical Association Yearbook*, XXI (October 1955), pp. 41–53.

Fireman, Floyd S.: "The Spiegelbergs of New Mexico: Merchants and Bankers, 1844–1893." *Southwestern Studies*, I (Winter 1964), pp. 1–48.

Fletcher, R. S.: "The Hard Winter in Montana, 1886–1887." *Agricultural History*, IV (October 1930), pp. 123–30.

Ford, Lee M.: "Bob Ford, Sun River Cowman." *Montana Magazine of History*, IX (January 1959), pp. 30–42.

Gard, Wayne: "The Fence Cutters." *Southwestern Historical Quarterly*, LI (July 1947), pp. 1–15.

Garnsey, Morris E.: "The Plains as a Region." *Western Humanities Review*, XIV (Winter 1960), pp. 61–8.

Gates, Paul W.: "The Role of the Land Speculator in Western Development." *Pennsylvania Magazine of History and Biography*, LXVI (1942), pp. 314–33.

Gressley, Gene M.: "The American Cattle Trust: A Study in Protest." *Pacific Historical Review*, XXX (February 1961), pp. 61–77.

———: "Teschemacher and deBillier Cattle Company." *Business History Review*, XXXIII (Summer 1959), pp. 121–37.

Haley, J. Evetts: "The Grass Lease Fight and Attempted Impeachment of the First Panhandle Judge." *Southwestern Historical Quarterly*, XXXVIII (July 1934), pp. 1–27.

Hayter, Earl: "An Iowa Farmer's Protective Association." *The Iowa Journal of History*, XXXVII (June 1934).

Hittson, John: "Cattle King of West Texas." *West Texas Historical Association Yearbook*, XXXVII (October 1961), pp. 70–81.

Jackson, W. Turrentine: "Administration of Thomas Moonlight, 1887–1889." *Annals of Wyoming*, XVII (July 1946), pp. 260–70.

———: "Railroad Relations of the Wyoming Stock Growers Association, 1873–1890." *Annals of Wyoming*, XIX (January 1947), pp. 3–23.

———: "The Wyoming Stock Growers Association, Its Years of Temporary Decline, 1886–1890." *Agricultural History*, XXII (October 1948), pp. 260–70.

———: "The Wyoming Stock Growers Association: Political Power in Wyoming Territory, 1873–1890." *Mississippi Valley Historical Review*, XXXIII (March 1947), pp. 571–94.

Jones, J. Lee, and Rupert N. Richardson: "Colorado City, the Cattlemen's Capital." *West Texas Historical Association Yearbook*, XIX (October 1943), pp. 36–63.

Josephson, Matthew: "Should American History Be Rewritten?" *The Saturday Review of Literature*, XXVII (February 6, 1954), pp. 9–10.

Larson, T. A.: "The Winter of 1886–1887 in Wyoming." *Annals of Wyoming*, XIV (January 1942), pp. 5–17.

Mattison, R. H.: "The Hard Winter and the Range Cattle Business." *Montana Magazine of History*, I (October 1951), pp. 5–21.

————: "Roosevelt and the Stockmen's Association." *North Dakota History*, XVII (April 1950), pp. 3–59.

McMechen, Edgar C.: "John Hittson, Cattle King." *The Colorado Magazine*, XI (September 1934), pp. 164–70.

Milligan, E. W.: "John Wesley Iliff." *The Westerners Brand Book*, VI (August 1950), pp. 1–16.

Nelson, Gerry: "Roosevelt Ranch Life in the Badlands." *North Dakota History*, XXIV (October 1957), pp. 171–4.

Oliphant, J. Orin: "Winter Losses of Cattle in the Oregon Country, 1847–1890." *Washington Historical Quarterly*, XXIII (January 1932), pp. 3–17.

Padgitt, James T.: "Captain Joseph C. Lea, the Father of Roswell." *West Texas Historical Association Yearbook*, XXV (October 1959), pp. 50–65.

————: "Early History of the New Mexico Military Institute." *West Texas Historical Association Yearbook*, XXXIV (October 1958), pp. 67–81.

————: "The Millers and Early Day Banking in Belton." *West Texas Historical Association Yearbook*, XXXII (October 1956), pp. 103–21.

Rippy, J. Fred: "British Investments in Texas Lands and Livestock," *Southwestern Historical Quarterly*, LVIII (January 1955), pp. 331–41.

Scott, P. G.: "John Powers, Bent County Pioneer." *Colorado Magazine*, VII (September 1930), pp. 183–7.

Shaw, Albert: "America's Millionaires and Their Public Gifts." *Review of Reviews*, VII (February 1893), pp. 48–60.

Spence, Clark C.: "Melbourne, the Australian Rain Wizard." *Annals of Wyoming*, XXXIII (April 1961), pp. 5–18.

Thompson, Albert W.: "The Great Prairie Cattle Company, Ltd." *Colorado Magazine*, XXII (March 1945), pp. 76–83.

Tipple, John: "The Anatomy of Prejudice." *Business History Review*, XXXIII (Winter 1959), pp. 510–23.

Wagoner, J. J.: "History of the Cattle Industry in South Arizona, 1540–1940." *University of Arizona Bulletin*, XXIII (April 1952), pp. 5–132.

Walter, Paul F.: "New Mexico's Pioneer Banks and Bankers." *New Mexico Historical Review*, XXI (July 1946), pp. 209–25.

————: "Ten Years After." *New Mexico Historical Review*, VII (October 1932), pp. 371–6.

Westermier, Clifford P.: "The Legal Status of the Colorado Cattlemen, 1867–87." *Colorado Magazine*, XXV (May 1949), pp.
109–18.

Westphall, Victor: "The Public Domain in New Mexico, 1854–1891."
New Mexico Historical Review, XXXIII (April 1958), pp. 138–
149.

Whitely, Phillip W.: "A Pioneer Story in Western Cover." *Brand
Book of the Denver Westerners*, VII (Denver, 1952), pp.
298–324.

Wright, Louis B.: "Franklin's Legacy to the Gilded Age." *Virginia
Quarterly Review*, XXII (Spring 1946), pp. 268–79.

Wyllie, Irwin G.: "The Reputation of the American Philanthro-
pists." *Social Service Review*, XXXII (September 1958), pp.
215–22.

PAMPHLETS

Albany Land and Cattle Company: *Prospectus*. Cheyenne; 1884.

American Cattle Trust: *Statement*. New York; 1890.

Ames Cattle Company: *Prospectus*. Boston; 1884.

Babbitt, A. T.: *Grazing Interests and the Beef Supply*. Cheyenne;
1884.

Capitol Freehold Land and Investment Company: *Prospectus*. Chicago; 1886.

Clay, John: *Coming Back to the Wagon*. Cheyenne; 1922.

De Kalb County Manufacturer. De Kalb; 1887.

Dodd, S. C. T.: *Aggregated Capital*. New York; 1893.

———: *Combinations: Their Uses and Abuses, with a History of
the Standard Oil Trust*. New York; 1888.

———: *A Statement of Pending Legislation and Its Consequences*.
New York; n.d.

———: *Trusts*. Boston; 1889.

Laramie County Historical Society: *Early Cheyenne Homes, 1880–
1890*. Cheyenne; 1962.

Robber's Roost Historical Society: *Pioneering on the Cheyenne
River*. Lusk, Wyo.; 1956.

Western Philanthropic Society of New York: *Prospectus*. New
York; 1879.

Yellowstone Cattle Company: *Prospectus*. Helena; 1883.

INTERVIEWS AND CORRESPONDENCE WITH CONTEMPORARIES

Interview with Carlile Bolton-Smith. November 12, 1963.
Interview with Colonel Padgitt. 1957 and 1962.
Interview with Harold Kountze. April 28, 1959.
Interview with Russell Thorp, August 10, 1959.
Mrs. Hebard Paine to Gene M. Gressley. May 20, 1958.

Secondary Materials

UNPUBLISHED THESES AND DISSERTATIONS

Bolino, August Constantine: "An Economic History of Idaho Territory, 1863–1890." Ph.D. dissertation, St. Louis University, 1957.
Boyce, Todd Vernon: "A History of the Beef Cattle Industry in the Inland Empire." M.A. thesis, State College of Washington, 1937.
Bright, Davilla: "Foreigners and Foreign Capital in the Cattle Industry of the United States." M.A. thesis, University of Oklahoma, 1935.
Brunson, Billy Bay: "The Texas Land and Development Company." Ph.D. dissertation, Texas Technological College, 1960.
Burleigh, David Robert: "Range Cattle Industry in Nebraska to 1890." M.A. thesis, University of Nebraska, 1937.
Cramer, Edison Henry: "Denver as the Financial Center of the Eastern Rocky Mountain Region." Ph.D. dissertation, Michigan University, 1940.
Evans, Samuel Lee: "Texas Agriculture, 1880–1930." Ph.D. dissertation, University of Texas, 1960.
Ferris, Buford E.: "An Institutional Approach to the Texas Cattle Ranch." M.A. thesis, University of Texas, 1939.
Hakola, John W.: "Samuel T. Hauser and the Economic Development of Montana." Ph.D. dissertation, Indiana University, 1961.
Hashem, Mohamad Zaki: "The Theory of Economic Development

of Under-Developed Countries, with a Study of the Development of the Egyptian Economy, 1927–1947." Ph.D. dissertation, Harvard University, 1950.

Hefferan, Vioalle Clark: "Thomas Benton Catron." M.A. thesis, University of New Mexico, 1940.

Hinton, Harwood Perry: "John Simpson Chisum, 1877–1884." M.A. thesis, Columbia University, 1955.

Hunter, John M.: "A Case Study of the Economic Development of an Under-Developed Country: Cuba, 1899–1935." Ph.D. dissertation, Harvard University, 1950.

Neil, William MacFarlane: "The Territory Governor in the Rocky Mountain West, 1861–1889." Ph.D. dissertation, University of Chicago, 1951.

Oliphant, James Orin: "The Range-Cattle Industry in the Oregon Country to 1890." Ph.D. dissertation, Harvard University, 1930.

Pearce, W. M.: "A History of the Matador Land and Cattle Company, Limited, from 1882–1915." Ph.D. dissertation, University of Texas, 1952.

Phillips, William Weiland: "The Life of Asle J. Gronna: A Self-Made Man of the Prairies." Ph.D. dissertation, University of Missouri, 1958.

Piccolo, Margaret Justine Lo: "Some Aspects of the Range Cattle Industry of Harney County, Oregon, 1870–1900." M.A. thesis, University of Oregon, 1962.

Prator, Moina Martha: "The Development of the Cattle Industry of the Great Plains States." M.A. thesis, University of Chicago, 1918.

Sluga, Mary Elizabeth: "The Political Life of Thomas Benton Catron, 1896–1921." M.A. thesis, University of New Mexico, 1941.

Sorensen, Barbara: "A King and a Prince among Pioneers: John and Edward Creighton." M.A. thesis, Creighton University, 1962.

Stevens, Thelma Walter: "History of Bailey County." M.A. thesis, Texas Technological College, 1939.

Straus, James Hartman: "The Entrepreneur: The Firm." Ph.D. dissertation, University of Wisconsin, 1945.

Toppin, Edgar Allan: "A Study of the Defense and Defenders of Big Business in America, 1900 to 1914." Ph.D. dissertation, Northwestern University, 1955.

Tsung-Yuan Logh, Arthur: "The Theory of Economic Development and Planning in an Under-Developed Country, as Applicable to China." Ph.D. dissertation, Illinois University, 1952.

Waters, William R.: "Entrepreneurship, Dualism and Causality: An

Appreciation of the Work of Joseph A. Schumpeter." Ph.D. dissertation, Georgetown University, 1952.

BOOKS

Adams, Ramon Frederick: *The Rampaging Herd*. Norman: University of Oklahoma Press; 1959.

Aitken, Hugh G. J.: *American Capital and Canadian Resources*. Cambridge: Harvard University Press; 1961.

Allen, Frederick Lewis: *The Great Pierpont Morgan*. New York: Harper; 1949.

Anderson, August: *Hyphenated; or, the Life of S. M. Swensen*. Austin: E. L. Steck; 1916.

Andrews, Frank Emerson: *Philanthropic Giving*. New York: Russell Sage Foundation; 1950.

Arps, Louisa W.: *Denver in Slices*. Denver: Sage Books; 1959.

Arrington, Leonard: *The Changing Economic Structure of the Mountain West, 1850–1950*. Logan: Utah State University Press; 1963.

———: *Great Basin Kingdom: An Economic History of the Latter-day Saints, 1830–1890*. Cambridge: Harvard University Press; 1958.

Barker, Charles A.: *Henry George*. Fairlawn, N.J.: Oxford University Press; 1955.

Bogue, Allan: *Money at Interest; the Farm Mortgage on the Middle Border*. Ithaca: Cornell University Press; 1955.

Bogue, Margaret B.: *Patterns from the Sod*. Springfield: Illinois State Historical Society; 1959.

Bray, Charles: *Financing the Western Cattle Industry*. Fort Collins, Colo.: 1928.

Bremner, Robert H.: *American Philanthropy*. Chicago: University of Chicago Press; 1960.

Bridges, Hal: *Iron Millionaire*. Philadelphia: University of Pennsylvania Press; 1952.

Buley, R. Carlyle: *The Equitable Life Assurance Society of the United States*. New York: Appleton-Century-Crofts; 1959.

Burcham, L. T.: *California Range Land*. Sacramento: Div. of Forestry, Dept. of Natural Resources, State of California; 1957.

Burns, Robert H., Andrew S. Gillespie, and Willing C. Richardson: *Wyoming's Pioneer Ranches*. Laramie, Wyo.: Top-of-the-World Press; 1955.

Carey, Fred: *Major Jim*. Omaha, Neb.: Omaha Printing Co.; 1930.

Caughey, John: *Hubert Howe Bancroft, Historian of the West.* Berkeley: University of California Press; 1946.

Century Association: *Clarence King Memoirs.* New York: Putnam's Sons; 1904.

Cochran, Thomas C.: *Railroad Leaders, 1845–1890: the Business Mind in Action.* Cambridge: Harvard University Press; 1953.

Commager, Henry S.: *The American Mind.* New Haven: Yale University Press; 1950.

Crawford, Lewis Ferandus: *Ranching Days in Dakota, and Custer's Black Hills Expedition of 1874.* Baltimore: Wirth Bros.; 1950.

Crichton, Kyle S.: *Law and Order, Ltd.* Santa Fe: New Mexican Publ.; 1928.

Cross, Joe: *Cattle Clatter.* Kansas City, Mo.: Walker Publications; 1938.

Current, Richard N.: *Pine Logs and Politics.* Madison: State Historical Society of Wisconsin; 1950.

Curry, George: *George Curry, 1861–1947; An Autobiography.* Edited by H. B. Hening. Albuquerque: University of New Mexico Press; 1958.

David, R. B.: *Malcolm Campbell, Sheriff.* Casper, Wyo.: Wyomingana, Inc.; 1932.

Decker, Leslie: *Railroads, Land and Politics.* Providence: Brown University Press; 1964.

Dennett, Tyler: *John Hay: From Poetry to Politics.* New York: Dodd, Mead & Co.; 1933.

Destler, Chester McArthur: *Henry Demarest Lloyd and the Empire of Reform.* Philadelphia: University of Pennsylvania Press; 1963.

Dictionary of American Biography. 22 vols. New York: Charles Scribner's Sons; 1928– .

Eaves, Charles, and C. A. Hutchinson: *Post City, Texas.* Austin: Texas State Historical Association; 1952.

Emmett, Chris: *Shanghai Pierce.* Norman: University of Oklahoma Press; 1953.

Fels, Rendigs: *American Business Cycles, 1865–1897.* Chapel Hill: University of North Carolina Press; 1959.

Fletcher, Robert H.: *Free Grass to Fences, the Montana Cattle Range Story.* New York: University Publishers; 1960.

———: *Organization of the Range Cattle Business in Eastern Montana.* Bozeman, Mont.: 1932.

Fosdick, Raymond B.: *The Story of the Rockefeller Foundation.* New York: Harper & Row; 1952.

Frink, Maurice: *Cow Country Cavalcade: Eighty Years of the*

Wyoming Stock Growers Association. Denver: Old West Publishing Co.; 1954.

————: W. Turrentine Jackson, and Agnes Wright Spring: *When Grass Was King.* Boulder: University of Colorado Press; 1956.

Gandy, Lewis C.: *The Tabors.* New York: The Press of the Pioneers; 1934.

Gard, Wayne: *The Chisholm Trail.* Norman: University of Oklahoma Press; 1954.

————: *Frontier Justice.* Norman: University of Oklahoma Press; 1949.

Gardiner, Charles Fox: *Doctor at Timberline.* Caldwell, Idaho: Caxton Printers; 1938.

Garnsey, Morris E.: *America's New Frontier.* New York: Alfred A. Knopf, Inc.; 1950.

Gates, Paul W.: *The Farmer's Age.* New York: Holt, Rinehart and Winston; 1960.

————: *Fifty Million Acres: Conflicts over Kansas Land Policy, 1854–1890.* Ithaca: Cornell University Press; 1954.

————: *The Illinois Central Railroad and Its Colonization Work.* Cambridge: Harvard University Press; 1934.

Gates, William B.: *Michigan Copper and Boston Dollars.* Cambridge: Harvard University Press; 1951.

Ginger, Ray: *Age of Excess; the United States from 1877 to 1914.* New York: The Macmillan Company; 1965.

Goodstein, Anita Shafer: *Henry W. Sage, 1814–1897: Biography of a Businessman.* Ithaca: Cornell University Press; 1962.

Green, Charles L.: *The Administration of the Public Domain in South Dakota.* Pierre, S.D.: 1940.

Grodinsky, Julius: *Jay Gould, His Business Career, 1887–1896.* Philadelphia: University of Pennsylvania Press; 1957.

Guernsey, Charles A.: *Wyoming Cowboy Days.* New York: G. P. Putnam's Sons; 1936.

Haley, J. Evetts: *Charles Goodnight.* Boston: Houghton Mifflin Company; 1936.

————: *Charles Shreiner.* Austin: Texas State Historical Association; 1944.

————: *The XIT Ranch of Texas, and the Early Days of the Llano Estacado.* Chicago: Lakeside Press; 1929; Norman: University of Oklahoma Press; 1953.

Hargreaves, Mary W.: *Dry Farming in the Northern Great Plains, 1900–1925.* Cambridge.: Harvard University Press; 1957.

Hidy, Ralph W.: *The House of Baring in American Trade and*

Finance; English Merchant Bankers at Work, 1763–1861. Cambridge: Harvard University Press; 1949.

———, and Muriel Hidy: *Pioneering in Big Business, 1882–1911.* New York: Harper & Row; 1955.

———, Frank E. Hill, and Allan Nevins: *Timber and Men.* New York: The Macmillan Company; 1963.

Hill, J. L.: *The End of the Cattle Trail.* Long Beach, Calif.: George W. Moyle; 1923.

Hofstadter, Richard: *Social Darwinism in American Thought.* Boston: Beacon Press; 1955.

Holden, W. C.: *The Spur Ranch.* Boston: Christopher Publishing House; 1934.

Hopkins, John A., Jr.: *Economic History of the Production of Beef Cattle in Iowa.* Iowa City: State Historical Society of Iowa; 1928.

Houck, U. G.: *The Bureau of Animal Industry of the United States Department of Agriculture: Its Establishment, Achievements and Current Activities.* Washington: Hayworth Printing Co.; 1924.

Howard, Joseph K.: *Montana; High, Wide and Handsome.* New Haven: Yale University Press; 1943.

Josephson, Matthew: *Edison; a Biography.* New York: McGraw-Hill Book Company; 1959.

———: *The Robber Barons; the Great American Capitalists, 1861–1901.* New York: Harcourt, Brace; 1934.

Keller, Morton: *The Life Insurance Enterprise, 1885–1910.* Cambridge: Belknap Press of Harvard University Press; 1963.

Kelly, James R.: *History of the New Mexico Military Institute.* Roswell, New Mex.: 1953.

Kirkland, Edward C.: *Business in the Gilded Age; The Conservatives' Balance Sheet.* Madison: University of Wisconsin Press; 1952.

———: *Industry Comes of Age.* New York: Holt, Rinehart and Winston; 1961.

———: *Men, Cities and Transportation, A Study in New England History, 1820–1900.* Cambridge: Harvard University Press; 1948.

Lambert, Oscar D.: *Stephen Benton Elkins.* Pittsburgh: University of Pittsburgh; 1955.

Larmer, Forrest M.: *Financing the Livestock Industry.* New York: The Macmillan Company; 1926.

Larson, Henrietta: *Jay Cooke.* Cambridge: Harvard University Press; 1936.

Larson, Orvin: *American Infidel.* New York: Citadel Press; 1962.

Latham, Hiram: *Trans-Missouri Stock Raising; the Pasture Lands of North America: Winter Grazing.* Denver: Old West Publishing Co.; 1962.

Leonard, J. W.: *Book of Chicagoans.* Chicago: Marquis; 1905.

Leslie, Anita: *The Remarkable Mr. Jerome.* New York: Holt; 1954.

Lewis, Willie Newbury: *Between Sun and Sod.* Clarendon, Tex.: Clarendon Press; 1938.

Lindsay, Charles: *The Big Horn Basin.* Lincoln, Neb.: 1932.

Lowitt, Richard: *A Merchant Prince of the Nineteenth Century.* New York: Columbia University Press; 1954.

Lurie, Edward: *Louis Agassiz.* Chicago: University of Chicago Press; 1960.

McCarty, John L.: *Maverick Town, the Story of Old Tascosa.* Norman: University of Oklahoma Press; 1946.

MacDonald, Dwight: *The Ford Foundation.* New York: Reynal; 1956.

Major, Nettie Leitch: *C. W. Post: The Hour and the Man.* Washington: Press of Judd and Detweiler; 1963.

Mattison, Ray H.: *Roosevelt's Dakota Ranches.* Bismarck: *Bismarck Tribune;* 1958.

Medbery, James K.: *Men and Mysteries of Wall Street.* Boston: Fields, Osgood and Co.; 1870.

Men in Business: Essays in the History of Entrepreneurship. Edited by William Miller. Cambridge: Harvard University Press; 1952.

Miller, Ernest C.: *Oil Mania.* Philadelphia: Dorrance and Co.; 1941.

Morgan, H. Wayne (ed.): *The Gilded Age: A Reappraisal.* Syracuse: Syracuse University Press; 1963.

National Cyclopedia of American Biography. 47 vols. (New York: J. T. White; 1893–   ).

Nelson, Oliver H.: *The Cowman's Southwest.* Edited by Angie Debo. Glendale, Calif.: A. H. Clark Company; 1953.

Nevins, Allan: *Abram S. Hewitt.* New York: Harper; 1935.

———: *Study in Power: John D. Rockefeller, Industrialist and Philanthropist.* 2 vols. New York: Charles Scribner's Sons; 1953.

Nordyke, Lewis: *Cattle Empire, The Fabulous Story of the 3,000,000 Acre XIT.* New York: William Morrow; 1949.

———: *Great Roundup, the Story of Texas and Southwestern Cowmen.* New York: William Morrow; 1955.

Osgood, Ernest S.: *The Day of the Cattlemen.* Minneapolis: University of Minnesota Press; 1929.

Overton, Richard C.: *Burlington West.* Cambridge: Harvard University Press; 1941.

Parish, William: *The Charles Ilfeld Company.* Cambridge: Harvard University Press; 1961.

Parrington, Vernon Louis: *Main Currents in American Thought*. New York: Harcourt, Brace & Co.; 1930.

Parsons Memorial and Historical Library Magazine. Compiled by Augustus Wilson. St. Louis: 1885.

Paul, Rodman W.: *Mining Frontiers of the Far West, 1848–1880*. New York: Holt, Rinehart and Winston; 1963.

Peake, Ora B.: *The Colorado Range Cattle Industry*. Glendale, Calif.: A. H. Clark Company; 1937.

Pearce, W. M.: *The Matador Land and Cattle Company*. Norman: University of Oklahoma Press; 1964.

Pelzer, Louis: *The Cattlemen's Frontier*. Glendale, Calif.: A. H. Clark Company; 1936.

Perloff, Harvey S., *et al.*: *Regions, Resources, and Economic Growth*. Baltimore: Johns Hopkins Press; 1960.

Pomeroy, Earl: *In Search of the Golden West*. New York: Alfred A. Knopf, Inc.; 1957.

Powell, Donald M.: *The Peralta Grant*. Norman: University of Oklahoma Press; 1960.

Press Reference Library, Western Edition. 2 vols. New York: International News Service; 1913–15.

Rich (Raymond) Associates: *American Foundations and Their Fields*. New York: American Foundations Information Service; 1959.

Robbins, Roy M.: *Our Landed Heritage*. Princeton: Princeton University Press; 1942.

Rogers, Henry M.: *Memories of Ninety Years*. Boston: Houghton Mifflin Co.; 1928.

Samuels, Ernest: *Henry Adams, the Middle Years*. Cambridge: Belknap Press of Harvard University Press; 1958.

Satterlee, Herbert L.: *J. Pierpont Morgan; an Intimate Portrait*. New York: The Macmillan Company; 1939.

Schatz, August Herman: *Long Horns Bring Culture*. Boston: Christopher Publishing House; 1961.

———: *Opening a Cow Country*. Ann Arbor, Mich.: Edwards Brothers; 1939.

Schmitt, Martin F. (ed.): *General George Crook, His Autobiography*. Norman: University of Oklahoma Press; 1946.

Shannon, Fred A.: *The Farmer's Last Frontier*. New York: Farrar & Rinehart; 1945.

Sheehan, Donald, and Harold Syrett (eds.): *Essays in American Historiography*. New York: Columbia University Press; 1960.

Sheffy, Lester F.: *The Francklyn Land and Cattle Company*. Austin: University of Texas Press; 1963.

Sheldon, Addison E.: *Land Systems and Land Policies in Nebraska.*
    Lincoln: The Society; 1936.
Shoemaker, Len: *Roaring Fork Valley.* Denver, Colo.: Sage Books;
    1958.
Spikes, Nellie W., and Temple A. Ellis: *Through the Years; A His-
    tory of Crosby County, Texas.* San Antonio: Naylor Co.; 1952.
Spring, Agnes Wright: *Cheyenne Club.* Kansas City: Don Ornduff;
    1961.
——: *Seventy Years. A Panoramic History of the Wyoming Stock
    Growers Association, Interwoven with Data Relative to the
    Cattle Industry in Wyoming.* Gillette, Wyo.: Wyoming Stock
    Growers Association; 1942.
Steinel, A. T., and D. W. Working: *History of Agriculture in Colo-
    rado.* Fort Collins, Colo.: State Agricultural College; 1926.
Stone, Wilbur F.: *History of Colorado.* 3 vols. Chicago: S. J. Clarke;
    1918.
Stout, Tom: *Montana, Its Story and Biography.* 3 vols. Chicago:
    American Historical Society; 1921.
Tebbel, John: *From Rags to Riches.* New York: The Macmillan
    Company; 1963.
Thayer, William R.: *Life and Letters of John Hay.* 2 vols. Boston:
    Houghton Mifflin Co.; 1915.
Towne, Charles W., and Edward N. Wentworth: *Cattle and Men.*
    Norman: University of Oklahoma Press; 1955.
Trenholm, Virginia: *Footprints on the Frontier.* Douglas, Wyo.:
    Douglas Enterprise Co.; 1945.
Wagoner, J. J.: *History of the Cattle Industry in Southern Arizona,
    1540–1940.* Tucson: University of Arizona; 1952.
Wakeley, Arthur C.: *Omaha: The Gate City, and Douglas County,
    Nebraska.* 2 vols. Chicago: S. J. Clarke; 1917.
Webb, Walter P.: *The Great Plains.* Boston: Ginn and Co.; 1931.
Wilkins, Thurman: *Clarence King.* New York: The Macmillan Com-
    pany; 1958.
Williamson, Harold F., and Arnold Daum: *The American Petroleum
    Industry; the Age of Illumination, 1859–1899.* Evanston, Ill.:
    Northwestern University Press; 1959.
Winkler, John K.: *Morgan the Magnificent; the Life of J. Pierpont
    Morgan (1837–1913).* New York: Vanguard Press; 1930.
Wyllie, Irvin G.: *The Self-Made Man in America; The Myth of Rags
    to Riches.* New Brunswick, N.J.: Rutgers University Press;
    1954.
Young, Mary E.: *Redskins, Ruffleshirts and Rednecks.* Norman:
    University of Oklahoma Press; 1961.

INDEX